DISORDERLY FAMILIES

DISORDERLY FAMILIES

Infamous Letters
from the Bastille Archives

ARLETTE FARGE *and* MICHEL FOUCAULT

Edited by Nancy Luxon
Translated by Thomas Scott-Railton
Afterword to the English Edition by Arlette Farge

University of Minnesota Press
Minneapolis
London

Originally published in French as *Le Désordre des familles: Lettres de cachet des Archives de la Bastille au XVIIIe siècle*, by Arlette Farge and Michel Foucault. Copyright Gallimard/Julliard, 1982 and 2014.

Cet ouvrage a bénéficié du soutien des Programmes d'aide à la publication de l'Institut Français. This work received support from the Institut Français through its publication program.

Published by the University of Minnesota Press
111 Third Avenue South, Suite 290
Minneapolis, MN 55401-2520
http://www.upress.umn.edu

A Cataloging-in-Publication record for this book is available from the Library of Congress.
ISBN: 978-0-8166-9534-8 (hc)

Printed in the United States of America on acid-free paper

The University of Minnesota is an equal-opportunity educator and employer.

22 21 20 19 18 17 16   10 9 8 7 6 5 4 3 2 1

This book was prepared in collaboration with Christiane Martin, who devoted herself to it until the end of her life. This task was completed by Éliane Allo, assistant at Collège de France. We thank her for her help and her important contribution to this project.

ARLETTE FARGE
and
MICHEL FOUCAULT

Contents

Translator's Preface

Translating these requests for *lettres de cachet* presented several challenges—or at the very least decisions. To translate them from French into English I first had to address the question of which English. After some consideration, the three main options seemed to be (1) to translate them literally, directly, preserving the archaic French syntax and language; (2) to render them in an equivalent eighteenth-century English; and (3) to bring them into modern English, my native language. Each of these choices had something to recommend it. The first would leave the lightest footprint and result in the most "authentic," albeit somewhat cumbersome, translations. Taking the second approach would offer the modern English reader the closest approximation of what French readers experienced when *Le Désordre des familles* was originally published in 1982—texts that were written in an outdated but not unfamiliar style, one that would correspond the closest to the era that had shaped both these letters and their authors.

If the first course could perhaps be said to be most authentic to the texts, adopting the third method would be the most authentic with regard to myself. I was not raised in a culture that spoke eighteenth-century English, and therefore I could only craft a likeness, at worst a simulacrum, of it—like an actor whose Scottish accent bears no relation to how people actually talk in Aberdeen, but rather reflects a Hollywood idea of how a Scotsman *should* sound. And so I should translate these requests into the language in which I speak and write. After all, when they were written, were not these appeals composed in the vernacular of the time?

But the incompatibility of these three paths, which appeared so stark when viewed at the level of abstraction, softened upon contact with the documents themselves. These elements were not mutually exclusive so much as in tension, or various considerations to navigate by, to keep in mind, while being guided by the same central concern that had motivated the people who had written—or dictated to a public scribe—these requests: making them heard. Not just in their written pleas, but in all that these pleas revealed about them lies a concern that is not merely linguistic but is also individual. If all the requests were literally translated into the same clumsy English, or literarily rendered into smooth English (be it eighteenth or twenty-first century), the difference between a letter written by an educated government clerk and one dictated by a nineteen-year-old gravedigger would be lost. The contrast between a public scribe's flowery introduction and an abused wife's pleading should be preserved. This sometimes meant rendering elegant French modes of address due to a royal official into an eighteenth-century English monarchical equivalent. At others times it meant conserving more literally the confusion of a jumbled account given by a furious and jilted husband.

With this as the central aim, I have created translations that are, I hope, as evocative, striking, and repetitive as the originals that passed across the lieutenant general's desk, only to later be placed in folders, and then boxes, where they would sit for two hundred years, before resurfacing once again on the archival reading-room tables of Arlette Farge and Michel Foucault, who recognized and respected the value of the voices captured within enough to have them reproduced unabridged.

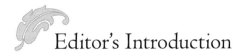 Editor's Introduction

Everything that's interesting takes place in the shadows.
Nothing is really known about people's true stories.
— CÉLINE

As originally published in 1982 by historian Arlette Farge and Michel
Foucault, *Le Désordre des familles* presented a selection of *lettres de cachet* (letters
of arrest)[1] with the aim of curating elements of a kind of popular memory
or "archive." The translator and I have decided to translate this as *Disorderly
Families*.[2] The volume reprinted *lettres de cachet* written in 1728 and 1758 per-
taining to roughly one hundred people, as well as twenty-four illustrations
bearing on the quotidian family and urban life of the Ancien Régime.[3] Divided into two sections, the volume collected letters all bearing on marital
strife and also on relations between parents and children; each section
opened with an interpretive essay. As a whole, the volume opened with a
jointly written introduction and closed with an essay titled "When Addressing the King." Foucault's consistent wish not to allow such materials to force
the reader to "consent to a 'declaration of tyranny'" meant that any interpretive apparatus around these letters must have a light touch.[4]

With murky historical origins, the *lettres de cachet* (often mistakenly glossed
as "poison-pen letters")[5] were letters addressed to the king, letters that invoked his absolute power to intervene in problems of marital and family life
by imprisoning family members on charges of theft, debauchery, drunkenness, infidelity, and other violations of civil order. Although some historians
date the letters' origins to the fourteenth century, or perhaps earlier, their
use by the king to intervene personally in the exercise of sovereignty dates to
the sixteenth century, and their frequency as a tool of royal administration
increased in the seventeenth century.[6] Often associated with the excesses of
royal absolutist power, historians initially viewed these letters as the prerogative of the king and upper aristocracy.[7] However, although some French
notables were arrested in this way (notoriously, Diderot and the Marquis
de Sade), most letters were penned by the poor and illiterate with the help
of hired scriveners. Many of the dossiers contained multiple letters; they included either repeated attempts to imprison a family member, or additional

testimonies from neighbors, the local curé, or police, or later requests that said family member be returned home. These requests for confinement were subsequently directed to and enforced by the local police—without any judicial interventions or possibility for self-defense. Taken as a whole, these letters offer a unique set of historical documents for a period in which the royal court, regional *parlements* (courts of appeal), Catholic church, and other elites dominate public record.[8] They provide a window onto the experience of ordinary lives touched by power.

HISTORY OF THE PROJECT

When Foucault first encountered these letters in the archives of the Bastille, he was fascinated by their explosive qualities—the stark contrast between their ornate openings and closing appeals (contributed by the scriveners) and the illiterate, rambling transcription of daily rancors and resentments that composed the actual plaint.[9] In an unpublished interview, Foucault describes these as "a model of writing, or a game, created by the staging of a plea and then its guttural cry—a game between the public audience and the eruption of a sort of spontaneity."[10] Elsewhere he describes them as "flash existences" or "poem-lives."[11] Each dossier offers a glimpse into a life at a crossroads—a life framed by the letter of indictment, the indignant responses from the social entourage of the accused, the laconic notes of the lieutenant general penned tersely in the margins. These dossiers are neither as voluminous as the memoirs of Herculine Barbin[12] nor as involved as the multiple testimonies around the parricide Pierre Rivière.[13] Instead, they lay bare the ligaments of power, sentiment, and moral conduct that constitute the heaving form of the social body. In so doing, these letters of arrest gesture toward the moments of agency, seized speech, and disavowal that resonate across the centuries with Foucault's work as part of the Prisons Information Group (Groupe d'information sur les prisons, or GIP).[14] In all cases, imprisonment arises from the moment of contact between public order and the obdurate with their own itineraries. Likewise, Arlette Farge's work consistently gestures toward the street as the eighteenth-century borderline between public and private, home and work, familial and social relationships; disturbance lingers around the threshold of these different sites and threatens to upset the order of things. These disturbances find their way into these letters when this contact becomes unbearable, relations have strained to breaking, and the resources of the neighborhood have become exhausted.

The collaboration between Farge and Foucault emerged from their different paths toward the material. As early as *History of Madness*, Foucault had been working with material from the period, including the *lettres de cachet*, albeit from a more institutional perspective. Many of the same institutions are there—the dungeons of Châtelet, the confinement of Charenton—along with the representatives of medical and police order.[15] While Foucault's intellectual interests moved in different directions, a research assistant slowly worked to transcribe a collection of letters.[16] Foucault does not write on them at length until "The Lives of Infamous Men."[17] That essay was written as an introduction for a differently conceived version of the volume, a version that was scrapped when Foucault fell out with editor Pierre Nora, then at Julliard.[18] Much more lyrical than the essay that now precedes the published letters, it concentrates on the movement from "fear and stupefaction" to intelligibility. That is, Foucault reflects on the reader's response that begins with aesthetic startlement, seizes the intensity of these fragmented lives, and then scaffolds up an interpretive framework to make even a fleeting sense of these poem-lives. If these lives are illuminated through their contact with power, they index both the clarity of power's gaze and the opacity of social relations that escapes beyond it. For these reasons, Deleuze calls this essay "a masterpiece."[19] In contrast to the more social-scientific language of the published volume, this essay evokes that "unending hum" that accompanies a discourse that stages scandals, shames, and secrets in the theater of power: "Characters out of Céline, trying to make themselves heard at Versailles," as Foucault writes.[20] The letters populate the eighteenth century with persons hitherto unseen and mute, and so imbue history with the "murmuring of a world."[21]

More than naive narrations of a brute reality, these letters actively stage personal resentments as questions of moralized civil order so as to justify sovereign intervention. Foucault was seized by the idea of presenting these as raw, tactile archival documents, documents whose immediacy might spark a bridge between popular past and present. Initially, he hoped to publish them without any interpretive apparatus. The letters would become *découpages*—collages from found fragments of shames and secrets, woven into cries, traps, and intrigues—whose effects arise kaleidoscopically with each reader.[22] Just as their writers resisted the social order encasing them, so would the letters remain to the side of any interpretive regime.[23] With these ideas in mind, Foucault sent Farge a letter proposing a collaboration.[24] Already he was familiar with Farge's first book, *Le Vol des aliments* (cited in *Discipline and Punish*), and they had subsequently met during the course of a May 1978 radio broadcast for her book *Vivre dans la rue à Paris au XVIIIe siècle* organized by historian Michelle Perrot.[25] Both books evidence what will become a constant theme in Farge's work: the challenge of vivifying a street-level view of the eighteenth century. Subsequent conversations with Farge, however, convinced him that more presentation was necessary to frame these texts and to sketch possible entry points for readers.[26] As a result, Farge and Foucault cowrote an introduction that treats the historical context of the letters. The introductions to each section (unattributed, although Farge will later admit to having written the first one, on marital discord)[27] outline a fluid social space crisscrossed by relations of gender and dependence, through which flow political, economic, and moral power. From their collaboration emerges the present volume.

All essays in this volume, but especially the concluding one, emphasize this prerevolutionary period as one on the cusp between disciplinary and governmental power. Echoing across the letters is the astonishing spectacle of ordinary people pleading for the king's intervention in their family life. Less the intrusion of royal power into the quotidian, the letters attest to "the distribution of that power through complex circuits and a whole interplay of petitions and responses."[28] In culling various patterns from the collected letters, Farge and Foucault's introductory essays consider the "staging of both oneself and one's partner in such a manner as to demonstrate the impossibility of shared existence."[29] Less the violation of ideals of marriage or family, such staging exposes "a whole field of confrontations that stemmed more from economic conflicts, physical violence, standing in the household, reputation in the neighborhood, and blows to a person's character."[30] These themes of domestic violence and separation, of assertions of individual judgment, and of excess resonated with the politics of 1981 and the election of President François Mitterrand. Rather than writing from nostalgia, Farge recalls that she and Foucault wrote "to pull from the past what's irregular and far from obvious in its representations, so as to bring the present to reexamine its own certainties."[31] These letters suggest the insufficiency of historical accounts premised on ideal families, popular disempowerment, and the emergence of a bourgeois public sphere. Instead, the letters reveal the disjuncture between events in daily life and the discursive constructions historians will later use to represent the period. Bluntly, letter writers seize phrases so as to seduce power, not to repel it: "Providing one knew how to play the game, every individual could become for the other a terrible and lawless monarch: *homo homini rex*."[32]

Previously, commentators starting with Frantz Funck-Brentano—the first to survey and index these letters in the early 1900s—had emphasized the absolutist nature of royal power and its miniature within the family.[33] Since then, many historians have backed away from both the claim that the eighteenth century is a long century of centralization and that familial patriarchy set the stage for its political extrapolation.[34] Instead, these letters attest to a series of tensions between different actors: between parents and children, husbands and wives, judicial and police orders, local *parlements* and royal power. One might reasonably argue that the letters and the accompanying essays elaborate Foucault's rather hasty claim in *Society Must Be Defended* that the political modes of discipline and governmentality came to exist simultaneously in the eighteenth century.[35] The nature, scope, and participation of power in this moment were volatile and subject to redirection. Pressures for democratizing access to sovereignty arose just as the police were consolidating and extending their administrative capacities into new domains. Rather than displaying an all-but-mute abjection of the vulnerable, the letters present actors at the intersection of mechanisms of power, ethics, and truth telling—actors who are willing to seize the jowls of power in the hopes of improving their lot.[36] Foucault describes that "political sovereignty penetrated into the most elementary dimension of the social body; the resources of an absolutist political power . . . could be brought into play between subject and subject . . . and in relations of interests, of profession, of rivalry, of love and hate."[37] Provocatively, Farge and Foucault claim that the paternal and political orders did not yet obviously overlap; that these letters do not demonstrate the abuse of royal power, but instead attest to the letters' popularity as a means to counter the social speech of scandal and rumor; and that the letters evince the political potentials of "speaking so as not to be spoken about."[38] The letters presented in *Disorderly Families* thus suggest an eighteenth century as caught between two different logics of politics: the sovereign and the governmental.[39] Like those they survey, the police are perched uneasily in between these two logics; their popular legitimacy demands a canny mediation of social relations within the neighborhood, even as their office takes its force from royal power.[40]

CIRCULATIONS OF GOODS, PEOPLE, AND POLICE

Watching over the human tide that surges across Paris, the police system has its own history and changing conceptions of "order." In March 1667, a royal edict disarticulated the previous functions of the civil lieutenant of Châtelet, that peculiar institution that was at once palace of justice, investigative police, and prison.[41] From these responsibilities, two lieutenancies were formed, one criminal and one civil. By 1674, the police lieutenancy became more clearly distinct from the jurisdiction of Châtelet, and by the 1760s the police had an established, threefold charge: assuring civil order and public safety (cleanliness, safety, circulation, building inspection, confiscation of arms, monitoring of gambling houses, prostitutes, and vagabonds); purging the city of all sources of disturbance (with attention to approved trade monopolies, conflict between master craftsmen and their workers, observation of holidays from work); and provisioning the city so as to prevent scarcity (regulation of markets, of price and quality of various commodities, of the circulation of goods—leading to the infamous *police des grains*).[42] Although the interactions of Châtelet and the lieutenancy were still closely entwined—through police reliance on the royal guard, not to mention the spats between police and provincial *parlements*—the lieutenant general reported directly to the king. Fairly high up in the hierarchy of royal administration, the lieutenant general rubbed elbows with the *parlement* of Paris, with members of the court, and with the king's advisers. He needed to be adept at negotiating the complicated political relations that traverse Paris, as well as at establishing an equilibrium between the overlapping judicial and police systems of the city. At the same time, however, the lieutenant general needed to have an ear and an eye turned toward the street, to attend to the circulations and movement of the city. To do so, the police would often draw on collaborators in the neighborhoods. The police sought information from innkeepers, building superintendents, master craftsmen, and local parish priests.[43] Poised between a hierarchized royal court and a social order in flux, the police sought to craft something recognizable as "order." Arguably, these negotiations are characteristic of the regulation of eighteenth-century daily life, rather than a centralized administration imposed from above.[44]

To maintain such order, the lieutenant general supervised forty-eight *commissaires* (two to three per neighborhood), who were themselves complemented by twenty *inspecteurs*.[45] They maintained a high degree of autonomy, and became part of the modernizing, yet still hierarchical, world of office. The regularization of the police, however fitful, contrasted with the patchwork of competing jurisdictions of other police units, such as the Guard (a military regiment under the Maison du Roi, with both mounted and foot patrols, as well as stationary posts), the Watch (a patrol of venal offices widely deemed incompetent), the mounted constabulary *(le maréchaussé)*, and the company of the Short Robe (that patrolled prisons) for enforcement.[46] If earlier lieutenant generals such as Nicolas de la Reynie and Marc-René d'Argenson sought to impose a social harmony or order on the city, by the time of Jean-Charles-Pierre Lenoir and Antoine de Sartine, the police recognize that they needed to adapt to the pulsating movements of Paris.[47] These circulations were multiple: in addition to the movements of people through licit and illicit spaces, the police were preoccupied with the physical conditions of travel, with the circulation of goods and services and the guild memberships and accreditation that accompany these flows. It is no surprise, then, that the police were actively involved in securing the provision of grain.[48] Second, to track these movements, the use of spies (known as *mouches* or *mouchards*—literally, "flies") as a source of information became more prevalent, starting with Lieutenant General Sartine. The use of spies varied, from requesting paid informants to proposition someone in the gardens of the Tuileries, to a months-long campaign to gain the trust of a bookstore owner selling clandestine printed material on the side. Such spying was felt by citizens to be too much and was defended by police as prophylactic and a means to avoid more repressive measures. Finally, the police themselves circulated through the city. In 1740, inspectors joined the *commissaires* so as to monitor different "at-risk" groups—in areas of morality, gambling, public safety (i.e., surveillance of foreigners), contraband, and so on—and this specialization was augmented under Lieutenant General Nicolas Berryer.[49] When Turmeau de la Morandière affirms in 1764 that the police must know where each body lives and sleeps, he seems to insist on a kind of omniscience, one "that sought to inject transparency into a body social constantly in movement and increasingly opaque."[50]

In their search for clarification of a constantly changing urban landscape— the word *éclaircissement* is used repeatedly to describe police investigations— the police develop their administration in two directions.[51] First, increasingly something like well-being—far more general than safety—becomes associated with both police administration and the city's population rather than royal benevolence. This sense of public well-being further moves away from the prerogatives of personal office that characterize the other policing units named above. Second, as the police carve up the city into zones, populations, and activities to monitor, their activities take on a politics of their own. They seize what is already a social space and make it into both their work space and a public space—even if any collective deemed "public" is in constant composition. Nonetheless, despite this apparent fluidity, Paris remained rather trapped by the sense that order was to be established through a watchful *bienvieillance*. Between popular suspicion of the police and their informants, and the internal tensions that pitted police against Châtelet, the Guard against the Watch, and superintendents against inspectors, the order sought by the police was precarious—a point underscored by the grain riots of 1748 and 1749, and the rumors of the 1750s that the police were kidnapping children and sending them to populate France's colonies.[52]

"WHEN ADDRESSING THE KING": CRAFTING A LETTER OF ARREST

Within this context of multiple and competing jurisdictions, circulations, and social networks, these letters *cachetées du cachet*—stamped with a seal—doubly marked the presence of a secret. Although most letters at the time were not sealed, the small red wax seal of the king physically attested to the secrecy and mystery of royal power. This spectacular power of the king leaves him alone capable of keeping secret these particular shames. The result, as Foucault comments, is an "extraordinary trajectory of the avowal *(aveu)*: the secret rises just to the grandeur of the king in order to be assured it will soon flee to the shadows just as the accused will flee to prison."[53] The letters display that striking and uneasy moment when those most vulnerable reveal themselves in an attempt to seduce power, not so as to bathe in its spectacle but instead to keep a secret hidden.

These letters authorized the police to arrest and imprison persons without bringing the matter before a court. Broadly, the letters can be divided into four categories: the rare ones that touch on affairs of state (such as treason); those resulting from police investigation (into prostitution, workshop disputes, libel, immorality in the theater); those that treat failures of military and religious discipline (drunkenness but also Jansenism); and those around family affairs.[54] Even the republican Malesherbes observes that letters in the second category "aim to protect society from those subjects who might be dangerous and would trouble right order and tranquility."[55] Although the first category initially garnered the most attention for their air of intrigue, the letters written by ordinary people about family matters were the most numerous by far.

Prominent families addressed their plaint directly to the king or the secretary of state of the Maison du Roi, and their request was examined within that royal council. By contrast, ordinary families sent their letters to the lieutenant general, who was charged with investigating the details, preparing a report, and then seeking the advice of the king and his council. Once approved, the lieutenant general determined the length of imprisonment. Caught between the formality and intimacy of addressing the king, the would-be letter writers—often with uncertain literacy—sought out the help of public scriveners, themselves reliant on *secrétaires*, or the letter-writing manuals that circulated as part of the popular *Bibliothèque bleue*. If aristocratic settings employed *secrétaires* as assistants, judicial stenographers, or confidants, then ordinary people made do with a politesse that betrayed its popular roots even as it sought to imitate discretion.[56] The result was frequently letters exquisitely penned in an ornate, baroque script that veered between finely wrought if formulaic salutations and the baldness of their demands and revendications. The salutations—spaciously indented, and often written halfway down the page—marked the social distance between writer and recipient on paper (itself a precious commodity). Some, more confident in their literacy, wrote their own letters and with uneven results. Across the letters, names are often spelled phonetically and inconsistently, spelling errors abound, and punctuation is abandoned. The result is a rush of written and oral language that blends intimacy and public speech.[57]

Initially, the prepared police reports were detailed and rather lengthy. As both the number of letters and the autonomy of the police grew, these reports shortened and often the police acted before formally requesting royal approval. Laconic scribbles in the margins occasionally hinted at police investigations. Police archives themselves swelled with police registers, written reports, and information bulletins produced through surveillance. Matching the perambulations of the population, these archival circulations made their way from the *mouches*, to the morality police, all the way to the lieutenant general. Order betrayed itself through constant movements, and public well-being became sought through furtive probing.

Indeed, the charges that strike contemporary ears as so distant and untimely—libertinage, vagabondage, debauchery—speak to the threats posed by being out of place and out of time. Where debauchery often gestured toward a sexual brazenness in women, the more general charge of *infâme* served as an epithet for a life in excess, as well as a euphemism for those trapped by police spies in homosexual activity.[58] Curiously, however, this activity seemed neither connected to an identity nor especially pursued by family members (and in this volume concern only the case of Nicolas Fieffé). Less than signs of moral depravity, these charges were claims about social relations splintered, deformed, or outright broken. Those accused of libertinage were faithless, bound to no principles or persons and so willing to wager. Debauchery captured excess, one that might signal a night of gaiety among the usually restrained, but a more fundamental tendency to indulgence or sexual brazenness among the others. In times of scarcity, vagabondage posed a special threat. Differently from the mendicants more permanently without means, vagabonds were the unknown who floated from town to town, unencumbered by responsibilities, social ties, or connections. They might well be *les gens sans-aveus*—those for whom nobody would speak, literally the "no-accounts" left unclaimed. Focused on these categories of beggars, vagabonds, and the *sans-aveus*, the royal edict of July 18, 1724, distinguished between the "true poor" *(le véritable pauvre)* and the criminally idle. For the first time, it provided royal funds for local hospitals that offered assistance for the "true poor" and served as workhouses for the putatively disreputable; the edict was motivated by the perceived belief that day laborers were scarce because of the appeal of being a lazy beggar. Enforced until 1733 as part of the Great Confinement *(Grand Renfermement)*, the edict was ultimately decided not to be effective, and royal officials sought other measures of surveillance.[59] By the end of the eighteenth century, the police specifically targeted inns and taverns, so as to use the proper identification and registration of guests to counter the rootlessness inherent to such sites. Within this context, the *lettres de cachet* sought to protect honor and to avoid scandal—again, to "speak before being spoken about."

Detention became a way to place people who were out of place, and to hide a secret in plain sight. Preoccupations with proper placement and order explain why so many sites—Bicêtre, Charenton, the Salpêtrière, Châtelet—are alternately referred to as prisons, châteaus, hospitals, or houses *(maisons)* of detention or healing. Initially, these sites indiscriminately sought to confine those misfits of whatever kind. All of these sites populate Foucault's earlier *History of Madness*, a book that narrates the movement from a general preoccupation with exclusion (and a simple distinction between reason and unreason) to a regime later dominated by more targeted classification and control. If initially these multiple and overlapping jurisdictions drew their authority from an equally byzantine set of political hierarchies, these conflicts later came to be seen as a different threat to order. No longer could prisoners, the poor, and the insane suffer the same kinds of exclusion and share the same spaces. By the nineteenth century and the 1806 Napoleonic Civil Code, confinement came to have different purposes for different populations.

CRITICAL RECEPTION AND INTERPRETIVE DEBATE

Upon its publication as part of the Archives Collection directed by historian Pierre Nora, *Le Désordre des familles* received little immediate attention. The volume's publication came during "a moment of complete silence by Foucault," according to Arlette Farge, one that was a transitional period in his work and health.[60] Some years later, Farge speculated that the initial slight reception resulted from disappointment that there were "too many texts and not enough Foucault" in the volume.[61] Nonetheless, there was sufficient popular interest that Farge and Foucault gave several radio addresses in which they discussed the project and its implications for thinking about power as something constituted "from below."[62] Critical reception to the book might be divided into two camps: a warm, if quiet, reception within the Anglophone press and a sniffy critical reception among French historians. In the first camp, one of the few extant reviews comes from Michael Ignatieff in the *Times Literary Supplement*, a review that describes the letters as a "poignant pantomime" of "intimate family life before [the king's] unseen gaze."[63] Even as Ignatieff emphasized the moving nature of the letters, French historians debated how to place them in conversation with the political and social dynamics of prerevolutionary France. In later interviews, Farge recounts that historian Emmanuel Todd likened the book to support for "Tea Party populism" *(un populisme poujadiste)*.[64]

At the moment of publication, Foucault was engulfed in serious dispute with leading French historians (mostly associated with the *Annales* school), including Jacques Léonard, Emmanuel Le Roy Ladurie, Robert Mandrou, and Emmanuel Todd himself, many of whom doubted his historical chops and questioned his collaboration on this volume with a female unknown. The book intervenes at the intersection of a series of debates around the French Revolution that turn to the Revolution as a touchstone for rethinking the nature of political and social relations.[65] These debates pressed on the challenges of continuity and rupture; the different connections one might draw between ordinary lives of individuals and extraordinary political conjunctures; as well as the disjuncture that divides lived experience during tumultuous times and its subsequent theorization. Already the 1970s and 1980s had witnessed the emergence of the Italian *microstoria* (cf. Carlo Ginzburg), the turn to the quotidian (cf. Michel de Certeau, Giovanni Levi), or the intransigently personal (cf. Jacques Le Goff).[66] Many of these historians, however, were skeptical of what they considered to be personal anecdote and instead used personal histories to illustrate large, slow-moving historical forces. In the French edition to his landmark *The Cheese and the Worms*, Ginzburg takes clear aim at Foucault and accuses him of an "aesthetic irrationalism" that is "the fruit of a refusal to analyze and interpret."[67] Foucault offers nothing but "populism 'through the looking glass'—a dark populism, but always populism."[68]

What to make of this sharp critique? Initially, the charge that the presentation of these letters "from below" was populist might seem warranted. After all, the practice of *découpage* risks overemphasizing the aesthetic and the anecdotal. It is further tempting to view these letters as claims made by antiheroic figures, or as a speech that escapes beyond the official discourse of power.[69] To read the letters in that light would be to sentimentalize them and to imbue these fragments with a sustained counterpower that they do not have. Farge claims that differently from Ginzburg, Levi, and even her mentor, historian Jacques Revel, she and Foucault sought to move social conflict into the foreground of their presentation. After all, as she and Foucault argue, the letters continued well into the eighteenth century owing to popular demand, and the practice ended only when local police became overburdened with requests. Indeed, the letters themselves participate in the staging of representations of suffering rather than simple storytelling. To consider the framing for *Disorderly Families*, one might recall the film review of *I, Pierre Rivière* as directed by René Allio: "[it] brings to life hidden inner worlds, revealing the post-medieval brutality perched on the edge of administrative and scientific modernity."[70] The letters that compose the volume vivify the same transitional moment between absolutist and administrative modes of power, the irruptions of domestic life into the social, and the perversities of presuming that psychological health be assessed in terms of family harmony. In retrospect, then, *Disorderly Families* attests to the movements that veer back and forth between disorder and order—movements that Farge will later argue characterize the very discipline of history.

On its own terms, *Disorderly Families* should be understood less as theory applied or as a one-off event than as a window onto the period preceding the Revolution. The letters bear witness to what Foucault describes in the lecture series *Abnormal* as "the power of normalization"—that these infamous lives are contoured by the effects of juridical struggles on the one hand, and emergent social norms on the other. Itinerants threatened to disrupt the fragile network of relations and lives that traversed the city, to the point that the lawyer for the comtesse de Mirabeau, as she requested a marital separation from her debauched husband in 1783, described him as a "bad son, bad husband, bad father, bad citizen, and dangerous subject."[71] Such charges of "bad conduct" were something other than efforts to exclude. With such a charge came the implication that a person didn't know his place—that his personal errancy led him to cross from public into private spaces and back again with little sense of how such itinerancy reverberated across his connections to others. Rather than simple, clear distinctions between private activities and public practices, French eighteenth-century life knew an entanglement of conducts, spaces, and orders. And yet these entanglements were also the condition of agency, of efforts to juxtapose intimate address and public claim, and so to use spectacular power to rectify the disorders of daily life.

Within the broader context of Farge and Foucault's other texts, then, the book challenges relations between so-called private and public, as well as usual accounts of the contact between these norms and power. The arrangement of these "familial letters," read alongside Farge and Foucault's essays, complicates the normative force of power and captures an eighteenth-century society in which public and private are thoroughly interpenetrated.[72] The letters represent an effort to use the terrain of social, written word—the language of scandal, rumor, actuality—so as to regulate those problems that irrupt in everyday life without necessarily demanding the direct gaze or intervention of public power. The gap, then, is more than a gap between discourses and practices. It traces the fracture within which lived experiences exceed efforts to be defined, contained, and ordered. In her subsequent books, Farge amplifies her work with these documents and others to capture the fluidity of a social space defined more by frontiers—frontiers that separate personal spaces inside the home or the workshop, for example, and the public life outside in the street—than by strict demarcations.[73] Such lives are fragile not because they define those unfortunates one can only console and classify, but because the itineraries they trace—through the quartiers of Paris, out past the drinking holes that pepper the city's gates, into nearby villages with the promise of escape—are transitory and teeter on the borderlands of public and private. Identities here are not settled, most noticeably in terms of gender and sexuality. Farge tartly emphasizes that women, both as letter writers and as social actors, agitate on their own behalf and demand (and receive) attention; it is not until the nineteenth century that the divide between public and private will be used to confine them.[74]

The phrasing that travels from Foucault's earlier work to this later enterprise is that of dangerous or "bad subjects."[75] These letters chart lives that teeter along the historical divide between "bad" and "dangerous" subjects, between those subjects excluded to the undifferentiated space of unreason, and those regulated according to increasingly medicalized norms.[76] The letters emerge from the history of madness charted in Foucault's earliest work—they are written from within the moment when the *représentance* (making present) of madness as unreason came into frictive contact with new practices of diagnosis and confinement enacted by the *lieutenance* (maintaining place) of the police.[77] Representation operated according to a logic of exclusion, policing according to a logic of regulation. From within this disjuncture emerges a peculiar political space. If, under the lieutenant general, the police sought both to control and to incite (leaving actions always already regulated), then through the representational power of the king, the terms of agency become inverted. Ordinary people could seize the incitement to speak in order to act: to protest, inveigh, and condemn. In an interview, Foucault explains: "It isn't true that in a given society, some people are *em*powered and below them are people who don't have *any* power at all."[78] Nonetheless, such seizures of speech were dangerous. Even the later French revolutionaries became nervous about outright prison abolition—

what might those imprisoned do if freed?—and preserved the family *lettres de cachet* even as they demanded that each letter be signed by more witnesses. These letters thus challenge contemporary readers to insist on the agency of lives lived on the margins of today's world, and the strategies and constraints for demanding political audience.[79]

Finally, the letters focus attention on what Foucault later refers to as "eventialization," a concept that Farge and other historians will subsequently develop. Mixing genres, Foucault describes the letters repeatedly as a "dramaturgy of the real" or "fragments of discourse trailing the reality they are a part of," a "mise-en-scène" of ordinary life.[80] This "theater of the quotidian" breaks up the solidity of institutions and reveals the rituals and strategies in play.[81] Such rhetorical staging also affects what counts as truth, by making visible the collective anonymity of the impersonal "they say" often associated with the institutional workings of power.[82] So argues Roger Chartier in *The Order of Books* (itself a play on Foucault's *The Order of Things* and on his inaugural lecture at the Collège de France, "The Order of Discourse").[83] For Chartier, by working with the layered patternings that emerge in the archives scholars can capture "the event" at both a discursive and a political level. He explains that "Apprehension of speech responds to an interest in reintroducing existences and singularities into historical discourse, in using words to draw scenes that are as many events."[84] Voice emerges not as the all-but-mute mutterings of the abject but as the condition of disjuncture: a disjuncture between the categories manipulated by actors in history and the concepts used in the course of (later) analysis. The *lettres de cachet* take on unusual importance, then, as they both seek access to the political scene and to wrangle over the terms of lived, political, and historical truths.

A final word on the editorial notes and translation. So that these poem-lives do not become leaden under the weight of scholarly commentary, the interpretive imprint of the English translation has been kept as unobtrusive as possible. A Glossary of Places and a Name Index come at the end of the volume, to clarify key places and historical figures as they flit in and out of the ordinary lives of the letter writers and to contextualize the family genealogies that underly the letters themselves. These sections make it possible to trace different itineraries—to move westward from Les Halles, past the putrefaction of the slaughterhouses to the salt merchants, trade depots, and prisons entangled in the areas around Grand Châtelet and its annex across the Seine, the Petit Châtelet. Likewise, as translator Thomas Scott-Railton explains in his preface, the translation has sought to preserve the slightly musty effect of certain eighteenth-century words and phrases that evoke a social context that haunts the present even as its material presence has dissipated. So, for example, the *marchand à cheveux* is translated as a "hair merchant," a figure slightly less elevated than *un perruquier* or wigmaker. Two phrases were especially difficult to grapple with. One is the translation of *aveu*, translated in volume I of *History of Sexuality* as "confession." However, *aveu* in French usually connotes a more straightforwardly judicial context: the context of avowal. The editors of Foucault's lectures on truth telling and juridical mechanisms of power, given at the Université Catholique de Louvain in 1981, argue for the use of *avowal* rather than *confession* so as to minimize the religious connotations of the latter. We have done the same. The two projects are nearly contemporaneous, and Foucault likewise writes of testimonies before a social entourage not limited to religious figures. Furthermore, the letters make clear that any attestations are staged for an emphatically public audience, rather than standing as private matters of conscience or soul. Consequently, where Farge and Foucault use *aveu*, translator Thomas Scott-Railton and I have decided to use "avowal" rather than "confession."

Second, and similarly, the phrase *rentrer en soi-même* is extraordinarily difficult to translate. Farge and Foucault comment numerous times in various interviews on the enigmatic beauty of the phrase. *Rentrer en soi-même* signals a return to one's self, so as to take stock of one's forces and start out anew. If *rentrer* has the sense of entering again, according to the 1762 *Dictionnaire de l'Académie française*, then *rentrer en soi-même* is a figure of speech whose definition evokes reflection *(se faire réflexion)* but is not purely cerebral. A concept that hovers between religious penitence, juridical evaluation, and social disapprobation, the connotations of the phrase change over the eighteenth and nineteenth centuries: from a sense of recollection (1764), to one of coming to one's senses (1833), to retiring into oneself (1876).[85] Thomas Scott-Railton and I considered numerous translations—from "enter into oneself" (which captures the spatiality important to thinking of the family as a site of social relations but is inelegant in English), to "turn inwards" (which suggests a stronger sense of withdrawal than perhaps existed at the time and has a contemporary, psychological tone), to "consult" or "search oneself" (often used in translations of Rousseau, who writes later in the eighteenth century than these letters). In the end, we settled on "to look within," which captures the movement of self-reflexivity and marks the interiority at stake with a question mark. What was asked of penitents was not quite the self-absorption of modern "soul-searching."[86] Instead, they were asked to use their forced isolation to reconsider their place within an emphatically social setting, and the morals that oriented them. Foucault refers to these letters in distinguishing various modes of self-cultivation that do not reduce to "know thyself," and so suggests that these returns have not yet taken on the confessional overtones of the late nineteenth century.[87]

DISORDERLY FAMILIES

Introduction

The idea that history is dedicated to "archival exactitude" and philosophy to the "architecture of ideas" is, to us, nothing short of preposterous. This is not how we work.[1]

One of us studied Parisian street life in the eighteenth century;[2] the other, the procedures for administrative imprisonment from the seventeenth century up to the Revolution.[3] Both of us came to work with what are called the "Archives of the Bastille," which are stored in the Bibliothèque de l'Arsenal.[4] These are, for the most part, dossiers concerning police matters that were compiled at the Bastille, scattered by the Revolution and later reassembled.[5]

Reading through these archives, the two of us had been struck by certain facts. First, there was the large number of these dossiers that pertained to *lettres de cachet*[6] and, more precisely, requests addressed either to the lieutenant of police or directly to the Maison du Roi that sought to obtain from the sovereign an "order" that would restrict an individual's freedom (sometimes through house arrest or exile, but more often than not through imprisonment).[7] We were also struck by the fact that, in many cases, these requests dealt with family matters that were altogether private: minor conflicts between parents and children, marital disagreements, the misbehavior of a spouse, the disorder of a boy or girl. It also became clear to us that the large majority of these requests came from modest, sometimes even quite poor, households—from the small-time vendor or artisan to the market gardener, the secondhand clothes seller, the domestic servant, or the day laborer.[8] Finally, we noticed that, despite the fragmentary nature of these archives, we could often find a whole series of related documents surrounding these requests for imprisonment: statements from neighbors, families, or entourages, the investigation of the police superintendent, the king's decision, requests for release coming from the victims of imprisonment or even from those who had initially requested it.[9]

For all of these reasons, it seemed to us that these documents could offer a fascinating peek into the landscape of daily life for the lower classes in Paris during the era of the absolute monarchy—or at the very least for a certain period of the Ancien Régime.[10] One might think that these *lettres de cachet* would offer documentation of royal absolutism, of the manner in which the monarch punished his enemies or helped an important family get rid of one of its members. Yet it was not royal anger that we found while combing through these dossiers, but rather the passions of the common people, at the center of which were family relationships—husbands and wives, parents and children.[11]

After a few words about the history of *lettres de cachet*, the way in which they functioned, and the reasons that guided our choices amid this mass of documents, we will provide the unabridged dossiers that we have selected: namely, those that concerned requests by a husband or wife for the imprisonment of a spouse or by parents for the imprisonment of their children, for the years 1728 and 1758. In a final chapter, we will indicate several perspectives that we believe emerge from this grouping of documents.

THE KING'S ORDERS

We must excavate the history of *lettres de cachet* from underneath thick layers of received wisdom, which remembers of them only that they served to imprison disloyal nobles or important vassals who were being troublesome—the *lettre de cachet* as a public act that served to eliminate an enemy of power without any other form of legal process.[12] History immortalized it by making it a symbol of the fall of the Bastille. What has eluded memory are the countless letters to the king that served an altogether different purpose than the affairs of the state.[13] In Paris, the creation of the police lieutenancy, responsible both for the city's police and for dispatching *lettres de cachet*, accentuated this phenomenon.[14] The lieutenants were quick to make use of this simple, flexible, fast, and formality-free means of arrest and imprisonment. It was a way of rapidly securing the person of the accused. The justice system was so unwieldy that perpetrators would often escape before a trial could be organized. It was only by a decree of *prise de corps* that a judge could order an arrest, except in cases of *in flagrante*.[15] Only then could the inquiry begin and the judge could only hear witnesses after subpoenaing them. It was therefore not uncommon for the prosecutor general to simply request incarceration directly by *lettre de cachet*.

The use of the *lettres de cachet* for police matters was therefore quite common in Paris. The term "police matter" (*affaire de police*)[16] was sufficiently vague and imprecise that a wide swath of cases could fall under its heading.

A conflict between master and apprentice could quickly become a police matter.[17] Public assembly was a royal crime, and throughout the sixteenth, seventeenth, and eighteenth centuries, laborers' associations were regularly prohibited by countless decrees, ordinances, and edicts. In order to enforce compliance with the ban on assembly, the king often made use of *lettres de cachet.* When it was just a case of a conflict between a single master and apprentice, ordinary judges would then take charge of the matter. Speed was of the essence, because the fear of disorder in the workshop outweighed the desire for regular procedures for determining guilt. Once again, the *lettre de cachet* was the simplest tool for discreetly and secretly imprisoning a headstrong laborer, one who demanded more from his master every payday or was quick to rebel.[18] This explicit usage of the royal letter partly explains the scarcity of labor conflicts in the judicial archives; to the contrary, it intimates the hypothesis—which would need to be proven—that a large body of conflicts may have been quickly hidden behind the hermetic leaden veil of the *lettres de cachet.* A police matter could be awfully convenient.

"Disturbing the peace" was sufficient reason for dispatching a *lettre.* Prostitution, for example, constituted disorder on the public thoroughfare, and the *lettre de cachet* was called upon to remedy this supposedly scandalous debauch; it made possible the regular raids that carted women off to the Salpêtrière hospital in front of jeering crowds. Actors would also experience the rigors of this form of jurisdiction that was not truly law: the "orders of the King for acts of theater" imprisoned in the For-l'Évêque those who were considered troublemakers for being bad actors.[19]

A document preserved in the Archives of the Bastille can give us a better understanding of how the orders of the king and the decisions of the police worked in tandem to clean up the capital: the register of inspector Poussot, kept regularly from 1738 to 1754.[20] Responsible for the neighborhood of Les Halles, Poussot recorded in alphabetical order the arrests carried out under his authority, and he included a good deal of information about those arrested (last name, first name, age, job, home, date of arrest, name of the authority that made the decision, reason for arrest, name of the prison).[21]

Of the 2,692 people arrested and detained in these records, 1,468 were taken on the king's orders, which is to say a little more than half. The others were imprisoned on the decision of the police.[22] Inspector Poussot was therefore working as a direct agent of the king, which differentiated him entirely from a police superintendent. He was not acting based on civil complaints, but on royal directions that permitted searches and arrests of suspected individuals. The inspector's lists offer a glimpse into the subjects who made the monarchy nervous and its rapid methods of responding.

As one turns the pages of this register, reading the names of all these men and women, noting the nicknames that are so common on these sheets, which tell us both so much and so little, a landscape begins to take shape. Almost three thousand people washed up on these pages, most of them young, more often than not born far from the capital. They exercised almost every trade except the noblest ones. They lie immobilized here after having known itinerancy, the precariousness of seasonal work, the heavy atmosphere of taverns and trafficking, the quick alliances made with others no more fortunate than they and just as tempted by malice, the swindles and the fraudulent deals that were accepted out of either haste or need, the bands that one joined in the countryside, and the women of the world to whom one attached one's misery as well as one's roguish ambitions. Swindlers, troops of undisciplined soldiers, beggars, women of chance, accomplished thieves, heads of gangs, and poor wretches—they are all here, filling the columns with their swift itineraries that were suddenly brought up short by arrest and imprisonment. But this was not the end of their journey: some escaped from prison, were freed or transferred, some returned, and some wandered until the end of their days, "roving the countryside" *(roulant les campagnes),* as it was called at the time. This is where this register's paradox lies: it freezes the lives of people quite suddenly, yet at the same time a feeling of incessant movement, of constant circulation, escapes from it. Not only does it deal mostly with migrants, but the information that can sometimes be learned about their backgrounds illustrates the extent to which this world was moving, fugitive, here and elsewhere; the bands of crooks that we can make out so clearly reinforce this impression of displacements both large and small, of fleetingness and elusiveness. Beneath Poussot's neat tableaus lies a mob of miscreants and wretches, an immense wave that breaks and spreads, that draws back up and escapes, or perhaps sinks in so as to better resume and reappear anew.[23]

It is also an image of Paris as seen through its nights; the searches carried out in furnished lodgings, rooms at inns, and closed spaces of ill repute are windows into nighttime life. An inspector could enter anywhere; he could interrupt someone's rest, surprise lovers or adulterers, demand of anyone that she justify her activities. Secure in this knowledge, he waited for nightfall to hunt his prey, certain that time and darkness were on his side.[24] Poussot meticulously assembles before us all of these ensnared beings, who no doubt naively believed that the night would protect them. Here we do not find thieves captured by the crowd, having snatched a fowl from the market, clothes from a vendor's stall, or laundry hanging from a washerwoman's clothesline, even if a few thieves of church linens have slipped in, having been caught in the act or identified by passersby. Instead, we see a mass of individuals who were often known to the police, whom they sought out based on indications from obsequious informants or higher authorities.[25] All that remained was to pluck them up once night had fallen in forbidden places, such as the gaming houses or the taverns that had not yet closed their shutters, or in places of sleep, such as furnished lodgings and inns—undoubtedly with the assistance of the records kept by innkeepers and hoteliers, who were under strict surveillance by the inspectors, and, moreover, did not mind receiving a little something for their troubles.

Nocturnal Paris enshrouded in its countless shadowy refuges the "scoundrel" who was so frightening and at the same time so fascinating, who always seemed to add debauch to his other evil deeds, who in truth could aptly be called a criminal, who knew the capital's thousand and one hideaways, using them to cloak his complicities, loot, and plots, who the bourgeois were persuaded represented the entirety of the people. He was in a certain sense a backdrop that justified police actions of all kinds, even the most sordid ones. Here in these documents we find assembled a population whose criminal activity was for the most part a way of living, one that did not much resemble the Paris of mornings and afternoons whose echoes can be found with the police superintendent.

The three thousand people arrested by Inspector Poussot's men in effect unveil the Paris that the dominant order refused. Behind these arrests, we can make out the desire of the police to be present in all of the capital's secret places, the desire for royal intervention at all levels, in the street as in the home.[26] At the same time, we can foresee the futility of such an undertaking once we start to understand in snatches how petty delinquency functioned. Furtive, moving, and already organized; delinquency, built around the model of a family (delinquency often ran in the family) or of a certain ritualization of male–female relationships, always seemed to rise from its own ashes. Neither the king's orders that struck into this elusive populace nor even death itself could interrupt these activities.

In a similar manner, a lack of military or religious discipline permitted the quick imprisonment of restless soldiers or clergy who were not faithful to the standard rules.[27] The number of clerics who were secreted away in this manner is very impressive: a study by Henri Debord places the number of *lettres de cachet* dispatched against clerics for France as a whole between 1741 and 1775 at 6,000 (in comparison with 17,000 to 18,000 letters dispatched against laypeople).[28] Even if these numbers are only approximate, their scale is remarkable.

It should also be noted that these royal letters had other powers besides imprisonment.[29] They could be appended to the actions of the court to complete, confirm, or increase the sentences given. Finally, the lieutenant general of the police would often use orders of the king to keep presumed thieves, whom ordinary justice could not convict for lack of evidence, incarcerated. The system of royal orders not only mirrored standard procedures but insinuated itself into them and modified them, perverting them from the inside.

AT THE FAMILY'S REQUEST

As a royal order, the family *lettre de cachet* was no different from others: like any social group, the family owed transparency to the king. Out of a need for order, private and public life melted into one another: the family was a privileged space where private tranquillity yielded a certain kind of public order. Thus, the king had the right to scrutinize its operation and its troubles.

The system of family repression that this authorized enclosed a particular site in the social order where a curious duel occurred—one in which the balance of power was often unequal—between the representatives of authority in the family and one of its members. The two parties did not fight alone; they tapped into their respective networks of social relationships, which would testify in their favor. The letter of imprisonment came to apply its punishment within a family fabric that was itself made up of relationships with others. And this is certainly one of the first characteristics that we should emphasize: the family *lettre de cachet,* despite the importance given to its secrecy, never concerned the family alone, demonstrating the ways in which the family was necessarily enmeshed with the world surrounding it and the impossibility for a family of ever remaining isolated, even if that was desired.

In Paris, family requests for imprisonment followed a procedure that was altogether specific to the capital: powerful families addressed their petition *(placet)* to the king himself or to a minister of the Maison du Roi.[30] In the royal council, in the effective presence of the king, the "petition" would be examined with care.[31]

The lower orders proceeded in an altogether different manner; they sent their petitions to the lieutenant general of the police, who examined them in his office, who oversaw the investigations and would hand down the rulings. This investigation would necessarily bring the affair to the attention of the superintendent of the neighborhood, who would delegate his power to gather information to a police inspector. The lower-class family, to a great extent permeated with its neighborhood and integrated into an intense urban life, cannot be severed neatly from these social capillaries. The root structure of the city, neighbors, superintendents, priests, merchants, and tenants formed a soil without which the family did not exist. Once he had informed himself in this manner, the police lieutenant drafted a detailed report for the minister and waited for the secretary of state for the Maison du Roi to send the order. Or, at least, this was the standard procedure under Louis XIV, but it was not long before it was warped and simplified under the reign of Louis XV.[32] We often see lieutenant generals drawing up only the briefest of notes and not even waiting for the royal response before taking it upon themselves to execute the orders of the king.

Going through the lieutenant general of the police was a Parisian invention, which also explains the constant slippage between ordinary judgments and royal orders, because in practice both were managed by the same person. In the provinces, forms of procedure differed. In Languedoc, for example, it was "military authority . . . that guarantees the order of families and, as protector of the rights of the nobility, it receives the complaints and recriminations of this class."[33] It received all the petitions from other circles as well: the imprisonment of a family member was not the prerogative of the aristocracy.

With the family *lettre de cachet* came the establishment of legalized private repression: royal authority would grant the legal authorization to imprison a given individual at the family's request, but would in no way pay the costs for the prisoner's detention. If you wished to have a relative punished without going through the ordinary public legal mechanisms, it was necessary, on the one hand, to supplicate the king and convince him of your woes such that he would deign to send the official order, and, on the other hand, to assist the king financially, as the royal administration could not be expected to bear the costs of imprisonment. The signature of the order was monetized: the money accompanying a tale of woe was an important piece of evidence in favor of conviction.

For contemporaries, this was traditional practice; it was a government function that was accepted and solicited—which explains the size of the dossiers for each case and the energetic insistence with which petitions were drafted. Writing to the lieutenant general of police to apprise him of the unbearable problems existing within your family was an adventure in the real sense of the word, especially if you were a member of the lower classes. You first had to find a public scribe who would transmit all of the details of a stormy and turbulent daily existence, couched in the standard forms of respect due to His Majesty.[34] Reading these dossiers, one is amazed by the sheer accumulation of domestic details and by the enormous amount of paperwork generated by this private unhappiness, which reflects intimacy and the dark shadows of family relationships. After the petitions came the testimony of neighbors. Sometimes they signed their names at the bottom and mentioned their professions, sometimes they wrote separately and spoke for themselves as to what they knew, had heard, or had seen. Distant members of the family, the innkeeper from the street-corner, the merchant grocer from the ground floor, or the tenants from across the hall were the principal signatories. In order to render a petition more convincing, one would do well to convince the parish curé, an influential person in the neighborhood, or the primary leaseholder, that feared, honored and hated guarantor of Parisian buildings.[35]

If it was a question of imprisoning a son or daughter and the father was dead or absent, the mother could make the request. In this case, she would surround herself with those close to her, and the "statement by the relatives" (*avis de parents*) would confer a greater weight to her undertaking. The petition was received by a secretary of the lieutenant general of the police who sent it to the superintendent and inspector of the neighborhood in question "in order to verify the facts and provide a report." Ordinarily, they were to conduct their investigations separately, but in reality, one of them took care of the work and wrote up a report on the petition, while the other commented on this report. The inspector listened to the witnesses, neighbors, and signatories; then the superintendent reported to the lieutenant general of the police. The level of detail in these reports varied by case and by superintendent. It was then the lieutenant's job to draw up his own report and send it to king's secretary. This was often purely a formality on his part; he would sometimes execute the order for imprisonment without having waited to receive a response.

1728–1758: A SURVEY

A close study of the Archives de la Bastille where documents of this type are found will reveal that they are incomplete. For one, we find very few requests for imprisonment for family reasons prior to the 1720s. What is more, these requests are also very scarce in the Archives de la Bastille for years after 1760.

In reality, these two facts do not share an explanation. At the end of the seventeenth century, and at the beginning of the eighteenth, political and religious affairs were the main focus in the king's orders that have been preserved: affairs of *convulsionnaires* and Jansenists, spies and foreign agents, and then a mass of small-time drawers of horoscopes, fortune tellers, "schemers," and restless souls.[36] The idea that *lettres de cachet* were used principally for public matters and only rarely for private family matters seems to be confirmed by Lenoir, lieutenant general of police—if we are to believe the account he gave after leaving his position, which is found in his papers preserved at the Municipal Library of Orléans:[37]

> The origin of the orders of the King called family *lettres de cachet* dates back to the administration of M. d'Argenson. Their usage was more common during the administration of M. Berryer and even more so during that of M. de Sartine than during my own. It was held at the time that the dishonor of an individual reflected on his family, and therefore the governments and politics came to the rescue of relatives who had a legitimate reason to fear that they might be dishonored. This measure is necessary in a large city like Paris where the youth are exposed to all of the dangers of corruption.[38]

We can therefore allow that the 1750s marked a real increase in the requests for incarceration for family reasons.

On the other hand, their near disappearance from the Archives de la Bastille after 1760 is more enigmatic. We know that Sartine, during the period at the end of the reign of Louis XV, and even Lenoir, despite his claims of using them "more restrictively," were reputed to have made wide-scale use of this type of procedure. Did not he himself say: "There were few families in Paris among whom there is not single a person who over the space of ten or twelve years did not seek recourse in the administrative magistrate of the general police in this city, for affairs concerning his honor." Moreover, in 1784, when Breteuil sent his famous memorandum limiting the practice, it is quite clear that at that moment it had not fallen into disuse.[39] Therefore, family petitions did not cease being sent in the 1760s, yet at that moment their trail disappears from the Archives de la Bastille. We must therefore assume that for the years in question the requests and the dossiers containing them were archived in a different manner, and then lost or dispersed over time.

We therefore have access to a rich trove of documentation for the 1720–60 period (which does not mean, of course, that these represent all of the petitions addressed by Parisian families over these forty years). We have selected two dates: 1728 and 1758, one at the beginning and one at the end of this period, separated by the thirty years of a generation. Certainly, the year 1758 coincides with the brief lieutenancy of Bertin de Bellisle, but a comparison with neighboring years (1756 and 1760) shows that, at least in this respect, his administration did not represent anything singular.[40] The documents from these two years (1728 and 1758) are plentiful enough, their convergence is clear enough, and, to be honest, they are repetitive enough that we can allow ourselves to think that we have a representative sample (even if they do not allow for quantitative evaluation).

An examination of the years 1728 and 1758 reveals that they contain 168 and 74 requests from families for imprisonment, respectively—the years 1756 and 1760 give us 67 and 76 dossiers of the same type of affairs—which is to say about one-fifth of the total requests for imprisonment. Even if these are precarious, uncertain, and undoubtedly far from the true quantitative reality, starting from them we can submerge ourselves in the registers and uncover through affair after affair the taut threads of a history of families that decided to expose themselves to the king in their suffering, revealing at the same time an intimacy where the tragic and the derisory are at every moment entwined.

Marital Discord

PUTTING AN END TO ONE'S MISERY

Fewer in number than requests from parents, as they represent only one-third of the incarceration requests from families, requests between spouses are surprising and significant, sometimes even elusive, documents. It is easy to see that they are, of course, full of traps that an analysis must both elude and employ. If a wife wished to have her spouse imprisoned, she needed to convince the king of the horror of her situation and present him with arguments that would both meet the formal requirements and be definitive. A husband had to do the same if he decided that his wife merited a royal order. One presented a staging of both oneself and one's partner in such a manner as to demonstrate the impossibility of shared existence. Inspectors, superintendents, and the lieutenant general of police would be the audience for this performance; it was on the basis of their indications that the royal signature would be granted. The stakes were high, and one did not denounce one's partner for trifles. The words used, the situations described, the accusations leveled may have been manifestations of the truth (it would in fact be up to the investigation to make the necessary verifications), but they also evoke that which one could not be asked to endure in conjugal life, and in this sense they proclaimed norms outside of which life together was no longer possible. Conversely, they illustrated—through the expressions of real lived experience or through crafted lies, it matters little—tableaus of conjugal life that were all so many expressive images.[1]

Behind these words, and even beyond proof of the precision of the facts, there hide collective expectations: neighbors, priests, families, men and women, molded by both their social and political statuses and by their relationships of dependency, echoed a certain archetypal representation of what family life should not be. From this, a consensus was created, and the petition delivered to the king would necessarily reflect the dark marks of disappointment, of bitterness. By marrying me, he should have . . . in marrying me, she should have . . . None of which he or she did; in fact, quite the opposite.

In any case, husband and wife alike made use of the *lettre de cachet*. Taking all the years as a whole, the numbers show that there are slightly more requests for the imprisonment of a partner from her than from him.[2] Although we should not attach too much importance to this minor difference, given the gaps in the sources and the small numbers involved, we should none-theless be attentive to the reciprocal possibility for this undertaking.[3] It is not nothing to be able to show that, contrary to expectations and received wisdom, women and men were on an even footing in this space of potential repression. And there was equality with respect to the royal decisions as well.[4] A woman's expectations of her marriage were just as important as a man's and the disappointment of these expectations was regarded similarly. The question that remains is whether there was a difference in the content of these expectations, and, if so, of what kind?

Putting this equality aside for the moment, we should be quick to empha-size the gravity of this undertaking. Requesting that your spouse be locked up was a significant act, one that was never done lightly and that arose only out of desperation and as a last resort, after numerous attempts at reconcilia-tion and appeals of all kinds addressed as much to neighbors as to the super-intendent. Petitions were never sent to the king immediately following mar-riage; they always came after a long period of shared existence. It was after an average of twelve years of marriage that a request was made, at the moment, one might say, when the ship was sinking, when all hope had crumbled, when an already difficult life now seemed definitively lost.[5] From that moment on, the only hope lay in separation, either with the request that it be permanent or in the hopes that it would elicit repentance and forgiveness. The alterna-tive was the following: never again living with one's spouse, the source of all of one's sorrows and woes, or waiting for punishment to imprint on his or her soul the desire to return to other proceedings.

Because of how long they had lived together before one of them addressed the king to put an end to their distress, he or she had—there was no doubt—much to say. Their life together, woven out of clashes and dissatisfaction, punctuated by births, illnesses, blows, failures, and infidelities, was heavy with events, overflowing with painful situations, violence, and passions. There was so much to tell the public scribes, so much to write to the lieutenant general of police, that no detail was overlooked—this unhappiness had not begun yesterday, after all. But one is also struck by their propriety; these texts may well pile on condemnations, wither with reproaches, accusations of villainy, and denunciations of abuse or disappointment, yet they remain marked by a certain restraint. Infamy and debauchery—and we have yet to attempt to define these terms—are brought out into the daylight, sometimes supported by details and proof, but never revealing anything whatsoever about the true intimacy of the couple—its sexual intimacy, for example.[6] A forbidden do-main, one to which even accusation, rage, and ruination did not give access. In fact, some even went so far as to express that it was impossible for them to say anything more, as if they had a secret of such extreme importance that it could never be told, not even be told to the king. A secret, or perhaps an expression of respect for the conjugal institution that forbade her from fully exposing her spouse.

"The supplicant cannot say anymore because she is this man's wife," writes Marie Millet, wife of François Dubois, commonly called Gilbert, tailor of clothes, sixty-two years old, "but she has every reason to fear for herself and children as much on the side of honor as of that of life."[7]

Another says: "I could say more but nevertheless he is my husband"; while the wife of Masson apologizes for accusing her husband François: "The supplicant would have kept silent about her husband's errors which are also to her own disgrace . . ."[8] revealing the way in which the accuser herself could be tarnished by her own denunciations.

Men were no more prone to provide excessive details of their conjugal lives, but they did not feel the need to invoke the law of silence. It is with women that we find this form of forced propriety that did not permit them to reveal all of the facts; perhaps this was a privileged means of indicating that, as unhappy wives, they were also under the sexual domination of their husbands, and that if such a thing were done, there is more that they could say.

In fact, was it not this same feminine and masculine propriety that stopped them from seeking recourse in ordinary justice? The justice system was *infamante*, shaming, while a secret told to the king remained private, protecting from dishonor.[9] One did not take one's spouse before the tribunals; this would have been scandalous. This is indeed what Alexandre Bonhomme, tapestry maker with Monsieur Delache, expressed when he learned about the detention at the Grand Châtelet of his wife Marie Pagez:

> But how great was the supplicant's surprise when the police inspector took her to superintendent Le Blanc, who sent her to the Grand Châtelet, to face ordinary justice for this supposed theft and thus the said supplicant was made informer on his wife, which cannot naturally be imagined on the part of a husband.[10]

Despite this refusal of ordinary justice and of a potential conventional detention after trial in the prisons of the Petit or Grand Châtelet, it is impossible to draw a strict line between the two domains of the legal system and of the *lettre de cachet*.[11] Many petitions confirm the impossibility of a complete decoupling of the two spheres: often husbands and wives had already complained to the neighborhood superintendent. These were not always full complaints filed in all due form, but she might have gone to the superintendent and brought to his attention what was going in her household.

The superintendent would have noted it down in his register, his agenda, or his notebook (these can be found in the Archives Nationales in the Archives des Commissaires du Châtelet), and then sometimes he would summon the spouse, give him an admonishment, essentially dispensing fatherly reprimands and threats and telling him not to do it again.[12] But nothing would come of it; later she would return with the same grief, the same woes, torn between the desire to have him imprisoned and the desire to stay with him so long as everything improved. Sometimes an actual crime would have been committed—a theft, a swindle, or a larceny—and this time the knave would be taken off to prison. But then he would return, and life would continue, up until the day when the thread snapped, when things had gone on too long, when what had been bearable was no longer so, and the threshold had been crossed. It is to the king that she would go, the only person capable of resolving the whole problem in its entirety, because he could deliver punishment without infamy as well as favor that bestowed a certain sort of social weight.

And even outside of these regular appearances before the legal system, the police superintendent remained central to the process of imprisonment by order of the king, given that the lieutenant general of police would order him to organize the investigation.[13] These were the "clarifications" (*éclaircissements*), some of which are included in the dossier.[14]

If the favor of the king could be requested, it could be paid for as well, or rather, it could be haggled over. The petitions, often sent by commoners, or even individuals close to destitution, would discuss the price, invoking pity and the considerable effort they had decided to undertake. Willingly, they would only consent to paying one hundred to 150 livres per year, which was very little, and it meant that their spouses had every chance of experiencing the atrocious conditions of Bicêtre hospital and the Salpêtrière rather than the comforts of certain religious houses.[15] Imprison for mercy's sake, but above all at the lowest possible cost: so the request was written, the words spoken, the steps taken.

THE PACT BROKEN

Now we must turn to the question of what made up this unbearable conjugal life, and what characterized a couple that refused to exist any longer because one of the partners was bad. What sort of person did he resemble when he was bad, to what ideal expectation had the unworthy partner not lived up? The dimensions of the unbearable emerge from the reading of these petitions—a meticulous, multiple, reading, attentive to every word, to the smallest detail, to the narration of situations and their convergences. What did spouses speak of when they wished to have a partner imprisoned? Their understanding, the behavior of their partners, their relationship with their family, with their work, with their neighbors, and the consequences of all this for the economic life of the couple. Through this, interlaced systems of values can be untangled one from another, as well as the order of their importance. The surface of the couple slowly comes into view; this picture, blurred upon first reading, comes into better focus little by little. The image becomes sharp, vivid. Although some doubts remain, some obscurities and queries persist, certain claims can nevertheless be expressed clearly.

As was clearly the case for the common expectation, shared by men and women alike, that a couple must reach a stable economic equilibrium, and that this was something for which both spouses were similarly responsible. Two-thirds of the petitions complained as much of a spouse's personal conduct, of her drunkenness or his debauchery, as about his or her economic behavior, often linking the two together. Simultaneously, in a single sweep, a spouse denounced the ruination of the household and a partner's indiscretions, invoking at once both the dissipation of goods and adulterous liaisons. It is clear that in shared life one expected a stable economic status, which cannot be asked to bear either the squandering of family resources or being obliged to descend in the social hierarchy. We often hear accusations that a spouse put an individual in a situation where she was obliged to become a domestic servant or he a day laborer, whereas before he had been a merchant silversmith or she a seamstress. "Selling household belongings" and "ruining one's trade" were grave accusations, ones that needed to be taken to the authorities. It should be added that a couple's expectations extended beyond economic stability: many petitions noted that there had been no improvement of the couple's material condition over time, and that this was intolerable. When it came to marriage, one also had the right to expect a certain economic progression over the course of the years. If this did not occur, it meant that something was wrong.

Only a third of the petitions implicate a spouse's poor personal conduct alone, without saying a word about the economic situation. For a large majority, it may have been possible to tolerate a partner who was a drunkard so long as this did not prevent the couple from maintaining themselves economically. Unless, of course, this drunkenness became scandalous, which was another problem. In most cases, the relationship of cause and effect was indicated by repeated trips to the tavern and sale of the household goods. And it was for this reason that imprisonment was requested: so that the inevitable march toward misery or beggary could be halted, the person responsible, who was preventing the other from properly carrying on his or her business, must be imprisoned. We must not forget that the people in question were not well-off, their economic vulnerability was such that the smallest blow to their resources threatened to plunge them into complete destitution. It did not take much to upend this unstable economic order, and the petitions often give the impression of describing fragile swimmers fighting to keep their heads above water.

The frequent conjunction of elements related to economic existence alongside others related to personal attitudes demonstrates the manner in which the conjugal bond was also a site. It was the site of socioeconomic establishment as much as it was the site of sexual and emotional understanding. The site of the body, of the heart, and that of social roles cannot be separated as neatly as one might wish; the couple was the intersection of these places, an expectation of harmony between them and a certainty that they were tightly interdependent on one another. In the slew of advice for marrying well and instructions for marriage transmitted in the peddled chapbooks that flooded city and countryside in the eighteenth century, this particular theme popped up time and again.[16] An accord between spouses required an economic adjustment between parties; it was not a bad thing for the man to be slightly more prosperous than the woman and they had to understand each other in order to make good on their shared resources. The idea that the couple was also an economic site, even among the poorest households, must not be taken to imply that love and attraction were excluded from it. More often than not they came to settle in this space, and they were created daily at the intersection of ties that were intense and sensitive, fragile and tenuous, fastened between appearances, benefit, respect, honor, and understanding. Marriage spoke of itself in terms of hope; happiness and livelihood became one and the same in order to create a good match. When the economic pact between husband and wife was broken, the rupture began.

Most of the time, understanding and honesty could create a satisfactory economic stability, albeit one that was often threatened—But only so long as it was not one of the partners that threatened it, and in the petitions there are details that are unmistakable. Certain thresholds, it would seem, could not be crossed: eating up the dowry of one's wife, going and collecting money for a spouse's labor before he did and then spending it, selling a spouse's belongings unbeknownst to her in order to drink and carouse. In the midst of all this disorder, one scene stands out as even more intolerable than the others, and its description alone seems enough to elicit a royal order: the removal of the bed. "He has sold even his bed"; "He has sold even his children's bed"; "She even took my bed." An essential, and singular, piece of furniture;[17] even when you had nothing, you still had your bed, whose symbolic function cannot be ignored. Its clandestine sale is the negation of cohabitation or a miserable deception with respect to the children. By selling the bed, one has done the irreparable and this wrong must be punished. Unmistakably, the loss of the bed is an economic loss as much as it is the deprivation of the sexual site.

Outrages, excesses, debauchery, bad conduct [*mauvaise conduite*], these terms give cadence to these texts without always allowing for much precision—as if they could always be substituted for one another, as if they were sufficient in themselves to make the infamy of another officially known.[18] And yet, these words refer to quite particular situations, thanks to which certain forms of debauchery or bad conduct can be outlined. Bad conduct is, in sum, when someone "takes to" pursuits other than her work, home, or the family's economic livelihood. She runs to the tavern, he comes home only occasionally, she goes off with soldiers, he commits swindles or leaves his job too often, she debauches herself in the company of women of ill repute. These are many forms of excess that share as a common trait that they were committed outside of the traditional geography of the spaces of labor and family. In lives already marked by itinerancy, the search for work and lodging, rhythmed by instability and long journeys on foot across the capital both day and night, bad conduct would be additional roaming on top of what was already required, adding disreputable absences to the habitual ones, further reinforcing these scattered lives, by bursting in a spectacular manner the already tangled map of their habitual trajectories.[19] Bad conduct was necessarily linked to different uses of spaces, shattering their precarious coherencies.

DEBAUCHERY: MASCULINE SPACES, FEMININE SPACES

At first glance, no clear differentiation between feminine and masculine misbehavior emerges. The petitions appear to maintain relatively similar criteria for the two sexes; drunkenness, the dissipation of goods, and debauchery were true of men and women alike.[20] Wives were not even particularly more insistent about idleness, as if masculine labor and feminine labor were both equally important, and men were no more defined by their occupations than women. Idleness was a vice that the two sexes shared in, which is normal, because a couple was also an association between two working people. Drunkenness was in no way a specifically masculine defect; husbands and wives both accused each other of it. Wine and *eau-de-vie*, those constant companions in misery, aggravated conjugal relations, destroyed their understanding, prevented trust, and led to all manner of economic disorders. It was an affliction that shattered all efforts undertaken toward potential economic stability.

In this outline of a common typology of bad conduct, in which men and women could be placed side by side with little differentiation, there are nonetheless still some meaningful dissimilarities and discordances. These bring out masculine and feminine roles more clearly and will help us specify what each partner expected of the other's conduct.

It was women who complained of blows, wounds, and physical abuse. They are the ones who evoked the cruelty of the knives, rulers, calipers, pokers, pots, and andirons used to vent the anger of their husbands. Often they had endured this for quite some time, frequently since the beginning of their marriages, already long ago, but were panicked when the day came when they felt that their lives were truly in danger. "The supplicant does not wish to die in the prime of life:" she was forty years old and had for thirteen years been married to a tailor who never ceased persecuting her and by whom she just narrowly "missed being killed by his blows."[21] And so she defended herself by informing the lieutenant general of the police "of the bad caliber of this cruel husband."

Three-quarters of the requests for imprisonment of husbands carried accusations of violence and abuse (only eight husbands out of seventy wished to invoke any abuse on the part of their spouses). The blow was the masculine weapon par excellence, one that could be denounced as intolerable, especially once the brutality took on shades of inhumanity. Moreover, the texts were not silent as to the atrocity of certain acts: "He horribly mistreats his wife and daughter"; "He has killed three babies in her body one after another"; "He knocks her out with blows then throws her into the stairwell"; "He has killed a first wife and mistreats his pregnant wife"; "He practices upon her abuses full of horrors"; "He gouged out her eye with his fireplace tongs . . ."

If the violence described is spectacular, it is because the women recounting it were already at the end of a long line of wounds and humiliations. They had nothing left to lose by exposing in this manner what their days and nights of sad cohabitation had been like, "of passions laden with violence." On the other hand, we do not hear them describe potential violence in sexual practices. Here the propriety of which we have already spoken appears to have held them back, and it is only through a few embarrassed, roundabout, vague, and in any case infrequent phrases that it seems we can make out their refusal of certain forms of sexuality. "He has employed bad usages toward her"; "He subjects her to shameful excesses of which his wife out of propriety cannot speak"; "He forces his wife knife in hand"; "He is indecent"; "He abuses her person," there is nothing precise in any of this. These words trace boundaries without describing what they are circling around, indicating that excesses and abuse of this kind did exist, but nothing that follows will truly reveal what they consisted of. Is it only a coincidence that these few phrases picked out from among so many others only appear in our dossier near the end of the 1750s, as if prior to this nothing of the kind had been allowed to come out? It's simply a question. On the other hand, men and women alike remarked on the venereal diseases of their spouses, sometimes with a certificate from a master of surgery as evidence, or an attestation from the hospital infirmary. Illnesses that in themselves were sufficient proof of the other's errant roamings and debauchery.

We have arrived at the most frequently employed word—*debauchery*—the word that flowed most often from the public writer's quill. A key word, but nonetheless an imprecise one, it seems to sum up all of the wrongs of the world without ever pausing to give them specific meaning, true content. However, a close reading of these texts reveals that when husbands and wives were designated to the king as debauched, this term connoted very different realities and situations. When a husband complained of his wife's debauchery, he almost always drew the same picture of her: an errant woman, depraved, of extremely bad conduct, with bad morals, who spends too much and enjoys the company of men. Often he would add to this that she had a penchant for drink or managed the household poorly. But if you read these marital complaints attentively, you will notice that this somewhat stereotyped picture of a woman of ill repute in fact covers two relatively distinct types of behavior. Of course, we do find violent and libertine women who drank and stole, sold the household's furniture, and insulted their husbands; but there are others who appear only to have wanted to leave to live with another man to whom they had become attached.

In these cases, the situation was relatively simple because it concerned a separation. And yet the husband would take pleasure in blackening the portrait of his wife. He piled detail upon detail to bring her image closer to that of a prostitute, as if he was afraid that he was not being convincing enough and would not obtain the king's order, as if he worried that the superintendent's or the inspector's investigation would find that his wife's liaison was not particularly dangerous at all. He was perhaps not wrong, as further research in the judicial archives can attest.

Sexual errancy troubled public order, this was clear, but the departure of a wife for another man was a more private and less serious event, one that the superintendent witnessed regularly. So long as there was no public scandal and the tranquillity of the neighborhood was not threatened, was it really necessary to open the king's prisons? The husband knew this; if he really wished to have his wife punished, then he would need to demonstrate that she had become a "public" woman, and that therefore this was not just a question of private order.

Angel or prostitute—there was no middle ground so long as divorce was not legally possible.[22] The petitions of husbands reflect this forced alternative rather well; covering one's wife's face with the dangerous mask of prostitution was done first to obscure one's own potential personal guilt in the face of a separation, and second to compel the authorities to punish her.

The debauched husband, as described by a wife, is one who lives day in and day out without constraints, leaving his job, sometimes staying out all night, returning home only at irregular intervals. He is a man who "goes with women," enjoys himself with them, gambles at the tavern, and then slinks back like a cat, exhausted by his nocturnal sabbaths. Women rarely accused their husbands of carrying on enduring and continuous liaisons with other women. Instead, a wife would paint a very fractured portrait of her husband, reporting him to be a roaming being, whose debauchery consisted of nomadic behavior of all kinds. "He takes to idleness, wine, *eau-de-vie*, and the feminine sex," affirmed the wife of Claude Rousseau in 1728.[23]

These wives' texts give the novel and interesting impression that they expected from their husbands a certain kind of genuine presence at their sides, consisting of work, understanding, and honesty, certainly, but also of time spent alongside each other, tending to the maintenance of the household. Suddenly, we can see married life in a new light; the well-worn image of the housewife is slightly broken in order to make place for a new, complementary, image: that of a woman who expects the presence of her husband in the home, and finds his repeated absences abnormal. And if this feminine expectation—this desire—was represented to the king, does it not mean that it was, despite everything, admissible to him?

What we can read in the petitions about relationships with children confirms this idea. Upending expectations that can rightly be suspected of being suffused with stereotypes, we notice that qualifying a woman as a "bad mother" was not an argument that was widely employed by husbands against their spouses. On the other hand, it is astonishing to see that women complained rather insistently of the little care that husbands provided to their children. One thing that was clear is that they would not tolerate it if he abused them, or if he abandoned them, or even, as one of them says, "that he does not particularly bother with them," neglects to take care of them, or tells them "indecent discourses." Taking care of his children was part of a husband's economic and civil duties; the mother needed him to shoulder this responsibility, and she let it be known when he did not. At the same time, the accusations contain an image of care and upbringing that it was necessary to emphasize. She no doubt felt this offense against her children in a very carnal way, and, at the same time, it was this sensibility that was important for her to signal. She and her children formed an emotional and economic group. If her husband did not take care of them, she was betrayed economically as much as bodily. Here again we see economic necessities interwoven with moral duties, and this is no simple thing.

Proportionally, the husband seemed more insistent that his wife maintain a positive attitude toward him than that he take good care of the children. Perhaps he was more confidant of her maternal attachment than her conjugal one? In any case, it was with regard to her duties toward him that he was more inclined to pass judgment.

Two additional justifications for imprisonment—madness and irreligiosity—were brought by women alone. A man's madness was, moreover, considered the unavoidable consequence of bad conduct and debauched roaming:

> Jeanne Catry represents very humbly to Your Grandeur that, having married the one named Antoine Chevalier a journeyman mason around forty-six years ago, he always showed some signs of madness, which have gotten worse year by year and which we attributed only to his debauchery and bad conduct, because he never behaved like an orderly man, having always spent everything that he earned at the tavern without any care for his family, and having always sold his belongings and those of his wife to go drinking at the tavern . . .[24]

Lack of religion was no more tolerable than signs of madness: "He fears neither God nor the devil"; "He does not go to Mass, and begs for supposed pilgrimages"; "He has sold even my blessed candles." These attitudes, piled on top of the others, clearly demonstrated a husband's infamy—attitudes that, in the texts, wives were never accused of by their husbands.

THE GAZE OF OTHERS

Debauchery, violence, bad conduct, madness, irreligion, drunkenness, and whorishness were all ways of finding oneself on the outside of reasonable spaces of honesty, harmony, and honor. In multiplying their accusations, husbands and wives clearly revealed all that went on outside of them, and it was this "elsewhere" that created scandal. Because a couple did not live alone with its children; a couple lived observed, supported, and accompanied by its neighbors, whether they were residents of the same building or street vendors, neighborhood superintendents or parish curés.[25] This was not all, for a couple also lived surrounded by its family. Relatives, brothers-in-law, and sisters-in-law continually reflected an image to a couple, one in which it wished to see a reflection of honor and dignity. The gaze of others stoked the intensity of the drama playing out between the partners, amplifying the tragic and the intolerable, indelibly marking a couple with hatred and disdain, or perhaps trust and affection. The request for imprisonment, then, became an act that was also undertaken for others, so that one could look at one's face in the mirror without shame. This meant that the scandal that the neighbors witnessed, and in which relatives were more or less involved, needed finally to come to an end. There is no scandal without the gaze of others, and in the near totality of cases the petitions were signed by neighbors, tenants, or priests. "The neighborhood has been scandalized by this excess, has suggested filing a complaint"; "She has become the public scandal of all of her neighbors"; "His honor on which his bread depends;" all these formulations indicate the capital importance of the entourage.[26]

Always present, an important actor in the drama that was enacted before its many eyes, the neighborhood was an essential component in a request. It was called as a witness in order to have someone punished, or perhaps it sprang up to defend the accused and reestablish the order of things, which had sometimes been upended by lies or dubious hearsay. It was in its name that certain spouses attempted to have their partners' paramours imprisoned at the same time, announcing loudly that this shameful concubinage was causing a scandal in the neighborhood and that the two guilty parties must be imprisoned at all costs. Pulled in one direction, requested in another, or acting on its own, and always quick to be emotionally swayed, the neighborhood was a necessary figure in the game that had been established, an indispensable pawn on the royal chessboard.

The moments when the neighborhood seemed the most active and most inclined to show solidarity, to take sides, even to be moved, were undoubtedly the instances when it had to assure the protection of a woman abused by her husband. In these specific cases, neighbors and merchants did not hesitate to sign the wife's petition, denouncing the husband as a savage, "bloodthirsty," creature, and even coming to her aid if they happened to witness the blows and injuries. A wife beaten by her husband could put the whole neighborhood in an uproar. "The whole neighborhood came to me asking that he be arrested right away," writes the police superintendent, "having brought her to death's door with his violent blows."

By contrast, it is interesting to note that a husband trying to have his wife imprisoned was more inclined to accompany his petition with the signatures of his relatives than of his neighbors. It is to family that he turned for justification, rather than to neighbors, as if he was much warier of the latter, frightened that they might easily side with her. A woman with children in her charge was not all that easy to imprison; by nature, a woman by nature inspired pity more easily than a man, and her imprisonment itself could also be a scandal.

THE IMPRISONMENT OBTAINED,
OR THE BEGINNING OF A STORY

So the petition went before the lieutenant general of police, everything written so as to sway him and result in imprisonment by royal favor. Thus the denunciation was formulated, the secret finally revealed: the words whispered to the writer were heavy with anger and fear, laden with hatred, but also sometimes hope and tenderness as well. Either way, they were always swollen with passion and they drew their strength from vividness of feeling. The theater of life did not end here: the petition sent to the king was the beginning of a long story of investigation, detention, retractions, and requests to be let free. Life continued, and each tableau made way for the next; these must also be told.

Each dossier offers a singular story to be uncovered, stories of conflict in which some fought to keep a spouse in prison or in a religious house for as long as possible, while others fought for their freedom. Each conflict had its own course, its own unique face and specific dramatic intensity. It is impossible, then, to make hasty generalizations; you must plunge into the reading of these many pages where numerous characters appear and then disappear, all engaged in shedding light on the event and positioning themselves as close as possible to fair solutions. You will read everything and its opposite in these muddled affairs, overflowing with details both derisory and moving—everything and its opposite, because those who took sides combed their memories for countless little facts that could potentially influence later decisions. The thickness of these dossiers shows that imprisonment left no one indifferent, and that it gave rise to an intense activity in which police superintendents, inspectors, relatives, friends, coworkers, bosses, and neighbors hurried to disentangle the enigmatic knotted threads of private life. Presented in this manner, private life allowed itself to be seen, visited, rifled through, and yet it never showed its true face with any certainty. It stepped forward in disguise, cloaked in many colors by those who would defend it and those who would blacken it. It will not unmask itself to our overly curious and often distorted prying. At the end of the story, we will never know who these people screaming out of torment and asking for love truly were.

And perhaps it is better this way; in uncovering too much, one always ends up simplifying. These lives unravel their outward appearances before our eyes without ever freeing themselves fully from the secret that had bound them together, and then wore them down.

What is left is the visible, the words written, the investigations undertaken, the letters sent.[27] They do not shed light on everything, but they can offer us an understanding of the singularity of these events.

OBSCURE "POLICE CLARIFICATIONS"

Reading the superintendent's reports—which are called "clarifications" [*éclaircissements*] without any trace of irony—concerning the petitions is enough to surprise you completely. Created to shed light on the "body of the crime" [*corps du délit*], they are so vague, so full of "more or less," and brief notes that you catch yourself dreaming about this police work, which is at once both tentacular and barely outlined. And yet, the superintendents did have help: they had so much other work—they were continually under pressure from the lieutenant general of police to remain as vigilant to street lighting as to the placement of stores, to street cleaning as to quarrels between soldiers—that they sent inspectors into the couple's neighborhood to provide a better account of the situation.[28] "More or less" is the rule here, and the reports indicate that sometimes summonses to appear were handed out, and sometimes not, that an inspector had vaguely interrogated the tavern keeper at the corner of the street or listened to a sister-in-law or brother. There is nothing systematic about any of this. It is a kind of calm disorder, where testimony, intuitions, and rumors were assembled pell-mell without any true classification. Here and there are a few promises to never do it again, fatherly admonitions, a little advice; elsewhere, orders to imprison, after having heard out one side or the other. In this register, there are often several reports per day. The task is decidedly a heavy one; how could it be meticulous and accomplished with rigor?

> September 10, 1779
> J. Cavour against her husband for misconduct and ill treatment.
> Summons to appear: the husband is agreed to having mistreated her in order to take from her a six-year-old child whom he wanted to have, as a result she gave up the child; he promised in my presence to leave her alone.

> September 17, 1779
> B. Coutin against his wife
> he, merchant tapestry maker and secondhand clothes vendor

[. . .] such that out of jealousy she never ceases to torment him and to hurl invectives at a woman named Bertrand with whom she suspects that he lives and the man named Leconte and his wife with whom she lodges.

I have seen the wife of the plaintiff and her words seemed to me to be devoid of any truthfulness, this woman seems to me to be ill advised, there are no swindles that she has not played on her husband, which are known to superintendent Mutel, it even seems that her father countenances her purloining of goods from her husband's shop, I did everything in my power to make her see reason but was unable to. As for the husband he certified to me that the account was truthful and told me that he did everything within his power to live in good faith with his wife, he is thought to be an honest man and his wife a very mean woman.

October 22, 1779

The Denis woman against her husband.

I have not heard from the opposing parties, the husband of the plaintiff did not show up to the summons, I was not able to conclude this affair.

October 25, 1779

François Jacob Pinson's wife a secondhand vendor rue des Petits-Carreaux, declares that the disturbance of her husband's spirit increases day by day and causes her to worry for her life, she requests imprisonment in the house of Monsieur Esquirol and offers to pay the pension.[29]

I have seen the Pinson woman who confirms the facts and has witnesses. The affair can be closed.[30]

It is true that they did not have the time to linger, these superintendents, over household quarrels, petty thefts, and arguments between spouses—later on they would say as much and would complain that they had been inundated with minor conjugal woes. But this was not the only reason. Imprecision was the medium in which the eighteenth-century police worked, blow by blow, never mastering the specifics of what was at stake in a given situation. Their goal was to be omnipresent, which is not synonymous with effectiveness, and this was not yet the era of classification, quantification, and strategizing. For the time being, the police responded to disorder by establishing themselves everywhere they could, which is not to say that they responded with order; the police clarifications were created in the image of their work.

From time to time, police investigations would be supplemented with certificates from parish curés, who were sometimes solicited in this type of affair. They were often satisfied to simply add their signatures to a request, but at times they also intervened directly. In October 1728, for example, the priest of Saint-Gervais hastened to send to the lieutenant general of police a statement against Jean Terrassin des Essarts, whose wife wished to have him imprisoned:

> I the undersigned, priest, doctor of theology, curé of Saint-Gervais in Paris, certify that one Jean Terrassin des Essarts, master clothes tailor in my parish, is a man of most disturbed mind and with and very bad conduct, that he scandalizes the whole neighborhood with the abuse that he gives his wife and the neighbors when they wish to come to her aid when he is abusing her.
>
> Made in Paris this October 3, 1728.
> Curé of Saint-Gervais.[31]

That same year, the priest of Saint-Paul supported a request in the opposite direction, by a husband against his wife:

> I the undersigned curé of Saint-Paul, certify that one Geneviève Alloché, wife of André Macé, master card maker in Paris, is a woman of wayward morals and of such scandalous conduct that I pray, in concert with her husband and her neighbors, Monsieur the Lieutenant of Police to have her imprisoned in the Hôpital général forever.
>
> In Paris this October 22, 1728.
> The curé of Saint-Paul.[32]

But these cases were not particularly frequent, and sadly it is impossible, given the gaps in the sources, to find a correlation between these interventions and their results. Did the parish curé exert true influence? Nothing in the archives would allow us to answer this question in either direction.[33] One interesting thing to note: certificates from priests and curés are more numerous after 1750 than before; but a more systematic examination would be necessary in order to confirm this.

The neighborhood, of course, either supported these requests or was indignant about them. Neighbors and merchants signed the bottom of petitions or even wrote separately if the scandal had truly shaken them to the point where they would band together to send a letter to the lieutenant general. Communities *[communautés]* of craftsmen also became involved in order to defend one of their own.[34]

My Lord,

The sworn members in charge of the Community of master and merchant fruit and orange sellers in Paris, most humbly beseech Your Grandeur that it might please him to order the release of one Alexandre Bruno, one of the masters of their community detained at present in château de Bicêtre. They will never cease to continue their wishes for the health and prosperity of Your Grandeur.[35]

Class solidarity? Perhaps, but sometimes a master would also come to the protection of his domestic servant or an employer would take the trouble to defend an employee.

Houdard, renter of coaches, represents very humbly to Your Highness that one of the coachmen of named Houdé was arrested Saturday February 28 1738 in his house rue des Boucheries based on false complaints made by his wife who in order to remove the presence of her husband has resorted to everything to surprise the religion of Your Highness.[36] The said supplicant dares to hope that Your Highness might wish to conduct inquiries into the life and morals of said Houdé and his wife, to know which of the two is in the wrong and should be punished . . .[37]

The police were always very sensitive to a neighborhood's atmosphere, to the manner in which it responded to events, spread rumors, became "agitated"; the inspectors would stroll through the streets and taverns to take the pulse of this strange figure that was the neighborhood. What they saw and heard was as important as the facts themselves, of which they could never have any formal proof. At times, a superintendent might even judge that an imprisonment was necessary in order to intimidate a neighborhood that took to disorder too quickly. In such a case, it was not the reactions of the neighborhood that were the source of the detention, but rather the neighborhood itself that was targeted by the placement of one of their own behind bars. This was the case for Catherine Louis, embroiderer, three months pregnant, imprisoned in 1756 at her family's request, about whom the superintendent writes: "Everyone says that this girl always behaved herself well . . . But the neighborhood still requires an example: it is full of a populace that can be restrained only by fear. How many useful subjects does the State not lose to the libertinage into which most of the girls of the lower orders give themselves."[38] Here at last we come upon the arbitrariness that one day the nation as a whole would no longer be willing to endure and with which it would refuse to be complicit.

THE SINGULAR STATUS OF REPENTANCE

In the meantime, the essence of the story after an order for imprisonment had been issued abided in the relationship that, despite everything, continued to exist between spouses over the course of the detention. Even if she had been taken away to the Sainte-Pélagie, the Salpêtrière, or Bicêtre, she still existed, and did everything in her power to make sure that he did not forget.[39] Some imprisoned wives wrote moving letters to their husbands; other spouses constantly haggled over the cost of a pension that they considered exorbitant, employing all kinds of arguments to demonstrate that the sum paid was sufficient for such an infamous person [*un infâme*] as this; others were quick to request a spouse's release, assuring the authorities of the detainee's repentance. Others still seemed stricken by the fate reserved for those from whom they had so ardently sought to distance themselves; one emphasizes the horror of the dungeons, the dampness of the cells in Bicêtre; another begs that visitors be allowed. The opposite also exists; husbands and wives find it irregular that it is so easy for their spouse to receive visits from bad influences "and demand an end to these comings and goings that are preventing the prisoner from "looking within himself" [*rentrer en lui-même*].[40] And in still other situations, if the rumor spread that a royal amnesty was going to be accorded in honor of the birth or marriage of the dauphin, or that powerful friends were looking to obtain the detainee's freedom, a spouse might rewrite a petition to confirm the request for detention, frightened and refusing to allow the "source of all ills and even more of dishonor" to return home.

In short, an intense and restless life continued to mark these couples, one composed of fits and starts or of hope, of regret and violence, or of fear and pity. And of meanness as well: some men and women were wrongly accused out of self-interest, despite having behaved irreproachably. They would have to struggle to make this known.

Each time that life stirred, an additional letter arrived to swell the dossier. These documents are so many surprising and contradictory cries. In these documents, certain traits are more visible than others; it is clear, for example, that wives were more likely to seek to have their husbands released than husbands were for their wives.[41] And these women did not attempt to conceal the economic reasons behind this: it was impossible to provide for the needs of their children while paying the pension, or there had been death in the family and the inheritance was being held up by the absence of the husband. Inheritance *oblige*.

In these requests for release, whether they came from the detainee or his family (parents were often the first ones to write the lieutenant general letters to this end, railing against their son- or daughter-in-law), as in the requests for continued detention, two words often recurred as a leitmotiv: repentance and correction: "He has shown signs of repentance"; "She says that she has been sufficiently corrected and it appears as if she will not start up again"; "He has asked for forgiveness"; "She has not yet begun to behave as she should"; "Despite everything, he remains incorrigible and should not be released."

Inevitably, these moral, even religious, tones concealed what were no doubt urgent economic realities. And yet, the arguments invoked deal with good behavior, the improvement of the soul, the amends by the guilty party through the severity of detention. Punishment was indeed necessary in order finally to bring things to a head, and the solitude of the dungeon was one of the best ways to bring about self-reflection and repentance for one's prior misdeeds.

How can we not be taken aback by the presence of repentance, which emerges so frequently in the texts? We know that in the eighteenth century the functioning of punishment had not yet annexed the realm of the soul, and that the legal system rested on an order of visible punishments that were inscribed onto the body of the delinquent or that made him invisible to the social body. People were marked, whipped, banished, put in shackles, displayed on the pillory, punished in galleys, upon gallows, or across the wheel, and the traces left on the body were visible reparation for the crime committed. While confession was the principal instrument that set the machinery of corporeal punishment in motion, at no time was the criminal ever asked to repent. And even if he did, this personal attitude was not the responsibility to the official system. How, then, to explain that repentance served as the key argument in the near totality of requests for imprisonment as in the requests for release? Was it that the wrong done could be erased by attention given to the soul and the recognition that one had taken the wrong path? Was it that the soul was now a principal locus of punishment, no longer the body alone? And what in the king was one looking to sway when one indicated to him the state of repentance of a subject imprisoned by his hand? Without any doubt, here we have an important personalization of the relationship between the king and his people. If punishment pierced to the very essence of a being, which is to say his soul, this represented an even more intense recognition of royal power and its ability to compel the internalization of its decisions—attitudes with which regular justice was little concerned. The king healed souls, his thaumaturgic function extended to this final point, further reinforcing, if it was necessary, the state of dependence of the subject on his king. To persuade the king that the bad in those he has punished had been blotted out was to reinforce his power to imprison as well as to release.

If there is a strategic element to this argument (repentance becomes a kind of magic key that justifies imprisonment until it is obtained and release once it has been), it should at the same time be emphasized that it also reveals an important component of relationships between individuals. What father and mother, husband and wife, ultimately expected from the guilty party was for them to renounce the wrong they had done, to integrate into their lives the norms dictated by their entourage. Here, repentance appears as one of the forms of living in society; if a breach in order was committed, punishment must extract from the accused both acquiescence and submission—submission to those around him, to an order that was necessarily recognized by royal authority, and therefore submission to the royal person. When nineteenth-century penal theory place amends and repentance at the center of its problematic, it was only incorporating into its system a preexisting social attitude.[42] The social group had made remorse and contrition into part of what was at stake in the function of punishment; the eighteenth-century *lettres de cachet* offer clear proof of this. The humanists and philanthropists of the nineteenth century were only institutionalizing this development. In this sense, they were not innovators, but perhaps simply more conscious than others of the importance that this parameter could have in the official course of justice. Perhaps it was also a means of personalizing the penalties applied by demanding that each person respond to them with a behavior of regret and rehabilitation, a personalization of punishment that was precisely what these requests for imprisonment sought after by offering to sovereign power the intimate details of their private lives.

Presented to the king in this manner, conjugal conflict was a public thing, and therefore a matter for the State to decide. Here, the confrontation between husband and wife had the same status as a betrayal of the king or an affront to religion. In itself, it was a story that in this era the king did not disdain; the encounter between man and woman effectively partook of the sacred, which legitimated the fact that their duel could go all the way to the person of the king. A quotidian and symbolic place, marriage definitively united two worlds that had negotiated their forms of power from the outset, where evidence of the seduction and fear of women were constantly intertwined, between which life and death both must pass. The stakes were of such importance that they could justifiably concern the king.

Later, and gradually, the king and his officers would tire of exercising their authority over these family stories, and they would no longer appear as a place of political decision. Then what would come to be called the head of the family (husband or father) would be instituted as the necessary figure of authority and responsibility. No more public light, whether arbitrary or not, would shine in on these private places; with some exceptions, the place of reproduction would from then on be managed by the male world.

The difference is an important one and this shift is meaningful. At the same time as the royal injustice of the *lettres de cachet* was denounced, with good cause, and family rifts became royal cases no longer, a domestic space where men would naturally lay down the rules began gradually to take shape. Detached from the field of public events, married life would obligate women to exit the stage. Between State and women, in this specific case, there was reciprocity no longer; their spaces had been severed in a quasi-definitive way. It was men who would assure the link between the two and who would, for this reason, relegate women to the confined space of private life. The Civil Code would represent the culmination of this movement.

 *Letters*

These texts have been grouped according to the themes discussed in the introduction. Within each theme, they are divided between 1728 and 1758, and within that, they are in alphabetical order. All of these documents come from the Archives de la Bastille, which are stored in the Bibliothèque de l'Arsenal (cited as Ars. Arch. Bastille). The writing of the era has been preserved.—Ed.

HOUSEHOLDS IN RUIN

Alexandre Bruno

My Lord,

Françoise Broüet, wife of Alexandre Bruno, merchant fruit and orange seller residing rue des Prêcheurs in the lodging of M. Maugnon, also a merchant fruit and orange seller, takes the respectful liberty of representing unto Your Highness that said Alexandre Bruno her husband, age seventy, leads a life of such debauchery, becoming drunk on wine every day and having done so for the twenty years she has been with him, he has consumed everything that she brought to the marriage and scandalized the whole neighborhood, as his debauches have driven him entirely out of his head, to which the neighbors will attest, such as the fact that yesterday he set the house on fire, M. the Superintendent Majurier arrived and invited the supplicant to do her diligences before Your Highness so that it might please you to order that said Alexandre Bruno be locked away in the hôpital de Bicêtre, the landlord, like M. the Superintendent did not wish for him sleep in the house for fear that something similar might happen again, she will never cease her wishes for the preservation and prosperity of Your Highness.

Ars. Arch. Bastille 11989, fol. 241 (1728)

My Lord,

Alexandre Bruno, master merchant fruit and orange seller of Paris, detained at present in the château de Bicêtre, most humbly beseeches Your Highness, that it may please him, seeing that his wife Françoise Brouet has made a certificate of retraction for her complaints brought against him, in consequence of which he is detained, seeing also that the relatives of said Bruno have given a leave *[permission]* in other certificates attached to the petition that the sworn members responsible for the Community had the honor of representing unto you, to order the release of the aforementioned Bruno, he will never cease to wish for the prosperity of Your Highness.

Ars. Arch. Bastille 11989, fol. 246 (1728)

My Lord,

The sworn members responsible for the Community of master and merchant fruit and orange sellers in Paris, most humbly beseech Your Highness that it might please you to order the release of one Alexandre Bruno, one of the masters of their Community at present detained in the château de Bicêtre. They will never cease to continue their wishes for the health and prosperity of Your Highness.

Mauge, Bollogniet, Moret
Tessard, Guillaume.

Ars. Arch. Bastille 11989, fol. 249 (1728)

Agnès Dujardins

To My Lord
the Lieutenant General of Police

My Lord,

Charles Bonnin, grave digger in the cemetery of the Saints-Innocents, most humbly remonstrates unto Your Highness that there is even more reason to pity him because his wife who has already been locked up in the prisons of the Grand Châtelet by order of M. the Lieutenant of the Criminal Police should have shown more orderly conduct than before and this had been the cause of her detention, but far from benefiting from it, she has for a long time been plunged into so terrible a disturbance *[dérangement]* that she has become the public scandal of all her neighbors and every day causes the total ruination of the supplicant as she has sold everything that was in his room, even his clothing, that of his young child, and her own in order to satisfy her drunkenness and that this has left the supplicant so distraught that he is currently lying in bed ill at his poor mother's who has a great deal of trouble simply subsisting where he was obliged to retire, his said wife having refused to open the door to him, she has been locked in there for three days drinking, he hopes that you might wish to show some regard by ordering that she be locked away at the hospital for the rest of her days and he will be obliged to pray God for the health and prosperity of Your Highness.

Signature: a cross.

I have the honor of certifying to My Lord the Lieutenant General of Police the truthfulness of the contents of the above. September 20, 1728.

Mettray, curé of Saint-Merry
[Accompanied by six other signatures.]

Ars. Arch. Bastille, not numbered (1728)

Geneviève Le Maître

Christophe Aymond journeyman carpenter residing rue Poissonnière in the lodging of Monsieur de Vitry, master ribbon maker, most humbly represents unto Your Highness that Geneviève Le Maître his wife of twelve years has thrice ruined him and destroyed his household through her unruly conduct and currently is no longer with the supplicant so as to have more liberty to live in debauchery, she is continually drunken and prostitutes herself publicly to the first passerby, she frequents only people of her ilk, with whom she eats up and dissipates everything that she can grab, such that in order to avoid the misfortune of which she is capable through her conduct which is unruly and given to all manner of vices, her own mother the widow Le Maître, and her family have joined the supplicant, to most humbly beseech Your Highness to have the charity to grant an order to have said Geneviève Le Maître locked up in the hospital. They will never cease their prayers for the preservation of Your Highness.

[On the back of the above petition:]
January 31, 1728.

I have written to one Le Maître, the wife of Aymond, against whom this petition was presented to you, but she has not seen fit to come speak with me.

All those who signed and certified this petition who are the mother, father-in-law and others in the family came to see me and assured me of the bad conduct *[mauvaise conduite]* of said Aymond wife and of her prostitution and constant drunkenness that she is at present a vagabond, without lodging, and it was only by happenstance that Monsieur Josse, officer of the short robe *[robe courte]*,[1] who was willing to carry the billet I had written her telling her to come speak with me knew where she retired at night. I therefore believe that there is reason to have her locked up in the hospital for correction.

The Superintendent Aubert.

Ars. Arch. Bastille 10998, fol. 231 (1728)

Marie Élisabeth Pied

To My Lord
the Lieutenant General of Police

My Lord,

Jacques Colot, sculptor, residing rue Montorgueil, cul-de-sac du Crucifix, Saint-Sauveur parish, most humbly represents unto Your Highness that he has the honor of presenting you with a petition on the subject of Marie Élisabeth Pied his wife, it was around seven weeks ago that you forwarded it to M. the Superintendent Aubert, who after hearing testimony, and after having added his report to the said petition, returned it to your residence *[votre hôtel]*, yet since that time the supplicant has been unable to receive any news of it, and had the honor of presenting you with a second petition around a month ago, but was unable to receive an audience, which has left the supplicant in the direst circumstances through the continuation of the bad life of his said wife, who every day sells and dissipates everything she can get her hands on of the supplicant's whom she has reduced to mendicancy, she is of greatly alienated wits, swears and blasphemes, threatens to kill him and his host as well as saying that they will only die by her hand which is repeated every day, and toward this effect she has a knife in hand at all moments, and this without his ever having given her the least reason, and even the son of the supplicant one Jean Colot age sixteen and a half follows the same principles as said mother, threatening the supplicant his father, swearing and blaspheming without the least respect, which has been going on for a number of years, because of which said Jean Colot his son was locked away in the hospital for six months, yet he will not give up his bad life and conduct, going so far as to steal from various persons anything he can get his hands on, which he dissipates with said mother, and they then return full of drink and eau-de-vie, quite often said Jean Colot stays out all night, and a few days ago, in concert with said mother, sold a piece of the supplicant's work that he was keeping in order to acquit himself of a debt, and they are currently off together spending this money, and as the remonstrances of the supplicant, those of his family, and of other persons of probity, have brought about no change to their bad conduct and to avoid the unfortunate consequences *[suites]* that might come of it, the supplicant appeals to Your authority, My Lord, and most respectfully beseeches you to order that said Marie Élisabeth Pied his wife and Jean Colot, his son, be locked up so that the supplicant's life will be safe.

He hopes for this grace of Your ordinary justice. He will continue his prayers for the preservation of Your Highness.

> Jacques Collot, Le Lanur, administrator of last
> rites at Saint-Sauveur; Andry, Louis Trouard,
> Lecanvin, Rousseau.

Ars. Arch. Bastille 11004, fol. 131 (1728)

Jacques Collot, sculptor, requests that Marie Élisabeth Pied, his wife and Jean Collot age sixteen and a half his son be locked away.

Declares that his wife is in a most outrageous debauchery, that she sells everything she can get her hands on and is reducing him to mendicancy, that she is of alienated wits, swears and blasphemes constantly, threatens to kill him and his host, and says they will die only by her hand, that his son does the same, and helps his mother at every opportunity, because of which he already spent six months in Bicêtre, that he steals from various persons all that he can and dissipates it with his mother, that often he stays out all night and is drunken, and finally, that he fears further misfortune.

This petition is signed by the supplicant and seven other people, two of whom are clerics of the Sacraments at Saint-Sauveur.

Superintendent Aubert responds that the facts are true, but also that this woman deserves to be locked away in the hospital, given that she is feeble-minded. And that the son who follows the bad example of his mother deserves to be locked up as well.

Ars. Arch. Bastille 11004, fol. 132 (1728)

> My Lord
> the Lieutenant General of Police

My Lord,

Jacques Colot journeyman sculptor, most humbly represents unto Your Highness that Marie Élisabeth Pied his spouse having the misfortune of being of alienated wits was by your order of the King locked away in the house of detention five months ago, which grieves said supplicant, as his wife had committed no wrong deed, which is why he beseeches Your Highness to have regard for this and to order that she be placed among the half-insane [*demi-insensés*], he hopes to receive this grace from your justice and your charity. He will continue his wishes and prayers for the health and prosperity of Your Highness.

[*On the back of the petition:*]

I beg you dearest sister to signify to me in returning this petition to me whether the requested grace can be granted. My dearest sister, I am quite perfectly your most humble and most obedient servant.

Ars. Arch. Bastille 11004, no folio (1728)

This November 15, 1728.

Marie Élizabeth Pied, thirty-nine, of Paris, wife of Jacques Collot, admitted by *lettre de cachet* granted in Versailles on July 31, 1728. The duration of her detention is not indicated. The letter holds until new order is given, signed Louis and below that Phelypeaux, brought by Monsieur Rivière, officer of the watch August 4, 1728: for the first time; for debauchery. This is the transcript extracted from our registers.

We see no inconvenience in sending this woman to the Innocents as her husband requests if My Lord finds it suitable.

At the Salpêtrière, this December 19, 1728.

Ars. Arch. Bastille 11004, no folio (1728)

His Excellence
My Lord the Cardinal de Fleury

Jacques Collot journeyman sculptor requests that Marie Élizabeth Pied his wife who was taken to the Salpêtrière by order of the King be placed among the insane. The Mother Superior does not see any objection to this.

I believe the requested order to be just.

Ars. Arch. Bastille 11004, no folio (1728)

Gilbert Dolat

To My Lord
the Lieutenant General of Police

My Lord,

Michel Caille, bourgeois from Paris and Louise Caille, his nineteen-year-old daughter, most humbly represent unto Your Highness that ever since said Louise Caille married Gilbert Dolat three years ago, there are no excesses to which he has not gone; he abused her on several occasions after having sold her furniture, he enlisted, and has not ceased to frequent the most crapulous company. No sooner had his relatives given him what he needed to clothe himself than he sold everything, and spent every penny of it, that two months ago he returned from the garrison where he had been, that he again sold everything up to the mattress that his mother had given him; and his conduct is so disturbed that the supplicants fear that from one moment to the next, he might do something to dishonor them. As the supplicant daughter is in a deplorable state, as the supplicant father has no means, as the mother of said Dolat and her family are still well willing to show the goodness of paying a modest pension to avoid the dishonor that would befall them, they beseech Your Highness that he might wish to dispatch his orders to have said Dolat locked up in the château de Bicêtre, offering to pay the most modest pension possible because through his expenses, which were extraordinary, he consumed and ruined his mother, her family and the supplicants in gratitude, will never cease to pray for the health and prosperity of My Lord.

The Dolat Caille wife, the father-in-law.

Ars. Arch. Bastille 11994, fol. 18 (1758)

Monsieur,

Consequent to the letters that you did me the honor of writing me, and through which you signified to me to verify the facts given in a petition that had been presented against Filbert Dolat and to send you what I learned on this subject, I brought the mother and sister of said Dolat residing rue des Mauvais-Garçons, to see me, they assured me that said Dolat was a perfect scoundrel, that it would be dangerous to leave him at liberty much longer. His mother added that for some time now she had not dared let him to sleep in the house, that she fed him during the day, that at night she gave him money to pay for a room, she gave me a letter according to which it would seem that he escaped from the hands of someone who had been charged with taking him to the Islands. The Dolat mother implored me to enclose it with the letter that I have the honor of writing you, to allow you to know the person against whom an order for imprisonment is being solicited and to further determine you to grant it. One Donet brother-in-law of the aforementioned Dolat testified to me that there was nothing he desired more for the honor of the family than that Filbert Dolat be locked up.

Ones Pinel and Fromentin, neighbors whom I brought in, assured me that said Dolat was the worst subject that they knew, that there was reason to fear that if he were not to be locked up then he would do some wicked deed.

Here Monsieur, are the circumstances and particulars that I was able to discover on the subject of Filbert Dolat.

With profound respect I am, Monsieur, Your most humble and most Obedient servant.

Greyel.
This June 24, 1758.

Ars. Arch. Bastille 11994, fol. 20 (1758)

Monsieur the Count de Saint Florentin

One Philibert Dolat was taken to Bicêtre by order of the King given on January 29, 1758, at the request of his mother, his wife, and his whole family because of his violence, excesses, outbursts, and his disturbed conduct.

He has since been released from the Bicêtre by virtue of a second order of the King of May 11, 1761, which exiled him at thirty leagues from Paris.

Far from obeying this order, he dissipated the money, and sold the belongings that his family had given him for his departure, and he still remains in Paris where he continues to make himself most suspect. Monsieur the Count de Saint Florentin is beseeched to dispatch an order to have him locked up in Bicêtre where he will be taken at the expense of his family who will pay a pension at the rate of one hundred pounds *[livres]* as before.

Ars. Arch. Bastille 11994, no folio (1758)

Chaban, June 2, 1761.

Monsieur,

I have the honor of reporting to you that one Philibert Dolat whom I exiled from Bicêtre on May 17 on the King's order that he remove himself from within thirty leagues of Paris, still remains in this city despite the fact that I had him told to obey the aforementioned order. His family who are most honest folk and who indeed wished that he effectively leave the city, worries that he might join in with thieves and that he might do them dishonor, they clothed him and gave him the sum of sixty livres so that he might go to Orléans to work his trade, but he went through the money, sold his belongings and remains in Paris.

(Police Report.)

Ars. Arch. Bastille 11994, no folio (1758)

From August 8, 1761

Monsieur,

I have the honor of reporting to you that consequent to the orders of the King dated June 14 last that you sent me, I arrested on the sixth of the present month, one Philibert Dolat heretofore an apprentice tailor, age thirty-six, native of Paris. He was taken in custody to the Petit Châtelet and the next day was transferred to the hospital by virtue of an order obtained by his family who are paying a pension of one hundred livres.

Nota: on May 17 last an order of the King dated the 11th was served that relegated the aforementioned Dolat to thirty leagues' distance.

(Police Report.)

Ars. Arch. Bastille 11994, fol. 28 (1758)

Marie Catherine Duhamel

To My Lord
the Lieutenant General of Police

My Lord,

Jean Mangerot, day laborer, residing rue Saint-Victor, Saint-Étienne-du-Mont parish, represents unto Your Highness that over fifteen years ago, he married Marie Catherine Duhamel, who is drunken every day, having sold everything in the room, even the beds of her children, to satisfy her passions and threatens her husband that she will do away with herself when he makes a few remonstrances to her, for which he has several times brought a complaint to Monsieur Roussel, police inspector.[2]

As this woman cannot control herself and as such conduct can only yield unfortunate consequences said Mangerot and family who always lived honorably, who never gave any cause for reproach, beseech Your Highness to grant an order to have said Marie Catherine Duhamel, wife of said Jean Mangerot, locked up in the hospital, which will restore tranquillity to an entire family who will never cease to wish for the preservation of the health of My Lord.

Jean Mangerot, her husband; Villeret,
brother-in-law; Buline, uncle and godfather
of the children; J. M. Lincelle, wife of
Pinard, cousin; Huline, Pinard.

Ars. Arch. Bastille 12007, fol. 151 (1758)

To My Lord
the Lieutenant General of Police

Monsieur, I have the honor of reporting to you that I have inquired into the conduct of Marie Catherine Duhamel, wife of Jean Mangerot, named in the present petition; I learned that around five years ago this woman fell into the most prejudicial sloth, gave herself to drink and neglected the care of her household and of her children, that in her drunkenness she talks only of throwing herself into the river, that her husband to recall her to her duty employed every means of kindness, continued to bring her his daily wages to provide for her and her children, wages that she most often used to satisfy her drunkenness, that after this it was not long before she had sold all of the furniture and effects that had made up her household, even the bed that the Huline wife had sent for her daughter to sleep in, and by this outrageous disturbance obliged her husband and the children to appeal to the mercy of charitable persons for lodging and food, and that currently all she seeks is the chance to steal so that she can always be drunk with wine, having even stolen laundry from a washerwoman, this was all certified to me by the persons who signed the present.

I am with profound respect,
this March 29, 1758, Ferrat.
(Police report on the petition.)

Ars. Arch. Bastille 12007, fol. 151 (1758)

The Mangerot wife whose husband requests her detention in the hospital owing to her bad conduct seems to me on the basis of the clarifications that I made on her account, to be a case for imprisonment her entire family attest as do her neighbors, to the truthfulness of the facts mentioned in the petition, this individual is they say almost always drunk. She has sold almost all of her household effects to obtain more drink, she is prone to theft; finally, when she is full of wine she is extremely violent and is capable of turning her fury against herself.

I am with a profound respect, Monsieur, Your most humble and obedient servant.

Superintendent Lemaire, April 20, 1758.

Ars. Arch. Bastille 12007, fol. 152 (1758)

To My Lord Bertin,
Lieutenant General of Police

My Lord,

Jean Mangerot day laborer, joined by the family of Marie Catherine Duhamel his spouse, had the honor of requesting and obtaining of Your Highness, Saturday 19 of the present month of May an order for the release from the house of detention of the Salpêtrière of said Marie Catherine Duhamel his said spouse, which Mme the mother superior remanded to My Lord with a letter, and told the supplicant that his wife was detained by order of the King: it has been a year now that she has been detained and what misfortunes he suffered from her bacchanals, having at that time been arrested by the guard and taken to Superintendent Rolland, then to the Châtelet, and by Your Order, transferred to the Salpêtrière. It is true My Lord that since her detention he has presented to you several petitions occasioned by the solicitation of her relatives, to the end of keeping her there, and that it is doubtless these same petitions that prompted the order of the King, but wishing to forget the past and be reunited with his wife, he beseeches you to grant him an order of the King for her release; a year of punishment being enough to make her look within herself [*rentrer en elle-même*], he will never cease to wish for Your preservation.

Ars. Arch. Bastille 12007, fol. 157 (1758)

Marie Anne Laville

To My Lord Bertin,
Lieutenant General of Police

My Lord,

François Sabin Parent, master saddler residing rue de Buci, faubourg Saint-Germain, Saint-Sulpice parish, in the lodging of Madame Germain, mistress saddle maker, where he has been obliged to work as a journeyman through the bad conduct of Marie Anne Laville his wife, has the honor of representing unto you that said Laville has lived in a most outrageous waywardness since he had the misfortune of marrying her ten years ago, which finally determined the plaintiff to make a complaint against his said wife to M. the Superintendent Laumonier August 19 last, and as the supplicant has since then learned that his said wife roams the streets of Paris, that she has become infatuated with wicked scoundrels to the point that she is now covered with leprosy from the top of her head down to her feet, and worried that as she had no resources on which to survive, she would sink to a new low, the supplicant had her arrested by the watch on Monday of the present month of September 1758 in a tavern on rue de la Huchette at 10 o'clock at night, and taken before the Superintendent Laumonier who sent her back by police order to Saint-Martin.

In these circumstances, the supplicant appeals to the authority of Your Highness who he beseeches to grant him an order to have her locked away in the hospital at his expense. The undersigned witnesses certify to M. the Superintendent Laumonier if My Lord sees fit, the truth of the facts that he has reported to you and they will not cease their wishes for the preservation of the precious days of Your Highness.

Widow Germondin, Canire, Deschamps,
François Sabin (Parent), Bazarne,
Clouët, Bertaug, Marie Joseph de la Ville,
F. Regnault, Marie Catherine Delaville

Ars. Arch. Bastille 12012, fol. 17 (1758)

To My Lord
the Lieutenant General of Police

My Lord,

François Sabin Parent, master saddler of Paris, takes the liberty to appeal to Your authority, to save him from the danger and opprobrium that threaten him. He had the misfortune of marrying a woman whose bad conduct led to her detention in the hôpital de la Salpêtrière, where she has been detained since September 7, 1758 and from where she is today on the eve of being released. This woman who is given, not only to the most shameful debauches, but even worse to the most grievous inclinations, which would have inevitably brought down Justice upon her in all its severity, as she continually threatened to have him murdered if he dared to oppose her will: threats that she often repeated to her family, even to her own sisters. After such excesses, what is there the supplicant would not have reason to expect, if she were to manage to obtain her freedom.

In these circumstances, My Lord, the supplicant requests in grace that you might wish to give your orders that this unfortunate woman remain where she is.

His means are quite limited because she reduced him to the necessity of having to go work for a master, and because he is responsible for raising and maintaining a child from their marriage: but even if it meant depriving himself of necessities, he will continue to pay the pension as he has up until now, as is shown by his most recent payment.

And he will redouble his wishes, My Lord, for the preservation of your days.

Ars. Arch. Bastille 12012, fol. 26 (1758)

Nicolas Martin

To My Lord,
the Lieutenant General of Police

My Lord,

Catherine Morin, wife of Nicolas Martin, peddler, residing in front of Saint-Hilaire at the Certain Well, has the honor of most respectfully representing unto Your Highness her just complaints against her husband who a year ago abandoned her to go off with a concubine who has a husband named Joinville commonly called Dandreville, who resides on rue Mouffetard, in the lodging of Mme Nobulau two down from the Hospitaliers, faubourg Saint-Marceau. For the thirteen or so years that she has been with him, he has never assisted her with the fruits of his labor, he received an inheritance of six hundred livres that he took to his concubine, instead of assisting his wife, he has not ceased abusing her cruelly, and has reduced her to the lowest misery, by selling her furniture, even the bed that she had provided, which he removed furtively, while she was sick in the Hôtel-Dieu, and every time that he encounters her in the street, he threatens to take her life; several complaints have been made to the Superintendent, and M. the curé of Saint-Médard will certify all of these facts.

In these circumstances, the supplicant appeals to the authority of Your Highness, and most humbly beseeches him to give his order to place said Martin in Bicêtre, along with his concubine and her husband who suffers this vice in his home, out of regard for the supplicant's life and the misfortunes they might commit in the future, the supplicant dares to hope for this grace from Your Justice: she will never cease to send up wishes for the preservation of the health and prosperity of My Lord.

Morin, Calagne, Bruret, Durief
current neighbor of said Joinville

Ars. Arch. Bastille 12008, fol. 18 (1758)

Report of September 13, 1758.

Quartier Saint-Benoît

Monsieur,

Following the orders that you did me the honor of addressing to me on the subject of the present complaint of one née Catherine Morin residing at the Certain Well in front of Saint-Hilaire against Monsieur Nicolas Martin her husband, I have listened to numerous witnesses whose depositions I have the honor of sending to you from which it would appear that said woman has just cause to complain of her husband who tried to murder her, who is disturbed, who insults the honest people she sees, who lives with a woman of ill repute *[mauvaise vie]* who is dangerous in her talk, and odious in her libertinage. The testimony of M. the curé of Saint-Médard confirms the justice of said wife's complaints against the accused who seem to have avoided being justly imprisoned.

Delajanière

Ars. Arch. Bastille 12008, no folio (1758)

Thérèse Pichard

To My Lord
the Lieutenant General of Police

My Lord,

Nicolas Pichard, journeyman miller residing rue Saint-German-l'Auxerrois, next to the signpost of the Red Rose beside and adjacent to the salt storage, represents most humbly unto Your Highness, that he has a wife one Thérèse Sivert of around seventeen years of age, who, in the absence of her husband the supplicant, obliged as he is to attend to his work to be able to subsist with honor and probity, as truthful individuals will testify, leads a life that is as shameful as it is dishonoring to her family, every day in all manner of taverns, with people of every ilk and no names, having destroyed her household in a shameful manner unworthy of a woman of probity; having sold her husband's clothes together with her own, obliged as he is to sleep elsewhere and even to preserve his life which is not safe owing to the threats of his wife when in her cups, that she will rob him of it by her own hands.

The supplicant, My Lord, has every reason to fear as much for his life as for the affront that said woman could cause against him and all his family, by the wicked company that she frequents and who cannot fail to be, in time, most noxious, he beseeches you with all possible insistence that you might wish to heed his just declaration and give your express orders that she be locked up in the hospital noting that the poverty to which he has been reduced leaves him in no state to pay a thing, he will continue his prayers to the Lord for the precious days of Your Highness.

> M. J. Lieurtant, Manjire, Nicolas
> Pichard, Delalfache, Richer, Garnier,
> Guedon.

Ars. Arch. Bastille 12012, fol. 213 (1758)

> To My Lord
> the Lieutenant General of Police

My Lord,

Nicolas Pichard, apprentice miller in Paris residing there rue Saint-Germain-l'Auxerrois has the honor of most humbly representing unto Your Highness that about nine months ago around the time of the All Saints' Day festival, Marie Thérèse Pichard was arrested and taken by Your order, at the instigation of her husband the supplicant, to the Hôpital général where she is presently detained, the supplicant hopes that she is fully corrected of the causes of her detention, he beseeches Your authority that it might please him to order her release from said Hôpital, he hopes for this grace from Your ordinary goodness, and he will thus never cease to raise his prayers to Heaven for the health and prosperity of Your Highness.

> Nicolas Pichard.

Ars. Arch. Bastille 12012, fol. 307 (1758)

THE IMPRISONMENT OF WIVES

Jeanne Lemoine

To My Lord Hérault,
Lieutenant General of Police

My Lord,

Jean Legris, clothes tailor with Monsieur Henry, tailor, Saint-Benoît cross-roads at the hôtel de Venise, most humbly represents unto Your Highness that one Jeanne Lemoine his wife is so terribly debauched as much by drink as by several larcenies she has committed, for which the supplicant as well as the father of said wife were obliged to make restitution on several different occasions. Said François Lemoine and his son, father of said wife, join their prayers with those of the supplicant that it might please you to grant them an order of the King to have said Jeanne Lemoine locked up in the hôpital de la Salpêtrière, which will forestall any further misfortunes from befalling her as well as her family since she has an extreme inclination for taking and grabbing all that she can, she would doubtless be caught in the act as she has already been several times, it would be an undignified affront to the supplicants as well as her family to be subjected to the rigor of the Laws, this grace would excite both him and her family to continue their prayers for the preservation of the health and prosperity of Your Highness.

Ars. Arch. Bastille 11018, fol. 440 (1728)

To My Lord
the Lieutenant General of Police

My Lord,

Jean Legris, tailor most humbly represents unto Your Highness that after Jeanne Lemoine, his wife, appeared before You and even as she left Your chambers she swore and declared with an oath that she would persist and live a life four times worse than she had heretofore, even going so far as to brag that she would take my life or have it taken at the hour that I would least expect it and several among messieurs your officers were witnesses to this and even since then she has stolen some effects that I represented unto you in a previous memoir and as he is utterly unsafe, the supplicant has no other recourse than Your Highness to restore order, he will continue his wishes and prayers for the preservation of Your Health.

Ars. Arch. Bastille 11018, fol. 446 (1728)

To My Lord
the Lieutenant General of Police

My Lord,

Jean Legris, most humbly represents unto Your Highness that Jeanne Lemoine, his wife, having recovered from an illness brought on a month ago by her debauches of wine and eau-de-vie that caused the great misfortune that she gave birth to a dead and deformed child. This I certified and certify with a certificate from the midwife that I had the honor of presenting unto you and placing in your hands. I beseech, My Lord, that he might wish to grant me the grace that he promised me for this wretched woman and fearing further like misfortunes and others things of which she is capable. Said wife has appeared before Your Highness four or five times, if My Lord might wish to have the charity to deliver some order on her subject the whole family and I could only continue our wishes and prayers for the preservation of Your health.

J. Legris, J. Adolphe Langé, Carlot.

Ars Arch. Bastille 11018, fol. 451 (1728)

Jean Le Gris master tailor requests that his wife Jeanne be arrested and locked away in the hospital. He declares that she is drunken every day, that she steals everything she can get her hands on, that there is reason to fear that she might dishonor the family by coming to a dire end. Superintendent Parent reports that the declaration in the petition is truthful. He adds that it is also true that this woman took several items and sold them. I have summoned her before me three times, but she did not appear, and could not be found in order to be summoned. Therefore I think there is reason to arrest her.

[*In the margins:*]

1) Take her by force, this April 17, 1728.

2) The woman appeared completely ill, Monsieur took pity on her and told the husband that he would grant his demand at a later time. This April 21, 1728.

Ars. Arch. Bastille 11018, no folio (1728)

Geneviève Macé

To My Lord
the Lieutenant General of Police

André Macé, master cardmaker, residing rue Saint-Antoine across from the little door to Saint-Paul most humbly represents unto Your Highness that he has the misfortune of having for a wife Geneviève Alloché who has for seven to eight years thrown herself into a terrible debauchery, because of which she absented herself from the supplicant and led a most unruly life, she was heretofore arrested during a nighttime visit by M. the Superintendent Divot and locked up in the hospital from where she was released on the promise that she would live better in the future. After a month, she was arrested once again with another woman, one Champenois, and placed in the prisons of the Grand Châtelet for having together taken all of the furniture from a room at five or six o'clock in the morning. The Champenois woman was released from prison as was said Geneviève Alloché, who is currently ill in the Hôtel-Dieu in the Legat Wing and as the mother superior has no hope of recalling said woman to her duty, he beseeches you My Lord in virtue of the above and the certificates enclosed herein to give orders for her to be kept in said Hôtel-Dieu until the order comes for her to be locked up in the hospital. He will continue his wishes for the preservation of Your perfect Highness.

Ars. Arch. Bastille 11021, fol. 12 (1728)

I the undersigned curé of Saint-Paul, certify that one Geneviève Alloché wife of André Macé, master card maker in Paris, is a woman of unruly morals and of such scandalous conduct that I pray, in concert with her husband and her neighbors, Monsieur the Lieutenant of Police to have her locked up in the Hôpital général forever.

> In Paris this October 22, 1728,
> the curé of Saint-Paul.

Ars. Arch. Bastille 11021, fol. 13 (1728)

I the undersigned, chaplain to His Excellency My Lord the Cardinal of Noailles, certify to all concerned that one M. G. Alloché, wife of André Macé, master card maker of Paris, has already been locked up at the Hôpital général for her bad conduct and that I even wrote a letter to immediately recommend that she not be released at the end of a certain period of time because we had evidence that she would be incorrigible from our several previous experiences of her.

Given the present certificate to the Archbishopric October 22, 1728,

> Berthod.

Ars. Arch. Bastille 11021, fol. 14 (1728)

Anne Doisteau

To My Lord
the Lieutenant General of Police

My Lord,

Michel Pierre Corneille journeyman woodcarver [*tabletier*] residing on the main street of Faubourg-Saint-Antoine has the honor to most humbly represent unto Your Highness, that the bad conduct and considerable disturbance of Anne Doisteau his wife who by inclination is taken not only to prostitution, but even to commit the actions that are most contrary to probity have obliged the supplicant who, albeit indigent, makes it his duty to live with honor, to bring his complaints to your tribunal upon which and after they were verified exactly it pleased you to grant an order of the King by virtue of which said wife was arrested November 30, 1756 and taken to the Salpêtrière where she was detained until the month of August 1757 because the supplicant was no longer in a state to pay any pension whatsoever, it pleased Your Highness to have her released: upon her promises and the greatest declarations that she would live with her husband in the future in the exact image of a good wife, he, touched with compassion at seeing her reduced to such a sad situation took her into his house, counting that his clemency and the correction she had just endured would have changed her but far from it, she spent only three months in their union; which is to say up until she was cured of the ulcers that she had acquired from the bad air, then she began her libertine life anew and even went further still by casting aside her mask and leading a life of continual debauchery, and what is even worse still, she has taken to theft, and threatens her husband that she will have him murdered.

The supplicant and his spouse's family fearing for their honor having both one and the other lived in the most exact probity since time immemorial, take the liberty of appealing to the goodness and the justice of Your Highness to shelter him from this danger by having this woman so inclined to vices locked up. They will never cease to wish and pray for the conservation of your precious health.

M. P. Corneille, Marguerite Desoteau,
Laure Perlot (cousin), Marie Doriteau
(cousin).

I certify that Mme Corneille, did me wrong while working for me.

Dernier (used clothing merchant),
Patipas, Mason, Pubi.

While working in my house she did me wrong (wife of Pubi).

Ars. Arch. Bastille 11992, fol. 96 (1758)

Duchesne

To the King,

Sire,

Overcome by the weight of a most excessive pain, Duchesne one of the clerks of M. the Procurator General of the Parlement de Paris, dares with humble and respectful confidence throw himself at the feet of Your Majesty to implore his Justice against the evilest of all women. If the least of Your Majesty's subjects has never appealed in vain to Your Supreme Authority, if Your Majesty has never failed to listen favorably to the just complaints that were brought to the feet of His throne by all of his unjustifiably oppressed subjects, and if he never sent anyone away with the pain of seeing a just request rejected, what hope can this unfortunate man not entertain, who reduced to the last extremity today appeals to Your Majesty, after having exhausted every means of kindness, remonstrance and consideration, to recall to her duty a woman devoid of any sentiment of Religion, honor, probity or even humanity? Such is, Sire, the state of the unhappy man who dares to raise his plaintive voice to the ears of Your Majesty.

The supplicant born to honest parents and to one of the first families of the burg of Argenteuil, after receiving an honest upbringing, and having completed all his studies with some success, thought in 1749 that he could contract a legitimate marriage with one Marguerite Gobet of the city of Premerye Nivernais who was staying at the time with one of her relatives in Paris. As reasons of convenience impelled him to make this alliance even though he did not receive a sou in dowry from this wife, nor any hope for such in the future, the first years of his marriage were fairly calm and peaceful, without any of the altercations that arise ordinarily or any quarrels occasioned by the loss of means, or the enmity caused by libertinism. But the tranquillity that the supplicant had initially enjoyed was short-lived, and the good conduct of this woman at the beginning had soon changed into the most frightful and universal disorder.

The wicked company that she frequented despite the supplicant and behind his back found in her a quite particular disposition to debauchery, she did not waste any time in following the wicked example given by these companions, such that ever since she went astray there have been no debauches, no excesses to which she has not given herself and does not continue to give herself still every day, excited in this by one Donis wigmaker residing rue Percée, a man who has fallen into drunkenness and is known as such in his neighborhood, whom she continues to frequent despite the supplicant and whom she forces the supplicant to frequent.

If on the one hand, Sire, the profound respect with which I am filled for the sacred person of Your Majesty prevents me from entering into the exact details of all of the abominations with which this woman has tarnished my honor and sullied my life, upon which she has already made several attempts, as she even attempted to make me cut my own throat, while I was shaving, by pushing my arm, and throwing something upon the razor, and took my sword to stab me while I was in bed, this would seem in one way or another to authorize me today to implore Your Justice and Your Clemency, which, I dare say, would never have been more fittingly employed.

Gluttony [*excès de la bouche*] and wine being this woman's dominant passions, there are no means or iniquitous paths that she has not used to satisfy herself and she gives herself to them with an inconceivable blindness.

A deceiver and a liar to the last degree, there are no turns that she has not used to hide her wicked practices and ways; a truthful word will never leave her mouth. Become faithless and lawless [*sans foi ni loi*], nothing is sacred to her, she no longer knows any yoke of Religion, having trampled it under her feet, it is not astonishing that she cares naught for that of the household and that she respects no one. With such dispositions, the darkest misdeeds seem as a game to her, and as, ever since she gave herself to all these excesses, I have never ceased to continually employ every manner of conciliation to cause her to give up her waywardness and look within herself, it is impossible to conceive of the fury and outbursts to which she abandons herself instead of heeding me: the cruelest indignities, and all manner of abuse are all that she gives me for my remonstrances and that I receive for all of the pains that I have taken to make her change her ways. And every day I am threatened with being murdered or poisoned by this woman, if I dare to complain and attend to my own security. Also it did me no good to take my complaint before M. the Procurator General, and M. the Attorney General his brother who were willing to take the trouble to reprimand this woman themselves on the subject of her disorderliness and she was able to justify herself only with lies, guile and calumny that she contrived against me.

But alas, Sire, must not I fear that I am tiring Your Majesty with the humiliating narrative of the extreme evils that I suffer from such a monster, in the midst of the laborious and important tasks to which Your Majesty is unreservedly and uninterruptedly devoted for the continuation of the Glory of His Crown, and for the defense of His People? And will it be allowed me to declare unto Your Majesty that there are no days, either in the morning when I leave for my office, or at night when I return from it, that this woman inspired by some evil spirit, and out of her own bad character, does not vomit out against me a thousand maledictions and imprecations, which are my recompense for feeding and maintaining her in her indolence as much as I can given my lowly means, that she does not spew opprobriums, insults and infamies of all kinds, and does not do me the most bloody outrage by calumniously accusing me of having committed the most horrible and detestable crimes, and does so in the presence of all those that her disorderliness scandalously attracts to my home, to witness her horrors and my affliction. There are no lies and calumnies that she has not employed to discredit me and to destroy me in the minds of my protectors. I have no other goods or revenues on which to subsist and with which to provide for her subsistence than my honor, the probity that I have always observed to this day, and my employment with M. the procurator general. She has had the cruelty and the temerity to come several times to my office to outrage and insult me in the presence of his secretaries, and to accuse me of having committed some baseness, which has never been true of me, and which was an invention of her fury and hatred alone, solely with the aim of blackening my reputation, and throwing me into ultimate despair.

Uncertain as I am of the eye with which Your Majesty will see my sad situation, I can only hesitate to continue my account of it, but nourished by the paternal goodness that Your Majesty makes known to the least of his unjustly oppressed subjects, and the Justice that he wishes to render throughout his Kingdom, to all those who request it, with humble trust I throw myself at His feet to ask for this Justice that is the most [illegible] learned from His Throne, and I dare to hope, Sire, that Your Majesty well instructed of the truth of all the facts that I have the honor of declaring to him and touched by compassion might wish to be so good as to secure my life and my honor by the means that he will judge most fit.

As what I have just, Sire, declared unto Your Majesty, is but a portion of the misfortunes that have cast me into the deepest despondency, I most humbly beseech him to allow me to bring the narrative to a close as succinctly as possible.

My lack of means does not permit me to supply this woman with all of the money that she wishes to spend in the excesses of her debauchery, she decided several years ago, to not only steal some of my effects consisting of linens, clothes, books and others things, and to sell them at the most shameful prices, without my knowledge and while I was occupied with the duties of my employ with M. the Procurator General, and doing so in order to satisfy her unbridled passion for wine, which has been taken to such an excess that she has not spared even her own clothes, which she continues to sell one after another toward this end, but what is more, she has had the baseness to sell several effects that did not belong to her, and even to misappropriate others to several persons for their sale, and used the money that came from this to feed her coarse passion, even to the point that she has not left me even a single sheet upon which to rest which has left me in a sadder state than even the lowliest mercenary.

I further presume, Sire, to declare unto Your Majesty that with no regard for the pregnant state in which this woman currently finds herself, and an advanced state at that, she has not set aside a single piece of linen to use in her upcoming childbirth, such is the horror and inconceivability of her blindness and frenzy for debauchery.

Such is, Sire, the excess of pain and despair to which I have fallen and been reduced from being forced to spend the rest of my days with a woman a thousand times worse than the most ferocious and cruel tiger or lion, and whose base deeds and crimes make me fear as much for her honor as for mine, if Your Majesty does not in his fatherly goodness have the charity to deprive her of a freedom that is so noxious to her and that she abuses every day more and more, or to grant me whatever employment that he will consider suitable, even if it be in the depths of the woods, where I could live far away from so fearsome and odious an object.

Stripped of everything my life is no longer safe, my honor on which my bread depends, is on the point of being ravished from me, by the darkest calumnies with which this woman poisons all my actions and the disgraceful deeds with which her entire life is filled. If I open my mouth to make her understand all the horror of her proceedings and the dishonor that is reflected on me by her excesses and her debauches, then there is no indignity, cruelty or abuse that she will not exercise upon me, not only during the little time that I am at home during the day, but even during almost every night, such that reduced to the cruelest despair I do not know where to turn for help from such anguish.

In fact it is inconceivable to think that a man from a good family and who has the sentiments of honor that accompany an honest upbringing might, without any means, survive alongside a woman without Religion, nor honorable sentiments, devoted to drunkenness and to the spirit of dissipation that is its result, constantly filled with rage and an implacable hatred against her husband, and what is more, prone to criminal thefts. It is too much, Sire, if I am permitted to represent this unto Your Majesty to leave such crimes unpunished, and Your Majesty is too much the enemy of injustice and crime, not to bring down the full weight of his avenging arm, and of his sovereign Justice upon one of his subjects who would be found and convicted of such iniquity.

In these sad circumstances, all that remains, Sire, is for me to implore Your mercy and Your Justice, and to beseech Your Majesty, with tears and the humblest and most vigorous insistence, to take pity upon my sad state, by returning my life to me, Your Majesty would impose upon me the happy necessity of being eternally grateful for such a great favor, and of continually raising my wishes to the Lord, for the prosperity of His Arms, the continuation and the Glory of His Crown, and for the precious preservation of His Sacred Person, and of all of His August and Royal Family.

Signed Duchesne.

Ars. Arch. Bastille 11994, fol. 178–183 (1758)

Raymond Lafond

To My Lord
the Lieutenant General of Police

My Lord,

One Lafond in whose favor the Baron de Zurlauben had the goodness of speaking to My Lord, has the honor of most humbly representing unto you that having been instructed that his wife was conducting herself most scandalously, he followed her five times to the same place, and there discovered by the host's testimony that she had rented a room, that she occupied it only during the day with a fellow whom she passed off as her husband.

The relatives of said woman convinced of her bad conduct join with her husband to pray that His Grandeur might wish to give the order to have her locked up and that this be done by order of the King, so that she could be released only at her husband's will.

The supplicants convinced of your fairness will never cease to wish for the preservation of Your Highness.

Raymond Lafond; Marin
(relative of said woman).

Ars. Arch. Bastille 12002, fol. 63 (1758)

Paris this February 10, 1758.

Monsieur,

I only see the appearances of libertinage in the conduct of the Lafond wife and I was not able to find proof of the scandal of which her husband complains in the petition that I have the honor of sending you.

Lussan, who rents furnished rooms on rue de l'Évesque, is the only one who speaks unfavorably of this woman, saying that on November 22 last, he rented to a woman, one Frédéric, one of his rooms on the fourth floor for her and her husband the manservant of M. the Count de Botta and that for this he received an *écu*; that this woman only reappeared fifteen days later with the Frédéric man and that both of them returned seven or eight times during weekends and that they only were there from 3 o'clock in the afternoon until 8, that he is unaware of what they might have done together in this room, or if the husband might not have given reason for his wife's estrangement either through his bad humor or otherwise.

As nothing is straightforward about this matter and there is no one whom I could address to receive clarifications concerning either the scandalous conduct, or the theft that this wife appears accused of by her husband, I esteem with Your permission, Monsieur, that there is no cause to grant Lafond the order that he solicits.

I beseech that you will be so good as to receive the assurances of my most respectful attachment.

Clérieu.

Ars. Arch. Bastille 12002, fol. 64–65 (1758)

Paris, this February 14, 1758.
Sir,

M. de Zurlauben to whose residence I took myself this morning, spoke to me of the bad conduct and the weaknesses of Lafond's wife, in such a way as to leave nothing to be desired in assuring you, Sir, that the husband has very firm grounds for requesting that his wife be arrested and placed in the hospital.

M. de Zurlauben spoke of the theft with so many precautions that I foresee the impossibility of ever receiving a declaration from him.

I therefore esteem, Monsieur, that the hospital must be in all respects, this woman's lot.

I beseech you, Monsieur, to receive this with every assurance of my most respectful attachment.

Clérieu.

Ars. Arch. Bastille 12002 fol. 66 (1758)

This July 19, 1760.

It is true, Sir, that I requested of M. Bertin your predecessor, an order to place in the hospital the wife of one Lafond heretofore my cook, I had strong reasons for soliciting the imprisonment of this woman then, but as her husband is no longer in my service and that it was in part on his insistence that I went to these extremities, I no longer have the same motives to interest myself in what concerns either him or her, I will always be delighted to receive news of you. I pray you to continue to honor me with our friendship and to be persuaded of the respect with which I have the honor of being, Sir, Your most humble and most obedient servant.

De Zurlauben.

Ars. Arch. Bastille 120002, fol. 75 (1758)

To My Lord
the Lieutenant General of Police

My Lord,

One Lafond, justifiably detained in the hospital for her libertinage by order of the King, requests her freedom.

1°) It has been over two years that she has borne the punishment for her crime.

2°) Her health has been much affected.

3°) Her husband, taking advantage of her absence has sold and eaten up all the furniture, even the belongings that she had in her room.

4°) Dame Saint Thecle, officer of the house of detention will give a very positive account of her conduct and her kindness.

5°) M. de Zurlauben no longer takes any interest in this affair.

Ars. Arch. Bastille 12002, fol. 81–82 (1758)

Françoise Le Roy

To My Lord Berryer,
State Councillor,
Lieutenant General of Police

My Lord,

One Flamand domestic with Mme de Beauvais, rue de la Chaise, has the honor of representing unto Your Highness, that Françoise Le Roy, his legitimate spouse has for six months led a most scandalous life, she frequents an apprentice wigmaker residing with a master wigmaker rue Saint-Étienne-des-Grez, who even calls himself a surgeon, the supplicant's wife through this liaison has emptied everything from her room and even sold most of it.

The supplicant responsible for a child to feed implores your goodness and your order that his wife be locked away in the hospital, these prompt and just orders will restore the safety of his life. He has joined the signatures of honest folks who attest to her bad conduct, he hopes for this grace and will wish for the preservation of Your Highness.

His wife is currently on rue Saint-Étienne-des-Grez.

> Flamand, Martin, Jadoy (relative of the
> wife), Pezele, Formager.

Ars. Arch. Bastille 11996, fol. 109 (1758)

In Paris, this October 27.

My husband,

I write you these lines to tell you of my unhappy fate and being caught in a state where I cannot appear before you, I have fled and you will find nothing amiss in the room, I took only my own affairs. I told everyone that I know that I was entering into a household to be the chambermaid of a madame who is in a convent on rue Saint-Jacques so if you wish to instruct the world of that fact you would be [illegible], there is no one in the world who knows this but me so you need not worry that some will laugh at your expense. You were very unlucky to marry a woman such as myself, you can sell the room to feed the child the only thing that I recommend in God is do not abandon the child because the poor unhappy little boy it is not his fault.

Ask Mme Veras for the key to your trunk, I left it in her hands, you will find a nightshirt in your trunk, the room keys are with Mme Masila.

I will not write you any further as I am lost forever, I sleep like a pig on a bale of straw where I have already endured much misery by my own fault and by my bad conduct.

I conclude and I pray you in God to not abandon that poor little boy.

> Flamand Wife

> To My Lord Bertin, State Councillor
> and Lieutenant General of Police

My Lord,

Flamand domestic to M. de Beauvais has the honor of most respectfully representing unto you that he obtained orders two and half months ago to have Françoise Le Roy, his wife, locked up in the Salpêtrière, as today he is about to depart for the countryside with his master, he would desire the release of his wife whom he believes has been sufficiently corrected for her mischief to bring her with him, therefore he implores your goodness to grant him this grace and he will wish for the preservation of My Lord.

> J. Flamand.

Ars. Arch. Bastille 11996, fol. 117 (1758)

Anne Marotte

To My Lord Bertin, State Councillor,
Lieutenant General of Police

My Lord,

Pierre Cyr Franquet, journeyman metalsmith, most humbly beseeches that it might please you, My Lord, to grant him an order to have Anne Marotte, his wife, a mistress seamstress residing rue Planche-Mibray with a used-clothing merchant, locked up in the Hôpital général, she had been detained there by order of M. Berryer on August 31, 1754. She escaped on September 27, 1756, despite the attentions that were shown her as stated in the certificate from the officer of the Saint-Élisabeth dormitory, enclosed herein, several persons had complained that she sold the laundry and other objects that she had been given for her work, in order to avoid worse to come, the supplicant throws himself at Your feet, and Hopes for this grace from Your Justice, as he is in no state to pay a pension, in gratitude for which he will continue his wishes and prayers for the health and prosperity of Your Highness.

Merlin, Calin, Pierre Cyr Franquet.

Ars. Arch. Bastille 11997, fol. 34 (1758)

I an officer of the Saint-Élizabeth dormitory of the Hôpital général certify that one Anne Marotte wife of Pierre Franquet, admitted to our house on July 1, 1754, she was detained here by order of M. Berryer on August 31, 1754. She escaped September 27, 1756, despite all of the attentions that I showed her by procuring her the means to earn something she decided, instead of saving up, she indebted herself and took advantage of my goodness to trick me by escaping I have since learned that she escaped with nothing, neither to pay what she owed nor for herself.

Made in the Salpêtrière, this October 28, 1756.

Mother Agnès.

Ars. Arch. Bastille 11997, no folio (1758)

Marie Pagez

To My Lord,
the Count de Saint Florentin,
Minister and State Secretary

My Lord,

One Alexandre Bonhomme, upholsterer *[tapissier]* with Monsieur Delache, rue Hautefeuille, where he has been for seventeen years, has the honor of most humbly representing unto Your Highness, that he has the misfortune of having for a wife one Marie Pagez who during a trip to Vienna he was obliged to make with the Count de Stainville[3] gave herself to libertinage, left Paris, and went to reside in Versailles with one of her aunts; that the supplicant upon his return and in concert with his wife's relatives, addressed himself to the police inspector Monsieur de Villegaudin in order to have her placed in the hôpital de la Salpêtrière, she learned of the supplicant's undertaking, left Versailles and returned to Paris, where she met a female individual unknown to her, who accosted her, and who brought her back to sleep at the house of a woman, who had declared that she had lost two old sheets and wickedly imagined that said Pagez might have taken part in the theft of these sheets, which had already been stolen before she had returned to Paris. Meanwhile the supplicant having learned that his wife was in Paris, and where she was residing, went to alert Monsieur de la Villegaudin that he believed he had an order of the King to place her in the Salpêtrière; but how great was the supplicant's surprise when this police inspector took her to Superintendent Le Blanc, who sent her to the Grand Châtelet, to face ordinary justice for this supposed theft and thus said supplicant was made informer on his wife, which cannot naturally be imagined on the part of a husband. The supplicant, and the whole Pagez family all honest people some of whom are at Court, most humbly beseech Your Highness that you might wish to grant a *lettre de cachet* such that said Marie Pagez, be transferred to the hôpital de la Salpêtrière, where the small pension will be paid for her. All will pray and wish for the health and prosperity of Your Highness.

This March 21, 1758:
order for transfer to the hospital
(Police Report).

Ars. Arch. Bastille 11988, no number (1758)

Catherine Robiche

To My Lord
the Lieutenant General of Police

My Lord,

Charles Louis Botot, journeyman bookbinder residing rue des Carmes, Saint-Hilaire parish in the house of M. Sauvage, master bookbinder, brings unto Your Highness his just complaints against his wife Catherine Robiche commonly called Jereme, whose disturbed conduct is given to excess having been locked away three times already for her bad morals. She currently leads so depraved a life that there are no terms strong enough to describe it. It is to avoid most the dangerous consequences, that the whole family of said Robiche, has joined with the declarant, and all of the neighbors, to most humbly beseech My Lord, that you might wish to hand down your orders to put in a secure place, a woman who makes such pernicious usage of her freedom. All the undersigned suppliants will wish to heaven for the preservation of Your Highness.

Florimond Charles Louis Botot,
M. Sauvage, L'hobereau the younger.

I beseech My Lord, to have regard for the account in the present petition. Your Highness can trust those who have signed above, and whose probity is well recognized. November 25, 1758.

Bellanger, curé of Saint-Hilaire.

Ars. Arch. Bastille 11988, fol. 319 (1758)

Declaration made under oath before God on the memoir presented to My Lord the Lieutenant General of Police November 29, 1758, by Charles Louis Botot journeyman bookbinder against Catherine Robiche commonly called Jereme his wife said memoir was forwarded to us by My Lord the Lieutenant General of Police on October 8 to verify the facts.

This Wednesday December 12, 1758, 10 o'clock in the morning, Charles Louis Botot age thirty-one, journeyman bookbinder residing rue des Carmes, Saint-Hilaire-au-Mont parish, after swearing to tell the truth, having heard said memoir presented by him against his wife read aloud.

He declares that it was around eight years ago—he was married to said Robiche commonly called Jereme who as a girl had been locked up in the hospital twice for disturbed conduct (of which the plaintiff had been unaware) that since her marriage said Jereme gave herself to wine and libertinage dissipated what little he earned, sold some effects, linens and belongings, then abandoned him last year and discovered a trick for keeping the place she had retired to unknown for the space of four and a half months, part of which time, she worked as a domestic in the village of Mary-sur-Marne without ever having received any reason for discontent from him the complainant her Husband that about a month ago, she retired to said hospital where she is currently in the linen-spinning room at this occasion he the complainant, fearing that said Jereme upon leaving the hospital would abandon herself to some bad deed was obliged to appeal to the authority of My Lord the Lieutenant General of Police, said Botot declares that there is no motive of hatred in this undertaking and that he has tried everything to live in peace with said wife and has signed the declaration.

Signed C. L. Botot.

Ars. Arch. Bastille 11988, fol. 320 (1758)

THE DEBAUCHERY OF HUSBANDS

Antoine Chevalier

To My Lord Hérault,
Lieutenant General of the Police

My Lord,

Jeanne Catry represents most humbly unto Your Highness, that having married one Antoine Chevalier journeyman mason around forty-six years ago, he had always given some signs of madness, which have gotten worse year by year and which we attributed only to his debauchery and bad conduct, because he never behaved like an orderly man, having always spent everything that he earned at the tavern without any concern for his family, and having always sold his belongings and those of his wife to go drinking at the tavern; but My Lord, since for the last few years this madness, accompanied by this bad conduct has increased to such a point that said Antoine Chevalier often returns home at all hours of the night, completely naked, without hat, without clothes, even without shoes, which he leaves at the tavern to pay for what he spends with the first passerby, even perfect strangers, and as he commits a thousand extravagances at home even though he is seventy-four years old the supplicant who is a poor woman reduced to mendicancy by the behavior of her husband, was counseled by all the undersigned neighbors to most respectfully beseech that Your Highness might wish to have the charity to have said Antoine Chevalier her husband locked up, she dares to hope for this grace from Your goodness, My Lord, and she will be obliged to pray the Lord for your health and prosperity.

Charles Cousin, Pierre Roussette, J.-P. Catry.

Ars. Arch. Bastille 11004, fol. 12 (1728)

To My Lord
the Lieutenant General of Police

My Lord,

Very humbly represents unto Your Highness, Antoine Chevalier, journeyman mason age seventy-eight, who in the month of August 1728 was seized and taken to the house of detention of Bicêtre where he is held in the dungeons, on these orders, he dares to say with certainty that ill-intentioned individuals misled Your Highness's Religion,[4] because he has the advantage of having always behaved irreproachably and at all times provided for the subsistence of his wife and family through his labor; these facts are certified by all of his family, friends and the principal inhabitants of the neighborhood of rue des Vieilles-Tuileries where he resided; the ignominy of being seized in the neighborhood where he was born and has lived his whole life, the solitude and horror of the dungeons, the supplicant's old age, and his good conduct have brought him the compassion of all, especially his family.

The infirmities inseparable from old age no longer permit him to work, his family is in no state to provide him with all of the necessary support, he can hope only for the few comforts that their means permit them to furnish him, but they are not at liberty to do so because he is secreted away in the dungeon; in this situation, he throws himself at the feet of Your Highness alongside all of his family, friends and the principal inhabitants of neighborhood, and beseeches that it might please you to order that he be placed in the yard and to grant his family the freedom to see him, they will continue their hopes and prayers for the prosperity and good health of Your Highness.

> Louis Deschamps, Raphaël Long,
> Jacques Sigie, André Sibire, Coussin,
> L. Léonard (friend), Delavoix, F. Jeandarme,
> Cresseau, Charles Bassille (friend),
> Delaunay, master of the journeyman
> employee.

Ars. Arch. Bastille 11004, fol. 15 (1728)

> To My Lord Hérault,
> Lieutenant General of Police

My Lord,

Jeanne Catry, wife of Antoine Chevalier journeyman mason, most humbly thanks Your Highness, for the goodness and charity he showed by having locked away Antoine Chevalier, her husband, age seventy-eight, who is detained in Bicêtre by order of the King, for whom she prays God, that his confinement will convert him, and because she asked you for this grace, My Lord, solely out of a spirit of religion, and as she learned with great pain, that he had been placed in the dungeons, and as a result deprived of the aid that she and his family might procure him, and that this is contrary to her intentions, she comes today, My Lord, to ask that he have the freedom of the courtyard, because he is neither libertine nor evildoer, being of such an advanced age that he is so to speak demented; in such circumstances, said Jeanne Catry hopes that Your Highness will grant her this grace and she will pray the Lord for the preservation of Your Highness.

> Signed by three people (illegible).

[*Note on the back of the petition:*]

Send him over to the deserving poor [*bon pauvres*].

Ars. Arch. Bastille 11004, fol. 16 (1728)

To My Lord Hérault,
Lieutenant General of Police

My Lord,

Jeanne Catry represents unto Your Highness that one Antoine Chevalier her husband who has been in Bicêtre since the month of August 1728, at the supplicant's request, recognizing his errors and being most repentant assures the supplicant that he will live with her until the end of his days with all the orderliness required of an honest man, if Your Highness would wish to show him the grace of granting his release and as she is touched with compassion for her husband and as she has reason to expect that said Chevalier being over the age of seventy-five, will keep all of these promises, she beseeches You most humbly, My Lord, that it might please you to be so good as to order the release of said Chevalier her husband so that he might finish the few days he has left to live at her side.

Both she and he will redouble their hopes and prayers for the preservation of Your Highness.

Ars. Arch. Bastille 11004, fol. 21 (1728)

Defay

To My Lord
the Lieutenant General of Police

My Lord,

Margueritte Ferrand, native of Orléans, comes to throw herself at the feet of Your Highness, with tears in her eyes to beseech him to regard her with a compassionate eye, she has the misfortune of having a husband one Defay also a native of said area of Orléans who lost his wits completely five years ago, committing a thousand extravagances, wishing at every moment to kill her, as the supplicant is responsible for five children, and has exhausted herself bringing succor to said husband she finds herself obliged to implore Your Highness's authority to obtain from him an order to place him in Bicêtre until his mind is healthy again, as her life is not safe, neither hers nor that of her children, and being in no state to pay any pension for this, having ruined herself entirely for said husband, and being obliged to work by the sweat of her body to provide for the subsistence of her five children, the supplicant advances nothing that has not been signed and approved by Monsieur the Coadjutor of the city of Orléans and by several persons from the city who are currently here for their business and she will never cease to offer to the

Heavens, with her family, her hopes and prayers for the health and prosperity of Your Highness.

> M. Ferrand, Foucher,
> J.-D. Gaucher, Dubois.

Ars. Arch. Bastille 11006, fol. 98 (1728)

I pray you, Monsieur, to have pity on the person who will have the honor of presenting you with this billet, she is responsible for a husband who has fallen into madness (*démence*), and for five children, her husband eats their subsistence up every day with his expenses.

I ask you in grace that it might please you to have him taken to the Bicêtre while awaiting the order of the King, never have I seen a woman more pitiable or more worthy of your charity.

I have the honor of being with the most respectful attachment, My Lord, Your most humble and most obedient servant.

> My Lord [illegible] Coadjutor of Orléans.
> This August 6, 1728.

Ars. Arch. Bastille 11006, fol. 101 (1728)

Duplessis

> To My Lord
> the Lieutenant General of Police

My Lord,

Marie Marguerite Fournier, wife of Duplessis most humbly represents unto Your Highness that she had the misfortune around thirty or so years ago of marrying said Duplessis from whom she has received every grief and abuse.

Said Duplessis has already been imprisoned three times in Bicêtre for his bad conduct and his debauchery and every day the supplicant his wife fears that some grievous misfortune might befall her as he threatens her daily that he will kill her, having even beaten her today the 18th of July 1728 which has left her dangerously wounded as their neighbors will testify to Your Highness in order to most humbly beseech him to be so good as to order that said Duplessis be locked up so as to avoid the misfortunes with which he threatens her and she will continue her prayers for the preservation and the health of Your Highness.

[In the margins:]
I certify that my vicar having been called yesterday to confess the supplicant, told me that she was dangerously wounded, and that to avoid an even greater

misfortune it would be suitable to imprison her husband who threatens her most shockingly.

In Paris July 19, 1728,

R. Poumart, curé of Saint-Médard.

Ars. Arch. Bastille 11009, fol. 61 (1728)

I the undersigned sworn master surgeon of Paris certify to all concerned that today July 18, 1728, I went to the home of Mme Duplessis, rue du Chardonnier Faubourg Saint-Marcel whom I found infirm in bed suffering from a quantity of blows inflicted by her husband and I examined her; first I found a wound on her head made by a fire shovel that begins in the middle and superior section of the parietal and extends to the middle and inferior section of the same bone in the place where it joins with the temporal which the wound has penetrated up to the first table where the periosteum is entirely separated from the bone then upon examination of her body I found several blows given by the same instrument particularly in the extremities both superior and inferior where I found several contusions and gashes because of which she is in great danger of dying said patient complains that she has been beaten several times by her husband which is certified by her neighbors and that he has already been locked up in Bicêtre for a similar matter, in testimony whereof I issued the present report the very same day for all legal purposes.

in Paris this July 19, 1728,

Süe, sworn surgeon.

Ars. Arch. Bastille 11009, fol. 62 (1728)

This July 20, 1728,

to Monsieur Rossignol[5]

I cannot refuse alongside M. the curé of Saint-Médard and the other persons of probity who have signed the enclosed petition, to provide the supplicants with an attestation of the Truth of the repeated violence of Louis Barthélemy Peau commonly called Duplessis and particularly of the violence he committed yesterday with regard to his wife; the whole neighborhood came to me requesting that he be arrested forthwith as he had brought her to death's door with his violent blows as you will see, Monsieur, from the report of the surgeon who examined and bandaged her wounds. This woman has received the sacraments and is currently in great danger, this villain is prone to excesses of this kind, especially when he is drunken, which is constantly, he has already been brought to the hospital twice for his misconduct. And all those who know him wish for him to be locked up in this most recent case no less so than they did the previous times reporting that he is capable of murder and of all things on certain days of his debauchery.

I am with a most profound respect, Monsieur, Your most humble and most obedient servant.

July 19, 1728.
Guillotte.

Ars. Arch. Bastille 11009, no folio (1728)

Henry Petit

To My Lord
the Lieutenant General of Police

My Lord,

Marie Lecocq, wife of Henry Petit, day laborer residing within the walls of the Quinze-Vingts hospital, most humbly represents unto Your Highness, that for the eighteen years that they have been together, there is no excess of harshness that her husband has not used to deprive her of her freedom to earn her bread, her life itself is in no way safe, either from abuse, atrocious oaths, always roused by wine, smashing, breaking all of the furniture up until he sold it in order to sustain his debauches; he has even gone to find the supplicant among the infirm where she is kept, and insults the infirm to the point that she is now finally forced to bring her complaint, certified by the heads and principal officers of the house, that it might please you, My Lord, in Your good justice, to avoid further great misfortune, as he has narrowly missed setting fire to his room several times, to order that he be arrested and locked away forever, the poor supplicant will wish along with her children for the health and prosperity of Your Highness.

I the undersigned Head *[chefier]* of the royal Hospital of Quinze-Vingts certify the contents of the present request to be truthful and worthy of the full attention of Monsieur the Lieutenant General of Police, in Paris, this March 16, 1728.

Gaucher.

Ars. Arch. Bastille 11025, fol. 151 (1728)

To My Lord
the Lieutenant General of Police

My Lord,

Marie Le Cocq, wife of Henry Petit day laborer, residing within the walls of the Quinze-Vingts, who was forced to bring you her complaints about the bad conduct of her husband and the enormous abuse that he exercises against her every day, her life is in no way safe as M. Le Cheveirer, Mssrs. the Masters and the Minister of this hospital have certified; even though Your Grace was so good as to summon him before him, and to forbid him from continuing his opprobrium, he now recidivates more than ever, notably on the 8th of the present month of July without the rescue of the officers of the house, she would have perished and he threatens her that her days will end only by his hand; finally My Lord, she cannot express the rigors and outrageous persecutions that she and her poor children endure which are shameful, she is constrained to importune Your Grace, to beseech him to interpose his authority, insomuch as it may please him, to have Monsieur Henry Petit arrested and locked away, to put an end to her pains, to avoid the greatest misfortune, and to provide her salvation, she requests that Henry Petit her husband be locked away, declares that despite the threats I made to him last June 8 he has redoubled his violence and that July 8, he would have killed her if not for her rescue by officers of the Quinze-Vingts. Superintendent Daminois offers his assurances that the account given in the petition is true, that the officers of the Quinze-Vingts used, remonstrances and threats in order to soften his ferocity, but without result. He even tore up the billet that I had sent to summon him before me a second time and threw the pieces in the face of the porter. As I now learn that he continues his violence, I believe that he must be arrested and taken to the hospital.

Ars. Arch. Bastille 11025, fol. 156 (1728)

Marie Lecocq requests that Henry Petit, her husband, a porter, be once again locked up in Bicêtre.

Declares that ever since he received his freedom four months ago on the occasion of Monsieur the Dauphin's birth, he has plunged back into his original debauches, that he gets drunk every day, sells everything up to the smallest of his children's belongings.

Finally, that he beats her with such violence that her life is not safe.

These facts are attested to by the Minister, the Master and the Head of the hospital of Quinze-Vingts. Messieurs Condé and Desclaire signify that they have learned that this individual is a dangerous subject.

It is true that Petit was placed in Bicêtre on August 23, 1728, by reason of the violence that he exercised toward his wife.

The supplicant complains in a new petition of her husband's fury, and she continues to request with insistence that he be locked away.

The petition is certified by the Master of the Quinze-Vingts.

Messieurs Desclaire and Condé signify that they have nothing to add to their earlier responses and to the certificates that the supplicant has produced. That unhappily for her, the facts are only too true.

Ars. Arch. Bastille 11025, fol. 159 (1728)

Germain Varillon

To My Lord
the Lieutenant General of Police

My Lord,

Claude Jacob wife of Germain Varillon, journeyman clockmaker at the cour du Palais, most humbly remonstrates unto Your Highness that ten years ago she had the misfortune of marrying said Varillon who since that time has been carried to all manner of debauchery, to the point of dissipating all his estate in the company of unruly people of his ilk, gambling and frequenting all of the academies[6] where he loses not only his own belongings, but also the watches and other things that were entrusted to him to repair which causes affronts every day and leads astray all his ordinary activities, the excesses, violence and assaults increase daily.

She is forced, My Lord, to address her complaints to you notably concerning a most recent outrage that he just exercised against the supplicant, the first of this month said Varillon being full of wine and almost dead drunk, began no doubt with premeditated design to insult her with every infamy that a man utters when he has a wicked design, the next day he brought a company of folks with him to dine and in the middle of the meal he had another quarrel during which she saw that he had premeditated this with this company because one of the troop insulted her at every turn giving her pinches and saying insults to her, and the next day, the third day of his debauchery, said Varillon still repeating the same insults beat her with a number of blows and among others punched her right ear with extraordinary violence wishing to kill her. Without the rescue of her neighbors who restrained him as these are daily occurrences and all too well known to the neighborhood where they have lived and as her life is in no way safe, she appeals, My Lord, to your authority and good justice in order to oblige Varillon to become orderly *[se ranger]*, to live and conduct himself in a different manner in the future, all of the neighbors will certify the truth of these facts, she hopes for this grace from My Lord and will pray God for the health and prosperity of Your Highness.

Cotelle, Duclos, Guillieu, Bultot,
Chanteveau, the younger; Champion, François Jean,
Jacquet Fromaget, Louise Boileau,
mother of said Varillon.

Ars. Arch. Bastille 11030, fol. 107 (1728)

Germain Varillon clockmaker, declares that Cl. Jacob his wife wishing to free herself from the reproaches he had been making to her on the subject of her bad conduct with one Balthazar, took pains to ruin him.

That to begin, she had him arrested by the watch and taken to the Conciergerie on the pretense of alleged assaults after she had pillaged all the effects, merchandise, works and furniture from the shop.

That as soon as he was released he filed a complaint of the above facts with Superintendent de la Fosse, and presented his request to Monsieur the Civil Lieutenant, to receive permission to carry out an inquiry, to open the door of his apartment and seize and lay claim to his furniture and merchandise.

That since then his wife fraudulently obtained a letter of the King to have him taken to the hospital, finally that an interdiction has been placed that consumes the rent of the apartment where the furniture is and that it is in his interests to have it lifted.

He requests that he be permitted to name a representative of his choosing in order to defend his interests.

Superintendent de la Fosse replies that there would be no inconvenience to granting said Varillon that which he requests, but on the condition that this take place before Monsieur Honnet the Bursar of Bicêtre so as to be certain that he will not be made to commit some acts against his wife to destroy or prejudice her rights, it is most essential that this be observed in the present circumstance for the reciprocal interests of both parties.

(Police Report.)

Ars. Arch. Bastille 11030, fol. 116–117 (1728)

To My Lord Hérault,
Lieutenant General of Police

My Lord,

The widow Varillon at present wife of Monsieur Duhamel, distributor of mineral Waters, most humbly remonstrates that she is the mother of Germain Varillon of thirty-one years of age, that she spared nothing to procure for him an upbringing conforming to his birth *[conforme à sa naissance]*, having had him learn the trade of clockmaker, she procured an honest marriage for him, that for the ten years he has been married to Claude Jacob as chaste as she is virtuous he has never ceased frequenting taverns, or the games where he consumed the small estate of his marriage, that he continually beats his wife and that several times he has put her in danger of death and even beaten the supplicant who always restrained the just complaints of her daughter-in-law, in the hopes that he could be brought back by means of gentleness, but her pains were useless, his disorder increases every day and he has such an excess of it that his unruliness could only be attributed to madness as his judgment is no healthier than that of his father deceased at Bicêtre at age thirty-five of this illness of madness.

Around eight days ago a petition was presented unto Your Highness certified by witnesses that testifies to the extravagances of said Varillon; the supplicant and her daughter-in-law would have waited without importuning you if said Varillon in a continuation of his madness, had not yesterday, the 20th of the present month of 1728, created a scandal that could bring shameful consequences.

It was around five months ago that Varillon lacking money and promising to behave drew up a billet of Partnership with Michel Balthazar, master clockmaker at the cour du Palais, to the effect that they would share in work and profits, he not being a master, for at least two months, Balthazar has remonstrated with him that his debauches, games, absences, and poor management interrupted their work, but neither Balthazar's remonstrances, his wife's prayers, nor his mother's reprimands had any effect, and instead of looking within himself, he beat Balthazar several times, and carried invective to the greatest excess. On said day, February 20 of the month, 6 o'clock at night, without respect or care for the rules, he came to the cour du Palais shop where, like a madman, he burst into insults, broke the window of said Balthazar's shop, beat him and assaulted him such that said Balthazar was obliged to make a complaint with Monsieur Bailly du Palais, who informed of the disorder caused by Varillon, had him arrested and taken to the Conciergerie where is at present.

Things being in this state, the wife of said Varillon, and said Balthazar were counseled to appear before You, My Lord, in order to avoid the fees that they could not bear owing to their indigence, the mother and the daughter-in-law to avoid shame and affront and said Balthazar to preserve his life which would not be safe if said Varillon were to be freed, to beseech Your Highness to obtain from His Majesty an order such that said Varillon remain locked up until new order is given. They will continue their prayers for the preservation of Your days, and have signed the present, along with other neighbors February 21, 1728.

We the undersigned, each certify in what concerns us that we know of said Varillon's disturbances.

Claude Jaquot, wife of said Varillon;
Pommeri, brother-in-law; Lameret, neighbor;
Vodeine, neighbor; Fouquet, cousin;
Charlesreau, neighbor.

Ars. Arch. Bastille 11030, fol. 102 (1728)

Louise Boileau, widow Varillon, requests the freedom of Germain Varillon her son, offers to look after him, and declares that her affairs are withering away every day because of the death of his father-in-law five months ago.

Germain Varillon was taken to the hospital by order of March 14 last because of his violence toward his wife, and that he was given to all manner of debauches.

His wife does not request his release in the least.

When a first petition was presented by the mother in the month of June and was communicated to Superintendent de La Fosse, he had horrible things to say on this individual's account.

And upon a second petition presented last month the same superintendent signified that he had spoken with the woman who made several requests some of which were just, that as penance cannot last forever, he believes that Varillon can be granted his freedom, that he will speak to him as is suitable in order to arrange his affairs with his wife, that with regard to the discussions of his family, he must take his case before the judge.

Ars. Arch. Bastille 11030, fol. 131 (1728)

Memoir

The wife of one Varillon, journeyman clockmaker, detained by order of the King in the prisons of the Bicêtre since March 14 last, having learned that he was having his freedom solicited beseeches most humbly Mgr the Count de Maurepas, that as her husband is a man given to all manner of vices and capable of going to extremities that might dishonor her and all her family, to have the goodness not to grant him this, and to order that he be held until through a long captivity, one could find in him different sentiments than those that gave rise to his imprisonment.

Ars. Arch. Bastille 11030, fol. 114 (1728)

Jean Terrassin des Essarts

To My Lord
the Lieutenant General of Police

My Lord,

One Magdeleine Dessessart, wife of Jean Terrassin Dessessart, master clothes tailor has the honor of presenting unto Your Highness that for thirteen years of marriage she has received only abuse from her husband, as he is a very disturbed man, who is daily drunken, which carries him to the extremities of madness, that she is not safe with him, having several times narrowly missed being killed by his blows—of which she has made complaints to M. the Superintendent Dinot—and that she is in no state to be able to subsist owing to his disturbance, which is seen by and known to all of the neighbors who are ready to testify upon this subject.

The supplicant hopes that My Lord might wish to do her justice, she will continue her prayers for the health and prosperity of Your Highness.

> Nisole Genier (host of said lodger),
> Widow Carrée, M. Carrée (wife of Genier),
> Marie Le Noury (lodger), J. Antoine
> Nollet (licentiate in theology), Bausneuil.

Ars. Arch. Bastille 11006, fol. 266 (1728)

I the undersigned, priest, doctor of theology, curé of Saint-Gervais in Paris, certify that one Jean Terrassin des Essarts, master clothes tailor in my parish is a man of most disturbed wits and of very bad behavior, that he scandalizes the whole neighborhood with the abuse that he does to his wife and the neighbors when they wish to come to her aid when he is abusing her.

> Made in Paris this October 3, 1728.
> Curé of Saint-Gervais.

Ars. Arch. Bastille 11006, fol. 267 (1728)

My Lord,

Madeleine Dessarle, wife of Jean Terrassin Dessessart, clothes tailor has the honor of representing unto Your Highness that she had the honor of presenting him with a petition with a copy of the complaints that she made against her husband before M. the Superintendent Divot, enclosed with it was a certificate from M. the curé of Saint-Gervais on the subject of the abuse that she has received from him over thirteen years of marriage in response to this representation it pleased Your Highness to order his arrest three and a half months ago and to have him taken to Bicêtre, since that time the supplicant out of her natural goodness twice requested permission to see him in order to tend to his needs, but upon seeing him she received only terrible threats from him, he told her that if he was released, that she was sure to be killed by his hand, and as she narrowly missed dying several times including most recently when he would have stabbed her if he had not been stopped, to avoid this misfortune, she implores the ordinary goodness of My Lord that he might wish to order that his imprisonment be continued. The supplicant offers to pay a modest pension, being in no state to do more, owing to the unruliness of her husband, who reduced her to her extreme poverty and burdened her with debts, she will continue her wishes for the health of My Lord.

Ars. Arch. Bastille 11006, fol. 272–273 (1728)

To My Lord
the Lieutenant General of Police

My Lord,

Jean Terrassin Dessessarts, master clothes tailor in Paris, ordinarily residing place Basdoyeu, around forty-eight years of age and honest folks who
find themselves obliged to take his side and cause, as he has no relatives; most
humbly remonstrate unto Your Highness that whereas since his marriage he
has increased his estate greatly through his labors and his care, yet October 4
last he found himself arrested by order of the King and taken to the Bicêtre
by Monsieur Guillotte where he has been detained ever since in the dungeons
of this house like a criminal; the undersigned have always recognized him as
a very honest and irreproachable man and can attribute his detention only
to the solicitation of his wife, whom he made what she is today, and who
enjoys all his effects, and this under the pretext that he is inclined to drink,
but while this may be true, as he has no other vices besides that one, to which
he is presently no longer attached and for which he has been sufficiently
punished, it would not be just, with Your good pleasure, My Lord, that this
poor unhappy man perish in the dungeons in the prime of life as if he had
committed a much greater evil, it is for all these reasons that we beseech Your
Highness to grant the liberty of said Terrassin Dessessarts, and we will never
cease to continue our hopes for the health and prosperity of Your Highness.

Pareul, Dupuis, Langlois.

Ars. Arch. Bastille 11006, fol. 275 (1728)

There is every reason to think that the thing that disturbed the conduct
of Dessessarts was that of his wife who was never contented with a husband
and always has a male friend whom she still keeps today and she has already
left her husband since his detention, she had the furniture removed from the
two rooms during the night, furtively and has dissipated everything, the effects and papers of her husband that amounted to more than two thousand
livres, she gave birth to two children two months ago and let them die from
hunger fifteen days later without a wet nurse, as she only had them drink
milk from a wet nurse.

Ars. Arch. Bastille 11006, fol. 276 (1728)

To Monsieur Chappelin

I had myself informed, Monsieur, of the reasons that brought about the
order of the King by virtue of which one Dessessarts was taken to the hospital and through the verifications that I conducted myself I found that the

neighbors of this man, the curé, the Superintendent of the neighborhood, and a police officer, all unanimously report that this individual is a drunkard, a blasphemer, who in his neighborhood has committed the greatest violence not only against his wife whom he tried to kill with a knife, which a witness declares having disarmed him of, but also against his neighbors.

I believed that the public interest demanded that a man of this character be separated from civil society, which is what determined me to report this to M. the Cardinal de Fleury who judged it necessary to have him locked up; as to the conduct of his wife, of which the petition you did me the honor of sending to me makes mention, I am utterly ignorant as to whether she is bad, as her husband has not made any complaints in the past. What the husband's friends say about her today can only be regarded as most suspect, thus I am persuaded that you will think as I do that the detention of this Dessessarts is just, and that as he has not yet given any sign of repentance, nor have his wits been restored, it is not yet time to free him.

Ars. Arch. Bastille 11006, fol. 281 (1728)

Pierre Blot

To My Lord
the Lieutenant General of Police

My Lord,

Marianne Perrin, wife of Pierre Blot, residing rue de la Cordonnerie, in the residence of M. Le Tellier, wine merchant, Saint-Eustache parish, most humbly represents unto Your Highness that for the last six years said Blot has been feeble-minded, he was treated for three months at the Hôtel-Dieu, but instead of recovering, his wits became more disturbed such that he tried to kill the supplicant his wife and a daughter of around two months that the supplicant is nursing, and he abuses a daughter age eight and a half. In short, their lives are in no way safe. As all the neighborhood can confirm and attest to the truth, the supplicant appeals to Your Highness, that it would please you to give an order that said Pierre Blot be arrested and taken to the château de Bicêtre to the madhouse *[salle des fous]* as she fears the further ills that could only come of this, and she will never cease to continue her wishes for the preservation of the health of My Lord.

Tellier (primary leaseholder), Gervais.

[*On the same petition:*]

Monsieur, I have the honor of reporting to you that the complaints made by the wife of Pierre Blot against her husband are just, she has every reason to fear her husband's madness. It would be a charity to place him in Bicêtre; several attempts have been made to cure him but it appears to me that his ill [*mal*] is incurable, the present can be sent to Monsieur the Superintendent Machurin.

Pouffis, this March 12, 1758.

Ars. Arch. Bastille 11988, fol. 60 (1758)

To My Lord
the Lieutenant General of Police

My Lord,

Marianne Perrin, wife of Pierre Blot, porter in the flour market in la Halle, residing rue de la Cordonnnerie, Saint-Eustache parish, most humbly represents unto Your Highness that her husband is detained in the common prisoner's room [*salle de force*] of Bicêtre for being of slightly alienated wits, but that he never insulted anyone, nor committed any base deeds, it was only the supplicant along with her two children who suffered a little, he always offered his services to the public in the said Halles with honor and probity and as he has put himself in God's hands his spirit is completely calm as it would appear from the certificate of his confessor enclosed herein. This obliges the supplicant to appeal unto Your Highness, that it might please you, My Lord, to release said Pierre Blot her husband, so that he could return home to work as before and earn a living for his children, she dares to hope for this grace from Your ordinary Justice and she will never cease to pray God for the preservation and health of Your Highness.

C. Gervais, M. Vanogenne,
Griffault (baker), Gioibisce.

Ars. Arch. Bastille 11988, fol. 68 (1758)

I the undersigned, sacristan priest of the church of Bicêtre, certify to whom it may concern that I heard the confession of Pierre Blot, prisoner in the common prisoner's room of the Bicêtre.

This present certificate was given this July 18, 1758.

Guiard, priest.

Ars. Arch. Bastille 11988, fol. 67 (1758)

Louis Couillot

To My Lord Bertin,
Lieutenant General of Police

My Lord,

Suzanne Baillet, wife of Louis Couillot, domestic currently without a position and lodging with one Julien, domestic of Mlle Breanne, rue des Tournelles, porte Saint-Antoine.

Most humbly remonstrates unto Your Highness, that the extreme poverty to which she has been reduced through the awful disturbance of her husband, has barred the ordinary paths to obtain a legal separation *[séparation de corps]* from him, and obliges her to appeal unto Your authority and unto your justice to halt the course of the infinite mistreatments, abuses and humiliations that her cruel and inhuman husband began exercising against her upon the second year of their marriage, and that he still continues to make her suffer every day: these are so great in number and their details so full of horror that she will restrict herself to exposing only a small portion before Your Highness's eyes, but it will doubtless be sufficient to convince him of the necessity of protecting the supplicant, of placing her under his safeguard, and of preventing this barbaric husband from further attempts upon her life.

The supplicant was married in 1739, and in 1740 after five days in childbirth, her husband came in a state of drunkenness and seized her by the hair and began dragging her inhumanely around her room, he left her for dead, and if not for the prompt aid procured for her by Madame La Mare, a surgeon's wife who resided in the same house and who fortunately happened upon her, she would in fact have died.

In 1745, he had a venereal disease, he went from the doctors to the hospice of Charenton and he spent a great deal in the eyes of the supplicant who is the only one who brought anything to their union, as for him, he did not have anything before his marriage, nor since.

In 1746, the supplicant was then residing in the house of the Chevalier Le Noir, her husband came to beat her, up until this lord had him pursued so as to be arrested.

In 1751, he resolved to murder her, to this end he came at midnight to the house of M. and Mme Defilly in whose service the supplicant was working, he had armed himself with a large andiron with which he gave her three sizable gashes to the head, Monsieur Delpêche, master surgeon did such as to bandage the supplicant, and doubted for a long time that he would be able to save her. (*In the text here*: I attest that I bandaged and attended to the supplicant at this time, Delpuech.)

In 1757, she received from her husband the kick in her ribs without the care of Monsieur de la Taxe, master of surgery, she would have remained crippled by it for the rest of her life.

He robbed the supplicant in this same year of 1757, he took from her twelve pieces of silverware, two large spoons and ten silver goblets along with a thousand three hundred and twenty livres in gold and thirty-six livres in white silver, sheets, her nightgown, in short he reduced her to mendicancy having carried away all that she possessed, with the exception of a bed, a dresser and a few belongings.

Finally, he came July last to take from the supplicant all that she had left, he tried to break down her door and lost his temper, cursing and insulting her. That these facts are true and real is attested unto Your Highness by the supplicant's neighbors. Those who know her give her reason to hope that you might by your authority and your justice wish to compensate for the insufficiency and the impossibility of appealing to the law to free her from the tyranny of a cruel and inhuman husband, who every day seeks to take her life, either by having him locked away, or by expressly forbidding him under grave penalties to ever set foot in the supplicant's house. She will never cease to wish for the precious preservation and prosperity of Your Highness.

Desilly de Cameron (retired infantry officer);
Pentus (former neighbor), Latasse
(Master in surgery), Mlle Lataste (former
neighbor), Mlle Pentus (mistress midwife,
former neighbor), Mlle Pentus
(seamstress, former neighbor).

I, former landlady certify that Mme Bouillet occupied a room for thirteen years with all of the conduct of a perfectly honest woman where she was beaten by her husband,

Mlle Boileau, Mme Gralet
(former neighbor and wood merchant).

Ars. Arch. Bastille 11992, fol. 120–121 (1758)

François Dubois

To My Lord
the Lieutenant General of Police

My Lord,

Marie Millet, wife of François Dubois, heretofore clothes tailor, residing rue de la Huchette, Saint-Séverin parish at the Trois Chandeliers, most humbly represents unto Your Highness, that for a number of years said Dubois having left and abandoned his trade, has given himself entirely to drunkenness, in such a manner that he is always drunken, and continually roams the streets both day and night, without her knowing from where he steals to satisfy this unfortunate passion and to survive, because after he carried off everything that he could get his hands on from his household and of his effects, she sees no other resources he might have than asking for alms from passersby in the street, he is in short like a man who is capable of anything [*un homme déterminé*]; and with whom the supplicant and her children are in no way safe, not only, this unfortunate family, but also the neighbors who arrive to calm the constant scandal that he creates each time he returns at whatever hour it may be, the supplicant cannot say more because she is this man's wife; but she has every reason to fear for herself and her children as much on the side of honor as that of life, so long as this man remains free; she comes to throw herself at the feet of Your Highness, to most humbly beseech that you might wish to dispatch an order to have said Dubois locked away; and all her family will never cease to offer up to heaven their wishes and their prayers for the preservation of Your Highness.

Ten people from the parish have signed,
+ the curé (archpriest) and the Dubois wife.

I the undersigned doctor of the Sorbonne, archpriest of Paris, curé of Saint-Séverin, certify that the six people who signed here alongside me are from my parish, bourgeois from my parish and honest folk, who can be trusted January 22, 1758,

Daumet de Brisson.

Ars. Arch. Bastille 11994, fol. 65 (1758)

From October 26, 1761.

To My Lord
the Lieutenant General of Police

My Lord,

Marie Millet, wife of François Dubois commonly called Gilbert age sixty-two, most humbly represents unto Your Highness that for a number of years her said husband has taken his most irregular conduct to so outrageous a point that it will now be the fourth time that he has been prosecuted in a different criminal jurisdiction and what is more he was locked away by Police order for eighteen months in the château de Bicêtre, which clearly proves his bad conduct and how far astray he has gone. The supplicant and all of her family have made the greatest efforts to ensure that her said husband be locked up for the rest of his days, in order to avert the troublesome consequences of such reprehensible conduct, police detective M. de la Villegaudin can report unto Your Highness the truth of the above declaration, because it was he himself who arrested him previously and took him to Bicêtre.

In such unpleasant circumstances and without any other foreseeable means of averting the evils that such conduct can occasion, the supplicant appeals once again to Your Justice and ordinary equity, My Lord, so that it might please you to give the orders to bring to the château de Bicêtre said François Dubois commonly called Gilbert, currently detained for the fourth time for a criminal matter in the prisons of the Grand Châtelet from where the supplicant has just learned that he has obtained his release; Your Highness filled with concern for the public good will feel more than anyone the danger of letting this man out into the streets of Paris, and one can envisage only grievous and shameful consequences for the family if he were to obtain his freedom, and that the life of the supplicant and the lives of her children are in no way safe; the whole family will redouble their wishes for the preservation of Your Highness.

> Signed by the Dubois wife, the curé and
> several witnesses from the parish.

Ars. Arch Bastille 11994, no folio (1758)

Monsieur the Count de Saint Florentin

One Marie Millet, wife of François Dubois commonly called Gilbert requests that her husband age sixty-two and heretofore clothes tailor, be taken to Bicêtre.

She declares that he was already locked up on her request in the month of February 1758 because of his bad conduct his dissipation and his violence: that he was released, without her participation, in the month of July the following year; that ever since he has continued to lead a most unruly life that he was arrested four times for criminal matters, that it would be dangerous to leave him in society and that her life and those of her children are in no way safe.

The conclusion of the inquiry that I had carried out by the neighborhood Superintendent and detective was that this declaration is truthful, that this man is given to theft and drunkenness, that his wife is reduced to such misery that she is in no state to pay his pension, and that said Dubois has no other relatives in Paris other than his children who join their mother in soliciting this order. Which is further supported by the signatures of the curé and several other persons.

> (Police Report.)

Ars. Arch. Bastille 11994, no folio (1758)

To My Lord
the Lieutenant General of Police

My Lord,

Marie Millet, wife of François Dubois commonly called Gilbert age sixty-two, most humbly represents unto Your Highness that for a number of years her husband has taken his most irregular conduct to so outrageous a point that it will now be the fourth time that he has been prosecuted in a different criminal jurisdiction and what is more he was locked away by Police order for eighteen months in the château de Bicêtre, which clearly proves his bad conduct and how astray he has gone. The supplicant and all of her family have made the greatest efforts to ensure that her said husband be locked away for the rest of his days, in order to avert the unpleasant consequences of such reprehensible conduct, M. de la Villegaudin police detective can report unto Your Highness of the truth of the above attestation, because it was he himself who arrested him previously and took him to Bicêtre.

In such unpleasant circumstance and without any other foreseeable means of averting the evils that such conduct can occasion, the supplicant appeals once again to Your Justice and ordinary equity, My Lord, so that it might please you to give the orders to bring to the château de Bicêtre said François Dubois commonly called Gilbert, currently detained for the fourth time for a criminal matter in the prisons of the Grand Châtelet from where the supplicant has just learned that he has obtained his release; Your Highness filled with concern for the public good will feel more than anyone the danger of letting this man out into the streets of Paris, and one can imagine only grievous and shameful consequences for the family if he were to obtain his freedom, and that the life of the supplicant and the lives of her children are in no way safe; the whole family will redouble their wishes for the preservation of Your Highness.

M. Leclerc, Ricard (son-in-law), Bourdon,
Cave the elder, Besolle.

I the undersigned doctor of the Sorbonne, archpriest of Paris, certify that all those who have signed the petition are from my parish in Bagneux.

This October 16, 1761.
Daumat de Brisson.

Ars. Arch. Bastille 11994, fol 74 (1758)

THE TALE OF A REQUEST

Vincent Croyseau

To My Lord
the Lieutenant General of Police

My Lord,

Margueritte Le Maire wife of Vincent Croyseau cobbler residing rue des Canettes, Madeleine en la Cité parish, most humbly remonstrates unto Your Highness that around seventeen years or so ago she married said Croyseau, and he after having spent time during his marriage living calmly was unable to stop himself from making known his debauches, his oaths, and his blasphemies, which led to the supplicant appealing to all of her relatives both on his side and on hers to testify to the truth and to request of My Lord that after having been informed of the acts committed by said Croyseau of which the supplicant gives proof through the undersigned to grant the order that he judges fit. This would be the means to put her in a state to see to her salvation and to purge the public of a man who seeks only to make an affront to his family by coming to a shameful end, the supplicant will continue her wishes and prayers for the health and prosperity of Your Highness.

Margueritte Le Maire (wife of said man).

I certify the truth of the facts declared in the above petition and that said Croyseau is a very bad subject [*mauvais sujet*] who deserves to be locked up, so that he no longer has occasion to continue his libertinage.

In Paris this April 7, 1728.
Duhamel, archpriest and curé of Sainte-
Madeleine, Pierre Croyseau (brother of said man),
Nicolas Ancelée (brother of said man).

Ars. Arch. Bastille 11005, fol. 111 (1728)

I pray Superintendent Isabeau to inquire into the conduct of the individual against whom the complaint was made and to signify to me his thoughts on his account. This April 5, 1728.

After having conducted a precise inquiry, Monsieur, into the conduct of this individual, all that remains is for me to certify to you that his own brothers request his correction. That M. the curé of the Madelaine who wrote and signed the certificate dated at the bottom of this petition, assured me that several times he urged him to live honestly, without any success. And finally that the certificates from several people of the diocese of Blois appear to me to be of such authenticity, that there is no reason to doubt that this man merits this punishment.

Superintendent Ysabeau.
May 20, 1728.

Ars. Arch. Bastille 11005, no folio (1728)

To My Lord
the Lieutenant General of Police

My Lord,

Margueritte Le Maire wife of Vincent Croyseau and Pierre Croyseau his brother and family most humbly represent unto Your Highness that at their request said Vincent Croyseau was arrested and locked up in the Bicêtre by order of the King where he has been detained for eleven months and as it appears that he has settled himself [*s'être rangé*] and promised to live peacefully, that even his governors are satisfied of him, they beseech you, My Lord, to grant them his freedom.

They hope for this grace and will continue their wishes for the preservation of Your perfect health.

Margueritte Le Maire (wife of
Croyseau), Pierre Croyseau (his brother).

Ars. Arch. Bastille 11005, fol. 119 (1728)

Marie Anne Goulard

To Monsieur Rossignol,
June 28, 1728

Monsieur,

In accordance with the honor of your orders, I inquired into the conduct of one Marie Anne Goulard, wife of Monsieur de Valence, fencing master in Orléans where he resides, he is around twenty years of age; it was almost a year ago that said Monsieur de Valence married said Goulard who was in service at the time, as soon as she was married she took out a lease for a part of the house in the name of her husband, obliged him to furnish it and once all of this had been done, she soon began to host gambling and to receive all manner of persons indiscriminately, one Grandlour who keeps the other part of the house a woman of very bad conduct had soon procured for her as many acquaintances as she wanted, she began by taking into her house a young man from the provinces named Guirard who was in Paris to study law of whom she ate up and made him sell everything he had, his family was alerted to this by the Messieurs of Saint-Sulpice, his father wrote him saying that he must turn away from this or else he would disinherit him; she currently sees one Chabrolle, notary clerk and two abbots, one of whom is called Du Plessis, and the other Mousseau, not to mention the others whose names are unknown, not long ago she moved from rue Princesse where she resided and went into the cloister of Saint-Benoît where she can do a great deal of harm, with regard to all the youth, who go to school there.

This June 26, 1728.

Haynier.

Ars. Arch. Bastille 11030, fol. 59–60 (1728)

Marie Anne Goulard requests the revocation of an order of the King from August 6, 1728, that her husband obtained to have her placed in the hospital.

Declares that on June 8, 1727, she married Monsieur Valence, fencing master who lived with her on good terms for five months.

But ever since this time he has never ceased acting badly toward her without her ever being able to penetrate into the reason why.

Finally, that she was very surprised to learn that while he was in Orléans, he was having an order for her detention solicited in Paris.

To prove her good conduct she offers the attestation of her neighbors.

And what is more there is the retraction by her husband who declared before a notary that he only complained of his wife in a rush of anger and that he only had her detention solicited upon the counsel of ill-meaning persons, that he recognizes that she is of good morals.

It is stated that Monsieur de Valence obtained an order of the King on August 6, 1728, to have his wife locked up for her bad conduct. Although today the husband tells a different story the disturbance of his wife is no less certain nor even notorious.

But perhaps the fear of being locked up will convince her to lead a more orderly life.

Ars. Arch. Bastille 11030, fol. 69 (1728)

I the undersigned certify that I attended to the administration of last rites which were given yesterday at 11 o'clock at night to Mme de Valence who was at death's door, that we had all the trouble in the world obtaining from her husband a cloth to receive Our Lord and that after the rites had been administered, having told him to consider the state to which he had reduced his wife who was at death's door, he replied to me that this was not what was going on, that I having replied to him that he therefore had no regard for the administration of last rites he said to me again on this subject that he would not suffer their putting on an act in his home.

Made in Paris this August 31, 1728.

Chabrol.

Ars. Arch. Bastille 11030, fol. 75 (1728)

On April 6 last, an order of the King was dispatched to have one Goulard the wife of Valence taken to the hospital, her husband first complained of her bad conduct and requested the order. She changed neighborhoods, going to live in the cloister of Saint-Benoît, the curé of this same parish strongly complained of the scandal that she was causing. All of the facts were verified and found true.

Valence gave a retraction to his wife and requested that she not be arrested. Monsieur ordered Monsieur Haynier to stay the order's execution.

The Valence wife absented herself and requested the revocation of the order that had been dispatched against her.

She feigned illness, returned to Paris, requested a confessor saying that she was at the extremity, she even received her last rites. Monsieur Haynier verified that the illness was feigned, that it was a game played upon the counsel of one Chabrol notary clerk who lives in bad commerce *[mauvais commerce]* with the Valence woman. Finally, she presented unto M. the Civil Lieutenant a request to obtain a separation from her husband and had the furniture seized. The husband requests that his wife be locked away.

Ars. Arch. Bastille 11030, no folio (1728)

Françoise Marguerite Gruyot

To My Lord

the Lieutenant General of Police

My Lord,

Pierre Verdeau, master glazier in Paris, residing there on rue de Verneuil, Saint-Sulpice parish, most humbly represents unto Your Highness that around ten years ago he had the misfortune of marrying Marguerite Gruyot, that instead of living as an honest wife, she has for the last several years, abandoned herself to all manner of debauchery, and has carried off furniture and effects from the supplicant's house in order to sustain this, which utterly undermined the supplicant's establishment which is why upon his justified complaints, the most recent dating from September 6, 1727, n° III, Your Highness had her locked up in the hospital from where she has now been released. The supplicant who did not doubt that the good instructions that she received there would have made her chaste, would have forgiven her and brought her back into his home, but she abandoned herself anew and contracted a wicked illness; she, unbeknownst to the supplicant, had gone to find the surgeon of the house, who refused to undertake her treatment, because of which she was forced to present herself to the Hôtel-Dieu, from where she was sent back to Bicêtre where she is at present, in the infirmary, for such debauchery so many times repeated, and without hope of return, the supplicant most humbly dares to beseech Your Highness, that he might wish to order that said Marguerite Gruyot remain in the hospital for so long as it will please God to keep her alive, or for as long as it will please the supplicant, and he will continue his wishes and prayers for the prosperity and health of Your Highness.

Ars. Arch. Bastille 11012, fol. 373 (1728)

François Manceau

To My Lord Hérault,
Lieutenant General of Police

My Lord,

Claude Mevillon, wife of François Manceau merchant grocer residing rue Mouffetard most humbly represents unto Your Highness that having by virtue of Your Ordinance had her husband locked up in Charenton for his debauches where he remained for three months, and upon the beautiful promises that he made to change his conduct, the supplicant obtained his release from Your goodness, but far from this correction having made him behave himself, he becomes more unruly every day, he is continually drunken, destroys their whole household and drunken or not showers the supplicant with insults, abuse and threatens to do even worse, the whole neighborhood is witness to the scandal that he causes, for this the supplicant once again implores My Lord's authority that it might please him to have said Manceau locked away in Charenton where he was before with the offer that she will pay his pension, and she will continue her prayers for the health of Your Highness.

Jean Lhost, Fr. de Bourg, Couturieux,
Catela, Cl. Mevillon.

I certify that the undersigned are my parishioners and people worthy of trust.

N. Poumard, curé of Saint-Médard.

Ars. Arch. Bastille 11021, fol. 112 (1728)

To My Lord
the Lieutenant General of Police

My Lord,

Claude Mevillon having had the honor of presenting a petition unto Your Highness nine months ago in which she beseeched you My Lord to have one François Manceau her husband locked up; you had the goodness of granting her this grace and of having him locked up by Your order in Charenton where he is detained.

And as said Manceau has promised the supplicant his wife that he would no longer fall into this disorder and would settle into his duty and live with her in their union and conduct himself in an orderly manner, the supplicant most humbly comes to beseech Your Highness to be so good as to give your orders so that said François Manceau be released so that he might return to his house with the supplicant his wife, this grace would oblige both of them to pray God their whole lives for the preservation of the health and prosperity of Your Highness.

Claude Mevillon.

Ars. Arch. Bastille 11021, fol. 117 (1728)

Marie Trouvé

To My Lord
the Lieutenant General of Police

My Lord,

One Michel Lecuyer, domestic of Mme le Mouche, residing rue de l'Hirondelle, Saint-André-des-Arts parish, most humbly remonstrates unto Your Highness, that around two months ago he had the honor of presenting you with a petition against Marie Trouvé his wife, and one Pierre Foulon commonly called La Forêt, domestic, on the subject of the scandalous disturbance of said Lecuyer wife with said La Forêt, even the threats made and almost executed to take said Lecuyer husband's life, you were so good as to forward this petition to Monsieur Haynier, officer, so that he would carry out all the inquiries necessary on this subject and make his report; Mgr the Chief Judge *[premier président]* having in the meantime ordered that the children of said Lecuyer and his wife be taken to the hospital in order to retrieve them from the upbringing of so libertine a mother, he did not obtain a response to said petition and that after his children were taken from the arms of this cruel mother *[marâtre]*, she carried off all of the furniture and went with said La Forest in order to continue her debauches undisturbed and to lead a libertine life, that said La Forest continues to seek out ways to murder the supplicant, making no scruple of bragging about this publicly.

Considering this, My Lord, it might please you to have said Laforest arrested as a vagabond (said Pierre Foulon commonly called Laforest retired three months ago to the residence of M. de Culans who resides rue Ferou, faubourg Saint-Germain as a domestic, only after the publication of the King's edict against vagabonds) accused of scandal five or six years ago, he was already imprisoned for the mischief for which he was convicted, and similarly to have the supplicant's wife locked up in the Hôpital général, in order to absolutely suppress this public scandal, and to place the supplicant's life in safety, and he will continue to raise his wishes to Heaven for the prosperity, preservation and health of Your Highness.

Ars. Arch. Bastille 11018, fol. 167 (1728)

> To Monsieur Hérault,
> Lieutenant General of Police

Monsieur,

I certify that Marie Trouvé wife of Lecuyer nursed my son and that after that she was my domestic and that she acquitted herself of all of her duties as a good and honorable woman and that I saw her to be chaste and sensible, and I often heard it said that the husband of said Marie Trouvé was ridiculous and full of false ideas that he wishes to pass for the truth out of his wish that his wife remain locked away.

The supplicant hopes for every justice from Your equity.

> Le Defossé,
> gentleman ordinary servant of the King.

Ars. Arch. Bastille 11018, fol. 171 (1728)

Monsieur,

I had the honor around two months ago of making a report to you concerning a petition that had been presented unto you by one Michel Lecuyer, domestic of Mme la Mouche, relative of M. the Chief Judge, on the subject of the libertinage and bad commerce of his wife with one La Forest, even of the repeated attempts of said La Forest on the life of said Lescuyer according to the inquiries that I carried out on your orders at the time: M. the Chief Judge who takes part in this affair requested that I inform him of the said inquiries that I had carried out on this subject and to report to him which I did not obey; I presented all of this to the office of M. Rossignol; M. the Chief Judge nonetheless ordered that the two children be taken from the arms of this libertine and had them placed in the hospital; this made no impression upon her, she still continued her same commerce with said La Forest who for his part is even more insolent than before, daily threatening said Lecuyer that he will beat him to death with a club which obliges him to beseech you once again to obtain an order of the King to have his wife locked up as well as said Laforest who is a very bad subject, who for his part is married and lives very badly with his wife, having sold her furniture several times, he currently lodges with said Lecuyer wife and he has dissipated a portion of her effects after her children were taken from her, I believe, Monsieur, that there would be justice in having said Lecuyer wife as well as Laforest locked up.

Haynier, April 29, 1728.

Ars. Arch. Bastille 11018, fol. 174–175 (1728)

I the undersigned priest, doctor of theology of the Faculté de Paris and Vice-gerent of the Saint-Côme parish, certify that Marie Trouvé, wife of Michel Lecuyer, has behaved like a most disturbed woman during the time that she has resided in our parish, despite the warnings that I gave her and the promises that she had made me in Paris.

De la Roche.

Ars. Arch. Bastille 11018, fol. 178 (1728)

Michel Lecuyer, domestic of Mme la Mouche, relative of M. the Chief Judge, requests that Marie Trouvé, his wife be arrested and taken to the hospital.

Declares that his wife has given herself to a scandalous debauchery with one Pierre Foulon commonly called Laforest, domestic.

That Laforest threatens to murder him.

That the chief judge had all of the children placed in the hospital to remove them from such an unruly mother and that immediately afterwards, she had all of the furniture carried off, which she took to the residence of Laforest where she lives as his wife.

The petition is signed by the Husband.

A wide inquiry conducted by Monsieur Heymier found that the curé of Saint-André-des-Arts, M. Hébert, priest who assists in the same parish, and nine people with whom he spoke, assured him that they all knew perfectly well of the debauchery of l'Ecuyer's wife with one Foulon commonly called Laforest, of the violence that Laforest had several times exercised against Lecuyer, and of the threats he made that he would kill him, in these circumstances, I think that there is justice in having this Marie Trouvé locked up in the hospital, even more so as M. the acting priest of Saint-Cosme and Monsieur Hebert signify by their certificates that the efforts they made to withdraw her from her debauches were in vain.

Ars. Arch. Bastille 11018, fol. 185–186 (1728)

I can assure you Monsieur that the wife of my lackey is the most wretched, meanest and most debauched woman that one could find. I know this beyond any doubt having inquired into her in several places where she had lived before I prayed M. the chief judge to have the two little girls placed in the hospital to remove them from a such a disgraceful mother, as for Lecuyer I can assure you that he is the best man in the world who did everything that he could to live correctly with her but she cannot suffer him and she stubbornly remains with a scoundrel who has a wife whom he beats and he threatens my lackey that he will kill him such that I never have him go out at night there is also a poor creature who knows that he has her removed from several posts and for a several days he has beaten her and all of this because she went to testify as to what she knew about the commerce of my lackey's wife with this wretched man.

It was he who makes every effort to have her released but I can assure you that this would be to authorize vice and to tell you the truth that man should be locked up along with her, as there is every reason to fear him.

Here, Monsieur, are things as they truly are.

I will always confess a perfect gratitude for the manner you have used with me. I wish with all my heart that I might signify to you the respect and esteem with which I am, Monsieur, Your most humble and most obedient servant.

Rousseau de la Mouche.

Ars. Arch. Bastille 11018, fol. 186 (1728)

I had thought it fitting, Monsieur, to pray you to leave the wife of Lecuyer my lackey in the hospital to make penance for her wrongs, but as her confessor has for several months now given a very good account of her sentiments and that the confessor of l'Ecuyer has counseled him to request her return, I conform myself to their opinions and pray You Monsieur, that you might wish to have them released as soon as possible so that she will be grateful to her husband and that this would engage her to be obliged to him and to be more chaste, I also wish that you would be so good as to have him told that you are granting him this grace at my prayer. Do not also refuse me the grace of believing myself with much respect, Monsieur, Your most humble and most obedient servant.

Rousseau de la Mouche.

Ars. Arch. Bastille 11018, fol. 190 (1728)

Jean Baptiste Boissier

To My Lord
the Lieutenant General of Police

My Lord,

Jean Baptiste Boissier, invalid soldier and clerk in the Stockings Manufactory of the Hôtel des Invalides for eleven years takes the liberty to most humbly beseech Your Highness to grant him an order of the King to have Françoise Lesquoy, his wife, locked up in the house of correction of the Salpêtrière, with the promise of paying Mssrs. the administrators one hundred livres per year for her subsistence up until, and as long as it will take for her to look within, and to give signs of repentance for her past bad conduct, what leads, My Lord, the supplicant to do her this grace, is that said Françoise Lesquoy becomes more insolent day by day and that she is not at all sorry for what she has done that after three rulings dismissed all the requests she had made to separate herself from him both bed and board, and having been unable to obtain the smallest [illegible], she refused to return with him, after having been legally ordered to do so; that she obstinately insists on wishing to live with her father and her mother who are capable of giving her only the worst advice, that he has every reason to fear that in continuing to frequent her younger sister who has become a prostitute of the first order, she might in the future give herself to ever greater unruliness than in the past and she is capable of dishonoring herself before God and before men as well as the supplicant, or that she might occasion or incite some unpleasant affair, all of these considerations, My Lord, that Religion and honor have suggested to the supplicant, are also motives that should urge Your Highness to grant him the grace that he takes the liberty of requesting of you and by granting it, you would be doing him a most powerful grace for which he offers God his wishes and prayers for the health and prosperity of Your Highness.

Ars. Arch. Bastille 11988, fol. 121 (1758)

July 10, 1759.

To My Lord
the Lieutenant General of Police

My Lord,

Nicolas Lesquoy, bourgeois of Paris lodging in a furnished room, rue du Plâtre, has the honor of representing unto Your Highness, that having had the misfortune of marrying his daughter, Françoise Lesquoy, to Jean Baptiste Boissier, currently an invalid soldier, who had the cruelty to drive out his wife after a few months of marriage after having subjected her to the cruelest abuse. This unfortunate woman withdrew to the house of the supplicant her father, where she remained for five years, her husband having then been enjoined, by a higher order from the police given with full knowledge of the facts, to leave his wife alone at the house of her parents.

During this interval of five years, J. B. Boissier led a libertine and wayward life: but finally overcome with remorse and shame, he came like a false prodigal son to throw himself at the knees of his father-in-law who he artfully seduced with his promises.

His wife, witnessing and touched by his repentance, succumbed to an inclination that carried her off: the two spouses were reunited. The wife by her assiduous care and her kindness for a time held the unrestrained and bad inclinations of her husband at bay. All the persons who knew them rushed to do them favors at this time: but the good conduct of the wife always played the greatest part. They received permission to sell tobacco and then eau-de-vie in the Invalides; and from this small business they amassed in only a few years, this even the husband admits, around thirty thousand livres.

He, drunk with a wealth that his libertinage had always hidden from him, soon began to abuse it. He spread the majority of his fortune into incestuous and unknown arms. This bad conduct brought discord back into the home. Threats were followed by blows and blows by threats.

The complaints of an unfortunate wife, her screams, her pains, her ardent representations were unable to return her husband's spirit and heart to her. He had become as much spendthrift as he was cruel, one would hardly even dare to say that he had made good use of a quarter of their fortune. This wife, finally, unable to resist the abuse of her husband any longer, and even at risk to her life, withdrew herself from his barbaric power by taking flight.

Meanwhile her husband, accompanied by Superintendent Renaudin, was making scandalous searches for her person vomiting out a thousand insults against her. The true motive that animates him is to sacrifice his wife to his vengeance; and his pretext is marital authority. Under cover of this title of which he has made himself unworthy, he has complaints drawn up to cover his shame and his blackness, and in order to manage a means of escaping the return to his wife of the small sum of money that she was able to amass by her care, or to give her the assistance that she lacks completely and that is her right to demand.

But, My Lord, under the wings of your protection could she worry any longer of being victim to so many cruelties and injustices.

An unfortunate father, overcome with pain, comes to place at the feet of Your Highness, the bitter complaints of a daughter, of an unhappy spouse, who, from the depths of her refuge, where a cruel husband pursues her in order to cause her to suffer the harshest torments that is unless he dares to make an attempt on her life, crying out for vengeance and justice.

In these circumstances, My Lord, may it please Your Highness to forbid Jean Batiste Boissier currently an invalid soldier, as did M. Berryer your respectable predecessor, in full knowledge of the facts, from troubling Françoise Lesquoy, his wife, or to make or have made any search for her by himself, or by any officer of the law at his request alone: given the harm and the abuse that he has almost continually exercised against her, and as her life is in imminent peril, without prejudice to her other rights: and the suppliant will continue his wishes for the prosperity of Your Highness.

[*On the same petition:*]

This July 26, 1759.

Monsieur, the present memoir that was presented by one Lesquoy, father of the Boissié wife, against whom her husband has complained, does not merit any attention, he is a father who is overindulgent with his children, and as to the rights of said Boissier against his wife, he is on the firmest ground and we should trust the attestations of all the superior officers of the Invalides hospital under whose observation said Boissier and his wife have been for several years and who have always condemned the wife's conduct.

(Illegible signature.)

Ars. Arch. Bastille 11988, fol. 132–133 (1758)

Jean Baptiste Boissier has the honor of representing unto you that he married Françoise Lesquoy in 1747, the mother of said Françoise Lesquoy gave said Boissier twelve louis upon marrying her daughter.

Fifteen days later, she forced her daughter to return the twelve louis, this was the beginning of their first disaster.

Said Boissier seeing the wicked ways of his wife's mother made up his mind to bring his wife into his household, near where he exercises the trade of fruit seller on rue de Jouy, quartier Saint-Paul it was here that said Lescoy came in the absence of said Boissier and carried off household effects to the value of around one thousand five hundred livres for which said Boissier made a complaint to M. the Superintendent de Roche Brune. After that said Lescoy retrieved his daughter back to his house where he kept her for three years while Boissier handled his household affairs well said Lescoy never ceased troubling his household and gossiping even to the point of bearing false witness against said Boissier in order to take, by order of M. Berryer, everything that he had in his house.

Here the goodness of M. the curé of Caillou and M. the Provost of the Hotel was required as they had misled the Religion of M. de Berryer.

During the time that said Françoise Boissier was with her father, she took forty-two gold louis and brought them to one of her brothers who was a master joiner and after that she went to find said Boissier in the Invalides so as to give the impression that he had taken them in malice so that the father would have the right to ask for them back.

As God does not leave anything unpunished, the brother profited so little from this sum, that he went bankrupt the next year after having eaten up the estate of his wife no longer wishing to see her. Like all of this family, the poor woman was obliged to place herself in servitude to live.

The cause of the current distress of said Boissier, it is that his wife became jealous of her sister who leads a most dishonest life and mocks her need for polish and fancy dress. She gave her sister a disgust for domesticity and said Boissier wife told her husband that she wished to quit his business in the Invalides, imagining the pleasures of the Boulevard and say that in the Hotel one had to [illegible] all desires—all by the bad advice of her sister.

Said Boissier had always showed good manners to his wife and he earned a good living and he bore large expenditures even having the complaisance to give her recreation from time to time and taking her to the Comédie[7] and all the while he hoped that it was just that her sister was putting ideas in her head.

Said Boissier having given everything due to honor and pleasure to his wife she took money several times that she gives in secret to her sister, most recently she took eight gold louis with which she bought handkerchiefs, bonnets and laces unbeknownst to her husband on July 9 of the current year, I was brought a Persian dress that said Boissier wife had ordered made and of whose purchase the husband was utterly unaware. All of this was well devised with her sister, they broke in and carried off a value of eight thousand livres for which said Boissier brought a complaint on the 8th of July of the present year, said burglary took place during the High Mass so that they would not be seen by anyone and she went to meet with said sister who was waiting for her at rue de Grenelle at the corner of rue de Bourgogne with another fellow who was in a carriage. Said Boissier wife carried off the sum of a thousand livres that did not belong to her husband and she was well aware of this.

Said sister an accomplice to the theft spent every day of the week with the fellow circling around the Hotel in order to pick out the day for the theft that they committed.

During this time said Boissier wife solicited workers to engage her husband to go for a stroll and during this week at said sister's house she carried out several misdeeds.

The day of the Octave of the Blessed Sacrament they plotted during the services to agree upon how they would go about carrying off the effects, they remained in the room of said Boissier not wishing to attend any services.

If My Lord might wish to be so good in his justice as to reduce the pride of these Lescoys who have always deceived everyone and to place the wife of said Boissier in the hospital with a small estate that he would provide for her in order to remove her from bad company, owing that said wife has never had reason to complain of him.

Which is why the interest of the father and mother has always been to retrieve their daughter along with whatever estate said Boissier their son-in-law might have.

Ars. Arch. Bastille 11988, fol. 137–138 (1758)

My Lord,

One Lesquoy, residing in Paris, rue de la paroisse Saint-Séverin, my penitent for around twelve or thirteen years, came to find me in a state of extreme affliction over the deplorable situation of her daughter, wife of Boissier a soldier in the Invalides, so that I might write Your Highness that he might be touched by this situation. I cannot refuse my involvement in her suffering, especially knowing her character, her tenderness and her good morals, I do myself the honor of writing unto Your Highness in all truthfulness that which might engage him to be favorable toward this afflicted mother, her daughter is guilty of nothing more than removing herself from her husband's home in order to find safe haven at her parents' from the wicked proceedings of her husband this determined said parents to counsel her to turn herself over to the Châtelet prisons while waiting for the *lettre de cachet* that was to be executed against her rest and tranquillity to be halted, thus, I dare to beseech Your Highness to show her this grace, she is worthy of it for her good conduct, past and present.

You would wish, if it would please you, to grant this grace that I solicit as a reward for her sensible and good conduct.

I have the honor of being with the respect that I owe you, Monsieur, of Your Highness, Your Most Humble and Most Obedient Servant.

Br. Mileare,
in place Maubert.

Ars. Arch. Bastille 11988, fol. 155–156 (1758)

To My Lord,
the Lieutenant General of Police

My Lord,

Françoise Lesquoy, wife of Jean Baptiste Boissier, invalid soldier, detained in the prisons of the Petit Châtelet returns to again implore Your Highness's mercy, beseeching him that he might procure her release; she knows that her husband accuses her of having carried off a value of eighteen thousand Francs, to wit five thousand livres in shares and five thousand livres in both silverware and silver coin and that he used every means to persuade her judges of this. But the exact truth is that all the supplicant took, when she was obliged to escape from his house was four hundred silver livres and enough silverware to be able to subsist for a little while up until she was able to find employment: the silverware having been recognized when she tried to relieve herself of it was returned to her husband, therefore the wrong that she did him is quite small especially because she brought much more to the marriage and the supplicant's father and mother gave him a second dowry in order to lift Boissier back up at a time when his affairs were going poorly; the supplicant's father who has exhausted himself up until the present to provide for her needs in the prisons where it costs forty-five livres per month for her room alone, finds it impossible to continue this charitable aid; the supplicant will then, if she is kept any longer find herself in the cruel necessity of going to the hay *[se mettre à la paille]*[8] and of seeing herself mixed in with all manner of wretches. She therefore hopes that Your Highness, always just and equitable, will recognize the truth and put an end to the supplicant's torments by giving her back her freedom, and she will never cease to wish for the preservation of Your Highness.

Ars. Arch. Bastille 11988, fol. 174 (1758)

On the 8th of July last, said Françoise Lesquoy took from the supplicant more than eight thousand livres, in gold, in silver and in other effects a portion of which belonged to a dyer residing rue de Grenelle, faubourg Saint-Germain, and she had herself made two sets of men's clothes, dressed thusly, she went to lodge the very same day of her escape with one Baptiste who is known as a debauched woman, instead of retiring to the house of her father and mother, she took a fake name, after Baptiste's she lodged in furnished rooms in different locations, namely rue de Saint-Merri, at the porte de Saint-Denis, at Saint-Germain-en-Laye, at Chaillot where she spent the greater part of the money that she had stolen from her husband by breaking into the armoire where it was locked away. All of these facts, My Lord, and several others have been proven and noted through all of the proceedings carried out from the first of September before M. the Civil Lieutenant of Paris, up to the present day, thus everything that the supplicant takes the liberty of advancing is pure truth, he believes that he has reason to hope that you would be so good as to hear his Most humble request, and that said Françoise Lesquoy, his wife, will be locked up in the house of corrections of the Salpêtrière as she deserves.

Ars. Arch. Bastille 11988, fol. 182 (1758)

To My Lord
the Lieutenant General of Police

My Lord,

Jean Baptiste Boissier, invalid soldier and clerk at the Stockings Manufactory of said Hotel for around twelve years, has the honor of most respectfully beseeching Your Highness, to give no regard to the solicitations of Françoise Lesquoy his wife, who proposes that the order of the King by virtue of which she is locked away in the house of correction of the Salpêtrière be revoked and to not make any decision without first having had the goodness of having the facts presented against said Lesquoy reported to him, either by writing to M. the Count de la Serre, Governor, or to M. de Sarty the Intendant of said Hôtel or by having represented to him the three sentences that the supplicant obtained before Mgr the Civil Lieutenant at the Châtelet in Paris against said Lesquoy who has still not given any sign of repentance since she was locked away by the counsel of her parents who are with her every day and provide her with absolutely everything that she desires, at the expense of the eight thousand livres that she carried off from her husband, and this for the third time.

The supplicant desires that by continuing to pay up until she has given him signs of true repentance.

He will never cease to wish to the Heavens for the health and preservation of My Lord.

Jean Baptiste Boissier.

Ars. Arch. Bastille 11988, fol. 185 (1758)

To My Lord
the Lieutenant General of Police

September 18, 1760.

My Lord,

Jean Baptiste Boissier invalid has the honor of beseeching Your Highness to give no regard to the solicitations that Françoise Lesquoy makes and her parents, that they say they will have revoked the order of the King by virtue of which she is locked away in the Salpêtrière revoked and that said woman grows more and more insolent every day.

M. de Mallebas, curé and Rector of said House told the supplicant that she was not maturing [*mûrissait*] and that it would be doing her wrong to release her and that neither her parents, nor others, should see her, so that she might be able to look within herself, the way things are, My Lord, releasing said woman and her being still in concert with her parents, would be to expose the supplicant to having his throat cut or in a transport of anger himself cutting the throat of someone he might find with his wife, all of these considerations, My Lord, well weighed before God and in no way suggested to the supplicant by any hatred, nor ill will toward his wife, give him hope that Your Highness will ratify his most humble request and that the supplicant after having experienced a great loss and being daily involved in proceedings that cause him expenses and the neglect of his work, he beseeches Your Highness to put an end to his pains, he will never cease to Wish to Heaven for the preservation of the health of My Lord.

Jean Baptiste Boissier.

Ars. Arch. Bastille 11988, fol. 186 (1758)

To My Lord
the Lieutenant General of Police

My Lord,

One Nicolas Lesquoy and one Jeanne Valvé his wife, merchant fruit sellers in this city of Paris take the liberty of representing most humbly unto Your Highness that having married one of their daughters to one Jean Baptiste Boissier, soldier in the Invalides of this city in the hopes that by this she would be loved and treated as he had sworn and promised, and that he would live and lead a Christian life with her, for as long as he would live, said Lesquoy and Valvé's hopes were soon frustrated when, six months after their marriage, having established themselves with the dowry promised and by them delivered, they saw in their house and heard it told of their said daughter that she was constantly abused by her husband.

Having justly complained to them of the abuse, of the dissipation of the dowry, of the nakedness to which he had reduced her, and of the impossibility of living with him any longer without being exposed to the danger of losing her life and receiving her death from his cruel and Jewish hand, they could not stop themselves from retaking, reclothing and rescuing their said daughter, four years after they had retaken, reclothed and fed her, it pleased her husband to ask for his wife once again with the promise that he would treat her differently than he had and to lead an edifying life with her. Her father and mother hoping that this promise would be carried out, granted the return of their daughter, and they gave her back to him with a new dowry of four thousand livres in silver coin, furniture and silverware so that he could see to their reestablishment and profit.

As soon as this man saw that he was well reestablished, with his wife's new dowry, and profiting well from the pains and vigilance of this same wife, although she conducted herself sensibly before him and everyone, he continued to abuse her and to deprive her even of her necessities, and she on her side constantly complained to this same father and mother, who always told her to have endless patience and to suffer everything for the love of God; but after having suffered for the space of eight years in which she lived, traded and commerced with this inhuman man, seeing herself still deprived of the necessities of life and continually threatened with a mortal blow, without being counseled by anyone, she withdrew from the house and sought refuge with a laundrywoman, a woman of great age and similar honor, with a few pieces of her own silverware, as she was without clothes or money to dress herself or to provide for her necessities, she went to the silversmiths to sell them the silverware, someone saw this purchase and alerted her husband, he removed everything and took it back to his house declaring that he would have his wife who had been his victim locked up; she, in order to avert the accomplishment of his barbarous design, brought him before the law so that they would be declared separated totally and in perpetuity, while waiting for this ordinance to be given, she entered the Petit Châtelet and stayed there up until she had obtained her release and return to the house of her father and mother in order to be free pending the judges' decision; while she was there, her cruel husband, had her seized and locked up in the Salpêtrière where she has been for month, crying and trembling; in order that she might be released, she and her father and mother, beseech Your Highness most humbly to order her release and they will never cease wishing to Heaven for your health.

Ars. Arch. Bastille 11988, fol. 195 (1758)

To My Lord
the Lieutenant General of Police

My Lord,

Jean Baptiste Boissier, invalid and clerk at the Stockings Manufactory of the royal Hotel of the Invalides. He most humbly beseeches Your Highness to give no regard to the solicitations that might be made on behalf of Françoise Lesquoy his wife who has been detained in the Salpêtrière for over a year and a half, who has given no sign of repentance and persists in the sentiment of wishing to live with her sister, who is a libertine and who had to be locked up for her bad conduct and was released by a gentleman of standing, she says that she will have her protectors revoke the order of the King by virtue of which her sister is locked away.

The supplicant, My Lord, again appeals to your Justice to preserve his life and his honor, let her stay where she is because she has not wished to be good.

My Lord, the supplicant will never cease to offer his Wishes to Heaven for Your Health.

Jean Baptiste Boissier.

Ars. Arch. Bastille 11988, fol. 208 (1758)

In Paris May 29, 1762.

After the letter, Monsieur, that you did me the honor of writing me, I summoned one Boissier invalid soldier and told him your intentions and those of M. the Count de Saint Florentin on the subject of his wife detained in the Hôpital général, he seemed to me to be far from willing to consent to her release, he even brought me a memoir that I have the honor of sending you and by which you will see that he claims that the father and mother of this woman who offer to take responsibility for her are not in any state to feed her; as for him, whose modest employment furnishes him only with enough to maintain himself quite humbly, he says that he is not in a situation to do so nor does he wish to give anything to this woman.

I have the honor of being with a most perfect attachment, Monsieur, Your most humble and most obedient servant.

Laserre.

Ars. Arch. Bastille 11988, fol. 211 (1758)

October 28, 1762.

Monsieur,

M. the Count de Saint Florentin did me the honor of granting me the freedom of one Lesquoy, I was astonished when I did not see arrive the order that would have granted it to her.

I was told that her husband employed at the Stockings Manufactory of the Invalides had solicited M. de La Serre to obtain another prolongation of this woman's detention. I assure you Monsieur, that this scoundrel of a man abuses the credulity of M. the governor. I offered you proofs the last time that you came into our house of the meanness and heinousness of the husband of this poor creature. Some of our sisters are willing to say what they have heard which is completely to the advantage of this woman.

I had not thought it useful to inform you of this given the promises that M. de Saint Florentin and you, Monsieur, had made me.

I hope that you will not revoke her freedom and I will be doubly grateful for this.

I am with respect, Monsieur, Your most humble and most obedient servant.

De M. Cousson.

Ars. Arch. Bastille 11988, fol. 216 (1758)

My Lord,

Nicolas Lesquoy and his wife, come to throw themselves at Your Highness's feet to most humbly beseech him that he might wish to remember Françoise Lesquoy their daughter, wife of Jean Baptiste Boissier, invalid soldier, who has kept her at the Salpêtrière for around two years by virtue of an order of the King that he obtained through the protection of M. the Governor of the Invalides to whom he made a false declaration; it is true that the state of despair to which he reduced her every day forced her to take the poorly considered path of withdrawing herself from his cruelty by suddenly abandoning the cruelest of husbands and by carrying off a few effects that have been, since then, returned to her husband.

This wrong, My Lord, is not worth her being deprived of her freedom forever and being locked away in a place intended for people convicted of the most awful debauchery, she has never ceased to be an honest woman, her husband is in no state to offer the slightest proof otherwise.

In these circumstances, My Lord, the supplicants who are without protection hope that you might wish to act in their favor as Your Highness generously does for the unfortunate who request justice and by this means procure their daughter's freedom and permit the supplicants to take her in with them, this grace that is requested of Your Highness by a father and mother who are reduced to despair and fall into tears at seeing their daughter in the saddest of situations engages them to offer to Heaven the most sincere Wishes for the preservation of Your Highness.

Ars. Arch. Bastille 11988, fol. 218 (1758)

To My Lord
the Lieutenant General of Police

My Lord,

Nicolas Lesquoy has the honor of representing unto you that flattered by the hope that you had the charity to give for the freedom of Françoise Lesquoy his daughter, wife of Boissier invalid, detained for around three years in the Salpêtrière, he beseeches you to remember this unfortunate captive.

If you would so deign, My Lord, return her to her father and mother who will answer to you as to the regularity of her conduct and who pray along with her for your preservation and prosperity.

Nicolas Lesquoy and his wife.

Ars. Arch. Bastille 11988, fol. 222 (1758)

Madeleine Tiquet

To My Lord Bertin,
Lieutenant General of Police

My Lord,

Charles Tiquet, clerk on the farms of the King, residing faubourg Saint-Martin lodging with Monsieur Prouselle, stockings merchant, has for a wife Madeleine Tiquet, vendor of small household items and lender of money on interest without the supplicant's consent, moreover she engages in bad commerce [*mauvais commerce*][9] for which, owing to her proven disturbances Your predecessor, My Lord, three years ago gave the order to have said woman arrested, along with one Turgis who was arrested, placed the House of Detention and he left in exile and she has since then escaped.

After this, she judged fit to unite with one Guaudissart, lender of money on interest and to live with him in concubinage and maintain their bad commerce; learning that she was just arrested July 2, 1758, along with Monsieur Godibert by M. Dupuis and placed in For-l'Évêque. Owing to the representations he hopes of from Your Highness and to obtain that she be transferred to the hospital, fearing every danger from this mean woman that she might dishonor the family, he dares to expect this grace from your goodness; and he will pray God for Your Highness.

Charles Tiquet.

Ars. Arch. Bastille 12017, fol. 78 (1758)

To Monsieur the Count
de Saint Florentin,
Minister and State Secretary

My Lord,

The relatives and friends of Madeleine Pillon, wife of Tiquet, detained in the Salpêtrière for fifteen months, have the honor of most humbly representing unto Your Highness that they have taken the liberty of addressing unto him several memoirs, with certificates enclosed herein to beseech him to order the freedom of said woman against whom there exists no complaints now that retractions have been presented to the offices of the Police and who could only remain detained by the blackness of Tiquet guard of the Barrières, her husband, who pays her no pension, who refuses her all aid, as well as his accomplices at the Pitié that allow him to better continue his outrageous libertinage, thus the supplicants implore the integrity of Your ordinary Justice, My Lord, to order her release or to have her transferred to the Châtelet if she is guilty of some crime, so that she might go to trial and they will never cease to wish and pray for the preservation of the days of Your Highness.

Ars. Arch. Bastille 12017, fol. 110 (1758)

The relatives of the Tiquet wife have presented several petitions requesting her freedom, on the pretext that the detention of this woman has no other motive than a signal animosity, and a false declaration on the part of her husband against her.

Upon the inquiries that were made into this subject at the time of M. Bertin it was noted that independent of her dishonesty and her swindles in affairs of moneylending on interest for which she had been taken to For-l'Évêque June 18, 1758, she was a libertine, who in 1753 lived scandalously with a crook named Turgès who was placed in Bicêtre for the swindles they concocted together: and that since then, this Turgès has been replaced by one Guaudissart another crook and swindler, with whom she carried on the same life, and she was found in bed with him, when she was on the request of her husband, transferred by virtue of the King of July 30, 1758, from For-l'Évêque where she had been, to the Salpêtrière where she is at present.

It has resulted from new inquiries that I had made into the subject of these said petitions, that those who take an interest in the Tiquet wife, and who claim to be her relatives, appear in truth to be only intermediaries, as none of these supposed relatives made themselves known and not a single one of them who signed the petitions could be found. No relative is known to the Tiquet wife other than her mother known as the little Lallemand who died in the hospital where she was detained for her swindles and a sister who is known as a woman of the world *[fille du monde]* who goes by the name Saint-Christ. It further resulted that said Tiquet, her husband, who opposes her freedom deserves to have his request heeded as he is considered a most honest man, and is regarded as such in his employment as a clerk at the Barrières that he has exercised for ten years.

Ars. Arch. Bastille 12017, fol. 114 (1758)

2 Parents and Children

The documents seem to indicate the existence of a "critical" moment in parent–child relations; a phase in family life when recourse to the *lettre de cachet* became more frequent, and when, in conflicts with their offspring, parents were more willing to appeal to the authority of administrative power. Taking the years 1728 and 1758 together, the age distribution of the sons and daughters whose imprisonment was requested is as follows:

Less than 17 years old: 6
From 17 to 19: 13
From 20 to 22: 20
From [23] to 25: 26
From 26 to 28: 15
From 29 to 31: 7
Over the age of 31: 6

Although the absolute numbers are quite different, it does not appear that the age distribution changes if we look at boys and girls separately, or if we distinguish between 1728 and 1758. At the very most we could note that in the latter year there were fewer requests toward the higher end of the age scale (only 2 over the age of twenty-eight, whereas there were 11 in 1728) and slightly more toward the lower end (12 against 9). Given the small number of documents at our disposal, however, these variations remain quite speculative. Nevertheless, these numbers do seem to indicate that the period when children are between twenty and twenty-five years of age represented a "critical phase." This was the undoubtedly the moment when the system by which children depended on their parents was already sufficiently strained that the latter no longer felt that they could impose their authority immediately or exact punishment and retaliate on their own, yet still considered that it remained within their rights to control their children's behavior. They were still, to certain extent, responsible for their children and their behavior still reflected if not their sovereignty, then at least their authority. Here we have one of the innumerable forms of the difficulty involved in reaching a reciprocal accommodation between the generations in Western society, dating back to the Middle Ages. The rising age at marriage, a trend that began in the sixteenth century, was certainly one element underlying the tensions of this era. Here we see the turmoil of young men and women who were offered neither any specific activity nor full-fledged access to adult life; and inversely the inability of many parents to exert authority over their children, to whom they denied autonomy while at the same time having trouble providing for their needs. This period in which their children reached twenty/twenty-five years of age therefore represented a trying time for the family unit, a moment when the coexistence of generations became the greatest struggle, when the problems that it posed, as well as the means of resolving them, no longer fit neatly within the framework constituted by the family. What was required of children by their state of dependence was not compensated for by benefits that would have rendered it tolerable. What is more, their independence could only be acquired at the price of a total break, along with the economic risks (when it came time for marriage, or inheritance) that this would entail.

Between their children and themselves, parents had neither the ability nor the will to provoke the intervention of the judicial apparatus: it was weighty and slow; it was always costly and often dishonoring. And, in any event, could it act upon the small disturbances that they wished to stifle? But families also lacked the weapons that would have allowed them to enforce the sovereignty of the paterfamilias. The recourse to administrative intervention can therefore easily be explained. The authority of the family thus found its support in the principle of the monarchy. But not in the form of the reproduction or extension of its authority. It was at the point of greatest conflict in family life, when discord was at its most violent and was the most difficult to manage, that those who represented authority in the family turned to the king, imploring him to exercise his own—which the royal administration did, although not without prudence and a certain wariness that grew increasingly pronounced, it would seem, as the century unfolded. It is not where the family hierarchy was at its most vigorous that the figure of state power asserted itself most firmly; as intermediary, backer, and secular arm of paternal authority, it intervened where the economic and institutional structure of the family showed itself incapable of resolving the problems inherent to the existence of an extended youth.

CONFLICTS OF INTEREST

The forms that these conflicts took deserve closer study. In the year 1728, 28 requests for imprisonment were made by both parents acting together; 57 requests indicated that the child had been orphaned of his father and mother or had lost one of the two. In 1758, 8 requests were made in the name of father and mother together; 25 indicated that at least one of the parents had disappeared. In situations of the latter kind, it is easy to imagine how there came to be conflicts of interest: these broke out when the moment came for the parents to turn over the money held in guardianship *[les comptes de tutelle]*, or when the children of the first bed *[d'un premier lit]* asserted their rights against their stepparents or the children of the second marriage. Certain dossiers offer quite stark examples of this: countering the *lettre de cachet* solicited against him, the interested party attested to the selfish and dishonest calculations of those around him. Louis Bellavoine, already prohibited from receiving his inheritance and threatened with imprisonment, protested by saying that his mother had gambled all of her money away, that she depended on him for her subsistence, and that she dreaded that he would get married. Vincent Bérard drafted a *placet* so as to have the royal order against him revoked: his father, after the death of his mother, refused him "the most urgent help," he "used the same hardness with his younger son," he wishes to "considerably advantage his daughter," he has "a penchant for a woman who inspires in him such injudicious sentiments toward his children"; and if he himself, Vincent Bérard, did indeed take money from his father's money box, it was so that he could study law (his father having convinced his mother, on her deathbed, to disinherit Vincent). Magdeleine Blanchet was imprisoned for concubinage at the request of her father;[1] this "poor unfortunate girl" wrote to the lieutenant of police to point out that

> her father contracted a second marriage from which he had several children, which has caused him to be indifferent to those of the first bed, up to the point of doing everything to bring about their deaths and to frustrate them of their mother's estate; he has taken not only the estate that was supposed to go to them but also the estate that was reserved for them by law.

But perhaps, outside of explicit references—which presupposed the presence of at least some wealth and the existence of a certain social status—several conflicts, in more modest circles, were of a similar origin; it could be that many of the small domestic thefts of which the surviving parents complained were, in the eyes of those who committed them, a manner of recuperating what was legitimately theirs. Similarly, one could argue that these moral denunciations concealed a desire to be rid of a child whose presence and support had become a burden when one wished to remarry. Second marriages and a child's majority do plausibly represent particularly thorny situations, ones to which internment offered a solution.

We might expect that during this same tense period, the marriage of children—or at least their desire to marry—would represent an aggravating factor in family crises. Yet this was not the case, outside of a few exceptions, all of which involved families that were either relatively well-to-do or that had a strong sense of their social standing. In appeals from common people, the possibility of a bad marriage did not show up as a motive for requesting imprisonment. What about concubinage, then? It appears in the petitions from 1728 far more often than in those from 1758 (20 to 4), and concerning girls far more than boys (15 to 5 in 1728).

Yet it is remarkable that, with the exception of one or two cases, the fact that a daughter was living with a man outside of marriage did not constitute for her parents the sole or even the principal reason for a request for imprisonment. What made for an unbearable scandal was almost always something that could be called "qualified" concubinage: either it was with a man who was already married (as was the case with Marie Joseph Coquerel, Magdeleine Blanchet, and Anne Hubert), or especially it led to the birth of illegitimate children. Even then it was not sufficient on its own to justify imprisonment. It always had to be part of a larger constellation, of which it was not necessarily the most serious element: debauchery in general, a multiplicity of liaisons (and anything that would give rise to suspicions of prostitution), various deceptions, and violence all played far more important roles.

What emerges out of these dossiers is not a "politics" of families centered on marriage (perhaps this was a feature of the aristocratic order, but it was certainly not a problem of the common people), but rather a relatively convergent and coherent ensemble of reactions to a series of traits that were both recognized and rejected as constituting "bad conduct." Within the family there was, between parents and children, old and young, a whole field of confrontations that stemmed more from economic conflicts, physical violence, standing in the household, reputation in the neighborhood, and blows to a person's character, than from marriage, than from the difference between a "good" marriage and "shameful" concubinage. One left it up to others to imprison their children for not making a suitable marriage or for demeaning themselves. One had them incarcerated because they were a disturbance.

DISTURBANCE

It would be interesting to compare this notion of "disturbance" with that of "dissipation," which would be so frequently employed in the nineteenth century in the moralizing of the poor. Dissipation fundamentally came down to temporal behavior; a "dissipated" laborer did not know how to prepare for the future, he spent his paycheck as soon as he got it, he did not practice thrift, anticipate the possibility of illness or the threat of unemployment, did not make provisions for old age or the education of his children. To counter dissipation, the poor must be taught the continuity of time, the accumulation of small profits, in short, the economy of life. Disturbance, for its part, involved primarily spatial behaviors. It would seem that these forms of behavior alarmed parents beyond anything else. The future was only invoked in the form of troublesome consequences down the line: crime, death, ruin, and sometimes, albeit rarely, the difficulties that the bad behavior of certain children would cause for the establishment of their siblings. In contrast, the pressure point for the conflict between children and parents was located at the boundaries of the family space.

It is not easy to delimit this space precisely.[2] It involved, of course, the living space, as well as the neighbors, the neighborhood. But it also consisted of the reach of reputation in a general manner: all of the places where one might still hear talk about these compromising characters, and places from which they might return, wretched, threatening, or with a "shameful" conviction hanging around their necks. It is significant that those who signed these requests for imprisonment, besides the direct relatives if they were still living, were not those who were close by blood, but essentially those who belonged to this space: living in the same building, being neighbors, belonging to a neighborhood, the fact that they had welcomed, at one point, the suspects, gave them the right to sign these petitions.

As for the "disturbed" young people, they shuffled restlessly between the different regions of this space, coming and going, entering and exiting.[3] Some created a scandal at their own doorstep, installing themselves in a tavern or place of prostitution where anyone could recognize them. But many of them would "absent themselves, staying out all night," roaming, roving about the country, vagabonding alone or with others. Above all, they are agitated people. The existence of Antoine Cotte is one example among others.[4] For ten years, he has "done nothing besides rove about the country, abandoning his mother who felt tenderness for him, . . . enlisted with three different captains, . . . has always continued to act the vagabond, roaming at night under pure pretexts," has become a lackey, took himself to Rouen, returned to Paris, went to Saint-Denis, was arrested there as a deserter. After his release we can see him travel to Versailles, to Paris, to Beaumont, to Senlis. But it was not always necessary for absence to take the form of this continual roaming across the country. Frequently, not returning home for the night represented reprehensible behavior, even for a boy. Edme Joseph Eli, at nineteen and a half years of age, carries on like a "libertine and debauches himself and spends his night who knows where," without his father or mother "being able to learn where he sleeps, which makes the supplicants fear for the worst."

When it came to girls, vagabonding in the strict sense of the word was cited less frequently, even if they did sometimes roam from region to region, accompanying a lover or a group of soldiers, as was the case with Marie-Françoise Coucher.[5] The simple fact of having "been absent" for a few weeks or months was enough to motivate a request from her parents. On the part of girls, the thing that seemed to be the true equivalent of instability for boys and their providing for themselves by dubious means, was, of course, a multiplicity of new "adventures." The word *prostitution* comes up fairly regularly, but it risks giving the wrong impression. Sometimes it seems to be used to emphatically designate one or several extramarital liaisons; in other cases (as if the parents were slightly reticent to talk about it when it was the real thing), we should understand that it was indeed a question of prostitution, involving the frequenting of seedy locales or the company of women of appallingly ill repute. What seemed most unbearable for families was when their daughter settled close to them, in the neighborhood or nearby, and displayed a multiplicity of liaisons, a succession of protectors, or a still more episodic procession of lovers. The entourage could not ignore this scandal, and the other residents were supposedly indignant. The apotheosis of scandal was reached when the regular clients or friends of the girl were soldiers of the guard.[6]

At the other pole of motives for imprisonment was the behavior of children within the internal space of the family. In a number of dossiers, the house appeared as a site of war, of extreme violence, of brutality. Two themes come up time and again, more often than not in conjunction with one another: insults, oaths, threats, blows, on the one hand, and, on the other, theft, robbery, money extorted by cunning or by force. Large sums were rarely involved, as the protagonists were by and large poor. By far the most commonly described situation was theft, under threat, of a little money or a few belongings; the scoundrel has created an atmosphere of terror in the home, he hits and he takes. For boys, drunkenness was very often pointed to as the reason for this behavior; he comes home drunk, he steals so that he can continue to get drunk. So the widow Barbion complained of her son, of around twenty-five years of age: he "is often drunk, utters execrable oaths, breaks and smashes everything in the house, and not satisfied with this disorder threatens the supplicant that he will kill her, sometimes with his tongs, sometimes with his knife." Louis Henry, age twenty-one, "goes roaming with them after dark, often staying out all night, and when he returns to his father's after eleven o'clock or midnight, he is so drunk that he will not hear reason, he curses and renounces God and makes threats to kill his sister";

"who knows where he gets the money to supply his debauches as he does not work, and his parents are in no state to give him any"; "several times he has been convicted of theft from the houses of masters to whom he had been apprenticed"; "and he even pushes his unruliness so far as to carry off what he can from his father's, threatening him and telling him that he will put to the test which of the two will be the stronger."

Violence was mentioned less frequently when it came to girls. But it did appear in several instances, in the form of threats, in the form of theft (sometimes with a lover as an accomplice), and even once as a suspected murder. But it seems that the basic danger that a daughter presented was not so much domestic trouble as the external damage she could cause to a family's good reputation. Problems with work were, with only three or four exceptions, never cited with regard to girls. In contrast, "disturbances" during apprenticeships were common in the lives of the boys whose imprisonment was being requested. Apprenticeship was a sensitive point for several reasons: because it implied an expenditure on the part of the family that the young man's bad conduct could squander; because it constituted a test of the honesty and the personal value of the apprentice; because he represented the honor of the family to the outside world; because his parents were repeatedly compelled to repair the damages or the indiscretions that he might have committed.[7] The mother of Pierre Germain Béranger had placed him with a wigmaker where he showed himself to be a gambler, a thief, a drunkard; then she took him back to teach him the craft of mercery.[8] But he "stole from her daily, and would have ruined her utterly if he had remained any longer." She then placed him with a merchant mercer where he took six hundred livres that had to be reimbursed. The same things happened when he wanted to enter into an order, and then again when he enlisted.

In most of these dossiers we can notice a pulsation: agitated, violent, thieving, threatening his mother (he beats her only occasionally), picking the lock of his father's safe, selling the store's merchandise under the table, coming home at night drunk. The boy's presence in the home was excessive, but as soon as he left he entered a domain full of risks where the worst could happen and from which the family sought to retrieve him, so that they might reestablish their control over him. As for a girl, although she may have left home and settled elsewhere, either with a married man or in semi-prostitution, she caused trouble for the family through her bad reputation, gossip, and scandal. These were neither fully internal conflicts (as would be opposing one's parents in the matter of marriage, refusing to work, or disputes of personal interest), nor clean breaks (which would perhaps have been more acceptable if they were definitive). These were comings and goings, the back-and-forth of a pendulum, drawing away and then coming back through disappearances and returns, false exits[9] and noisy reentrances. Many of these youth are less reminiscent of the adventures of Gil Blas[10] or the stubborn passion of Des Grieux[11] than the permanent "disturbance" of one Pierre Lalande, who "keeps the entire household in fear," returned to his father's before his apprenticeship was even over, showed "the most complete disobedience, drinking left and right, giving himself entirely to sloth, vagabonding, staying out all night, haunting taverns, billiard games, gambling on the bridges and behaving most dissolutely," selling his father's clothes and his own cobbler's tools.

CONFLICTS AT THE THRESHOLD

Most of these cases are what we might call "conflicts at the threshold." At the threshold of adulthood, at the threshold of the house; at the threshold between dependence and independence. Naturally, these provoked two contradictory reactions: definitive expulsion—let us be rid of this child and never hear her spoken of again; or complete reabsorption—we are willing for her to come back to us, but on the condition that she has repented and will behave herself. Of the two, the second solution was often seen as preferable. Families requested imprisonment, which they well knew would be temporary—given that they often had to pay a pension and in cases where they did not, the administration was careful not to burden itself with non-paying prisoners (although in truth we should take into account cases of the "forgotten" [*oublis*], which were not rare: pensions whose payment was neglected, pensioners who remained locked away without anyone paying them any mind). In this case, imprisonment in itself was supposed to provoke repentance and lead the incarcerated person to resipiscence.[12] Punishment was a lesson unto itself. Moreover, because parents, who had obtained the *lettre de cachet*, had at least partial control over their child's release, this appears to have been more of a "contract" for good behavior than the "recognition" of psychological and moral improvement. The boy or girl gave signs of repentance, promised to behave as they should, sometimes even wrote letters certifying their goodwill. At times the administration pushed for reconciliation by affirming that the pensioner was now behaving himself. Imprisonment was modeled upon the punitive framework traditionally applied to children: punishment, repentance, promises of obedience, and, on the side of parents, forgiveness and forgetting.

DEPARTURE FOR THE ISLANDS

At the other extreme, we can find requests for the Islands.[13] These represented a desire for a complete and definitive break. Nothing was known of the Islands; it was very difficult to send letters back, one almost never returned, and, another advantage for the family, there was no pension to pay. We should nonetheless notice that these requests from parents were not large in number (eight in 1728 and four in 1758; only two in total concerning girls) and that they were not always granted. We can also observe that in several cases the families involved were large and poor, and that in some instances it was the extended family who desired this definitive departure, either against the mother's will or because there was no longer anyone left to pay the pension for incarceration. Being sent to the Islands had a profound resonance in the imagination of the lower orders. Invisible but real, the Islands were a "non-place" where the mark of the wrong done disappeared in silence. It was on the horizon of this whole system of punishment as the ultimate threat, the one that would be invoked when patience had run out, after so many promises of improvement had showed themselves to be empty. Not the least of the paradoxes was that the establishment of moral discipline and the improvement of these exiles, many of whom were never to return, was one of the concerns most frequently invoked—if not one of the most important—by the governor. It seems as if "there is more preoccupation over there with correcting those who risk staying there forever than there is here with transforming those who will one day be released from the houses of imprisonment."

Rousseau de Villejouin, governor of la Désirade, wrote in 1753:[14]

> My Lord, I received the letter that you did me the honor of writing me as well as the copies of the edict issued regarding families that contained bad subjects [*mauvais sujets*] who His Majesty wished to allow the dispatching of to la Désirade, I will follow it in all of its points and will give my attention to correcting the faults of these young expatriated individuals, I will observe them closely, I will neglect nothing in making them turn inwards and I will direct them with firmness, it is quite necessary My Lord, and I take it upon myself to present unto you, that huts be built in the places destined to receive these individuals, I will have them built at the lowest cost . . .

The governor regularly requested that he be granted subsidies for his prisoners, while simultaneously expressing surprise at the ease with which he was, in general, able to oversee them: "Since their stay on this island began, I have had no reason to complain of any misconduct by these young people in general, I have prescribed for them rules for their walks and for their behavior . . . they promise me marvels, I will observe them closely."

In July 1756, the island of la Désirade contained forty-five bad subjects, in 1766, there would be fifty-four of them. They were sorted into three classes, based on their conduct and the governor's hope that they might show improvement. But Rousseau de Villejouin was constantly amazed at the lack of care that their families showed them:

> Here is the list of the forty-five bad subjects that I have sorted into three classes, if those in the first and a portion of the second continue to behave themselves well I believe that they will be in a position to return to the order of society, but if their parents continue to show them such cruelty I do not see, My Lord, how they will be able to survive, as few of them receive any aid, as to those in the third class, I believe them to be without the resources such that we could expect improvement from them. All of these youths have endured much misery, soldier's rations and the care of the King are not sufficient for them, this does not ordinarily return men to their sentiments.

THE HONOR OF FAMILIES

The sensitivity of parents to the "disturbance" of their children reveals just how fragile the outside surface of the family unit was. The "crises" between parents and children seemed for the most part to have been determined by two simultaneous impossibilities: the impossibility of parents being able to effectively control their offspring, to provide for them economically, to make room for their comings and goings, and, in the wide sense of the term, to "lodge" them; but also the impossibility of extricating themselves from their problems and disidentifying themselves from them. How far, outside of their home, could parents exercise power? In whom, outside of the legal ties of responsibility, did they have to recognize themselves?

We might be surprised by the insistence with which reasons of "honor" were invoked in these documents that display, with a great deal of detail, the small disorders of family life. This is even more surprising in light of the fact that what was at stake was obtaining an incarceration in houses such as the Saint-Lazare or the Hôpital général, of which the least we could say is that at the time their reputations were hardly positive.[15] It is remarkable that all of these common people—penniless merchants, extremely modest artisans, domestic day laborers—sought recourse in a rhetoric of honor that could very well be found among the wealthy bourgeoisie or the aristocracy.

Of course, we must account for the extent to which this was required when one addressed the king or his representatives in order to request a favor. That a family of secondhand clothes sellers had to invoke its honor to have their drunkard and loudmouth of a son imprisoned was a condition imposed by the genre of the *lettre de cachet* itself. How could the benevolence of the Sovereign be solicited for such a small affair, if not by pointing to a category that one knew to be essential to all those who had any importance and "standing" in the world? But we should not conclude from this that all we have here are simply more or less forced forms of conventional expression alone. Even for those who employed it in set phrases, the vocabulary of honor had a precise meaning. It was through it that parents sought to establish, to recognize themselves, and to have recognized by the authorities the nonjuridical rights and duties that linked them to their children. In a way, this was the family's self-concept (to be understood here as the parent–child structure) in search of itself, elaborating itself and attempting to have itself validated by political power.

I. From this point of view, the question of the relationship to the justice system is quite significant. It was very rare that imprisonment was requested in the wake of a genuine criminal offense, in order to help the culprit and his family escape the shame of a punishment. Withdrawing a delinquent from regular justice through administrative imprisonment was a grace that the king reserved for the powerful. The dossiers published here offer only a few requests of this kind. On the other hand, as humble as a family may have been, it considered it both its right and its duty to alert the authorities and solicit the imprisonment of one of its children if his or her conduct was such that it might lead to a genuine criminal offense: the shame of the family would then be consummated. The justice system was to be avoided through preemptive measures. The focus of parents was not on interrupting the mechanisms of justice but on preventing them from being set in motion in the first place. Their honor itself was at stake.

And this calculus was not just acceptable to the administration, it received explicit approval; it had been part of the spirit in which the lieutenancy of police had been established. It was not only a question of taking minor affairs off the hands of certain judicial bodies, as well as hastening the resolution of these affairs, but also of intervening at a level prior to involvement with the justice system. Tranquillity and public order were to be among its primary concerns. The Decree of 1667, which created the police lieutenancy of Paris, already expressed it thus: "Police consists in assuring the calm of the rest of the public and of individuals, . . . and to call each individual according to his condition and his duty." And only a century later,

Vattel wrote in *The Law of Nations*: "The internal police consists in the attention of the prince and magistrates to preserve everything in order . . . By a wise police, the sovereign accustoms the people to order and obedience, and preserves peace, tranquillity, and concord among the citizens."[16] Moreover, in order to attain this goal, it was indeed necessary that the police not have to wait for disorder to have reached the point of provoking judicial action. They needed to intervene before the justice system became involved, through intervention in minor troubles, in unrest that preceded crimes, in what were called "offenses of nonsurveillance."

Honor, for families, and public order, for the administration, constituted two methods of aiming at the same result: the establishment of a permanent regulation of the behavior of individuals, and particularly of turbulent youths, through mechanisms that operated in the interstices of the justice system's apparatus, machinery that from the State's perspective was heavy, uncertain, and, moreover, whose relative independence sometimes led it to be recalcitrant; machinery that from the point of view of parents was dangerous, costly, and often shaming. We can see the procedure of the *lettre de cachet* as an interplay and adjustment between these two concerns. Families requested the imprisonment of a son or daughter who threatened to bring dishonor upon them if the justice system were ever to step in. In order to make this threat of dishonor tangible, they described all of the disorders that made this eventuality seem probable. Then the police administration would investigate and judge in relation to what the good order and tranquillity of a neighborhood or a city ought to be. Finally, imprisonment was obtained at the intersection of these two requirements; the honor of families was thus recognized as a necessity of public order. The law of parents, the family as the source of nonjudicial authority over children, even if they were no longer minors, would be validated by public power, to the extent that their internal sense of honor coincided with the rules of collective order.

In the case of the aristocracy, the arrogance of honor allowed them to request exemptions from the common law. The modest honor of the lower orders was taught—and the practice of the *lettres de cachet* was one of the instruments of this instruction—that it existed, as a real honor, that it too deserved to be recognized, but on the condition that it fit in neatly alongside the principles of order maintained by the State administration, which, far from being exceptions to the justice system, guaranteed the necessary and permanent foundations of its effective exercise.

2. But we must not think that fear of the justice system and its shameful consequences was the only way by which parents displayed their concern for honor. It was important to them to show that they had been, through-

out their difficult relationship with their children, good parents. It was a question of dignity. Being a "good parent" meant showing care for one's offspring, despite the worries and torments that they might be causing. The mother of Pierre Germain Béranger "loved her child tenderly despite all the grief that he had already given her"; the mother of Cotte felt "tenderness" toward her son and had on many occasions shown him "a mother's kindness." It also meant showing patience, indulgence, when a son or daughter committed their first vagaries. At times these overly fond parents had been misled by false repentance. But many of them wish to remind the reader that they have nothing for which to reproach themselves, that they performed the duties of their position: they made "the efforts" necessary to bring their children back to virtue, they gave salutary advice, they combined "honest remonstrance" with "charitable aid." And now that all of the resources of their patience had been exhausted, their affection could be seen in the sorrow they displayed when requesting incarceration: they have "tears in their eyes," they are "filled with the deepest pain." Next to these expressions filled with pathos, the portrait given of the child to be imprisoned breathes, it cannot be denied, hatred. Their children were "rogues, scoundrels, cheats, crooks, deceivers, villains"; they wished to punish "the most unworthy object imaginable." This dramatic contrast between the finest parents and such unworthy offspring can leave one a little skeptical of the accuracy of the depictions presented and the sincerity of the affections expressed.

PARENTAL ETHICS

In any event, these texts should not be read as authentic expressions of deeply held feeling. Rather, they are manifestations of the existence of a model, a framework, prescribing good parental behavior, what people believed one should say in order to be seen as a good father or a good mother. From this perspective, it is interesting to compare the dossiers from 1758 with those from 1728. Once again, the fragmentary character of the documentation prevents us from arriving at any certainties, but it does indeed appear that between the two series we can notice several differences that offer evidence of a certain common evolution.

In 1728, parents emphasized their affection, their attachment, their tenderness. In 1758, they especially emphasized the good upbringing that they had given their children.[17] For example, a stepfather presented as evidence against two girls, ages fifteen and seventeen, who were on the point of dishonoring their family, "the good upbringing that he had always endeavored to give them out of tenderness for them and out of consideration for the memory of his wife." A traveling wine merchant "spared no expense" in "obtaining an education for his son," and he "employed every kind approach to recall him to his duty." Le Perrier, a bourgeois of Paris, "until the present day spared no expense" to give Jeanne, his illegitimate daughter, "all possible education"; he even apprenticed her to a seamstress twice. One gets the impression that from 1728 to 1758, the way to manifest attachment to one's children shifted toward the fulfillment of a duty of one's role as parents, that of education. Parents were no longer good parents simply because they loved their children, but because they raised them properly. Was this a tactical concern, an attempt to justify oneself in the eyes of the administration, to adequately demonstrate that there was no more that one could do? This seems quite plausible. But this concern itself is indicative of a certain normative representation of parenting, on the basis of which the supplicants thought they could obtain the support of the authorities. Moreover, in the year 1758 (and the neighboring years, 1756–60, bear this out), there were fewer requests for the imprisonment of children over the age of twenty-five and more for children under the age of twenty. We can therefore advance the hypothesis—which would, of course, be subject to various verifications—that family ethics gradually came to be recentered around the duty of education. Love for one's children was to be demonstrated first and foremost in fulfilling educative duties, and it was having performed this role correctly that could validate parents in the eyes of the administration.

We could add to this that the hope that imprisonment would lead to the correction of the imprisoned subjects appears to be formulated more clearly and more frequently in 1758 than in 1728. Thus, the drama of Good and Evil, of Good Parents coping with Rabid Children that the older documents seem to portray appears to have been modified to a certain extent in the more recent ones. Family dramas were no less intense, but perhaps their stakes were more clearly pedagogical. As if in requesting State intervention into an affair between parents and children, one was not only implying the powerlessness of the former in the face of the dangerous frenzy of the latter, but also suggesting, quietly, a certain division of labor. It was up to the parents to educate, raise, and take care of their children in the proper manner. But if, once these tasks had been fulfilled, success was not the result, if a child betrayed all of these efforts on her behalf, then it became legitimate and just for the State to intervene. We should not forget the objective of allowing parents to avoid the shameful mechanisms of the justice system. It was also a question of prolonging an educational effort, of proper development, that had been disturbed by the child's recalcitrance. This would explain the seemingly increasingly frequent appearance in these requests of notions such as "bad inclinations, natural predispositions, dangerous inclinations," being of "bad fiber." These were certainly no more precise, more objective, or less impassioned than the terms "crook, knave," and "scoundrel" that were so common in 1728; but they indicate a change in focus and in the object itself. It was upon a certain form of character, extraordinary and inaccessible to parental education, that the administration was asked to intervene. Imprisonment was not only requested in order to circumvent ordinary and rule-governed justice, it was also to complete the interrupted parental education. It would seem that there was a desire to add to its parajudicial role an instructive and corrective function in which State intervention stepped in for the family. In turn, these families tended to mix the language of honor with a language of training and good education in order to incite public power to enter into the game out of its own interests. The bad conduct of children was perceived as a stain on the family's honor, which, insofar as this honor was an element of public order, would indeed interest the government; maintaining the good conduct of children appeared to be a goal shared by both families and the State because it was in the general interest.

We can observe the idea taking shape that a family's honor no longer simply demanded that its reputation not be tarnished by its children, but that it also consisted in something more positive: the proper education of these same children. As evidence of this evolution, which the documents cited here indicate in a very fragmentary manner, we could cite the *Causes de la dépopulation* by abbé Jaubert (1767).[18] He saw the educational role of the family and the mechanisms of administrative control as tightly interconnected. Magistrates should be tasked with judging the responsibility of parents in the wrongs committed by their children. Within their families, fathers should follow extremely precise rules for punishment, but at the same time, this should not prevent them from "making themselves more loved than feared," from entering into the hearts of their sons in order to become their friends and confidants. However, the young people who left their families for their studies would be subject to a police, which would "learn where they live, be attentive to them, watch over their actions, light their way, and observe whether they were frequenting criminal or dangerous company, if they were going to too many plays," etc.[19]

Letters

THE DISRUPTION OF AFFAIRS

Jean Allis

To My Lord
the Lieutenant General of Police

Antoinette Pauline Valancier, daughter of Claude Valancier merchant in Paris humbly represents unto Your Highness that Jean François Allis son of Claude Allis and Jeanne Miard whose father and mother are also merchants in Paris residing rue du Cygne sought the supplicant's hand in marriage a few years ago, in 1728 her father's business called him to London in England, where the supplicant accompanied him; the love that said Allis the younger had for her gave him occasion to come find her in the city of London where in the presence and with the consent of the supplicant's father they received the sacrament of marriage in all the requisite conditions in the chapel and from the chaplain of His Exc. Mgr the ambassador of Portugal, in the presence of witnesses on August 23, 1728; after the consummation of the marriage, said Allis the younger and his wife returned to Paris where after a time the fury of the Allis parents became so bold that they had their children placed in an awful prison on the sole pretext of having disobeyed them; the supplicant was released from there on the 31st of December last at the solicitation of several relatives and friends, and as said Allis the younger has been detained in the horrors of the prison since December 27 for a single disobedience of his father and mother who (in order to satisfy their ambition) found a way to surprise the religion of Your Highness, to whom we have given certificates of the life and morals of said Allis the younger who does not merit any punishment, on the contrary, he has all of the characteristics of an honest man by whom the supplicant is now four months pregnant following an authentic marriage that said Allis father and mother deserve no less than God's punishment for wishing for its destruction; given these considerations, My Lord may it please Your Highness to have no regard for the temerity of said Allis father and mother and order his release from the prisons of For-l'Évêque, the supplicant and her husband will never cease to wish for the precious days of Your Highness.

Ars. Arch. Bastille 10998, fol. 48 (1728)

We certify that we know Jean François Allis son of Claude Allis and Jeanne Miard merchants residing in Paris on rue du Cygne in Saint-Eustache parish, to be a boy of whom only the most advantageous things can be said having always known him for conduct worthy of praise by all honest folk and for having been very useful to his father and mother in their trade and if we are summoned before the magistrates to testify as to what we declare in the present certificate, we will present ourselves whenever it is deemed necessary and will swear to tell the truth.

[Sixteen signatures.]

Ars. Arch. Bastille 10998, fol. 49 (1728)

To My Lord
the Lieutenant General of Police

Antoinette Pauline Valancier daughter of a merchant in Blois and Jean François Allis also son of a merchant in Paris most respectfully represent unto Your Highness that she was made prisoner along with her husband and both were taken to For-l'Évêque by Superintendent de Launay and Monsieur Leclerc by virtue of her having married Jean François Allis without the consent of his father and mother who wish to have the marriage annulled under the pretext that they were married in London under the protection of the Ambassador of Portugal who had allowed the marriage sacrament to be administered by one of his chaplains in his chapel.

The supplicant dares hope that Your Highness would be willing to lend a favorable ear to the reasons that brought about this marriage.

Antoinette Pauline Valancier first made her husband's acquaintance in 1724. They loved each other from the very beginning of their acquaintance, they saw each other for a year with the plan of marrying each other and during this whole time their fathers and mothers approved of their children's undertaking.

But the disruption of the business of the supplicant's father that occurred near the end of the year 1725 brought about a change in the sentiments of her husband's father and mother who thereafter began proposing other matches to their son who never wished to accept any of them as they had made reciprocal promises to each other during that time that still held. The misfortunes of the supplicant's father having obliged him to absent himself and flee to a foreign country, she resolved by a movement of tenderness in the hopes that she might find a way to establish herself and to see her father again, was able to join him without the knowledge of her husband, who nonetheless learned of her departure after she had been in the country of Liège for two months, he went to find her and in a certain sense constrained her to marry him, and they traveled to London with the supplicant's father where they were married as can be seen by the marriage certificate, which is ready to be represented unto Your Highness, and the consummation was carried out on the 23d of August last by which the supplicant now finds herself three and a half months pregnant.

The solicitations of her husband at the time engaged her to return to Paris with him to work, which today is the cause of all the supplicant's pain as she is persecuted by her father-in-law and her mother-in-law who wish to mislead Your Highness's religion with the awful calumnies that they direct against the supplicant who has no reason to reproach herself when it comes to honor. And it will be easy for Your Highness to have himself informed of the facts contained in the certificate enclosed herein, as she has always been a reasonable and very chaste girl.

The supplicant dares to flatter herself that Your Highness will be touched by compassion and might wish to protect her against the violent persecution of her parents and order the release of her husband and herself to live together and work their trade as honest folk without being a burden on any person and they ask nothing of their father and mother and we will never cease to pray the Lord for the prosperity and health of Your Highness.

Jean François Allis,
Valancier, Allis wife.

Ars. Arch. Bastille 10998, fol. 52 (1728)

We certify that we have been perfectly acquainted with Antoinette Pauline Valancier, daughter of Claude Valancier merchant stocking maker [illegible] for around fifteen years we have always known her to be a reasonable and quite sensible girl on whose subject only very advantageous things can be said and if we are summoned before the magistrate to testify in person as to her conduct past and present we are telling the truth.

[Twelve signatures.]

Ars. Arch. Bastille 10998, fol. 51 (1728)

To My Lord
the Lieutenant General of Police

Claude Allis, master silk worker *[ferandinier]* and Jeanne Miard his wife residing rue du Cygne, most humbly remonstrate unto Your Highness that they have two sons and took great care in providing them with a upbringing; that one of them, named Jean François Allis age twenty-six, far from answering to this, let himself be debauched by Toinette Valancier, daughter of Valancier, Capuchin, stockings merchant, who escaped to Holland where their son was debauched four years ago when they lured him to them and their said son took from them a bill of exchange for three hundred livres with M. Joffrin secretary of the King and in Laon he received the sum of four hundred twenty-five *livres* from monsieur Legros merchant in Laon and they went off to Holland and from there to England and after six months of libertinage and absence they returned not long ago and continue to live together and are on the verge of leaving; and as it is in the suppliants' interest to arrest the disorderliness of their son with said Valancier so as to forestall the shameful and grievous consequences that might arrive, because of this they made a complaint with M. the Superintendent de Launay at rue Quincampoix and were advised to appeal unto the authority of Your Highness to obtain an order of the King to have them placed in Bicêtre and the Valancier girl in the hospital, and the suppliants will wish for the health and prosperity of Your Highness.

Claude Allis father,
Jeanne Miard mother.

Ars. Arch. Bastille 10998, fol. 58 (1728)

To My Lord
the Lieutenant General of Police

Claude Allis merchant manufacturer in Paris and Jeanne Miard his wife most respectfully represent unto Your Highness that you granted them an order to have their son made prisoner in For-l'Évêque where he has been detained from the 27th of the month of December last because of his disobedience and that this same son having sincerely repented for his past wrongs and now declaring according to the attached letter addressed to the suppliants that he detaches himself entirely from everything that he has done up until the present and that in the future they will have no reason to complain, the suppliants dare to take the liberty to request the release of their son from Your Grace so that he might return to their home they hope that they will be fully satisfied with him as he is most necessary to their trade, they will never cease to wish for the health and prosperity of Your Highness.

Claude Allis father,
Jeanne Miard mother.

Ars. Arch. Bastille 10998, fol. 62 (1728)

My dearest father and my dear mother,

This missive is so that I might have the honor of assuring you of my most humble respect and to pray you to be so good as to forgive a son who was disobedient, and who recognizes his wrongs I pray you my dear father and my dear mother to be so good as to have me released and that I renounce all that displeased you and as proof of the contentment that I can give you, is that I renounce the woman who displeased you and I will only do as you wish and will leave here only with you. So my dear father I pray you to be so good as to forgive me I await this grace of you, I remain in all respects, my very dear father and my dear mother your most obedient servant and son.

In For-l'Évêque January 23, 1729.

Ars. Arch. Bastille 10998, fol. 63 (1728)

To My Lord
the Count de Maurepas,[1]
Minister State Secretary

My Lord,

Jean François Allis, age twenty six and Toinette Pauline Valancier both children of merchants represent most respectfully unto Your Highness that they were made prisoners in For-l'Évêque, the 27th of the month of December last by order of M. the Lieutenant General of Police upon a complaint made before the Superintendent de Launay by Claude Allis and Jeanne Miard father and mother of the supplicant, their son, who married Antoinette Pauline Valancier on August 23 last which was consummated the same day by which the supplicant now finds herself around four months pregnant.

As today the father and mother of the supplicant wish to annul the marriage made in London under the protection of the ambassador of Portugal who had allowed the sacrament of marriage to be administered unto them by one of his chaplains in the chapel without their consent and as they have no power over Antoinette Pauline Valancier, she received her freedom the last day of December last, and they currently solicit an order of the King to have their son locked up in a place where he will not be able to speak with anyone to reduce him by force to give his consent to an annulment of the marriage.

But the supplicants who are constant to one another and love each other mutually appeal unto Your Highness hoping that you might wish to sympathize with the extreme pain that they already feel in the fear they will see themselves separated forever and that Your Highness might wish to grant them his protection and not issue any order for the supplicant to be locked up as he has never committed any base deeds as it is easy for Your Highness to see from the certificate enclosed herein signed by his merchant in Paris.

The supplicants who see themselves reduced to the most awful misery, one of them in the depths of a prison, subsisting only on the bread of the King and the other who must importune several persons who help her subsist out of consideration for her being with child both implore the clemency of

Your Highness persuaded that you will grant the supplicant's freedom to put them in a state where they could subsist off their labor. They will never cease to wish for the health and prosperity of Your Highness.

[No signature.]

Ars. Arch. Bastille 10998, fol. 65 (1728).

To Monsieur
the Count de Maurepas

Jean François Allis is a young man of twenty-six who made the passage to England after having robbed his father and mother and there married one Valancier who is said to be the daughter of a Capuchin who quit his convent long ago and established himself as a merchant in Paris but out of fear that his wife would not keep a secret that was so important to him made the passage to London with his daughter whom he married to said Allis around five months ago without the consent of his parents, the marriage ceremony was carried out by the chaplain of the ambassador of Portugal.

As the father and mother design to have the marriage of their son annulled and as they fear that they might return to the foreign country

I gave an order on December 27, 1728, to arrest said Allis and have him taken to prison.

M. the Count de Maurepas is beseeched to have a formal order dispatched to authorize the one that I gave.

Ars. Arch. Bastille 10998, fol. 69 (1728)

Louis Bellavoine

To Monsieur
the Superintendent General of police

The Bellavoine family comes to implore your authority to beseech you to procure for them an order of the King to have Monsieur Bellavoine locked up in Saint-Lazare or in the château de Guise owing that his libertinage and his bad conduct are on the point of dishonoring himself as well as his family if His Majesty does not have the kindness to come to its rescue.

Monsieur Bellavoine is twenty-seven years old, and was denied his rights of majority as soon as he came of age and since his denial a brother has overseen his funds, from which he receives only the income. He is currently in debauched commerce with a woman named Thoinette Louison widow of Leboulin, whom he made his family believe that he was seeking in marriage to which the supplicants had acquiesced, believing her to be of good life and morals; but as they have learned that her conduct is among the most irregular, that several complaints have been made against her with M. the Superintendent Parant, and that she has even had several children from her debauches and is currently raising one of them in her home.

The supplicants hope that Your Highness will grant them the honor of his protection, as he is the recourse of afflicted families. They have made every effort and remonstrance, he did not leave his debauchery with said Thoinette Louison, and they currently live as man and wife. He even had the baseness to say to his family that he wanted to recognize the child of said Thoinette Louison, as being his own; if you would be so good, Monsieur, as to write to M. the curé of Saint-Sulpice to obtain the child's baptismal certificate it will be easy to learn that what the supplicants advance is only too true, Monsieur Vanneroux is even acquainted with the content of the present memoir and can give a report of it to Your Highness, if you see fit. It would be quite a misfortune for a family to see itself dishonored, which said Louis Bellavoine desires quite against their wishes and which he would accomplish if Your Highness does not put a halt to it by favoring their request; the supplicants hope for this grace from you and will continue their wishes for the health and prosperity of Your Highness.

[Four illegible signatures.]

Ars. Arch. Bastille 10999, fol. 230 (1728)

Monsieur Bellavoine against whom these complaints are made is a foul potion [*un bien mauvais médicament*] among honest folk; his debauchery with Mademoiselle Loison is manifest, their concubinage is brazen and causes great scandal. Madame Rivou, a merchant fruit seller is perfectly acquainted with the matter, she assured me that Mademoiselle Loison is a debauched woman, and that her father who is secretary to M. the Intendant of Perpignan was on the verge of soliciting an order to have her locked away in some religious community.[2]

June 17, 1728, Vanneroux.

Ars. Arch. Bastille 10999, fol. 231 (1728)

To My Lord
the Superintendent General of Police

Monsieur,

Humbly beseeches Louis Bellavoine age twenty-seven and a half and remonstrates unto you that having been warned that Madame his mother had solicited her relatives to unite and surprise your judgment to obtain a *lettre de cachet* to have him locked away, which comes from vengeance and personal interests on the part of his mother owing that she is dependent on him for the income which his mother said she would pay him, she has been reduced to extreme misery having gambled and dissipated her estate which can be proved by the ordinance and fine that it pleased you Monsieur to have posted against her in the year 1726 which obliges the supplicant to appeal unto your justice, Monsieur, in order to forestall the trap that she and her relatives wish to lay for him by preventing him from marrying Madame de Sébolin despite the fact that he received their consent by a decision from M. the Civil Lieutenant, a copy of which is enclosed herein.

To these causes the supplicant has every hope of your Equity, Monsieur, and you will do justice.

Ars. Arch. Bastille 10999, fol. 234 (1728)

The widow Bellavoine and all the family request

that Louis Bellavoine be locked away in the château de Guise where the family will pay for his pension and his transportation according to the instructions of His Excellency;

that ever since Louis Bellavoine reached adulthood he has shown scandalous conduct through his unruly acts and the dissipation of his estate;

that he uses all manner of artifices to borrow money;

that it was around eight years ago that he tried to marry a public woman;

that at that point his family denied him his rights of majority;

that to bring grief to his family he enlisted in the French Guards;

that his bad conduct obliged [illegible] his captain to have him locked away in Bicêtre for six months;

that believing that he had been corrected by this six-month detention they released him;

that he immediately returned to his debauches and took as a concubine a young widow who bore him a child and who is pregnant once again;

that he enlisted once again with M. de Levy the Captain of the Guards and this was fourteen months ago;

that M. de Contade had him placed in prison a few months ago;

that at last they obtained his discharge, and an order from M. de Contade to turn him over to them.

The petition is signed by his mother, by two paternal uncles.

This young man has long been known to be a rowdy, a swindler, and a debauchee I think that the order is just.

Ars. Arch. Bastille, fol. 239 (1728)

Vincent Bérard

Letter written by M. Bérard
in Grenoble December 7, 1727, to
Monsieur Perrin in Paris

Monsieur,

I appeal unto you as one of my dearest friends to help me avenge the theft, the perfidy and the ingratitude of my eldest son with whom you are acquainted after having placed him in a position to be received as a lawyer, having supported him during his long stay in Valence, as it was only on the last holidays that he returned with a rank; I was endeavoring to have him received by the Parlement before Christmas; he just stole from me during the night of the 5th to the 6th of this month all of the gold, silver and jewels that I had and fled, and as it appears he went to Paris, where he found the habits that have spoiled him entirely, I justly beseech you to approach M. the Lieutenant General of Police and if you see fit, to have the order given for his arrest, so that I might be returned my estate and have him punished if I may; he will no doubt arrive by the post, by the coach or by the stagecoach; he only left this city yesterday, the sixth: thus I count that so long as he sojourns in Lyon this letter will reach you before he arrives in Paris, and that by your care he will be seized before he arrives; I give you full powers to make this seizure, even to take the money, silver and jewels and to repay everyone concerned and you will reimburse yourself exactly for everything that you will have provided; I am assured that in Paris this kind of scoundrel can be found by the good care of M. the Lieutenant General of Police with the aid of your ordinary goodness and diligence; I hope that you will have regard for my misfortune, as it is very great; you know that I suffered a similar misfortune before and I did not expect that a son for whom I spent so much in Paris and elsewhere and who I hoped would sustain me during my last days, would be capable of such an enterprise, of ruining me and ruining himself at a time when I was working only for him and to provide him with all of the estate and advantages that I could; he is a barbarian and an executioner who merits severe punishment; I am sending you his description; and he will no doubt have changed clothes and put on a blond wig and other things to disguise himself; but he will not find a way to change his face and height; in the name of God please have regard to my prayer, without any regard or consideration for him and with secrecy so that he not be alerted, I give you the power to have him put in prison, until he will have returned to me all that he has taken from me; you must not listen to him because he is a deceiver, an imposter and without reason, as the temper and vanity that he possesses as well as his spirit of debauchery, you know this better than others owing to the kindness that you showed him in the past, are such that he merits no attention than to be punished, I count on you as on myself and I am always most perfectly Monsieur your most humble and most obedient servant.

Bérard.

Ars. Arch. Bastille 11000, fol. 32–33 (1728)

Letter written by M. Bérard of Grenoble
January 15, 1728, to Monsieur Perrin

Monsieur,

I received the honor of your letter of the 7th of this month. Despite the perfidies of my son, I am delighted that he gave in to good and took a path befitting an honest man, and that if there remains in him the least good feeling toward a father whom he crushed and ruined he will return me my money to pay my deposits and my debts and avert my demise, and the pain of seeing me tormented by seizures and the sale of furniture that cannot be avoided and to help me at the same time to repair a portion of the wrongs that he did me during the little time that I have left to live, which will not be long, because it is impossible to resist the dagger he has stuck in my breast, since his design was to bring about my demise it would have been better if he had taken my life all at once, rather than wound me as grievously as he did causing me to waste away along with all the rest of my family. He must have seen that the majority of this money was not mine, that it belonged to several persons and parties and others who entrusted and deposited it with me for business and why dishonor me without reason to go to Paris to gamble, drink, and eat and perhaps other even more wicked things did I ever ask or demand anything harsh or unjust of him. I have only ever spoken to him for his own good and benefit, could he have a better friend than I, nor anyone in whom he could have more trust or hope or who would be less susceptible to vengeance toward him, even if he does not wish to take advantage of this. I am to be pitied and so is he and I will pray my whole life for the Lord to have pity on him; nonetheless I pray him to have pity and compassion for me, to write you and give you all of the money that his duty and a remnant of his natural bond to me should inspire in him, to send it me as soon as possible to rescue me and insure me against the lawsuits and seizures with which I am threatened by those who lost the money that they had placed with me, and other creditors, so that I do not succumb under the weight of my overwhelming pain; after his theft it would not have taken much for him to learn of my death, which would not be advantageous to him in these circumstances because perhaps I will be forced not to follow my inclination toward him, which would harm him greatly; I speak to you as a friend and in confidence because you are the only one who knows the secret of my misfortune and as you been so good as to take the part of my interests and his let him put himself in my position for a moment and immediately do me the justice that he would wish to have done unto him in a similar case. I will await your news with impatience, and I will always be most perfectly your most humble and most obedient servant.

Bérard.

Ars. Arch. Bastille 11000, fol. 31 (1728)

Letter to M. Bérard, of Grenoble,
February 19, 1728, to Monsieur Perrin

Monsieur,

I received the honor of your letter of the 13th of this month, which informs me that you saw my son the night of Fat Tuesday, and that you spoke sternly to him; that he told you that he had written me which is false, he is a most skillful scoundrel in whom one should have no faith, as I had the honor of writing you in my last missive and that it was necessary that he not be spared in any way nor should any regard be given to what he says because he seeks only to continue his libertinage and to deceive the whole world and to consume my money, after which he will ask for alms or do something worse; he is drunk on all the sins and he treats me like a rogue because he refuses me help in my present need after having stolen all of my estate and those of others at a time when I counted on him and when I acted only for his benefit and was making a suitable plan for my family at the end of my career; and this is how I am repaid with a son for whom I took so many pains and such care in raising in the hopes that I could make an honest man of him, as such, Monsieur, I beseech you to help me as you have promised and oblige him to return my money before he sinks into the mire, and have him arrested without delay, and oblige him to do this without consideration, because I will not hide anything from you, I [illegible] from all sides and I will take a violent path whose effects he will suffer, he will choke on his debauchery for a long time and will learn to correct himself; there is no agreement to be reached; he must return my money to you as soon as possible, because he wishes to perish and to continue to abuse me, I will follow him to the grave, in a manner suited to a spirit as odious as his, do not in any way believe that he wants to do good nor that he will keep his word, you have known him for a long time and I even better, he is a man dominated by vice from which he will never extricate himself too bad for him, thus do me a service, I have no regard or consideration for him, I have counted on you and on what you promised me in your letter, without which I would have taken other measures; should I be so unfortunate that you will abandon me to spare an impostor, a cheat and a scoundrel of this kind, if you had had him arrested upon his arrival, you could have compelled him to return my estate to me, I hope that you will have regard for my pain, I will not fail in my gratitude, nor to signify to you how much I am and will be my whole life, Monsieur, your most humble and most obedient servant.

Bérard.

Ars. Arch. Bastille 11000, fol. 29 (1728)

My Lord,

I took the liberty of appealing to the justice of Your Highness February 14 last in order to file a complaint concerning the theft and robbery that Vincent Bérard my son committed against me with false keys and cruel artifices the night of the 4th to the 6th of December last taking both the estate that others had deposited with me and my own; as the sad state to which he reduced me did not permit me to follow him and hoping that in your equity, and charity Your Grace would have him arrested and fearing that by deceit and imposture he might again suspend the effect of your orders so as to have time to continue his debauches and consume the money, I again take the liberty of renewing my complaints, and of supplicating Your Highness, My Lord, to have regard for the prayer of an unhappy father, crushed and ruined along with his family by the debauches and dissipations of a son on whose behalf he used every suitable means to oblige him to give in to virtue without any success. It would perhaps be better if I were the guilty one; but I have committed no wrong, and I am above suspicion, and it is with extreme pain that I have been obliged to expose my son's vices and to acquaint you with a portion of them. I beseech Your Highness to trust in what I have the honor of writing him in purest truth, to forgive my liberty and to forever allow me to say that I am with most profound respect, of Your Highness the most humble and most obedient servant.

Bérard, procurator of the Parliament of Grenoble.
in Grenoble March 11, 1728.

Ars. Arch. Bastille 11000, fol. 23 (1728)

To Monsieur Hérault,
Lieutenant General of Police

My Lord,

Barthélemy Bérard, procurator at the Parliament of Grenoble most humbly remonstrates unto Your Highness that on the night of the 5th to the 6th of December 1727 he had the misfortune of being robbed by Vincent Bérard his son who stole from him more than eight hundred gold and silver livres along with a ring with six diamonds and who then fled to Paris, the next day he sent letters in all directions and among others the Monsieur Perrin his friend in Paris to pray him to implore the authority of Your Highness who had the goodness of ordering the arrest of his said son who had come to Paris.

Monsieur Perrin, believing that his representations to the son would recall him to his duty, judged it fitting to first take this part and to this effect had in the month of January last spoken and remonstrated with this son about the misfortune and cruel extremities to which he was reducing his father and himself; this son promised to immediately return to Grenoble and to return the money to his father if his father would be willing to forgive him and assure him so in a letter in response to the one he would send him on this subject.

The supplicant to whom Monsieur Perrin reported the news of this conversation waited with impatience for this letter from his son like a good and tender father; but as he saw that this son as fickle as he is unnatural from whom he received no letter had invented this supposed letter and restitution so as to continue his debauches and dissipations unmolested he again wrote to Monsieur Perrin the two letters of the 14th and 28th of February last copies of which are enclosed herein in which he once again called out for the justice of Your Highness and most humbly beseeched him to give his orders to have him arrested which will reestablish the deplorable state of this poor seventy-year-old father and of his family who have all been ruined by this theft and halt the debauches and dissipations of this unhappy son; and the supplicant like all of his family and those who had entrusted him with a portion of this money will continue their prayers for the health and prosperity of Your Highness.

Perrin, bearer of orders and letters for the
supplicant, rue de la Verrerie
lodging with Monsieur Mol, tapestry maker.

Ars. Arch. Bastille 11000, fol. 25 (1728)

Vincent Bérard, of Grenoble age twenty-three,
Graduate in civil law,
Requests the revocation of an order of the King obtained by his father.
He represents that out of his greed that had gone to the point of refusing him the most urgent help after the death of his mother, whether it be for his food, his maintenance or the continuance of his studies;
that the supplicant found himself reduced to abandoning the house of

his father and coming to Paris where for ten years he worked for lawyers and procurators;

that he used the same hardness with his younger son who also quit the paternal house and that his father took an inheritance that an uncle had left this young man;

that the intention of his father is to considerably advantage his daughter to the prejudice of his two sons;

that his father who is a procurator is very rich, he has acquired credit both among his relatives and among other individuals of the city of Grenoble such that he has one and all at his disposal and has had his request to obtain orders supported by different persons who did not dare resist him because of their reliance upon him and out of their fear that he might cross them in their own affairs which are in his hands and that he therefore finds himself the victim of this deference;

that moreover his father has a penchant for a woman who inspires in him such injudicious sentiments as these toward his children;

that he admits that his fault was to have taken from a sum of two thousand that he found by chance in his father's study, a sum of one thousand five hundred that he employed to continue his legal studies, and to obtain his diploma, and that nonetheless it this was on this pretext alone that the order was obtained, but the use he made of this money should fully justify his conduct he is beyond any suspicion his emulation having always carried him to [illegible].

Finally that he is less sensitive to the fact that his father convinced his mother an hour before she died to remove him from her inheritance, so that the largest part of the estate would go to him alone, than to the lack of tenderness that he has for him and his unconcern for his advancement.

He brings three certificates that certify his good morals and the assiduousness he has shown in his legal studies.

[*In the margins:*]
I wrote to Monsieur Pillevault to suspend the execution of this order on September 4, 1728.

[*This is the summary of a long petition from the son.*]
Ars. Arch. Bastille 11000, fol. 39 (1728)

Claude Housse

> To My Lord
> the Lieutenant General of Police

My Lord,

Jean Housse bourgeois of Paris and Claude l'Espée his spouse residing rue Saint-Honoré in Saint-Roch parish, most humbly represent unto Your Highness that they have a son named Claude Housse, over twenty-four years of age, whom they placed with Monsieur Jacques Fainet in Rouen, more than three years ago, who since he has been there "has made much mischief" by gambling the money that said Fainet gave him for merchandise; among others, he once lost a thousand nine hundred livres for which the supplicants have already paid a sum of a thousand one hundred livres and since then, he lost a sum of one thousand two hundred livres as it was reported to the supplicants, and other things of this nature and as the supplicants whose honor and probity is known to everyone, fear that through this son's conduct, some affront to them might occur, as this is a vice that leads to others; they appeal unto Your Highness, to beseech him that he might wish to give an order to have him locked away, and they will pray God for the preservation of Your Highness.

Ars. Arch. Bastille 11013, no folio (1728)

> To My Lord
> the Lieutenant General of Police

My Lord,

Jean Housse, merchant in Paris, Saint-Roch parish and Claude Lespée his wife and all his family, beseech Your Highness to grant them permission to retrieve their son currently a pensioner in the house of Bicêtre who was placed there by Your Order at their request following the prayer they made unto you, and they also beseech you, My Lord, to grant them this grace as promptly as it would be possible as they have a most advantageous opportunity for his departure for he has been provided employment that requires that he leave this instant otherwise it might be given to someone else, they hope for this grace, from My Lord, they will continue their wishes and prayers for the continuation of Your Health.

Ars. Arch. Bastille 11013, fol. 141–142 (1728)

François Roy

To My Lord Hérault,
Lieutenant General of Police
of the City of Paris

Vincent Roy and Catherine Galenby, merchants residing faubourg de Saint-Symphorien, city of Tours, humbly beseech and represent unto You that they have a son of around twenty-nine to thirty years of age named François Roy, who since the age of eighteen has given them all of the pain that can be inflicted upon a father and a mother and even an entire family, having enlisted three times in the last ten years and their having discharged him as many times; he has already cost them more than six thousand francs by his mad and imbecilic ways, which has ruined the supplicants entirely, and left them in no condition to raise their other children, and to complete this misfortune he deserted six months ago; to avoid what might have happened if they had left him in this situation, the aforementioned supplicants made one final effort and at last obtained his leave by way of money; said François Roy who is no way fit to serve His Majesty in this state because of his indisposition, and the nature of his imbecility has since this time done them all possible dishonor, he goes from door to door howling like an animal, and he is absolutely incapable of taking any profession, without which the supplicants are in no state to sustain him as their family is a large one; considering this, My Lord, might it please You to order that said François Roy be locked away in Bicêtre to make penance for his wrongs; the supplicants will never cease to pray the Lord for the preservation of Your Highness.

Ars. Arch. Bastille 11019, fol. 157 (1728)

My Lord the Archbishop of Tours

My Lord,

I did not fail to suggest to Mgr the cardinal de Fleury the order that you did me the honor of requesting of me to have François Leroy locked up in the hospital, His Eminence was well willing to grant it. I will receive this order directly but I will not be able to have it executed until you have had the kindness of signifying me whether this young libertine is in Paris or in the provinces; in the latter case, I will dispatch an officer of your choosing to make this arrest whose expenses as well as those for his transportation will have to be paid by the family, unless it judges it more suitable to send the young man to this city where I will have him arrested right away, in order to avoid by this means, the object of the expenses that I would, in such a circumstance, put onto the King's account. You know all the sentiments of my devotion with which I have . . .

Ars. Arch. Bastille 11019, fol. 163 (1728)

I have just learned, Monsieur, that Monsieur Leroy de Tours whom you were so good as to place in Bicêtre at the recommendation of Mgr the archbishop has enlisted in the regiment of Piémont once again. This has placed his poor mother in despair. M. the archbishop tells me that he has written to you again about this matter if you could keep him where he is, he declares unto you that you would be doing a great charity, because this unfortunate man costs immense sums to his poor mother who is dying of worry. If I could flatter myself that you still have some goodness toward me, I will unite my prayers with those of Our Archbishop, I can assure You that no one in the world is more respectfully devoted, Monsieur, Your most humble and most obedient servant.

The abbé of Peseux,
Tours this November 6, 1733.

If I had thought that M. Hérault might still remember my name, I would beseech you to assure him of my most humble respect.

Ars. Arch. Bastille 11019, fol. 166–167 (1728)

To My Lord
the Lieutenant General of Police

My Lord,

Charles Chahan, master vinegar maker in Paris, most humbly represents unto Your Highness, that he has been asked by the letter of Monsieur Vincent Roy, merchant in Tours, and by his wife who is a relative of his, to most humbly beseech you to order that François Roy, their son detained and imprisoned in Bicêtre for more than fifteen months on your orders have the liberty of the Courtyards of said Bicêtre, and Your Highness he also beseeches you to order M. the Bursar that said Roy not be given the freedom to leave, nor that any officer be allowed to enlist him under any pretext whatsoever even when this Roy wishes to do so, and that he be given the ordinary fare and that he be employed inside the house in the jobs that suit him such that he might enjoy the benefits that You grant to those who work and the supplicants will continue their wishes for the prosperity of Your Highness.

Ars. Arch. Bastille 11019, fol. 168 (1728)

Mgr the archbishop of Tours requests by his letter enclosed herein that one François Roy who is in the hospital by an order of the King of October 18 for disturbed wits be kept there for a long time. He declares that he has given new signs of disturbance by enlisting himself again and that if he leaves he will not join the Regiment, but will have his neck broken!

I also wish that Monsieur would intervene to have this most recent enlistment revoked.

Ars. Arch. Bastille 11019, fol. 170 (1728)

One François Roy de Tours did not enlist, but he was seen by a captain of the Piémont regiment with the permission of Monsieur and in his presence; I do not remember the name of this captain, but only that no enlistment took place and that such a thing is not done in Bicêtre except by order of the King, so if there had been an enlistment, he would have been deceived by a blank form with his signature, which prisoners will sometimes have passed to officers by those who are released: I put a note next to the file on François Roy of the intentions of Monsieur for when an order of the King might arrive to have him handed over to an officer, he will only be released after I have had the honor of reporting it to you.

This November 23, 1728.
Haynier.

Ars. Arch. Bastille 11019, fol. 171 (1728)

Jean Baptiste Carnavillier

Memoir for Monsieur de Sainfrée

After a series of libertinages and awful disorders the honest family of Jean Baptiste Carnavillier, of Orléans, addresses itself to M. de Barentin, currently the intendant of this generality, who obtained the *lettre de cachet* of November 22, 1758, and who had him taken to Bicêtre, at the expense of three of the supplicants from the family who paid his pension.

The most comfortable of the three has died and his inheritors no longer wish to bear this burden; the second of the three does not have, he says, the means and the third, who is the widow Basseville, a seamstress with a family to support has had up until now a great deal of difficulty in paying her share and through the desertion of the two others, it is now impossible for her to fulfill the entire obligation.

She most humbly beseeches My Lord the Procurator General that, owing to the infamous and notorious conduct of said Jeanbaptiste Carnavillier and the impossibility Madame Basseville finds herself in with regard to paying his pension alone or in its entirety, he be placed on the bread of the King or transported to the colonies, such that as residents of Orléans, his spotless family will not have the pain of watching him receive the punishment that he would incur, both for the acts of which he is already guilty as for the crimes that he would probably commit, if he were to be released.

Nonetheless we will continue the payment of his pension, up until his embarkation if this is so ordered by My Lord the Procurator General.

Ars. Arch. Bastille 11990, fol. 224 (1758)

In Bicêtre June 17, 1763.

Jean Baptiste Carnavillier, no profession, married, forty-one years of age, from Orléans, Saint-Victor parish, held as a prisoner in Bicêtre since October 24, 1758, where he was transferred from the convent of the Récollets d'Orléans by virtue of an order of the King given in Versailles on the 5th of said month and year, countersigned by Phelypeaux, to the effect that he should be received and detained up until new order by His Majesty by means of a pension of a hundred twenty livres a year that would be paid by his family.

Said pension was reduced to one hundred livres by order of M. the count de Saint Florentin on the date of January 30, 1761.

Monsieur Germain Carnavillier, relative of said Jean Baptiste, merchant grocer in Orléans, rue Bourgogne, across from and in the parish of Notre-Dame-du-Chemin, is the one who always paid said pension until the 24th of August last, since which time I have not touched any of it because said grocer says that he and all of his relatives are immiserated and unable to continue paying this pension, and that for this reason they consent that said Jean Baptiste Carnavillier be given his freedom.

Upon which I took away the wine and surplus food that this prisoner was being given because of said pension.

It has been around five years that this individual has been detained here. He has always behaved himself peacefully, therefore I think that he is a case for release, even if his pension were to be paid in full, even more so because this is the first time he has been locked away here and his charge is simply: convicted of theft.

Haynier.

Ars. Arch. Bastille 11990, fol. 226 (1758)

SHAMEFUL CONCUBINAGE

Magdeleine Blanchet

To Monsieur
the Lieutenant General of Police

Pierre Blanchet, bourgeois from the city of Sézanne en Brie and at present in Paris finds himself obliged to give you an account of the unhappy and infamous life that for several years one Magdelaine Blanchet his daughter has led with one Hotton who calls himself an apprentice furrier with whom this unhappy girl has had five or six children even though said Hotton is married, this criminal life has obliged his wife to leave Paris owing to the abuse that she received every day from her husband; the supplicant has spared nothing to retrieve his daughter from this scandalous life, having himself gone to bring her back more than two years ago, but no sooner had she arrived in the paternal home than she returned to the side of said Hotton; the supplicant's tale is only too true this is what obliges him to most humbly beseech you to have said Magdelaine Blanchet locked up so that she might make a penance proportional to his troubles, as for the justice that you will grant the supplicant, he will not cease to continue his wishes and prayers for the health and prosperity of Your Highness.

Blanchet father.

[*On the back*: A report confirming this from Malavoine in 1727.]
Ars. Arch. Bastille 11004, no folio (1728)

From Paris this March 4, 1723.

I assure you, Monsieur and dearest father, that I am in a quite pitiful state when I think of my obligations toward you and my dear mother of the kindness that you have shown me, and thus for which I will be grateful my entire life; I cannot console myself for having increased the misfortune of giving such grief as I have, I will never console myself of this in all my days, my life will be as languishing as it had seemed easy to me when I was with you, God alone can support me in my pains, I ask of him the grace, and will never in my life cease doing so of preserving you both. Do not refuse me your benediction I ask this of you my dearest father in the name of God and of all the tenderness you have always shown me, I do not dare to hope to hear any precious news of you, this is a favor of which I am not worthy and I hope that M. the Dean [*doyen*] will often give me news of you. I shall add to the obligations that I also have toward monsieur his brother who came before me as a true friend, took a part in my suffering, his presence will support me in my misfortunes, I ask you for permission to assure my dearest mother of my most humble respect and I say with perfect submission with all the respect that I owe you my dearest father your most humble and most obedient servant daughter.

Magdeleine Blanchet.

Ars. Arch. Bastille 11000, fol. 163 (1728)

Madame,

I have the honor of once again soliciting your good heart to obtain from monsieur your husband, the pardon that Mademoiselle his daughter asks of him; she knows that she is guilty and as a consequence she is in the situation of the prodigal child; one cannot think ill of the approach that you have judged suitable for communicating an affair such as this to an afflicted father; but it is not suitable to defer, you would certainly become guilty before God our sovereign judge of the excesses to which said mademoiselle might take herself, if you do not lend your hand immediately to the design she has conceived to remove herself from her state; I do not know if it might not be fitting if monsieur your husband were to facilitate her the means of taking herself to Montmirail where it seems that she has the intention of locking herself away to make penance and see to her state, rather than having her return to the paternal home, where she has every reason to fear enduring many trials and tribulations. You will please be so good as to give this your attention. You will find in the present a letter from said mademoiselle in which she signifies to you her submission while nonetheless requesting a letter from monsieur her father before she will resolve herself to obey; what is more you may know that she does not have a cent; therefore see what it is you desire to do in this regard. Reply, if it would please you and as soon as possible to one who remains with respect your most humble and most obedient servant.

Graffart, vicar in Saint-Médard.
In Paris, March 13, 1723.

Ars. Arch Bastille 11000, fol. 164 (1728)

Monsieur,

I am persuaded that you will not find it wrong for me to appeal unto you on the subject of the unruliness of Magdeleine Margueritte Blanchet your daughter in concubinage with one Othon apprentice furrier by occupation, residing in our parish, a married man and whose wife is in Nantes in Brittany. This is the third child that they have had together, the most recent of whom was just baptized in these last few days. I hope, Monsieur, that employing all of the authority that God has given you as a father you will bring remedy to such disorder as this and that you would wish to let me know your wishes upon this matter. You understand, Monsieur, that it is necessary to return order to this situation and I am astonished that this has not yet been done; as for I who just learned of this you can well believe that I will neglect nothing once I have had the honor of your reply before which I have not thought it right to act, while awaiting it I remain with respect your most humble and most obedient servant.

Graffart, vicar of Saint-Médard.
In Paris, March 4, 1723.

Ars. Arch. Bastille 11000, fol. 167 (1728)

To My Lord
the Lieutenant General of Police

Madeleine Marguerite Blanchet adult daughter of Pierre Blanchet, bourgeois of the city of Sézanne in Brie and the late Madeleine Chauveau, detained by order of the king in the house of detention since the 18th of January last at the solicitation of Monsieur Blanchet her father who instead of doing her justice as to what he legitimately owes her and even to shelter himself from the just lawsuits that she was on the verge of bringing against him did, by false declarations surprise the religion of Your Highness, and obtained from him a *lettre de cachet*.

The supplicant remonstrates unto Your Highness that for the nine years she has been in Paris she was never helped by her father and having been abandoned entirely, she learned how to work in the fur trade through the care and assistance of Monsieur Hotton by whom she has one son who is today around eight years old and she has lived for about that long with honor and probity with said Hotton to support and raise her child.

At the beginning of 1723, the supplicant had M. Graffard vicar of Saint-Médard parish write her father to retrieve her back to him he consented to the second letter she remained with him for nine months having always been submitted to the will of her father who during this time gave her a false and invented account of the money in guardianship for her in her mother's estate, he wronged his daughter of more than five thousand livres giving her as her whole estate only seventy livres of rents instead of the eight thousand that should have gone to her out of the inheritance of her late mother, who had brought Blanchet sixteen thousand livres through the marriage from which the supplicant and a younger sister were born and after the alleged accounts were given and he had had her sign an act before a notary whose true import she only learned recently, said Blanchet her father abused her and chased her from his house and she was left to go wherever she saw fit, upon which she was obliged to resolve herself to serve in Coulommiers in the house of Mademoiselle Pidou, with the widow Fournel cabinetmaker, then with Monsieur Prieur spinner of gold threads [*tireur d'or*]. The high price of bread in 1725 left her penniless, in this state she wrote her father several times, praying him to send her some little kindness, or to signify to her what he wished her to do, but as he did not make any reply to her, necessity obliged her to return to said Honton where she has lived and worked until today, which was not unknown to her father.

This poor unfortunate woman most humbly beseeches Your Highness to observe that said Blanchet her father contracted a second marriage from which he had several children, which has caused him to be indifferent to those of the first bed, up to the point of doing everything to bring about their deaths and to frustrate them of their mother's estate; he has taken not only the estate that was supposed to go to them but also the estate that was reserved for them by law.

Considering this, My Lord may it please you to have the kindness and the charity of granting her freedom so that she can furnish proof of this to Your Highness to whom she submits herself entirely with regard to her fate, after her release, she also most humbly beseeches My Lord, that her father do her justice as to her mother's inheritance, otherwise she will be obliged to seek legal redress in court. She hopes for this grace from the equity of his Grandeur for whom she redoubles her wishes and prayers for the preservation of his health.

Ars. Arch. Bastille 11000, fol. 174 (1728)

Response to the memoir given to
Mgr the Lieutenant General of Police by
Madeleine Marguerite Blanchet

Said Blanchet must in no way give as a pretext for her release that her father did not do her justice and that it was in fear of lawsuits that she was on the verge of bringing against him that he requested a *lettre de cachet* for her arrest.

He reached a settlement with her over the money in guardianship that he owed her by the decision of a procurator in the bailiwick of Sézanne whom she herself selected, through said transaction it was found that her father owed her a sum of seventy livres and seven sous.

And if she had been wronged, nothing stopped her from suing.

She makes a false accusation when she says that for nine years, which she spent in Paris, she never received any help from her father. Several times he sent her gifts for which he has receipts and which were listed in said transaction.

With respect it is similarly false that it has only been nine years that she has been in Paris, and the only reason for this is to give the impression that it was one Hotton who debauched her first, as she says in her memoir that she has had a child by him who is now eight years old.

Let her correctly declare the time of her departure from Sézanne and the child's age, which she admits, and we will see that she had been in Paris for quite some time, when she became pregnant by the labors of said Hotton, we pray Mgr the Lieutenant of Police, to give leave to Monsieur Blanchet to explain the cause of his daughter's departure.

It is true that at the beginning of the year 1723 Monsieur Blanchet received letters from Monsieur Graffard, vicar of Saint-Médard, presented here, that advised him of his daughter's disorder, and her continued cohabitation with said Hotton, who is a married man and in a broken marriage with a woman who is currently in Nantes in Brittany and that he immediately set off to retrieve her from her debauchery, which he thought he had achieved by bringing her back home where she remained for around nine months, and where she was fed and maintained like the other children.

But she makes a false accusation when she says that she was abused and chased from there, said Monsieur Blanchet beseeches My Lord in grace to have himself informed of the truth of said declaration.

Despite the dishonor that she had done him Monsieur Blanchet had for her the same goodness that he had for his other children, and there is reason to believe that notwithstanding this she still maintained her debauched spirit because she had only just arrived in Coulommiers where persons of probity and friends of her family had found her an honest position with Mademoiselle Pidou with two hundred livres per year when she furtively left after three months to return to Paris.

Monsieur Blanchet does not know if she first went to the widow Fournel, cabinetmaker, and then to Monsieur Prieur gold embroiderer, what is true is that she returned as she admits she lives with the man from whom she already had a child, and who as I just said is a married man and in a broken marriage with his wife, what stronger proof of libertinage and debauchery could there be, independent of those that Monsieur Blanchet would perhaps find if he was taken to learn what she did in the ten years she has been in Paris.

It is in a vain attempt to excite compassion that she pretends that her father did not do her justice, that with these intentions and in order to frustrate her and her sister of her father's estate, he hid away his estate.

There is currently a court in the bailiwick of Sézanne that is about to make its judgment between her sister and him whose ruling he hopes will show that far from being wronged by the aforementioned transaction she was on the contrary quite favorably treated, but is this not *[rip in the document]* Monsieur Blanchet who is a man from one of the most important families of Sézanne and son of the Royal provost marshal of said city, did not importune Mgr the Lieutenant of Police over his daughter's first debauches; he believed it prudent that to maintain his honor he not spread the just resentments that he had conceived and moreover he even undertook this approach with joy when it seemed that he could believe that the return of his daughter to the city of Sézanne and into the paternal home could recall her to herself and turn her away from the unruliness of her conduct, but he could no longer remain silent once he learned that his unfortunate girl had left an honest position where she had been placed in order to return with even greater passion to her libertinage with the same man by whom she admits that she bore the shameful fruits of their debauches.

And he hopes that by all these considerations it might please Mgr the Lieutenant General of Police to give no regard to the complaints of this prostitute who asks for freedom only to be able to continue living in libertinage and to finish covering her family with ignominy.

Blanchet.

Ars. Arch. Bastille 11000, fol. 176 (1728)

Thérèse Boisselet

To My Lord Hérault,
Lieutenant General of Police

My Lord,

François Boisselet, journeyman cobbler and Louise Beley, his wife, residing rue des Lyonnais faubourg Saint-Marcel, Saint-Médard parish, most humbly represent unto Your Highness that Thérèse Boisselet their eldest daughter age twenty-six fell nine years ago into unruliness frequenting all manner of libertines, and conducting herself most scandalously and three or four years ago she debauched one Cochois whose wife is still alive and who is very abused because of said Boisselet who brought disorder to this household, having had a child by said Cochois and finding that others were obstacles to their debauches, his wife for him and her father and mother, the supplicants, for her they resolved to go off and arranged to meet at a later date, Cochois carried off all that was in his house and left to establish himself where no one knows, except for said Thérèse Boisselet who is preparing herself to go find him. All that is declared here and much more that it would be too long to tell is known to M. the curé and the undersigned neighbors and said Boisselet father and mother, overcome with pain at the debauched conduct of their said daughter and fearing that worse might yet arrive they most humbly pray My Lord to give your orders to have said Thérèse Boisselet locked up before she has disappeared. They will continue their prayers for the health and prosperity of Your Highness.

François Cochois, Louis Cochois,

François Boisselet.

I have the honor of certifying to My Lord the Lieutenant General of Police the truthfulness of content of the present petition that the conduct of the said Cochois and Thérèse Boisselet is a public scandal and I beseech him to make a [illegible] lock up said Boisselet. In Paris Oct. 2, 1728.

N. Dommart, curé of Saint-Médard.

Ars. Arch. Bastille 11000, fol. 226 (1728)

To Monsieur Rossignol,

at the office of Monsieur the Lieutenant of Police

Monsieur,

I am persuaded that you will not find it wrong that I insist once again on praying you to give your attention to having the Boisselet girl sent to the Salpêtrière a new scandal in the neighborhood has emerged on her account such that one Cauchois and said Boisselet having been found together Sunday night, were seriously beaten by the crowd; it would it seems to me be suitable not to defer making an example by dispensing punishment that could suppress any that the neighborhood might wish to give and anyone who might be disposed to follow such an example. I will take advantage of this occasion to assure you that no one is more sincerely, your most humble and most obedient servant.

Graffart, vicar of Saint-Médard.

I arrive, Monsieur, as my vicar writes his letter. I join my testimony to his, praying that you might wish to put an end to the scandal of which he speaks, regarding which I already signed a petition this summer.

Dommart, curé of Saint-Médard.

Ars. Arch. Bastille 11000, fol. 227 (1728)

To My Lord
the Lieutenant General of Police

My Lord,

François Boisselet, cobbler and Louise Beley his wife, residing rue des Lyonnais in Paris, father and mother of Thérèse Boisselet most respectfully remonstrate unto Your Highness that around six months ago Thérèse Boisselet was detained in the house of the Hôpital général for causes, means, and reasons known to his Grandeur who dispatched an order to have her placed where she is at present locked up. As she is in a deplorable state, as she is deserving of compassion and as she is so to speak eaten by vermin, for these reasons the supplicants humbly beseech the help of his Grandeur whom they humbly beseech to grant them an order granting said Thérèse Boisselet their daughter her freedom and placing her under the direction and loving gaze of her father and mother on the condition that she will behave herself better now than she has in the past in accordance with Christian doctrine and they will continue to pray the lord for the preservation, prosperity and health of Your Highness.

Ars. Arch. Bastille 11000, fol. 229 (1728)

Madeleine Chapé

To My Lord
the Lieutenant General of Police

My Lord,

François Saffard and Madeleine Belot his wife, grandfather and grandmother of Madeleine Chapé age twenty-one orphaned of both father and mother, most humbly represent unto Your Highness, that despite the good education they have provided her, she has always wished to follow her bad inclinations and her libertinage, such that she is today around seven months pregnant, said supplicants most humbly beseech you, My Lord, that you might wish to do them the grace of having said Madeleine Chapé locked away in the hospital in order to arrest the path of her libertinage that does dishonor to the supplicants they would be obliged to pray God for the preservation of Your Highness.

Saffard.

Ars. Arch. Bastille 11003, fol. 200 (1728)

To My Lord
the Lieutenant General of Police

My Lord,

François Saffard and Madeleine Belot his wife, officer in the fisheries, most humbly represent unto Your Highness that around two and a half years ago you were so good as to grant them an order to have one Marguerite M. Chapé their granddaughter age twenty, orphaned of father and mother, locked away for youthful libertinage alone. And as during the two and half years of her detention in the hospital, she has reflected as much as possible, and has become greatly repentant of her wrongs, requesting forgiveness from the suppliants grandfather, grandmother and her guardian, they beseech My Lord to be so good as to grant them her freedom, considering that it is time for them to establish her and finding this occasion to be a favorable one, they will never cease their wishes to Heaven for the precious preservation of Your Highness.

Saffard.

Ars. Arch. Bastille 11003, fol. 206 (1728)

Monsieur Guillotte will verify the content of this petition exactly and will promptly report to me on May 12, 1728.

Monsieur,

The suppliants were unable to indicate anyone who could give me proof of what they advance against their granddaughter, but as they are folk of true probity, he a retired subsacrist of the parish, we can have faith in what they say in this regard; according to their declarations, it is certain that Madelaine Chapé is a very bad subject plunged into debauchery, that she left their house where she had a most comfortable life to roam the bad areas of Paris where her grandmother went several times to find her to recall her to her duty, her grandfather is her guardian as well as that of a little brother who lives with them, they have no relatives on the paternal side except a strongly debauched uncle of bad morals and the entire estate of this girl consists in thirty livres of income, she is a seamstress by trade but does not work at all. Her grandmother tried to engage her to visit a midwife for her childbirth but she would not hear of it; it is said that she currently remains in a bad area on rue des Moineaux.

Guillotte.

Ars. Arch. Bastille 11003, no folio (1728)

I pray you my dearest sister, to signify me by sending over to me the petition by virtue of which this girl is detained in the Salpêtrière.

This October 24, 1730.

Madelaine Marguerite Chapé twenty-one years of age, of Paris, girl entered by *lettre de cachet* given in Compiègne, June 30, 1728, the time of her detention is not signified. Her letter holds until further order. Signed Louis and underneath that Phelippeaux;[3] brought by Monsieur Haynier, an officer of the Provost Marshal of the Island by virtue of My Lord's order, while awaiting the letter from the King June 13, 1728, that was brought by Monsieur Guillotte, officer of the provost marshal of the Island July 30, 1728, for the first time.[4] For libertinage. This is the content of our registers.

Bailly.

Ars. Arch. Bastille 11003, no folio (1728)

His Excellency My Lord
the Cardinal de Fleury

Magdelaine Marguerite Chapé was taken to the hospital by virtue of an order of the King of June 30, 1728, at the prayer of her family because of her libertinage.

Because the family requests her return and offers to take care of her, I think she can be freed.

Ars. Arch. Bastille 11003, no folio (1728)

Marie Joseph Coquerel

To My Lord
the Lieutenant General of Police

Monsieur,

Nicolas Coquerel, master ribbon maker in Paris, residing rue Neuve-Saint-Martin, Saint-Nicolas-des-Champs parish, humbly recounts unto Your Highness, that he had Marie Joseph Coquerel, his daughter, age twenty, locked up in the hospital because of her libertinage, debauchery and bad conduct with a married man from where she was released at Your Order on the occasion of the procession of Corpus Christi last, and as this unhappy girl has begun her debauches anew with the same man and as he cannot be the master of her and he fears the trouble that might come of her libertinage, he most humbly beseeches Your Highness to be so good as to give orders to have her arrested and locked up in said hospital for the rest of her days.

He will pray God alongside all his family for your health and prosperity. This will be the third time that she will have been locked up there for the same reason.

Des Champs, Benoist Maille, Nicolai Maille,
Veuve Cadet, Coquerelle.

Ars. Arch. Bastille 11004, fol. 240 (1728)

Nicolas Coquerel beseeches Monsieur to have Marie Joseph his daughter age twenty locked up in the hospital once again:

Declares that although she was already locked up before because of the debauched commerce she maintained with one Masson locksmith, married man, she has continued the same life since her release.

M. the curé of Saint-Nicolas-des-Champs and Superintendent Blanchard offer their assurances that the declaration is truthful.

Take by force this August 7, 1728.

An order of the King for the hospital this September 17, 1728.

Ars. Arch. Bastille 11004, no folio (1728)

Monsieur,

I have inquired as to the content of the present petition. And I learned from several people in the neighborhood that said Marie Joseph had been in the hospital for reasons of debauchery. The same neighbors assure us that since she left the hospital, she has not ceased her debauched commerce with a married man named Masson Sarrazin. In addition to what the neighbors have told me, I remarked that there was a certificate from M. the curé of Saint-Nicolas-des-Champs at the bottom of the present petition by which I esteem that there is reason to have her locked up in the hospital.

Superintendent Blanchard.

This August 2, 1728.

Ars. Arch. Bastille 11004, no folio (1728)

His Excellency My Lord

the Cardinal de Fleury

Nicolas Coquerel requests that Marie Joseph Coquerel his daughter, be arrested and taken to the hospital.

Declares that his daughter is twenty years old, that she has already been locked away in the hospital because of her scandalous commerce with one Masson a married man whose household she was ruining, that when she obtained her freedom she continued this same debauchery. This petition is certified by M. the curé of Saint-Nicolas-des-Champs, and Superintendent Blanchard attests to the truth of the facts, I was obliged to have her brought before me to have a talk with her, she was unable to disavow her debauchery therefore I think that she deserves to be arrested again and returned to the hospital.

Ars. Arch. Bastille 11004, no folio (1728)

Anne Hubert

To My Lord
the Lieutenant General of Police

My Lord,

Hubert, locksmith, residing rue Saint-André-des-Arts, Saint-Séverin parish, most humbly represents unto Your Highness, that unhappily for him, he has a daughter who is plunged into debauchery and vice, and has been for more than three years with one Pierre Malurier, and Anne Hubert, daughter of the supplicant, who said supplicant only learned three months ago had given birth. In the night said Malurier and said Hubert, came to rob the supplicant after having picked the lock of his door and abused him around six months ago, not satisfied with this, said Hubert again picked the lock of one Maréchal on rue de la Corne such that the supplicant's life is not safe as he is every day under the threat of losing his life at the hands of his daughter and said Malurier as several attempts have already been made on their part, in these circumstances the supplicant appeals unto Your Highness to beseech him most humbly to have locked up said Hubert his daughter who resides with said Malurier across from Saint-Denis-de-la-Charte in the house of one Tagon, lemonade maker [limonadier], on the fourth floor in the back.[5]

This is the grace that we hope of Your Justice, and said Hubert will continue his Wishes for the health and prosperity of Your Highness.

[On the same petition:]
I the undersigned first Archpriest of Paris and curé of Sainte-Marie-Madeleine en la Cité, certify that one Anne Hubert leads a scandalous life with one Pierre Malurier, that she gave birth from his labors around four months ago, that I went to her several times to put an end to this scandal, without having ever been able to win her over.

In Paris, this February 4, 1728.
Duhamel.

Ars. Arch. Bastille 11013, fol. 149 (1728)

Anne Catherine Seray

To My Lord
the Lieutenant General of Police

My Lord,

Gabriel Seray, master locksmith, and Anne Charlotte Muideblé his wife, residing in Mantes, most humbly represent unto Your Highness, that around four and a half years ago they married Anne Catherine Seray their daughter, to one Pierre Grambert, master tanner in Mantes, but since this time they have kept such a bad household, that they have dissipated everything the several times that the supplicants helped to reestablish them; and as both of them fell into libertinage they left one another, and for around six months said Seray their daughter has been in Paris with one Faucroy carpenter, a widower residing in this city on rue Poissonière in the house of Monsieur Martin pâtissier, she lives with this Faucroy in bad commerce.

As this conduct is shameful, which supremely dishonors her family, and as the supplicants with all their prohibitions and their care were unable to remedy this and put her on the right path, on the contrary, as they have reason to fear that even more trouble might come of this they most humbly beseech Your Highness that he might wish to authorize in advance an order to have said Anne Catherine Seray their daughter locked away in the hospital, while awaiting an order of the King for her to be detained there until she has been corrected of her libertine inclinations, and they will not cease their prayers for the preservation of Your Highness.

G. Seray.

Ars. Arch. Bastille 11028, fol. 165 (1728)

THE DISHONOR OF WAYWARDNESS

Barbe Blondel Duponchel

To My Lord
the Lieutenant General of Police

My Lord,

René Duponchel locksmith residing faubourg Saint-Antoine rue de Naples, most humbly represents unto Your Highness that he has a daughter named Barbe Blondel Duponchel age twenty-nine who conducts herself most wickedly as she even lived for a considerable time with a boy passing themselves off as husband and wife, from whom she even had a child, and they had lodged in the house of M. Gallois, master perfume maker, residing rue de la Lanterne, Sainte-Marie-Madeleine en la Cité parish where said fellow died about six weeks ago and as said Barbe Duponchel does not wish to be recalled to her duty, as she continues her bad life by not returning at night to the house of Monsieur Gallois who out of charity and to make her look within herself still lodges her in his house, which is attested to you by M. the curé of said parish, said René Duponchel beseeches you to give him the order to have her taken and placed in the house of the Salpêtrière for the rest of her days and he will continue his prayers for the health and prosperity of Your Highness.

Pierre Caillois, Marianne Dapert.

I certify the truth of the facts written in the above petition and that it would be a very good deed to imprison said Barbe du Ponchel lodged in my parish in Paris this May 5, 1728.

Duchanel, Archpriest
and curé of Sainte-Madeleine.

Ars. Arch. Bastille 11009, fol. 95 (1728)

Marc René Cailly

To My Lord
the Lieutenent General of Police

Jean Jacques Cailly lawyer in the Parlement and Marie Madeleine du Poys his wife most humbly beseech, stating that Marc René Cailly their son age twenty-one, forgetting the good upbringing that they gave him frequents only prostituted women and persons of ill repute with whom he has delivered himself to such an outrageous debauchery, that it is to be feared that the consequences for him will be dire, it is in order to forestall this that the suppliants, after having vainly remonstrated with their son to recall him to his duty, and that he live a more orderly life, appeal unto the authority of Monsieur.

In consideration of this, Monsieur, may it please you, to order that Marc René Cailly, the suppliants' son be taken to the house of the H. Fathers [*R. Pères*][6] of Saint-Lazare to be detained and corrected until he has shown signs of repentance; with the offer that the suppliants will pay his pension, they hope for this grace from the Justice of Monsieur, which could not be granted on a more just and necessary occasion.

Cailly, Dupoys Cailly.

Ars. Arch. Bastille 11003, fol. 26 (1728)

Cailly retired Superintendent of Châtelet most humbly beseeches Monsieur the Lieutenant General of Police that he might wish to grant the freedom of Marc René Cailly, detained by order of King in the house [*maison*] of Saint-Lazare where he appears to have made such good usage of his penance, that the supplicant dares to hope that he will behave himself sensibly in the exercise of his employment with M. D'Argenson that he was so good to give him.

Ars. Arch. Bastille 11003, fol. 30 (1728)

His Excellency My Lord
the Cardinal of Fleury

Marc René Cailly was taken to Saint-Lazare at the behest of his father by virtue of an order of the King from September 8, 1728, because of his libertinage.

But because his father requests his return, I believe that there is no disadvantage to his being released.

Ars. Arch. Bastille 11003, fol. 31 (1728)

Antoine Compère

To My Lord
the Lieutenant General of Police

My Lord,

Simon Compère, bourgeois from the city of Châlons in Champagne, most humbly represents unto you that Antoine one of his children, has for the last several years continued the greatest libertinage despite all of the care of the supplicant and his wife which makes them fear that trouble might come of this which would cause them as much dishonor as it would woe, which would cause the death of the supplicant's wife if the conduct of said Antoine were not to be promptly halted; this is what has obliged the supplicant to give the order to have said Antoine arrested in the city of Fismes, but as the supplicant cannot make said Antoine return to the city of Châlons because of the scandal that he would cause as much for the supplicant as for his other children who are all in a state to be established the supplicant has come to the decision to have said Antoine brought to Paris.

This is why, My Lord, the supplicant asks you with a most profound respect for the honor of Your Protection and most humbly beseeches you to order that said Antoine be taken to the house of detention to remain there for correction until said Antoine has shown signs that he recognizes his libertinage and a more orderly conduct.

And the petitioner, My Lord, will wish for you and Your Illustrious family.

Simon Compère.

Ars. Arch. Bastille 11004, fol. 197 (1728)

This March 27, 1728.

Saint-Martin Prison.

Monsieur,

I have the honor of forwarding unto you a petition that came to me from Châlons to be presented unto you on the subject of a young libertine age twenty-two named Antoine Compère along with the letters written to me on his subject including among others one from his brother dating from the 24th of the present month as I found that the petition did not offer enough explanation and was insufficient, I asked that I be sent a power of attorney from the father and the mother made before a notary, and certified by a judge of the area, which would explain the nature of the libertinage and disorderliness of this young man, but as the family had him arrested in Fismes and taken to Paris to Saint-Martin prison, the warden who knew that I was responsible for this matter told me that he could not keep him without a Committal, so as to not compromise himself before the Parlement and as I cannot do this without your order, I pray you to sign one to authorize this.

Commit him until the power of attorney arrives. I spoke with this libertine, he admitted to me that it was true that he took a silver cup and a goblet from his father, but that after reflection, he placed these effects in the hands of the curé of Saint-Étienne au Temple—in order to have them returned to his father. He also admits that he sold some candles and a pair of mules that he took from his father, he does not admit to the other things of which he is accused.

I am with a most profound respect Monsieur your [illegible].

Simonnet.

Ars. Arch. Bastille 11004, no folio (1728)

In Châlons, this May 24, 1728.

Monsieur,

Do I dare take the liberty of assuring you of my most humble respects although I do not have the honor of being known to You, I beseech you that you might wish to allow it.

M. Mouret to whom you took pains to write in reply to the letter that he had addressed to M. Simonet, communicated to me your letter dated May 16, 1728. I am sorry for the pains that you took to go see if the young man you signify had arrived by the Fismes stagecoach. He is currently in the Saint-Martin-des-Champs prison awaiting his fate.

I have the honor of telling you, Monsieur, that I have the misfortune of being the brother of this young man, I was unable to carry out the procedure contained in your letter, my father being absent.

I join my prayers with those of the family to beseech you that you might wish to do us a favor and grant us your help. I ask you in grace that you might wish to recommend to the warden of Saint-Martin prison, that he might hold him until we have done as you signified.

I warn you in advance that this brother conducts himself badly which led him to commit libertinage at the expense of others, which is to say that in order to give himself to his passion, he stole from several houses in the countryside, even some in Châlons, any effects that he could get his hands on even including a silver goblet from the home of a bourgeois of this city, he spent eight months selling everything that he was able to take from my father's house, and finally he bragged that he wished to roam the countryside and that he would absolutely not fail to give others something to talk about even saying that he would get himself arrested to dishonor his family, you can judge for yourself that this young man is insane.

Would it not be possible to have him arrested as a vagabond by the watch, I beseech you that you might wish to honor me with your response.

Compère, Receiver and Comptroller of fees,

charges, and reserves.

I reiterate that if this young man is given his freedom, the family will be dishonored entirely.

The warden will be paid what he is owed, be so good as to inform him of this and that he is to have my brother live on bread and water.

I will perhaps be happy enough to find occasions to show you my gratitude for all of your goodness.

Ars. Arch. Bastille 11004, fol. 194 (1728)

Simonnet

M. Rossignol will be so good as to obtain an order of the King to transfer Antoine Compère over twenty-three years of age from the prisons of Saint-Martin to the House of Bicêtre. In execution of the power of attorney of his father and his mother.

Ars. Arch. Bastille 11004, no folio (1728)

Marie Anne Lefébure

To My Lord

the Lieutenant General of Police

My Lord,

Jean Lefébure clerk in the *greffe des gens de Mainmorte*[7] in the diocese of Paris and Louise Magny his wife, most humbly represent unto Your Highness that they have twelve children to support and that they have the misfortune of having for their eldest a girl of around twenty-three years of age, disturbed, whom they were never able to correct and who on the 2nd of the month of November last absented herself from the paternal home and they have been unable to find her since; as we are persuaded that she is continuing a life of debauchery, we appeal unto Your Highness to obtain an order of the King to have her locked up in the hospital for several years in order to make penance for her wrongs, and we will pray to Heaven for the prosperity and health of Your Highness.

J. Lefébure, L. Magny.

We discovered on January 18, 1728, that said daughter is in a room with one Billam who had counseled her escape rue de Bourbon on the side of rue Saint-Denis, at the Saint-Sauveur signpost, on the third floor, at the end of a little hallway; she has changed her name, calls herself Mademoiselle Le Blond.

Ars. Arch. Bastille 11018, fol. 356 (1728)

Marie Françoise Le Normand

To My Lord
the Lieutenant General of Police

My Lord,

Médard Le Normand resident of Brunoy, Joseph Majoral, curé of said place, and the undersigned residents of it, most humbly beseech Your Highness that he might wish to order that Marie Françoise Le Normand daughter of said Médard Le Normand around eighteen years of age, be locked up in the hospital as a prostituted girl having been debauched by certain fellows with whom she abandoned herself to all manner of vices around a year ago and she committed several small thefts such as chickens and laundry from her father's neighbors and others. What is more, she escaped from the sight of her said father and the residents of said Brunoy for more than three months and could not be discovered, nor found that Monday last the 20th of the present month of September 1728 she was arrested a few leagues from here by her relatives themselves who took her to the prison of said Brunoy where she is currently, threatening that if she is freed she will burn down her father's house and that of the neighbors.

This is why the suppliants appeal unto the authority of Your Highness to forestall the dire consequences of such abandonment by which the father and stepmother with other children to support have been reduced nearly to mendicancy. And said suppliants My Lord, will never cease to wish to Heaven for the health and prosperity of Your Highness.

Signed: Mayort curé; Bovineau, Coret,
H. Garonne, Fournier, Feurrien, Guichard,
François Merglée, Dandelle, Duviniery,
procurator Pascal, Michel Pasquier,
Guillaume Cozeau.

Ars. Arch. Bastille 11019, fol. 31 (1728)

Laurent Michel Levasseur

To My Lord
the Lieutenant General of Police

My Lord,

Laurent Levasseur, merchant miller in Rouen, most humbly represents unto Your Highness, that trusting Laurent Michel Levasseur his nineteen-year-old son he sent him to fetch nine thousand livres of merchandise that he consumed and embezzled with harlots and libertines.

The supplicant once alerted to his son's debauchery came to Paris to recover his effects or the little of them that remained in his son's hands. He endeavored to find him in Paris and its surroundings through his searches. He has found his residence which he changes from day to day in fear of the correction that his father the supplicant wishes to give him. Consequent to the orders that he hopes Your Highness might wish to give him.

Levasseur, father; Dumarout, uncle.

Ars. Arch. Bastille 11019, fol. 335 (1728)

On the visit that I made a few days ago to Bicêtre I found, Monsieur, Laurent Michel Levasseur your son who has been in this house since the month of December 1728 because of his libertinage.

As this sanction seems sufficient, I think that you should make arrangements to obtain his freedom which I did not wish to propose without telling you first, or at least have him placed in a house where he will be better off.

I am, Monsieur, entirely yours.

Hérault.
In Paris this August 25, 1729.

Ars. Arch. Bastille 11019, fol. 336 (1728)

Louise Marguerite Pagin

To My Lord
the Lieutenant General of Police

My Lord,

one Pierre Pagin, dancing master in Paris, residing rue Sainte-Anne, Saint-Roch hill and parish, most humbly beseeches Your Highness, to grant him the grace that he dares to take the liberty of requesting of You on the subject of Louise Marguerite Pagin his eldest daughter, who for four and a half years has led a most disorderly and most scandalous life, having committed several thefts, frequented all manner of libertine men and women, and threatened to have me murdered by the soldiers of the watch with whom she traffics, I did everything I could to prevent all of these disorders, I was unable to put an end to them, and as she yet continues this same unruliness, this is, My Lord, what obliges me to appeal unto Your Highness to most humbly beseech you to be so good as to have her locked up for the rest of her life or sent to the Islands, I will redouble as will all my family, our wishes to Heaven for the health and prosperity of Your Highness.

We the undersigned Pierre Pagin (father of Louise Margueritte Pagin), Pierre Maillard (her uncle), Jean Coffiniez (her second cousin, on her mother's side), and Jean Pagin (cousin on her father's side), certify the present memoir truthful, without any reservations as to the above declaration in testimony whereof we have signed.

Ars. Arch. Bastille 11024. fol. 303 (1728)

Jeanne Cécile Pezan

To My Lord
the Lieutenant General of Police

Michel Pezan, merchant parchment maker and Marie Hélène Adam, his wife residing rue Saint-Germain-l'Auxerrois, have the honor of most humbly representing unto you, that they have the misfortune of having a daughter, named Jeanne Cécile Pezan, age twenty-one, who has plunged herself into an awful libertinage, having abandoned the paternal home in order to give herself entirely to debauchery, which she currently continues with the first passerby, and she vagabonds in Paris with all manner of persons. The supplicants, stricken by the liveliest pain, had presented you with a petition that had been sent to Monsieur the Superintendent Soucy, who is well acquainted with the bad conduct of their daughter, and of the justness of their complaint, he replied to the petition, which was then lost in your offices, this is what has obliged the supplicants to appeal unto Your Highness once again, through a second petition, seeing that the debauchery of their unhappy daughter is known and they most humbly request that after Monsieur the Superintendent Soucy will have given you an account of the conduct of said Cécile Pezan, you might have, if it would please you, be so good as to grant them an order of the King to have arrested said daughter who currently lives in a furnished room with an apprentice tailor with whom she lives in debauchery, then locked up in the hospital, Your Highness would be doing a great charity, and the supplicants will be obliged to pray the Lord for Your prosperity and health.

Marie Hélène Adam, Passault, J. Boudard,
Lanvoureux, Vinsant Rion, Étienne
Lolette, F. Le Michon, M. Rivière.

Ars. Arch. Bastille 11025, fol. 210 (1728)

Edme Joseph Eli

To My Lord Bertin,
Lieutenant General of Police

My Lord,

Joseph Eli, traveling wine merchant and his wife, residing place Maubert, most humbly remonstrate unto Your Highness that they have the misfortune of having for a son Edme Joseph Eli, age nineteen, for whose upbringing they spared no expense and after having employed every kind approach to recall him to his duty, they were unable to gain any change in his conduct, they have the sorrow of seeing that their son instead of behaving in an orderly manner passes his days in debauchery, frequenting a number of libertines with whom he libertines and debauches himself and spends his nights who knows where without the supplicants being able to learn where he sleeps, which has made the supplicants fear for the worst.

This is what obliges them to appeal unto the authority of Your Highness to beseech him to order that he be locked up in Bicêtre where he was already locked up last year as a punishment for his unruliness and to prevent him from dishonoring his family, and for this they wish to Heaven for the prosperity of Your Highness.

Eli (father).

This declaration is truthful, the father and the mother, my parishioners are honest folk; they deserve the kindness of Monsieur the Lieutenant General of Police.

Pregnault, curé of Saint-Étienne-du-Mont.

The petition is signed by Villy, Md Chapellier, Saint-Étienne-du-Mont parish, Philippe Thomas Morel, lawyer (knows the Eli son to be a vagabond), Megret, primary leaseholder.

Ars. Arch. Bastille 12000, fol. 36 (1758)

May 15, 1756.

Monsieur Chaban

Monsieur,

Enclosed is the petition that one Eli presented unto you to have his son locked up in Bicêtre. I postponed reporting unto you the clarifications that I made regarding the conduct of this young man for some time because the father and the mother having decided he would work for the masons, engaged me to wait until they had been assured of the changes that they hoped to see in him. But now they complain once again that their son continues to be disturbed, that he has completely abandoned their house where he no longer returns to sleep, that he sleeps in the market stalls of place Maubert to spend the night with other vagabonds like himself and that he has no occupation.

These facts as well as those in the memoir were attested to me by different persons who have spoken with a single voice about it. I therefore esteem, Monsieur, that there is no hindrance to granting the requested order.

I am with a profound respect Monsieur your most humble servant.

Superintendent Lemaire.

Ars. Arch. Bastille 12000, no folio (1758)

Marie Madeleine Hébert

To My Lord the Lieutenant General of Police

My Lord,

Anne Philippe Faure, laundrywoman residing quai des Ormes, place aux Veaux, lodging with a fruit seller at 22, Saint-Paul parish, has the honor of most humbly representing unto Your Highness, that having raised the five children of one of her sisters who were orphaned of father and mother from their most tender youth, that she nonetheless suffers despite the good example and instruction that she gave them, to see that M. M. Hébert her niece is abandoning herself to libertinage and has for several years conducted herself in a most disturbed manner dishonoring herself entirely, not wishing to listen to any remonstrance often returning with great scandal at midnight or one o'clock, which is for her aunt and all the family who raised her the subject of the bitterest pain and which finally resolved them seeing as there is no way to make her change, to appeal unto the Justice of Your Highness beseeching him that after having himself informed of the truth of these facts to have her arrested and locked up in the hospital by order of the King to avoid the dire consequences of such odious conduct, the supplicant who exhausted herself raising these children is in no state to bear any cost or pay a pension, being the only resource left to a destroyed family and particularly to the supplicant who hopes for this grace from Your Charity and natural equity and will wish for the health and prosperity of My Lord.

Anne Philippe Faure; Louis Faure, her
uncle; Savard, brother-in-law; Louis Hébert,
brother, J. B. Hébert, brother; Marie Coutant,
aunt; François Hébert, brother.

Ars. Arch. Bastille 12000, fol. 15 (1758)

April 4, 1758.

My dear friend Madelaine Hebere,

I am seizing the chance to put quill to paper to inquire as to the state of your health of which I am greatly worried, I have now sent you two letters to which you have made no reply you signified to me in your letter that you were angry with me. I myself am far angrier still to have written you two letters and for you to have made me no reply. I do not know if it is because I had asked you for money you should know that in the letters I send to my father I asked them as well, my dear friend when you send me three livres or indeed six livres that a poor solider such as myself, one does need such things in the state that I am in my dear friend; I think that you would give me such pleasure, I pray you in grace to give me this pleasure, I embrace you from the depths of my heart my dear friend, good-bye, I pray you to reply to me as soon as you have received this if you only knew in what anxiety; my dear friend, I pray you in grace to always be as faithful to me as you can; as for me, I am indeed, thank God, faithful toward you, I think that you are doing the same; I conclude by embracing you from the bottom of my heart. I pray you again in grace, my dear friend to answer me as soon as you have received this letter, to reply to me to remove me from the anxiety that I am in.

I am always your most humble and obedient and legitimate lover.

Thibault.

Here is my address:

Thibault, soldier in the regiment of the guards
2d battalion, Saint-Omer.

Ars. Arch. Bastille 12000, no folio (1758)

July 20, 1758.

Monsieur,

Anne Philippe Faure, washerwoman, who raised the five children of one of her sisters who had lost their father and their mother at a young age thought it her duty to present you with a petition to have locked up in the hospital Marie Madeleine Hébert, one of her nieces age twenty-four. This girl has unfortunately given herself to debauchery and has taken for one of her darling lovers one Thibault, soldier in the Guards. The departure of this soldier for Flanders led the relatives to think that their remonstrances might have an effect on the spirit of this girl whom they have urged in vain for four months to conduct herself properly.

Today, seeing that said M. M. Hébert continues to behave herself worse and worse and as she abandons herself to the first passerby, they think that there is no reason to delay the punishment she deserves.

I have listened to the uncles, aunts, brothers and brothers-in-law of this girl, all testify that her libertinage is complete.

In these circumstances, I found that said M. M. Hébert deserves to be locked away in the hospital she will be fortunate if she can draw principles of Religion from the instruction that she will receive so as to replace her conduct with a more regular one.

(Police report.)

Ars. Arch. Bastille 12000, fol. 24 (1758)

To My Lord
the Lieutenant General of Police

My Lord,

One Anne Philippe Faure, aunt of Marie Madeleine Hébert who had beseeched Your Highness that he might wish to place said niece in the house of the Salpêtrière, which she obtained from Your Highness on August 7, 1758, most humbly beseeches Your Highness that he might wish to grant her release so that she be placed according to her desire and that of all her family in the Communauté des Filles du Sauveur. This is what she desires of Your Highness as she wishes to Heaven for the health and prosperity of Your Highness.

Anne Philippe Faure.

Ars. Arch. Bastille 12000, fol. 31 (1758)

Marie Noëlle Rebours

To My Lord the Count de Saint Florentin,
Minister and Secretary of State

My Lord,

Jean Rebours commonly called Labonté, heretofore domestic of Mgr the Duke de Gesvres residing in Saint-Ouen, most humbly represents unto Your Highness that he has for a daughter one Marie Noëlle Rebours age nineteen, that for the last four to five years she has given herself to libertinage she does not attend Church, she is currently with a soldier in the French Guards, despite the good upbringing that he endeavored to provide her, and the remonstrances that he made to her to retrieve her from her disorders were unable to gain anything from her, on the contrary, she has lost her respect for her father, and out of fear that worse is yet to come, the supplicant was counseled to appeal unto Your Highness such that it might please you, My Lord, to grant an order of the King to have her locked up in the house of the hospital. He hopes for this grace from Your equity and the supplicant will continue his prayers for the preservation of the health of Your Highness.

Jeanne Bourti, La Goulette,
Geneviève Trouillet, François Compoint,
Eustache Compoint, Gabriel Dubois,
Coufens, P. Dumay, Le Meriel.

Ars. Arch. Bastille 12014, fol. 171 (1758)

I the undersigned, curé priest of Saint-Ouen-sur-Seine, certify that the one named in the petition enclosed herein has always conducted herself, while residing in my parish, in a manner that could only dishonor her parents, in testimony whereof I have signed.

In Saint-Ouen, this October 14, 1758.
Coulon.

Ars. Arch. Bastille 12014, fol. 172 (1758)

Monsieur,

In execution of the order that you addressed me, I had Monsieur Rebours and his family sign the petition that he presented to the minister against one Marie Noëlle Rebours his daughter, and I verified the declaration.

For five years this girl has led a life of the worst conduct during the trip that M. de Sachelles made to Saint-Ouen to the house of M. the Prince de Soubise, a few years ago, she made the acquaintance of men in uniform and since then has known no other society. The Swiss from Colombe, Courbevoie and Asnières each had her in turn; she then moved on to the French Guards. Her father forced her to return to his home several times; he attempted to make her look within herself, she seemed to be listening to him, promised that she would change and left the next day. Said Rebours is known as a perfectly honest man and it was only a few days ago he learned from trustworthy persons known to him and persons of faith the outlines of his daughter's story which prove that she has no more probity than she has modesty.

Prulhiere.

Ars. Arch. Bastille 12014, fol. 173 (1758)

To My Lord Bertin,
Lieutenant General of Police

Antoine Gilbert, innkeeper in Saint-Denis in France, beseeches you, My Lord, that you might wish to acquaint yourself with a memoir that should have been forwarded unto you by M. the Count de Saint Florentin for the freedom of Marie Noëlle Rebours his second cousin, who has been detained in the Salpêtrière since December 21, 1758, having been arrested by the mounted constabulary [*maréchaussée*] of Saint-Denis at the request of Jean Rebours her father all because of bad humor and to please his present wife the stepmother of said cousin, and without any legitimate grounds. The supplicant will be responsible for her conduct and for her morals, before the eyes of his wife, and of all his family. And will pray God for Your Highness.

Ars. Arch. Bastille 12014, fol. 175 (1758)

To My Lord the Count de Saint Florentin,
Minister and Secretary of State

My Lord,

Antoine Gilbert, innkeeper in Saint-Denis, and Nicolas Trerel, tavern keeper in Saint-Maur, the former a cousin of Marie Noëlle Rebours, native of Saint-Maur, and the latter her own uncle, most humbly represent unto Your Highness that to please a father's second wife who can rightly be regarded as a wicked stepmother [*marâtre*], Jean Rebours, father of said Marie Noëlle Rebours, was not ashamed to degrade nature by surprising the Religion of different persons so as to have his daughter taken, and even to affix the signatures of relatives that are completely false which brought a higher order to have his said daughter arrested, this was executed by the mounted constabulary in Saint-Denis on the 22d of December last and she is locked away in the hospital for correction like a wretch. The supplicants, on the contrary, My Lord, assure you that this unfortunate girl is innocent, and they present you with a certificate from different persons with whom she has resided who testify in her favor, an unworthy stepmother is behind this crime and a father established in Saint-Ouen who is too indulgent with her and who forgets the blood of his first bed, all her misfortune.

The supplicants stricken by pain implore your commiseration My Lord for this poor victim, the undersigned Guilbert requests again alongside others that he be allowed to take her in and care for her. They will pray the Lord for the preservation of Your Highness.

Ars. Arch. Bastille 12014, fol. 176 (1758)

My Lord,

I have the honor of informing Your Highness that Marie Noëlle Rebours, born in Saint-Ouen-sur-Seine, was arrested in Saint-Denis on December 22 last and then taken to the hospital for no other subject nor legitimate cause than a lack of uprightness and of sentiments of Jean Rebours, her father, and the woman he wed in his second marriage.

This unnatural father had his eldest son from his first marriage sent to the Islands, and hopes to be able to distance his daughter, who is currently locked up, in order to possess the meager estate of his children in peace.

As this girl is irreproachable, Nicolas Tresel, tavern keeper in Saint-Ouen, maternal uncle of said girl, and Antoine Gilbert, innkeeper in Saint-Denis, cousin of this girl, and who wish take her in, appeal unto Your authority and equity, My Lord, to obtain the freedom of said Marie Noëlle Rebours, offering Your Highness, the complete proof of what I have the honor of advancing. I have the honor of being with the most profound respect, My Lord, of Your Highness, the most humble and most obedient servant.

Deurdes, curé of the Island.
Island of Saint-Denis, June 21, 1759.

Ars. Arch. Bastille 12014, fol. 180–181 (1758)

My Lady,

I beg of you a thousand pardons for not having yet had the honor of presenting you with my respects at the beginning of this new year; several causes prevented me from doing so, I hope that you might wish to forgive me when I tell you the reasons this week at the latest.

I have a grace to request of you, I flatter myself that you might wish to grant it me, which is to speak to M. Chabannes, secretary of M. the Lieutenant of Police in order to have released from the Hôpital général a girl from my parish who has been detained there for around a month. One of her relatives offers to take her in with him and answers for her conduct according to the petition that was presented to M. de Saint Florentin and the certificates that I gave as to the life and morals of the man who wishes to take her in his charge.

I hope My Lady, that you would might wish to grant me this grace as well as that of believing myself with profound respect, My Lady, Your most humble and most obedient servant.

Coulon, curé of Saint-Ouen.
January 21, 1759.

Ars. Arch. Bastille 12014, fol. 183 (1758)

Marie Toussine Le Blanc

To My Lord
the Lieutenant General of Police

My Lord,

Jean-Baptiste Le Blanc, woodshop apprentice for Monsieur Rémy Robinet de Grenant, wood seller, and his wife, most respectfully declare unto Your

Highness that being quite certain of the disorderly conduct of Marie Toussine their daughter, they have decided to have her locked up to which effect they most humbly beseech that Your Highness might wish to give them an authorization to have her arrested and taken to the Salpêtrière, offering that come what may, despite their having nine other children to support, they will pay a pension; they will continue their Wishes for the preservation of Your Highness.

Vuilleret (wife of Le Blanc),
Vuilleret (maternal uncle),
Badin (paternal cousin).

I the undersigned priest serving the parish of Saint-Nicolas-du-Chardonnet, certify that the supplicants deserve to have their request, which was certified to me to be truthful, granted.

In Paris June 6, 1758,
Nommel, priest.

I certify the present supplication to be truthful.

Loreau, priest.

Ars. Arch. Bastille 12004, fol. 35 (1758)

I saw the relatives of Marie Toussine Le Blanc against whom her father and mother presented You with the petition enclosed herein.

It was unanimously attested to me that this young girl age nineteen has been prostituted for five years; that she began by going to the house of the Montigny woman from where her father and mother retrieved her; having escaped from their home a second time, she was kept by a man for a time and after that began offering herself to the first passerby; that this is the way she currently conducts herself in a room she occupies in the house of one Morel, lemonade seller rue Montmartre at the corner of the Boulevard.

In these circumstances, given the concurrence of the paternal and maternal relatives of this girl, alongside her father and mother, I esteem, Monsieur, with Your good pleasure, that there is reason to grant them their request for an order to have her locked up.

I am with profound respect, Monsieur, Your most humble and most obedient servant.

Superintendent Lemaire.
July 6, 1758.

Ars. Arch. Bastille 12004, fol. 37 (1758)

I certify that Mademoiselle Le Blanc resided in my house around six years ago in the capacity of a woman of the world [*fille du monde*] for the space of six weeks and that she had been brought me by one Geneviève Danton to whom I give eighteen livres to her mother when she learned that she was residing in my house, twelve livres per week she was perfectly acquainted with the trade that she carried on in my house in testimony whereof I have signed the present certificate and am ready to affirm this in the presence of magistrats if necessary.

In Paris the 1st of August 1758.
Montigni.

Ars. Arch. Bastille 12004, fol. 44 (1758)

I certify that Mademoiselle Le Blanc resided in my house during the time that I kept my house rue Mazarine for the space of three months in the capacity of a woman of the world with the consent of her father and mother who came to my house to see her and eat with her there. This father and mother invited me several times to their house, where I went with her and Monsieur Darnerl, surgeon, to arrange that I finally finding her a man to provide for her in testimony whereof I have signed the present certificate and am ready to declare this to the magistrate myself if this were to be necessary, in Paris the 1st of August 1758.

Jeanne Herment.

Ars. Arch. Bastille 12004, fol. 45 (1758)

I certify that Mademoiselle Le Blanc resided in my house for fifteen days in the capacity of a woman of the world around six years ago and she was brought to me by her mother and one Lucas when I resided rue des Boucheries-Saint-Honoré where her father as well as her mother came to see her in testimony whereof I have signed the present certificate and am ready to affirm this in front of the magistrate if necessary.

In Paris this 1st of August 1758.
Baudouïn.

I certify that the father of Mademoiselle Le Blanc told me around six weeks ago that he was very happy with his daughter, that she had just given him six gold louis to have her brother discharged from the French Guards and that she was ready to assist them in every way.

Baudouïn.

Ars. Arch. Bastille 12004, fol. 46 (1758)

I certify that Mademoiselle Marie Toussine Le Blanc resided in my house for the space of a year when I kept my house rue des Vieux-Augustins, this was around four years ago; that she was brought to me at the time by her mother and her grandmother so that I would receive her among my pensioners and that I gave her mother six livres a week, that her father and mother came to see her several times in my house, that the two of them both knew the life she was leading in my house, in testimony whereof I have signed the present certificate as containing the most exact truth and am ready to affirm this myself to the magistrate if necessary.

In Paris the 1st of August 1758.

Pequet.

Ars. Arch. Bastille 12004, fol. 47 (1758)

We the undersigned, certify that for the nearly eighteen months that Mademoiselle Le Blanc has resided in our neighborhood, we have never remarked anything scandalous about her conduct and on the contrary we declare that she has always behaved herself with great decency and prudence.

Made in Paris, rue Montmartre, near the Boulevard, this August 2, 1758.

B. Morel (lemonade seller), P. Buffet (domestic residing in the house of Monsieur Courtan), M. Isselot (haberdasher), Thierry (package officer [*officier emballeur*]), Mattrazon (neighbor), Dupont (tobacconist [*débitant de tabac*]), neighbor (beadle of Mr the Count de Courteu), Enfant (retired gendarme), Delamarre wife (baker), wife of Ducatelli (butler [*maître d'hôtel*]).

Ars. Arch. Bastille 12004, fol. 48 (1758)

To My Lord
the Lieutenant General of Police

My Lord,

Marie Toussine Le Blanc, arrested by order of the King the first of this month and taken to the Salpêtrière, throws herself upon the knees of Your Highness and has the honor of representing unto him that for the six years that she was out in the world, it was always with the knowledge of her father and mother who even profited from the product of her debauchery as it will be possible for Your Highness to have proven and reported to him by ones Montigni, Baudouin, Hermand and Hecquet, women who keep public houses where her father and mother came to see her, to eat and to receive money each week, and in several of which her mother had herself placed her to be a woman of the world, that having sought to end this life of libertinage, and having found a gallant man who retrieved her from it these same father and mother, wishing no doubt to deprive her of the furniture and effects in her possession, appealed unto the authority of Your Highness to have her arrested and punished for the wrongs that they shared in by their acquiescence.

The supplicant dares to assure you, My Lord, that in her neighborhood where she lodged porte Montmartre, she never caused any scandal. It is only with regret that she finds herself forced to make the turpitude of her parents known to Your Highness, she awaits her freedom from Your Charity, My Lord, and will never cease her prayers for the prosperity of Your Highness.

Marie Toussine le Blanc.

Ars. Arch. Bastille 12004, fol. 50 (1758)

My Lord,

Forever filled with gratitude for your goodness, I throw myself upon your knees, I kiss them and solicit before Your Highness, grace for a father and mother who are guilty before him, but whose punishment would bring my Death; I would not hesitate to return for a long time to the place from where I was released by your goodness, rather than to know that they were there for an instant, and in my captivity my respect for them would never cease, as well as the gratitude that I owe to the probity of Your Justice, grant their grace to my tears, My Lord, their misfortunes would be for me a second punishment for the wrongs that I might have committed; they have a family to support, she would be forced to distraction in the hospitals out of misery, this would be the height of my suffering.

I have every hope of Your Clemency, and I dare to assure you, My Lord, that Your Commiseration for my father and mother would give me back my Life. What sorrow it would be for me if I knew that they were in irons.

I have the honor of being with the most profound respect, of Your Highness, My Lord, your most humble and most obedient servant.

M. T. Le Blanc.
This August 8, 1758.

It is I, My Lord, who had the honor of presenting myself this morning to an audience with you for the same prayer.

Ars. Arch. Bastille 12004, fol. 52 (1758)

To My Lord
the Lieutenant General of Police

My Lord,

Jean Baptiste Le Blanc, woodshop apprentice residing in Paris, rue de Seine, Saint-Victor neighborhood, most humbly represents that the 15th of this month, Anne Villeret his wife, washerwoman, was taken from him and led by Your Orders to the hospital where she is detained.

The supplicant who never recognized anything in the conduct of his wife that could possibly have merited such an affront, can only attribute it to the most remarkable deception of the Religion of Your Highness.

In fact, My Lord, these blows certainly arise from the credit that the eldest daughter of the supplicant acquired for herself by her unruliness. Herself detained by reason of her debauches, a protector who is even more dangerous and criminal because his employment gives him reason to be honored by Your Confidence, has had the art of procuring her freedom and it was not long afterwards that the storm befell the mother.

That the innocent were substituted for the guilty in this way, that a valetudinarian woman was taken from the arms of her husband like this, that she was torn from the tears of nine children who are in the most awful indigence and for the most part of the most tender young age, it must no doubt have been, My Lord, that quite grave crimes were imputed to her.

All that the supplicant was able to learn about the causes of this detention, is that his daughter and the man who protects her told a few persons that the supplicant's wife had favored the daughter's debauchery. In order to convince you, My Lord, of all the horror that must [illegible] a calumny such as this, the supplicant takes the liberty of enclosing with this memoir copies of different acts that prove that the supplicant and his wife continually did all they could to retrieve this girl from the libertinage to which she gave herself by quitting their home.

These acts are the testimony of Monsieur Feury, police inspector, that of the supplicant's wife, the letter of M. Berryer, consequent to which an inquiry was carried out before Monsieur the superintendent de Rochebrune that he dispatched to Your Highness, and which offers full proof that the order was given at the time to seize the Rodolphe and Montingy women and that the supplicant's wife is in no way suspected of the calumnious facts that some dare impute against her today.

Your Highness must arm himself with severity against the authors of this accusation. The supplicant flatters himself that you would not have had, My Lord, any regard for the indecent cries of this daughter against her mother, if her allegations had not been supported by several fabricated documents of which the supplicant has no knowledge. He reserves the right to demonstrate their falsity in the case that Your Highness would judge it fit to order their communication. The protector of the supplicant's daughter no doubt made use of several misleading devices, of several specious proofs, to obtain the order in question.

It is worth recalling the fact that we would tend to presume they used the most illicit channels. When the supplicant had his daughter locked up, this gave rise to several rumors against the father of this daughter whom people claimed to know and to see coming to visit her every day; and it was to the supplicant that this was said, there was therefore already an assumed paternity.

In these circumstances, I hope that you might wish, My Lord, to revoke the order that you gave on this subject and that you might return a wife to the supplicant, and a mother to a large family whose need for her is even greater as she was rendering them the greatest aid, which provided for their subsistence. They will continue their wishes for the preservation of My Lord.

Ars. Arch. Bastille 12004, fol. 64–65 (1758)

Monsieur,

With eyes bathed in tears I throw myself at your knees and ask you for my mother's freedom: the shock that took me when I learned of her detention left me bedridden with a great fever, otherwise I would have gone to throw myself at your feet and I would not have left them until I had obtained the grace of your goodness, or else I would have died of the liveliest pain; that Your Justice, My Lord, might allow itself to bend; my mother has ten children to support, and when she was arrested at home by Monsieur Ferrat, one of your inspectors, one of them was at her breast who had to be taken away from her; what a dagger's blow for a mother!

And what wrong this will do to the poor innocent child; my parents were terribly wrong when they tried to mislead Your Highness about me, it is true, they deserved punishment, but it is a great soul that forgives, Your own, My Lord, is susceptible to clemency, I hope for its effects, without this I would succumb to my pain, and I would die of grief.

I have the honor of being with a most profound respect, My Lord, of Your Highness, the most humble and most obedient servant.

Marie Toussaint Le Blanc.

Ars. Arch. Bastille 12004, fol. 72 (1758)

To My Lord Bertin,
Lieutenant General of Police

My Lord,

Marie Le Blanc, eldest daughter has the honor of most respectfully representing unto you that ever since Marie Anne Villeret, her mother, was locked away by your order in the Salpêtrière, it has been impossible for her to care and provide for her seven brothers and sisters who are of very young age and who have an indispensable need for motherly care and as their poor mother was only arrested upon a false accusation, they all dare to throw themselves at the feet of Your Highness so that in consideration of this, My Lord, it would please you to look with pity upon the deplorable state of seven poor children who were deprived of motherly care and having no other cannot subsist.

And by an effect of Your ordinary Charity, order the release of their mother, they all offer their prayers to Heaven for the prosperity of Your Highness.

[*There are two orders for the arrest of the father of Marie Toussine, Jean Baptiste Le Blanc, followed by an order:* "Suspend the execution of this order, and for the present moment only execute that of the Le Blanc wife." (August 11, 1758).]

Ars. Arch. Bastille 12004, fol. 76 (1758)

To Monsieur Bertin

Monsieur,

Because you think that Marie Anne Villeret, wife of Jean Baptiste Le Blanc has been sufficiently punished, I enclose herein the order of the King that you suggested to have her released from the hospital.

I am always most perfectly, Monsieur, Your most humble and most obedient servant.

This August 29, 1758.
Florentin.

Ars. Arch. Bastille 12004, fol. 79 (1758)

Françoise Villette

To My Lord Bertin,
Lieutenant General of Police

My Lord,

Pierre Villette privileged surgeon and Anne Jacotin his spouse residing rue du Figuier passage Saint-Paul, have for a daughter Françoise Villette age twenty, who some time ago escaped at night from the house of the supplicant father and mother. They had not given her any legitimate cause, all this to lead the unruly life of a prostituted girl left and right; during this interval the suppliants retrieved her to their house to put her on a good Christian path, doing so with the voice of kindness. Despite this, she once again escaped through a window. She continues her wicked unruliness, everyone fearing from this daughter who dishonors the family, learning that she lives with one Charier, a faithless man [*homme sans aveu*], who sometimes works as a scribe outside the Palace, lodging together one day in one place, the next in another; the suppliants father and mother, beseech You, My Lord, that you might wish to order an inquiry into what is known to many honest folk and after this to grant them an order to have her arrested and placed in the Salpêtrière until such a time as God will do her the grace of making her recollect herself. They hope for this grace despite being in no state to pay a pension owing to the sad state in which they have fallen, in gratitude, they will never cease to pray God for the precious days of Your Highness.

Pierre Villette, father; Anne Jacotin, mother;
Antoine Henriquez.

Ars. Arch. Bastille 12018, fol. 232 (1758)

DOMESTIC VIOLENCE

Pierre Bechon

To Monsieur
the Lieutenant General of Police

Jacques Bechon, market gardener residing behind the Salpêtrière, Saint-Martin parish, most humbly represents unto Your Highness that he has a son named Pierre Bechon, age twenty-four, whose conduct has been most unruly for eight years, who leads a vagabond's life, who only comes into the suppliant's house to abuse him with dishonest and insolent words, which decorum does not permit the suppliant to repeat, along with oaths and blasphemy, stealing everything that he can take from the house, sometimes coming in through the windows, breaking into closets and chests, thus he fears that this bad conduct will have consequences that are even more troublesome and that are inevitable, he beseeches Your Highness to have the charity to watch over an oppressed father by having said Pierre Bechon his son locked away in Bicêtre, being in no state to pay his pension. He hopes for this grace from your ordinary clemency and will never cease his wishes and prayers to heaven for the prosperity and preservation of Your Highness.

Cosignatories: two sons-in-law.

[*On the back:*]

Prémontuel, Superintendent, esteems that there is reason to grant said Bechon senior what he requests.

The aunt of Bechon, wet nurse of Mme Herauch, assures that he is "a very bad subject."

Ars. Arch. Bastille 10999, fol. 202 (1728)

Sulpice Antoine Danville

To My Lord
the Lieutenant General of Police

Monsieur,

Madeleine Legrand, widow of eight years of Antoine Danville, artillery officer, most humbly represents unto Monsieur, that having several reasons to complain of the conduct of Sulpice Antoine Danville her son, native of the parish of Saint-Sulpice, around twenty-two years of age, as he took from his mother a diamond, a purse of tokens [*jetons*],[8] a half-dozen silver spoons and forks, a quantity of shirts and linens on various occasions, having even in his mother's absence broken into closets and commodes to remove and carry off everything in them, having even on the 9th of this month taken the habit, vest and stockings, hat and wig of a sick man in the Charité, where he himself had taken the novice's habit, which habit said monks then stripped him of for the reasons given in their certificates, and it is for all of these reasons that said Madeleine Legrand along with all the uncles, aunts, nephews, relatives and friends of said Sulpice Danville, most humbly beseech you, My Lord, that you might wish to give an order that he be locked away in a secure place to prevent him from further dishonoring his family by his crimes, whose punishment is reserved for justice.

There follow ten signatures.

Ars. Arch. Bastille 11005, fol. 164 (1728)

To Monsieur
the Lieutenant General of Police

My Lord,

The widow Danville, most humbly represents unto Your Highness that it pleased him—upon the supplicant's declaration—to grant an order, around two and a half months ago, to have her son Sulpice Antoine Danville locked away in Bicêtre, where he has been detained since that time, because of several youthful actions, that Your Highness, having granted to Monsieur from the Indies Company an order to remove several young people from Bicêtre for immediate departure, said Sulpice Antoine Danville was among the chosen and is on the list to be sent to the Islands. As the supplicant cannot see any other course to cause him to leave his youthful urges behind other than consenting to this, she most humbly beseeches, My Lord, to approve this and give the order that he be removed from Bicêtre so as to depart Monday next for the Islands, and she will never cease her prayers for the preservation of Your Highness.

Ars. Arch. Bastille 11005, fol. 170 (1728)

Pierre Ducauroy

> To My Lord Hérault,
> State Councillor
> Lieutenant General of Police

My Lord,

Christophe Le Moyne, glazier *[vitrier]*, and Anne Vincent, his wife, residing rue de la Roquette, faubourg Saint-Antoine, Sainte-Marguerite parish represent for the second time unto Your Highness that they have the misfortune of having a son-in-law named Pierre de Corrois, wigmaker, who keeps shop at the entrance to rue Charenton, who since November 10, 1722, when he married Marie Lemoyne, their daughter, has never ceased to abuse her with blows and atrocious insults, treating her like the lowliest wretch, constantly threatening to kill her, this man is a perfect drunkard, who has no fear of God, nor respect for anyone, and is searching for a means to bring about the supplicants' demise, insulting them in their home, breaking and smashing their furniture and merchandise, even to the point of attempting to take the supplicant's life, if he had not been rescued: the complaints that were twice brought before Monsieur the Superintendent de la Sarrie are proof of his bad conduct.

The supplicants seeing themselves insulted every day by this wretch and in mortal danger, presented Your Highness with a petition signed by bourgeois, merchants and retired subsacrists of the parish, certified by M. the curé concerning the scandalous life of said Corrois, said petition was recorded and replied to by said Monsieur the Superintendent de la Sarrie and on the books of Your Secretary, and it was then forwarded to Monsieur Rossignol who says he sent it to Monsieur Chapentrie, who cannot find it.

The supplicants seeing that said Corrois continues his violence with the same fury, that their lives are in no way safe, appeal unto the authority and Justice of My Lord, that it might please him to have him locked up by *lettre de cachet* in whatever place would please him, the supplicants who sought out, but in vain every possible means of recalling him to his duty, hope that Your

Highness, heeding these two petitions, will grant them what they dare to request of him for the safety of their lives, this will oblige them to wish for the preservation and prosperity of Your Highness.

> Christophe Le Moyne (father),
> Anne Vincent (his mother),
> Le Bègue (brother),
> Anne Le Moyne (sister).

Ars. Arch. Bastille 11007, fol. 177 (1728)

My Lord,

You have summoned to appear Monsieur Du Corois as well as the father and the mother of his wife, the father is quite ill, bedridden and his wife is partially paralyzed, in no state to appear before My Lord; as for Monsieur Du Caurroy, you will meet the most treacherous possible man, who upon the remonstrances of My Lord that you must indeed make he does not believe that he deserves to receive any, out of the high esteem that he has for himself, he will make beautiful promises to Your Highness, and once he will have returned it will be to injure his poor wife and to carry off everything, this would be leaving the lamb with the wolf, and he will have her poor father and mother abused by soldiers who are good friends and drinking companions of his, because he frequents only the dregs of the population, he waits only for the death of his father-in-law to put the poor mother out on the streets along with the other children in the home; be persuaded, My Lord, that we do this only out of great necessity, as his poor wife is so tormented by him that she is always in despair and she is a most hardworking woman and a good Christian, she stayed in the convent of Corbeil for year to become a nun, but the Lord did not allow it, she left and she is in hell. It would bring peace to a most afflicted family, if My Lord might wish to have this done without having him summoned before Your Highness; it would be better to let us die a slow death than to have a family perish all at once. There are better men than he locked away because we are in constant fear that he might make some affront to us through his wicked tempers and his dreadful outbursts and oaths.

We have brought two complaints before M. the Superintendent de la Sarrie. The father who made remonstrances and corrections to him that were useless, who had been astonished by his wicked tongue and beautiful promises, and who came two days later with his cane to strike the uncle of his wife on the head and it was his mother-in-law who parried the blow who received it on her hand. This is not the last of our complaints but he is a bad subject who fears neither God, nor law, who curses against his late father and mother when he is obligated to work.

She was alerted that he had sold his establishment and his furniture so that he could go off and leave her with no estate, if he had had the means to have them separated, he would have done so even though he still mocks those who have been separated by the law, he says that he could kill them and go off, I hope My Lord, that Your Highness will have pity on this poor afflicted family, the first petition that we had the honor of presenting was signed by good bourgeois and even the retired subsacrist, and by M. the curé of Sainte-Margueritte, and by M. de la Sarrie, we would be well obliged to pray God for your health and prosperity.

[*Below:*]
My Lord,

I despair that I am not able to throw myself at your knees to assure you that everything signified above is most truthful, and to assure you that my life is not safe and we could go on without end if we were not afraid of bothering you and I am the most unfortunate woman if Your Highness does not have pity on me.

I am, My Lord, with my perfect submission to your wishes your most obedient servant.

Marie Le Moyne.

Ars. Arch. Bastille 11007, fol. 177 (1728)

To My Lord
the Lieutenant General of Police

My Lord,

Marie Le Moine, wife of Pierre Ducauroy, master wigmaker established in faubourg Saint-Antoine at the entrance to rue Charenton, most humbly represents unto Your Highness that her husband has been detained in Bicêtre as of February 20, 1728, by an order of the King dispatched at the supplicant's request concerning some abuses and threats by him unto his spouse.

That as the supplicant and said Ducauroy can in no way reach an agreement nor concord together he prayed her to solicit his freedom, with the promise on his part to consent to the separation of bed and board that she requests, and to amicably return to her everything that she generally brought to the marriage.

Said Lemoine most humbly beseeches Your Highness that he might wish to grant the freedom of her husband on the condition of said separation and that he restore to her all that she had brought him, to leave her to live in peace on her own, in the house of her father and mother, she hopes that My Lord will be so good as to grant her this grace, and she will never cease her prayers for the preservation of Your Highness.

Ars. Arch. Bastille 11007, fol. 184 (1728)

To My Lord Hérault,
Lieutenant General of Police

My Lord,

Pierre Ducauroy, master wigmaker at the entrance to faubourg Saint-Antoine most humbly remonstrates unto Your Highness that since he has been arrested in Bicêtre he has learned that his spouse had hidden from him a letter that Your Highness had written him before his arrest, which must undoubtedly have made him seem in the mind of Your Highness to be an insolent and disobedient man, that their small disputes were caused by jealousy against his first apprentice who is currently the master of all his house, that all his effects are at the discretion of a young woman who could ruin him totally by misappropriating his money, his merchandise, and his furniture.

His said spouse just had the supplicant summoned before M. the Civil Lieutenant to have ordered the separation of bed and board that she requests; it is contrary to the rules for her to reside in the house after her request has been formulated and the decree obtained, the supplicant cannot provide for his interests and his defense if Your Highness does not have the charity to grant him his freedom, he promises that he has no vengeful design.

He will continue his Wishes for Your Highness.

Ars. Arch. Bastille 11007, fol. 186 (1728)

To My Lord Hérault,
Lieutenant General of Police

My Lord,

Pierre Ducauroy, merchant wigmaker at the entrance to faubourg Saint-Antoine, most humbly remonstrates unto Your Highness that in 1721 he married the niece of Monsieur Hue upon her departure from the convent, having only two thousand livres by marriage, the supplicant by his labor accrued earnings of eight thousand livres, having a well-stocked shop, and three apprentices to serve his customers; he saw himself in a state to do without his wife's parents and to live independently, this resolution to depend no longer upon their will stung them, the supplicant's wife stubborn in her resolve to subjugate him to this dependence despite his just reasons for withdrawing from it, forced him by her heedless words to administer a light punishment, without scandal and not shocking in the least, but far from recalling her to her duty, out of resentment she took her complaints to her parents who delighted by such a favorable occasion to execute their design of returning the supplicant into their dependence extracted from his wife her consent to solicit an order in the form of a *lettre de cachet* for the purpose of having him locked up in Bicêtre, that after such punishment and in fear of enduring another, he would become more circumspect, discourses such as this insinuated to a young woman of twenty-two are not without their charm when it comes to getting her consent to everything that is wanted of her, with this consent they obtained the order by which he was arrested on the 20th of this month; the truthful story that he declares unto Your Highness and the testimony that persons of honor and probity will give of his conduct lead him to hope that Your Highness will grant his freedom which is of infinite consequence to him as to both his honor and his shop which has been delivered to the care of three apprentices and abandoned to the care of a twenty-two-year-old woman who is hardly capable of maintaining it; as a detention such as this can ruin the fruit of the labor of several years, he hopes for his freedom from Your Justice, assuring him that he will bear no vengeful grudge for such an affront, he will continue his wishes for Your Highness.

> Cœurderay (stocking maker),
> Matispont (stocking maker),
> Delaucipure, Royer,
> Doirat (master cabinetmaker),
> Ballieux (master tailor),
> Michault, Barde.

Ars. Arch. Bastille 11007, fol. 188 (1728)

Jean Ducroux

> To My Lord
> the Lieutenant General of Police

Order of March 28, 1728.

My Lord,

Jean Ducroux, wine merchant in Paris, residing rue Saint-Germain-l'Auxerrois and Marie Françoise Dupont his wife, most humbly represent unto Your Highness, that they have the misfortune of having a son named Jean du Croux age twenty-four, who for several years has plunged himself into a true and extraordinary debauchery being continually drunk on wine and in this state insulting not only the supplicants, but also his brothers and sisters, having even abused and threatened them which several times obliged the supplicants to give him paternal reprimands to which he gave no heed nor paid any attention, that Thursday the 10th of the present month of February, being drunk on wine by afternoon as is his custom, he insulted the supplicants and swearing upon himself, told him that if he was not given account of his money in trust and given five thousand livres immediately, he would break and smash everything in the house and as he persevered in his outburst, the supplicant was obliged to seek out the watch at the barrier of Saint-Honoré, who upon arrival, took him before M. de Soucy, Superintendent who had him sent to For-l'Évêque until ordered otherwise and, as it is in the interest of the supplicants to arrest the course of such unruly conduct, they appeal unto Your Highness and most humbly beseech him to interpose his authority such that said son be locked up in the house of Saint-Lazare for correction;

they hope for this grace from Your Highness. They will continue their wishes for the preservation and health of My Lord, and have signed to serve as their consent.

Ducroux, E. M. Ducroux (sister and
wife of Ponson), M. F. Dupont.

Ars. Arch. Bastille 11007, fol. 259 (1728)

Monsieur,

I had promised you long ago to give you news of the situation with regard to Monsieur your son, I do this today with pleasure:

he just made his communion, it took six months to incline him to it, there is reason to believe that he did it correctly, charity obliges us not to think otherwise. It us up to you, Monsieur, to see now, what it is that you wish to do with this young man. It is useless enough for him to stay here any longer as he is good for very little *[c'est un esprit fort borné]*, it does not seem that any more can be gotten out of him or that we could discover whether he has changed or not; his conduct outside of here will tell.

I am most perfectly, Monsieur, Your most humble and most obedient servant.

Caillet, one of the priests
of the Congregation of the Mission,
this September 18, 1728.

Ars. Arch. Bastille 11007, fol. 263 (1728)

To My Lord
the Lieutenant General of Police

My Lord,

Jean Ducroux, wine merchant rue Saint-Germain-l'Auxerrois and Marie Françoise Dupont his wife, most humbly represent unto Your Highness, that in the month of March last, being tired of the irregular conduct of Jean Ducroux, their son age twenty-four, who was at that time a drunkard, they brought their complaints of this to M. de Soucy, Superintendent of the neighborhood, who had him taken to For-l'Évêque, and upon a petition that the supplicants had the honor of representing unto Your Highness, he was so good as to have him locked up in the house of Saint-Lazare by way of correction and with a pension which they have paid and where he is currently, and as the supplicants have every reason to believe that this detention has operated in him a change in his conduct, both from the letters of apology that he has written them and by the letter of the Father Superior and Corrector of the House, which assure and certify a perfect return and a total resignation to the wishes of his father and mother, this is what obliges them to appeal unto Your Highness and respectfully beseech him, to be so good as to give an order to procure the freedom of said Jean Ducroux, their son, they hope for this grace, even more so as there is no cause that retains him there.

They will continue their Wishes for the preservation and health of My Lord.

Ars. Arch. Bastille 11007, fol. 256 (1728)

This February 24, 1728.

Since the present petition was presented to you Monsieur, the family gathered, and they agreed to have the young man named in the petition who is a very bad subject taken to Saint-Lazare, especially since it has been more than three years that he has not frequented the sacraments. This is why it would be agreeable for you to give an order to have him released from For-l'Évêque, where the archers who led him there decided to imprison him, which they could not have done without my orders as is customary usage.

Monsieur Desclaire,
for the Superintendent de Soucy.

Ars. Arch. Bastille 11007, no folio (1728)

Antoine Duruet

To My Lord
the Lieutenant General of Police

My Lord,

Catherine Mosny, seafood merchant under the Petits Piliers of the Halles and widow of the late Edme Duruet, has the honor of most humbly declaring unto Your Highness that Antoine Duruet commonly called Valcant, her son, age twenty-seven leads the unruliest of lives, losing his respect for the supplicant his mother, and for an older brother, who is also the plantiff's son, and the intendant of M. de Torcy, going to the extreme of threatening to kill them, even drawing the bare sword that he now wears, to execute his wicked intention and especially when he is drunk, which is ordinary for him, and that at these times he even insults all passersby, and moreover he is worthless as heretofore considerable sums were spent to have him discharged and learn a trade which he never wished to do, nor does he intend to use it, preferring his debauches to work, the supplicant made the complaint enclosed herein before M. the Superintendent Aubert, she most humbly beseeches Your Highness to have him arrested by sending him to the Islands and she will along with her other sons wish for the health and prosperity of My Lord.

Catherine Mosny (Duruet wife, mother).

Ars. Arch. Bastille 11009, fol. 145 (1728)

Louis Henry

To My Lord
the Lieutenant General of Police

My Lord,

Louis Henry apprentice locksmith of twenty-one years of age, has been so disturbed over the last three or four years that because of his libertinage and his debauches, he could not stay with any master to finish his apprenticeship: he traffics with a band of vagabonds and libertines, he goes roaming with them after dark, often staying out all night, and when he returns to his father's place after eleven o'clock or midnight, he is so drunk that he will not hear reason, he curses and renounces God and threatens to kill his sister, which he attempted to execute on the 24th of last month, having armed himself to this effect with a fireplace shovel that his father took from him by force. Who knows where he gets the money to supply his debauches as he does not work, and his parents are in no state to give him any: several times he has been convicted of theft from the houses of masters to whom he had been apprenticed, and he even pushes his unruliness so far as to carry off what he can from his father's, threatening him and telling him that he will put to the test which of the two will be the stronger. When they threaten to have him locked up and to complain of this to Mssrs. the magistrates, he brazenly replies that he would like to be in Bicêtre, but that he does not fear or suffer any man. This is why his father and his mother most humbly beseech My Lord the Lieutenant General of Police that he might wish to give this his attention.

Signed Henry.

Ars. Arch. Bastille 11013, fol. 42 (1728)

Louis Henry apprentice locksmith who M. Hérault will be so good as to summon in order to speak to him himself did not return to his father's the night of Tuesday to Wednesday and last night he only returned after eleven o'clock at night, drunk, who knows where he got the money for this, cursing, renouncing God, threatening to kill all those who approached him and finally causing so much noise and disorder that the watch arrived and was then also insulted from the windows, but the officer did not see fit to seize him saying that he could not seize him from inside his father's house, but that if they wanted to cast him out, he would immediately have him seized for creating a public disturbance.

Ars. Arch. Bastille 11013, fol. 43 (1728)

To My Lord the Cardinal de Fleury

Marin Henry and his wife request that Louis Henry their son of around twenty-one or twenty-two years of age be locked away in the hospital.

They declare that their son is a locksmith by trade, but that for three or four years he has been unable to stay with any master to finish his apprenticeship, that he traffics with a band of libertines and vagabonds, going roaming with them at night, that he often stays out all night or only returns at eleven o'clock or midnight; drunk on wine, he renounces God, and threatens to kill his sister—which he would have done on the 25th of June last if his father had not disarmed him of a fireplace shovel, that they do not know where he gets the money to support his debauches, that he was convicted of several thefts from the houses to which he was apprenticed, that he steals from his father's house and that when his father reproaches him for this he replies that they will see who will be the stronger his father than him or him than his father. The petition is signed by the father, by the mother and by three masters whom he robbed. M. Thoru signifies that this said Louis Henry leads a most detestable life and requests that he be locked away; the Vice Principal of the Collège des Quatre-Nations also requests that he be locked away.

Ars. Arch. Bastille 11013, fol. 49 (1728)

Guillaume Sauvage

To My Lord
the Lieutenant General of Police

My Lord,

Louise de Laurent, widow of Jérôme Sauvage, ballet organizer [*faiseur de ballets*], residing on the Main street of Faubourg Saint-Antoine, most humbly represents unto Your Highness, that she has a son named Guillaume Sauvage age twenty-eight who on June 3, 1728, left Bicêtre hospital where he was locked up for a third time having swayed your equitable justice and promised to be an honest man. However since said day of his release said Sauvage has redoubled his violence toward the supplicant his mother to the point of threatening her and raising his hand to strike her; such that she is compelled to abandon her house and her work as her life is unsafe, because said Sauvage so as to exercise his violence with greater authority, has donned the uniform of a soldier of the French Guards and calls himself a soldier. This obliged the supplicant to take her complaints to Monsieur de la Gretez, sergeant in the French Guards, Commander of the Watch of said faubourg Saint-Antoine on the subject of her son's abuse.[9] Said Monsieur de la Gretez conveyed himself with the Guard right away and arrested said Sauvage in his soldier's clothes and had him taken to the prison of the abbey of Saint-Germain-des-Prés on August 3, 1728.

Considering this, My Lord, the supplicant most humbly requests of Your Highness, that said Sauvage be locked away once again in Bicêtre for the rest of his days in order to avoid the misfortunes that might arrive.

She will redouble her prayers for the preservation of your health.

Ars. Arch. Bastille 11028, fol. 129 (1728)

Monsieur,

In execution of the order of His Majesty that you did me the honor of delivering to me on the date of September 18, 1728, I took to the hospital one Guillaume Sauvage accused of having attempted to cut off his mother's head or arm with a billhook.[10] He claimed to be a solider in the Guards in the Company of M. de Courtemer and he was declared incapable of being so because of his behavior and his great libertinage. The mother of said Sauvage hopes that it would please Monsieur to send him to the Islands and Sauvage himself is willing. He says that he will not change, that his character is dyed in the wool. I have the honor of being with a profound respect Monsieur
[illegible] Dercoint.

Ars. Arch. Bastille 11028, no folio (1728)

Claude Carbonnet

To My Lord Bertin,
Councillor to the King in his Councils,
Master of Requests and Lieutenant General of Police

My Lord,

The widow Carbonnet, washerwoman residing in Vaubres represents unto you, aggrieved with suffering, that she has the misfortune of having a son Claude Carbonnet, age twenty-one, who for eighteen months has been a debauch and a perpetual drunkard who never ceases to torment and assault her, and who daily threatens to strangle her and bring about her demise and even to set fire to the house and throw himself from it afterwards. The above declaration is true and is known to M. de la Bernardière, commander of the Mounted Constabulary in the burg of la Reine, as well as the curé, mayor and residents of said place: that she the supplicant has always endured, not wishing to lose her son by complaining to the law; but as she has every reason to fear not only for her life, but also the evident dishonor that he would cause his well-regarded family. She most humbly beseeches Your Highness to grant an order of the King to have said Claude Carbonnet arrested and locked away in Bicêtre and from there, to have him transported to the Colonies. By granting her this grace, My Lord, you will protect the life of this mother from pain and preserve her family from the utmost affront with which this wretch threatens them, and she will never cease as well as her family her most ardent wishes for the health and prosperity of Your Highness.

Fouchard, Prior of Vauves;
G. Minand, Subsacrist; Le Blanc.

I the undersigned, procurator of the parish of Vambre, certify that I am acquainted with the facts given above.

(Illegible signature, Financial Procurator of
H.R.H. Mgr the Prince de Condé.)

Ars. Arch. Bastille 11990, fol. 197 (1758)

Memoir

Monsieur,

I have the honor of reporting to you that following your orders, I made a precise inquiry, in the village of Vamvres, into the content of the enclosed petition, and I learned that all of the facts declared within it are most truthful, it is, Monsieur, with good reason that the widow Carbonnet complains of her son's conduct; by which she is frequently abused. This wretch being almost always drunk; it is to be feared that this poor woman might die under the blows of this unnatural son who brought about his father's demise, according to what I learned from the principal inhabitants of the area who assure that they saw the son, armed with a pitchfork running after his father in the fields and abusing him.

I can assure you, Monsieur, that the signatures that are at the bottom of the petition are all truthful and that the inhabitants of Vamvres ardently desire their deliverance from Claude Carbonnet who is capable of setting fire to the village.

Labenardière.

In Bourg-la-Reine this June 11, 1758.

Ars. Arch. Bastille 11990, fol. 198 (1758)

Marie Antoinette Guichard

To My Lord the Count
de Saint Florentin
Minister and Secretary of State

My Lord,

Madame Guichard and her family request an order of the King to have Marie Antoinette Guichard, her daughter, placed in the hospital.

Marie Antoinette Guichard, adult daughter, around thirty years of age always showed the most violent inclinations from her most tender youth. Being still at a very young age she was one day on the point, in a moment of obstinacy, of stabbing herself with a knife had she not been stopped in time. At around sixteen years of age, she furtively left the house of her now widowed mother, to live in a clandestine room with a man for a great number of years until finally her mother, having discovered her retreat by a police investigation obliged her to return to her house, not long afterwards she was surprised, ready to throw herself out of one of her mother's windows; such that we were obliged to guard her day and night, for more than six months and during all this time, she stubbornly refused any food, so that she would die of starvation.

Since then, she has been taken by an infatuation for another who is a married man. And as all of her passions are tinged with violence, she has conceived of such jealousy against the wife of this individual, that she wished to engage him to quit his establishment in order to go off to live together far away otherwise she threatened that she would kill his wife and set fire to his house, saying that she was not frightened of dying after this like la Lescombat.[11] She made this speech a number of times to both sister and mother; and moreover she also told several other persons of her acquaintance, that she would only die at the Grève,[12] but that this did not worry her so long as she got what she wanted.

Two months ago after one of the furies that often seized her, she was on this occasion overcome by an illness of the nerves. We took advantage of this illness to engage first M. the curé of Saint-André in the parish where she lives, and then M. the curé of Saint-Benoist, to go to see her, so as to try to soften her spirit and bring her over to sentiments of Religion: these two pastors were unable to gain anything of her; she did not even wish to hear them.

Finally, her doctor having judged that baths might be useful to her, as she was not lodged comfortably to receive them where she lived, she was taken for this purpose to the Hôtel-Dieu where she remains. But the baths did not calm her furies; it was even necessary to interrupt them, the weakness of her temperament did not permit her to bear them any longer; and she does not dissimulate from her mother and sister, who go to see her at the Hôtel-Dieu every day, that she awaits only the moment of her release in order to execute her initial designs; she says this moreover with rage and despair that leave no doubt that this is what she would do if she were ever freed.

The nun in the ward where she is kept, has learned of some of her violence in this regard, having been witness to it.

What is more, in these circumstances, the mother and the family of this girl, justifiably alarmed by the grievous consequences that might come from this violence, and of the dishonor that would reflect upon each of them, if she put herself in the situation of being taken by the law, thus have a very great interest in her. This is what has decided them to throw themselves at My Lord's feet, to beseech him that he might wish to grant them an order of the King, to the effect of having said daughter Guichard locked up in the Salpêtrière and they will pay her pension.

> Widow Guichard (mother),
> Auneault (brother-in-law),
> Marie Geneviève Guichard,
> Renault wife (sister),
> Corranson (brother-in-law),
> Marie Marthe Guichard,
> Corranson wife (sister).

I have the honor of assuring Monsieur the Count de Saint Florentin that the family of Mademoiselle Guichard has just reasons for requesting her detention.

> Léger, curé of Saint-André-des-Arts.
> Sallé, lawyer of the Parliament,
> of the Academy of Berlin (friend).

Ars. Arch. Bastille 11999, fol. 146 (1758)

In Paris this February 28, 1758.

I pray Monsieur to have the charity of wishing to suspend the execution of the supplicant's *lettre de cachet*; Marie Antoinette Guichard who promises to calm herself and to no longer return to her past wrongs.

Moreover she is in no state to bear the punishment intended for her.

You would infinitely oblige your most humble servant widow Guichard, mother.

Ars. Arch. Bastille 11999, fol. 155 (1758)

> To My Lord Bertin,
> Lieutenant General of Police

My Lord,

Geneviève Antoinette Jore Desellarets, widow Guichard has the honor of representing unto you that consequent to an order of the King, which she obtained to have her daughter Marie Antoinette Guichard locked away for misconduct, she was taken on the 7th of this month to the Salpêtrière, by Monsieur De la Villegaudin: but it is important that no one have the liberty to speak to her so that she might live in a tranquillity suited to her state; this would not be possible if she were to see anyone, and especially Monsieur Salé, lawyer; because although he might appear to be a benefactor, it is nonetheless true, that he is the second infatuation of the supplicant's daughter and the married man in question in the memoir that she presented and that was even made and signed by said Monsieur Salé.

As the infatuation of this girl has gone to a point for which there are no examples, it is of great consequence that she not see the man who is its object, so that she might recover from it and recall herself to her duty *[rentrer dans son devoir]*.

It is with great pain that the supplicant finds herself reduced to the harsh necessity of naming Monsieur Salé, her obligations to his late father lead her to conceal many a thing, out of fear of doing injury to his state, gratitude wins out over the many complaints about him that she could make, and if it were not that he seemed to repent of her daughter's detention, telling her that things would not go as she imagined them and that he had a long arm, she would have kept a profound silence and would have locked away her pain inside herself: but fearing many things from his part, she appeals unto your protection, most humbly beseeching, My Lord, that you might wish not to grant anyone permission to see said Marie Antoinette Guichard, her daughter, and she will continue her wishes for your health and prosperity.

> Widow Guichard.

Ars. Arch. Bastille 11999, fol. 158 (1758)

My Lord,

The protection that you bestow upon the unfortunate and defenseless, today brings me to take the liberty of addressing a memoir unto you that I beseech you to read, if it would please you; and I do not doubt that you have sufficient goodness to offer me relief in the sad and painful situation in which I find myself.

I have the honor of being with most profound respect, My Lord, Your most humble and most obedient servant.

Widow Guichard.

In Paris this May 23, 1758.

Ars. Arch. Bastille 11999, fol. 159 (1758)

BAD APPRENTICES

Paul Robert Charpentier

To My Lord
the Lieutenant General of Police

My Lord,

Monsieur Charpentier, surgeon in Paris, and his wife, residing rue des Muriers, in the place Maubert neighborhood, has the honor of representing unto you most humbly and with the sharpest pain, that P. R. Charpentier their son age twenty-three has for several years given himself to debauchery and drunkenness with such excess that the Watch has already been obliged on several nights to bring him home.[13] That in order to provide for the nourishment of his vices, he takes from their home all the clothes and belongings that he can, and goes off to sell them. That having sold among other things, the month of June last, a new bedsheet that he carried off furtively, you were willing My Lord, to interpose Your authority to oblige the reseller who bought it off of him, to return it; that for forty-seven years Messieurs the Ecclesiastics of the Seminary of Saint-Nicolas have sought their service for surgery, and for their shaving, but that finding himself sixty-four years old and of very feeble eyesight, these Messieurs granted that their son would shave them, and this is the only custom that they have left that provides for their subsistence; and as they fear with all too much reason losing it through the bad conduct of their son, whose inclination to wickedness might excite him to steal from these Messieurs things he could sell to supply his drunkenness, that all their remonstrances, their threats and their corrections were unable to operate a change in him, that these even brought him to an excess of hatred against his father that cannot be expressed, and that he approaches none of the sacraments; it is in this troubled and deplorable situation, My Lord, that they appeal unto Your Justice and unto Your authority, and that they beseech that you might wish to have him placed in Bicêtre by *lettre de cachet*, and they will continue their wishes and prayers for your health and prosperity.

The truth of the above exposition is attested by the Messieurs of the Seminary.

Charpentier, Collet, Delasalle,
Levallois, Father Superior of said seminary,
Pagnier, priest of said seminary.

Ars. Arch. Bastille 11003, fol. 262 (1728)

To My Lord Hérault,
Lieutenant General of Police

My Lord,

Robert Charpentier, surgeon in Paris, most humbly remonstrates unto Your Highness, that seven months ago he had Paul Robert Charpentier his son placed in Bicêtre for correction by order of Your Highness.

The supplicant learned from several persons that his said son had looked within himself and that he promised to do his duty with obedience Messieurs from Saint-Nicolas-du-Chardonnet, Mssrs. Dolet, Delasalle and de Vallois counseled the supplicant to retrieve his son. This is what obliges the supplicant to most humbly beseech Your Highness to order that said supplicant's son be released from Bicêtre and returned to the supplicant his father, and he will continue his prayers for the prosperity of Your Highness.

Rollet, priest, Delasalle,
Le Vallois, Charpentier, father.

Ars. Arch. Bastille 11003, fol. 267 (1728)

In Saint-Nicolas this November 24th, 1729.

Monsieur,

I appeal unto you once again on the subject of a young libertine of our neighborhood one P. R. Charpentier around twenty-six years of age, he was arrested by M. de la Genièvre and led to Bicêtre where he spent close to eight months; appearing contrite and humbled you were so good as to have him released at my prayer in the month of June last, but his conversion was not long-lived, his passion for wine soon carried him to renew his old larcenies which obliges Robert Charpentier his father residing rue des Muriers and

Françoise Alary his mother to beseech you to have him locked away once again in Bicêtre and from there transferred to the Islands if possible, I request this grace of you for these poor and honest folk along with that of believing me in the sentiments of profound respect, Monsieur, your most humble and most obedient servant.

Rollet.

Ars. Arch. Bastille 11003, fol. 270 (1728)

His Excellency the Cardinal de Fleury

M. Rollet requests in the name of Robert Charpentier and his wife that Paul Robert Charpentier the younger be locked away once again in the hospital.

Declares that once this young man age twenty-six was released from Bicêtre, that he plunged again into his initial disorders which are wine and theft.

It was for similar causes that he was taken to the hospital by the order of October 30, 1728, from where he was released by the request of M. Rollet by the order of June 10, 1729, on the promise that he would behave himself. I think that the order is just.

Ars. Arch. Bastille 11003, no folio (1728)

Nicolas Dubuisson

To My Lord
the Lieutenant General of Police

My Lord,

François Dubuisson day laborer and Claude Lément his wife residing rue Saint-Martin, lodging with Monsieur Leblanc, master cobbler next to the Saint-Nicolas cemetery, most humbly represent unto Your Highness that Nicolas François Dubuisson, their son age twenty-four, has since the age of seven given himself to libertinage, stayed out all night, and been unwilling to learn his religion, they placed him in the cobbler's trade, where he caused his master all manner of displeasure without learning it as one must to be able to earn a living, he is debauched with wine, and with women of ill repute who gave him venereal diseases, and he spent three and a half months in Bicêtre being treated.

As he has not stopped recidivating, as he continually stays out all night, as he frequents vagabonds and in his debauchery seeks out quarrels with one and all, returning often with no hat, and with his clothes and garments torn, cursing and threatening that he will give people something to talk about, as he is incorrigible and as the supplicants have every reason to worry that so licentious a life might lead to the most grievous consequences, in order to arrest its course, the supplicants can only appeal unto the equity and authority of Your Highness, most humbly beseeching him to grant them an order to have their son locked away in Bicêtre, and they will never cease their wishes for the preservation of Your Highness.

Claude de Buisson (uncle),
Le Blanc, Blondeau, Étienne Bertin,
Aubert, Mantoz

[*On the same petition:*]
I the undersigned certify that he is a bad subject and that for his own good it would be suitable that he be locked up until such time as he is corrected.

In Paris this November 10, 1728.
Bonnet, curé of Saint-Nicolas-des-Champs.

Ars. Arch. Bastille 11007, fol. 167 (1728)

Louis Faucquet

To My Lord
the Lieutenant General of Police

My Lord,

Monsieur Faucquet, bourgeois of Paris, residing rue de Grenelle, Saint-Eustache parish, most humbly represents unto Your Highness that he has a grandson whom he placed in apprenticeship for haberdashery around fifteen months ago with M. Godert, rue Saint-Denis, he frequents persons of bad conduct and no faith [*sans aveu*] who have carried him to libertinage, such that the supplicant has every reason to fear that bad will come from the excesses of his disturbance and of his debauchery.

This is what obliges him to appeal unto Your Highness such that it might please My Lord, to permit him to have him placed in Saint-Lazare and he will pay his pension, he hopes that Your Highness might be willing to give his orders so that the supplicant will be able to reprimand the bad conduct of his grandson.

Faucquet.
December 1728.

Ars. Arch. Bastille 11010, fol. 329 (1728)

To My Lord
the Lieutenant General of Police

My Lord,

Louis Faucquet, bourgeois of Paris, residing rue de Grenelle and Laurent Bourton one of the twelve wine merchants privileged by the King residing rue des Poulies most humbly beseech Your Highness to retrieve from Saint-Lazare Louis Faucquet their grandson and brother-in-law whom they prayed you to have locked away six months ago, and who is detained by Your Order.

They will continue their prayers for the health of Your Highness.

Ars. Arch. Bastille 11010, fol. 333 (1728)

Nicolas Fieffé

To My Lord Hérault,
Lieutenant General of Police

My Lord,

Nicolas Fieffé, master boilermaker *[chaudronnier]*, and Marie Têtu, his wife, most humbly represent unto Your Highness, that they have a libertine and vagabond son who does not wish to remain in any shop to learn his trade which he does not yet know at the age of twenty-six, as he traffics with a great number of scoundrels and libertines like himself, the supplicants having always made every effort and many expenses against their means, having a large family to support, to attempt to recall him to his duty, have been unable to put an end to this, and they have the pain, after having exhausted themselves entirely, of seeing him give himself further and further to libertinage, from which they fear grievous consequences.

In these circumstances they most humbly beseech that it might please Your Highness to have him locked away to be sent to the Islands. The supplicants will continue their prayers for the preservation of Your Highness.

Fieffé, Marie Têtu.

Ars. Arch. Bastille 11010, fol. 228 (1728)

To Monsieur
the Lieutenant General of Police

My Lord,

Nicolas Fieffé, master boilermaker most humbly beseeches Your Highness that he might wish to grant the freedom and release of Nicolas Fieffé, his son, who is in the Dortoir de la Visitation of Bicêtre, who was placed there by Your Order, My Lord, at the supplicant's request so that he might work on his profession in the residence of the supplicant's brother, his uncle another master boilermaker. He will be obliged to continue his wishes for the preservation of Your Highness.

Fieffé.

Ars. Arch. Bastille 11010, fol. 231 (1728)

One Fiéfait son of a boilermaker is carrying on an awful libertinage. Or he prostitutes himself to infamous men of different conditions, with whom he commits infamies. He has commerced among others with ones Buiche, André, Aubry footman of M. de Charolais, with a chevalier of Saint-Louis and a young marquis residing on the Île Saint-Louis. When Buiche was arrested and André and Aubry were chased from Paris, he took fright, and appealed to an honest man who having shown him the unhappy state that he was in, sent him to a good ecclesiastic of Saint-Sulpice, but he did not profit from the sensible advice of either of the two. Instead of working at his profession, from morning to night, he has relations with the infamous *[des infâmes]*; it is therefore necessary to place him in correction, because in losing himself, he will lose several others of his age.

After having him arrested, it would be good to interrogate him on facts and articles, to learn from him the names of the other infamous that he knows. Monsieur Haymier knows several facts that will serve in his interrogation. Said Fiéfait sleeps in the home of a cook who resides rue d'Argenteuil in the residence of M. Josset boilermaker, I have not even mentioned the knaveries he commits to get money. These will be deduced in the memoir of facts and items about which he will have to be interrogated in order to identify his accomplices.

Ars. Arch. Bastille 11010, no folio (1728)

Monsieur,

I beseech you to make a decision against said Fiéffé, the enclosed memoir will show you how detestable he is; and I have verified and have had verified the facts contained within it. His poor family has complained of him for a long time. I did what I could to win him over by reason, and by kindness. I will provide the facts and items about which it would be good to interrogate him.

I am most sincerely, Monsieur your [Illegible].

Theru.

This October 3, 1728.

To Monsieur Rossignol,
Secretary of M. Hérault,
Lieutenant General of Police

This October 11, 1728.

Monsieur,

For several years, the Count de Labatu has been among the ranks of the most infamous corruptors and he must be in your papers, because he has been denounced before.

He was in the Conciergerie for a fairly long time during the period that M. d'Argenson was procurator general, and as this abominable man corrupted young libertine men who went there to prostitute themselves to him, I informed the magistrate but my opinion did not have the success that it deserved.

If M. Haymier brings you Monsieur Fiéfé to be interrogated, it would be a great evil to release him even more so as he is incorrigible, M. Rousselot and I beseech this of you.

Monsieur Alexandre is an insolent man I would be honored to tell you particularities about him that concern you and me as well.

If Monsieur Simonnet had any honor, he would not make use of such people, not Aumont, not Philippe, not Lerdun. Please be so good as not to cite me as to this article. I am most sincerely Monsieur your most humble and most obedient servant.

Theru.

Ars. Arch. Bastille 11010, fol. 220 (1728)

Michel Husart

To My Lord Hérault,
Lieutenant General of Police

My Lord,

Madeleine Rigot widow of Michel Husart, wine merchant rue Princesse faubourg Saint-Germain at the Grand Moyse,[14] most humbly represents unto Your Highness, that Michel Husart the supplicant's only son, age twenty-one, is an incorrigible libertine, inclined to baseness, even at the residence of his master, where the supplicant placed him, as is attested by M. Aubert pâtissier, with whom the supplicant had placed her only son, who remains abandoned to harlots of ill repute, with whom he eats up everything that he can steal from the supplicant, whom he threatened not long ago with horrible oaths and blasphemy, which he does regularly, especially when he is drunk, which is almost every day.

For all these causes and reasons, the supplicant appeals unto Your Justice, so that you might wish to order that Michel Husart the supplicant's only son be placed in correction in Bicêtre until said Michel Husart has been sufficiently corrected and thus avoid the misfortune of his falling into the hands of a more rigorous justice.

The supplicant having no aim or intention other than the amendment and correction of her said son Husart and she will redouble her prayers for your preservation, My Lord.

Husard, Girardan, Guérin,
Gadmèr, M. the abbé Piclot.

Ars. Arch. Bastille 11013, fol. 292 (1728)

To My Lord
the Lieutenant General of Police

My Lord,

Madeleine Bigot, widowed of her first marriage to the late Monsieur Uzart, wine merchant and caterer, currently the wife of M. de Montpoivin, first lieutenant in the company of M. the chevalier of the Watch most humbly remonstrates unto Your Highness that Michel Husart her son age twenty-four is detained in Bicêtre by order of the King for embezzling and as Monsieur de Malpoivin went to see said Husart and he made him all of the promises that a young man can make to a stepfather and said that if he had done any wrong he was well repented of it, that in the future he would do the best that he could and that his mother and stepfather would be satisfied with him.

This is why, My Lord, the supplicant requests of Your Highness, along with said Monsieur de Malpoivin, the freedom of her son and they will continue their wishes and their prayers for the health and prosperity of My Lord.

Madeleine Bigot, Marie Madeleine Huzard,
M. Poyrier, Lavallet, Pascal, Huilley.

Ars. Arch. Bastille 11013, fol. 298 (1728)

Louis Rolet

To My Lord
the Lieutenant General of Police

My Lord,

Louise Rolet, a nun in the Orphelines of faubourg Saint-Germain has the honor of representing unto you that she has the affliction of having for a nephew Louis Rolet age fifteen and a half, his father died a manservant, surgeon to M. de Villard, captain of the guards who had had the woe of being forced to have his wife Louise Phelippeaux locked up in the hospital where she is currently detained the bad conduct of his son whom he was unable to recall to his duty despite the good upbringing that he had endeavored to give him, having had him finish a portion of his studies was the cause of his death, the supplicant hoping to put an end to this placed him with honest folk who did not wish to keep him because of his bad inclinations and his oaths, he stole twenty-four livres from the residence of one Hérouard woman where he was in a pension to which he would often not return at night and most recently he was absent for seven months, upon his return he stole a silver spoon, the supplicant burdened by this child engaged the widow Gaubert to receive him until he might be placed with a master, he was placed with one Hardy, master marbler [*marbrier*] who did not wish to keep him on because of his oaths. Said Gaubert had such goodness for the supplicant that she took him back in, since his arrival in her residence, she has noticed that several of her effects have gone missing and she no longer wishes to keep him on as much for his oaths as for his insolents replies, in this circumstance the supplicant appeals unto Your goodness, My Lord, that it might please you to have said Louis Rolet locked up in Bicêtre by your authority. This is the only means of saving the supplicant from having to see her nephew punished by the law and herself dishonored, which would be a considerable wrong to the sister of said Rolet who behaves herself very sensibly and whom the supplicant has placed in apprenticeship with a mistress laundrywoman, she will employ her prayers for the preservation of the health of Your Highness.

Gaudert, mistress laundrywoman;
the sister Louise Rolet, her aunt, a nun
in the Orphelines; Hardy, marbler.

EXILES

Jacques Barbion

To My Lord Hérault,
Lieutenant General of Police

The widow Barbion residing rue de Paradis in the residence of Monsieur Georges Tacheron, master roast meat seller [*rôtisseur*] humbly represents unto Your Highness that one Jacques Barbion, of around twenty-five years of age, journeyman mason, one of her four children, has already done her several wicked turns, is often drunk, utters execrable oaths, breaks and smashes everything in the house, and not satisfied with this disorder threatens the supplicant that he will kill her, sometimes with his tongs, sometimes with his knife; in the sad situation to which the supplicant finds herself reduced, at every moment on the verge of dying at the hands of an unnatural son, she appeals unto Your Highness's authority and most humbly beseeches him to order that said Jacques Barbion be arrested and put in a secure place and then sent to Mississipy at the first opportunity so as to avoid the misfortunes that might follow from his disorder. And the supplicant will wish every day for the prosperity and preservation of the precious health of Your Highness.

Eight signatures including
Claude Barbion his uncle.
Ernault, curé of Saint-Jean.

The sad contents of the present petition are truthful and said Jacques Barbion is known by all residents of the neighborhood to be a true libertine and he is even suspected of theft which was certified to me by the residents of the old rue du Temple, by several bourgeois who stopped said Barbion from beating his mother several times.

Gobillard (officer).

Ars. Arch. Bastille 10999, fol. 49 (1728)

Pierre Germain Béranger

Monsieur,

I have the honor of sending you the memoir enclosed herein to have a libertine locked up while awaiting the opportunity to have him sent to the colonies; you will find four times more evidence than would be needed for this punishment; he is the relative of a man of mine whose family he distresses, by his wicked excesses; I pray you to use your authority and to have this rascal placed somewhere where he will suffer what his disorders deserve.[15] Along with this we present to you the discharge that we obtained from his captain because he was enlisted in the army.

The chevalier d'Orléans.

M. Hérault.

Ars. Arch. Bastille 11000, fol. 6 (1728)

To My Lord Hérault,
Lieutenant General of Police

The supplicant was left widowed by Béranger, wigmaker, with three children of whom the eldest is named Pierre Germain Béranger, who from the age of twelve on gave his mother every grief imaginable; she placed him in Saint-Lazare to correct him; upon his release she placed him with a wigmaker, where he immediately returned to his bad habits which are gambling, theft, drunkenness, etc.

The supplicant remarried after three years of widowhood to save herself a crust of bread, and practiced the trade of haberdashery; she thought to do well by bringing her son back into her home to avoid the loss of his honor, which she was unable to guarantee, as My Lord will notice and if it would please him. This libertine promised to please her so that she would give him an apprentice haberdasher's certificate. The supplicant loved her child tenderly despite all the grief that he had already given her, she made him an apprentice, kept him in her home, unhappily for her and for her other children he resided there for two years, during which time he stole from her daily, and would have ruined her utterly if he had remained any longer.

The supplicant believing that he would behave himself better in the house of another, as he knew his trade and was able to work, placed him with M. Cochin, man of a probity, haberdasher at the porte Saint-Jacques, he counterfeited himself for three months, then this libertine stole six hundred livres that the supplicant was obliged to pay back to save the life of her son and the honor of the family; for which she received a receipt from said Monsieur Cochin, which her son knew of and signed attesting to this theft. This rogue not knowing how to trap his mother, feigned that he wished to become a clergyman, to this effect he deceived several persons of probity, who, believing in good faith what this scoundrel had told them, showered his mother with good reasons, and said to her that she would have to answer before God as to what would become of her son, if she opposed herself to his vocation, and did not help him to accomplish this good design, that he was in earnest, that he wished to convert himself and by this put his conscience to rest, and safeguard his reputation. The supplicant who had known of the bad conduct of her son for years could not help but fall into the trap, she gave him everything that was generally necessary to enter in the convent of Yverneaux, on November 12, 1722. This wretch stayed there for only three months saying that this order did not please him and that he would prefer to be a Premonstratensian.[16]

The supplicant who did not wish to have reason to reproach herself gave her son everything that he had requested to enter the Order of the Premonstratensians: there he took the cloth; but this miserable being who in fact was only looking to trick his mother soon made his treachery known, which obliged these messieurs to chase him from their house after six months of novitiate.

This rogue not daring to return to his mother's again had others approach her about his entering into the convent of Basse Fontaine. She was again so weak as to consent to this; he remained there for only a month, the Superior knowing that he was a bad subject, put him out, and gave him back the money that his mother had paid for his pension.

This libertine returned to Paris, sold his books and all his belongings, ate up the money along with the pension that had been returned to him, in less than a month and no longer daring to speak to his mother, he enlisted in the month of September 1723 in the company of M. Huvet, captain in the regiment of Lyonnais. The supplicant whom he had not seen while he was in Paris, upon his return from Basse Fontaine was surprised to learn from a letter he wrote her from Douai that he was garrisoned there and to ask her for things he needed. Again against the advice of her relatives she sent him more than a hundred livres of belongings. These the scoundrel sold as soon as he received them to supply his debauches, which never ceased no matter where he went.

The supplicant was counseled to let a few years in the service pass so that he would suffer, but she sent him a pension of a hundred livres that she paid regularly every three months.

What made the pain of this poor mother complete, is that in the month of August last this wretched son came to Paris to threaten her that he would kill her and her husband, if she did not retrieve him from the service and above all if she did not give him the money he was demanding of her.

The supplicant to parry the blow appealed to all her friends for the money to get a full discharge for her son and to pay all of the debts that he had contracted both by borrowing and by the guard duties that he has his comrades perform for him and by all that he spends in Paris every day.

She appeals unto your kindness, My Lord, and most humbly beseeches you to facilitate a *lettre de cachet* to have her son locked away and sent to the Islands at the first opportunity, without which she and her husband will never have any rest, nor will their lives be safe.

Ars. Arch. Bastille 11000, fol. 8 (1728)

Pierre Pasquier

To My Lord
the Lieutenant General of Police

My Lord,

The relatives of Pierre Pasquier, son of the late Jacques Pasquier master cobbler in Paris and of Jeanne Candide, of around twenty-four years of age and prisoner in the prisons of the Grand Châtelet most humbly remonstrate unto Your Highness that even though said Pasquier was without means from his youth onwards he received all possible instruction, the supplicants have no knowledge of the pernicious company that he frequents and do not know the causes of his detention, nevertheless they know and have known that said Pasquier ever since the death of his mother eleven years ago, has always had bad inclinations, that he is most inclined to debauchery and frequents women and girls of ill repute, even debauching women and girls of renown, that he curses and blasphemes the sacred name of God and that when some of the supplicants remonstrate with him about his excessive conduct he hurls the most atrocious insults at them. And as the supplicants are from an honest family, it would be most troublesome to them if said Pasquier inclined as he is to debauchery came to frequent faithless persons, vagabonds, or even thieves and resellers and were to be severely punished by the law, to avoid this affront they desire that said Pasquier be sent to the Islands.

On these grounds, may it please Your Highness that after reading the interrogation of said Pasquier he condem him to the Islands for the rest of his days, this grace that the supplicants await of your ordinary charity will make them redouble their wishes for the health and prosperity of Your Highness.

> Françoise Pasquier, sister; Jacob, brother-
> in-law; Anne Élisabeth Candide, maternal
> aunt; Guillaume Menu, brother-in-law;
> Louis Coutellier, uncle through M. T.
> Candide my wife.

I have the honor of certifying to My Lord the Lieutenant General of Police, that the content of the present memoir is truthful and that it would be charity to remove from said Pasquier the opportunity for debauchery and libertinage by sending him to the Islands.

> L. Metta, curé of Saint-Merry.

Ars. Arch. Bastille 11024, fol. 125 (1728)

Jacques André Pellerin

> To My Lord Hérault,
> Lieutenant General of Police

My Lord,

The widow Pellerin merchant upholsterer *[tapissier]* in Paris with five children to support of which four are girls and one a boy most humbly represents unto Your Highness that said son one Jacques André Pellerin more than twenty-three years of age has for some time led a most unruly, scandalous, life, risking affront to the family by his bad conduct notwithstanding all her remonstrances as well as those of his uncles. This obliges her to most humbly beseech Your Highness, My Lord, joined by his uncles who have signed the present alongside her to give your orders that he be locked up and then sent at the first opportunity to the Islands for three years, with said widow offering to pay the costs of his transportation to the port of embarkation and she will continue along with all of her family her wishes for the preservation of Your Highness.

Mary, paternal uncle; Meusnier, paternal
uncle; Lange, maternal uncle;
Jeanne Maillot, widow Pellerin, mother.

Ars. Arch. Bastille 11025, fol. 23 (1728)

Simon Symphorien Barbot

To My Lord
the Lieutenant General of Police

My Lord,

Simon Barbot master saddler rue de Grenelle, faubourg Saint-Germain, and Marie Madeleine Marthe Barré his wife, stricken with pain at seeing themselves obliged to bring their complaints to Your Highness against Simon Symphorien Barbot their son, journeyman saddler, age twenty-five and a half, who harbors within himself every bad inclination.

He stole, around eighteen months ago a ring on the quai de la Mégisserie, he was locked up for this in Châtelet, his father's probity and his protectors retrieved him from this unhappy matter. A few days ago he stole a pair of shoe buckles with diamonds from the residence of M. Goizet, merchant silversmith across from the Châtelet; he takes everything that he can from the house of the supplicants to satisfy his passions.

His father twice had him cured of a secret illness and he is almost always drunk; in short, he is a truly intemperate man.

The supplicants implore Your protection, My Lord, to have him locked away in Bicêtre by means of a pension of one hundred livres that they will pay until he wishes to enlist himself in the Indies Company or for the Islands. With good reason they fear seeing him die on the scaffold.

They hope that you might wish to grant them this grace and they will continue to address their wishes to Heaven for the health and prosperity of Your Highness.

Barbot.

Ars. Arch. Bastille 11986, fol. 37 (1758)

To My Lord
the Lieutenant General of Police

My Lord,

Barbot, master saddler rue de Grenelle faubourg Saint-Germain had the honor of most respectfully representing unto Your Highness, the 17th of last month by the petition that he took the liberty of presenting to you, that the odious conduct of his eldest son, age twenty-six, was causing him the most mortal grief; it pleased you, My Lord, to order Mssrs. Chenu and Bulot to verify the facts declared unto Your Highness, the officers were convinced of their truthfulness and had the honor of reporting this to You, the supplicant learned that you, My Lord, decreed that another house than Bicêtre be chosen.

He dares to represent that being responsible for his children whom he raised with honor and a great deal of pains, his means do not permit him to pay a pension greater than that of one hundred livres.

He hopes for this grace of your goodness, and will wish for the preservation of Your Highness.

F. Barbot.

Ars. Arch. Bastille 11986, fol. 42 (1758)

In Paris June 18, 1759.

To Monsieur de Chabot

Monsieur,

I have the honor of addressing you the enclosed consent of the family of one Symphorien Barbot detained in Bicêtre since January 15 last and whom I enlisted in the service of the Indies Company.

If you judge it suitable to grant me his freedom, I will have him depart with my first review.

I am with respect, Monsieur, Your most humble and most obedient servant.

Bouchez.

Ars. Arch. Bastille 11986, fol. 47 (1758)

Jean Antoine Lacour

To My Lord Bertin,
Lieutenant General of Police

My Lord,

Joseph Lacour, master saddler, residing rue des Rosiers, faubourg Saint-Germain, Saint-Sulpice parish, represents unto Your Highness that Jean Antoine Lacour his son by the late Élisabeth Faure his mother, who saw to his upbringing, having placed him in a pension, first with Monsieur Grumeau in Maison near Charenton, then with Monsieur Guillemain in Vincennes, who also keeps a pension, there he stayed until his first communion, then with his consent he was brought back to his father's to learn the trade of saddling. And to inspire him he sent him every day to Monsieur Jaurel sculptor to learn to draw. Having made himself known in said house for his bad conduct he was obliged to retrieve him from there. And making similar usage in the supplicant's house he decided on his own to enlist in the regiment of Auvergne and then he was sent back for not being tall enough. He went to M. the curé of Saint-Sulpice to obtain a certificate for passage to the Islands. Having presented himself with this to the Indies Company and to the officers and not having been unsuccessful he enlisted himself in the Fichier Compagnie of M. de Rochemont. Being quartered, in the city of Chartres, he had M. Levesque solicited seeing as the supplicant has the honor of working. And he bought him his discharge, upon his return to Paris he asked to continue his trade. The supplicant placed him with his godfather Monsieur Faucher rue des Moineaux, butte Saint-Roch where he remained only a very little while. He declared to his godfather that he did not wish to work any longer, that he wanted to be a Brother of the Charity. The Messieurs of the Charity did not want him as they were acquainted with him. The supplicant tried every other approach. And placed in pension in the convent of Verneaux in Bris-Comte-Robert, he remained for three months and ten days and then left furtively and went to present himself to the Capuchins rue Saint-Jacques, took the robe on September 6, 1757, and left on January 17, 1758, as they did not find him a very good subject for them; he asked to work once again, he returned to his godfather's and remained only a few days, they do not know where he might be, and fear every danger for this child in view of his past troubles who might find himself in bad company that could dishonor the family.

The supplicant, a father appeals unto Your Highness beseeching him most humbly to order that inquiries be made after which he would grant him an order of the King to have him arrested and deposited in Bicêtre. Up until Your Highness grants the supplicant another order to have him enlisted for the Islands. He dares to hope for this grace and justice along with all his family and they will pray God for the precious days of Your Highness.

Lacour.

Ars. Arch. Bastille 12002, fol. 48 (1758)

February 22, 1757.

Monsieur,

Dear nephew, we have received your letter it gave us great pleasure to learn some precious news of you as well as the grief that your knave of a son is giving you and us as well, you ask us for our consent to have him sent to the Islands, we consent to this wholeheartedly, if you had wished to listen to us, he would have left a long time ago if it had been up to us. We are not doing all that well. Is there anything else that we might send you. M. and Mme Escottier send their regards to you and all our friends.

Marie Faure.

Ars. Arch. Bastille 12002, fol. no number (1728)

FAMILY HONOR

Étienne Dupuis

To My Lord
the Lieutenant General of Police

My Lord,

Raimond Dupuis, bourgeois of Paris, and his wife most humbly remonstrate unto Your Highness, that they exhausted themselves giving as happy an upbringing as was possible for them to all their children, as they had several to support, but their misfortune was having one Étienne Dupuis, age twenty-two, the youngest of his children, who since his tender youth, up until the present only ever gave signs of libertinage, and the supplicants were obliged to suffer this with pains and expenses; in the Hope that he would change his life, but on the contrary, he debauches himself further and further, he is out of control, as he consorts with several vagabonds; in the fear that one of these days they will witness a spectacle before their eyes; as honor has always run in their family; although fortune has forgotten them when it comes to money, their honor has always protected them from all misfortunes and disasters; the supplicants come, with tears in their eyes (and with the consent of the relatives who signed the bottom of the petition), to implore Your Justice and Your Authority, My Lord, to most humbly beseech him that he might wish to grant them an order of the King to dispatch him to the Islands so that this would give him cause to change his life, especially because he is capable of supporting himself, as he knows the trade of wood sculpting, of which he has acquitted himself quite well. The supplicants dare to flatter themselves of this grace full of Justice, and they will not fail to wish to Heaven for the health and prosperity of Your Highness.

> Charles Blezé (uncle), Raymond Blezzé (second cousin), François Blezzé (second cousin), Marianne Thévenin (aunt), Charles de Solor (uncle, bourgeois of Paris), Marie Thérèse Thévenin (aunt), Charles Jobert (uncle), M. Beaufort.

Ars. Arch. Bastille 11009, fol. 130 (1728)

From Malesherbes, the second of April 1728.

My dear wife,

I just received your letter from which I learned of the ill state of your health which pains me greatly, as for myself, I am not yet well and I have hope that in a little time, with the help of God, my strength will return. I am most worried to learn that our son Étienne cannot correct himself of his wicked inclinations, and that he even had the effrontery to steal a goblet and a silver cup from you and that he has reached the unnatural point of having made an attempt upon your life, having climbed up onto the roof of your house, in order to enter into your room, I do not know of any other means to avoid a horrific spectacle at our doorstep than that of endeavoring to obtain his departure for the Islands so as to safeguard the honor of our family by sending him away. He has a good trade that will serve him well if God shows him the grace of having him return an honest man, of which I despair after all of the grief that he has given us from his most tender childhood, up to his present adulthood. I give you my consent to have this done, thus you may act in virtue of my present letter.

I embrace you and wish you better health and a little more rest once you have been delivered from the continual state of worry that you are in and I am, my dear wife, your husband.

> Dupuis.

Ars. Arch. Bastille 11009, fol. 132 (1728)

> To My Lord
> the Lieutenant General of Police

My Lord,

The widow Paillard, worker with men's clothes, residing rue de la Lune near Bonne-Nouvelle takes the liberty of most humbly representing unto Your Highness that three months ago one Dupuis obtained from My Lord an order to have locked away in Bicêtre Étienne Dupuis her son, journeyman sculptor age twenty-two, who was without employ at the time and who had abandoned his mother despite being at his ease, believing her to be an obstacle to his irregular conduct, her husband being absent; as since this time several master sculptors whom he has served, knowing him to be a good worker and of most loyal and well-behaved conduct, as is shown by their certificates enclosed herein wish to give him work, the supplicant who raised him and who has almost always taken care of him since his childhood, dares to most humbly beseech Your Highness, that he might wish to grant the freedom of said Étienne Dupuis to continue to work in his profession as he did before she hopes for this grace from the equity and the Justice and Charity of My Lord, and she will redouble her wishes to Heaven for the prosperity and Health of Your Highness.

[*On the back of the petition:*]

I recognize that said Dupuis worked for me very faithfully. Demarignery.

I recognize that said Dupuis worked for me with faithfulness. Delguierre, master sculptor.

I certify that one Dupuis sculptor worked in my house with all faithfulness in testimony whereof I have signed.

Nicolas Saussay, Master sculptor.

Ars. Arch. Bastille 11009, fol. 138 (1728)

The widow Paillard, worker with men's clothes, requests the freedom of Étienne Dupuis, journeyman sculptor, age twenty-two, her son, declares that she only had him arrested because without work he was too much abandoned to himself. But that now several masters who had employed him offer to give him work, the petition is signed by three of these masters, the Bursar of Bicêtre gives a good account of him, he was taken there by order of the King on the 17th of April last as a libertine given to brazen debauchery.

(Report by the Superintendent of police.)

Ars. Arch. Bastille 11009, fol. 140 (1728)

Jeanne Le Perrier

To My Lord Hérault,
Lieutenant General of Police

My Lord,

Monsieur Le Perrier, bourgeois of Paris, most humbly represents unto Your Highness that one Jeanne Le Perrier his illegitimate daughter [*fille du côté gauche]* and aged twenty-four decides to lead a life of the greatest excess even though the supplicant has up until now spared nothing to provide her all possible education. Twice he placed her in apprenticeship for the trade of seamstressing but she did not wish to remain with the first mistress, nor with the second, who is Mlle de Saint Laurent where her situation was quite good.

Nonetheless she left there six months before her time was up without informing the supplicant her father, and as this girl has only libertinage in mind anyway and as she continues to reside in a small room rue Parcheminerie with one baker grocer on the fourth floor, where a boy currently sleeps with her, and that when the supplicant and others remonstrate with her about her bad conduct, she threatens them daily that she will have them murdered and poisoned, and she even caused a public scandal in the church of Saint-Séverin, as the Beadle chased off her lover and her having noticed that they arranged to meet there; she also threatened the Beadle with similar threats, this is why the supplicant beseeches Your Highness that he might wish to order that she be arrested and taken to the hospital and he will continue his prayers for the preservation of Your Highness.

Not knowing how to sign I made my cross +

Paper merchant on rue Saint-Jacques, Le Perrier.

Ars. Arch. Bastille 11099, fol. 71 (1728)

Marguerite Massé

Marie Gauthier, widow of Joseph Massé, surgeon residing rue des Canettes faubourg Saint-Germain in the residence of Monsieur Jolly surgeon most humbly declares unto Your Highness that she has the misfortune of having a daughter Marguerite Massé age twenty-eight who is abandoned to all manner of unruliness she is currently detained in Sainte-Valère for the second time from where the supplicant wishes to have her released, owing to the bad example that she creates in the community. As this girl belongs to an honest family that she dishonors with her bad conduct, and as we have reason to fear that she will continue her libertinage, if she were to return to the world, the supplicant most humbly requests of Your Highness that he would deign to grant her a *lettre de cachet* to have mademoiselle Marguerite Massé locked up for the rest of her days in the Hôpital général where she has already been detained three different times for the space of eight years for wicked morals. The supplicant will be obliged to redouble her wishes for the continuance of the health of Your Highness.

My Lord,

Following Your Orders I verified the facts given in the petition enclosed herein, it is true that Marguerite Massé wishes to leave the house of Saint-Valère without offering any reason according to what I was told by the Mother Superior who similarly assured me that she sometimes had very high humors, but that nonetheless she would apologize afterwards.

Finally, this mother superior, has already separated her from the others and is waiting rather impatiently for her relatives to take her out of her hands.

I similarly saw the mother and the other relatives who signed the petition and who not only certify its contents, but also add that this girl has always given herself to the most infamous debauchery, that she was absent for three years, that she was found in a wicked place, then placed in Saint-Valère itself where she appeared to be of good will and she stayed there until springtime when the urge took her again, as it has today, to leave and as it was feared that she would plunge back into debauchery once more, she was transferred to the hospital where she stayed for three years, that, once released, she continued her debauchery, was returned to the hospital where she stayed another three years and that upon her release she promised to behave herself, that they had her placed in Saint-Valère once again where she is currently and where she wishes to leave without giving any reason, moreover her relatives appear to be most honest folk.

I am with a most profound respect, Monsieur, Your most humble and most obedient servant.

Grillotte.
This August 13, 1728.

Ars. Arch. Bastille 11021, fol. 317 (1728)

Marie Anne Félicité Martin

To My Lord
the Lieutenant General of Police

My Lord,

Anne Catherine Denis wife separated in bed and board from René Martin, she a mistress midwife, most humbly represents unto Your Highness that M. A. Félicité Martin her daughter age nineteen years gives herself to libertinage and debauchery with the first passerby and to scandalous prostitution near where she lives both rue de Bussy and the whole neighborhood, in such a manner that she dishonors and does considerable wrong to the supplicant in the profession that she practices in order to subsist, taking advantage of the fact that her mother is in no state to pay a pension to have her locked away. This is why the supplicant in this deplorable state most humbly beseeches Your Highness that you might wish to have said Marie Anne Félicité Martin locked away in the Salpêtrière and to deliver the orders necessary for this. She will continue her wishes for the prosperity and preservation of Your Highness.

De Mouchy, René Martin,
Gebert, Landais.

Monsieur, I have the honor of reporting to you that the facts contained in this petition are the most exact truth as one Anne Félicité Martin age nineteen against whom her parents complain that she is a libertine whose bad conduct began at the age of ten; she has now taken this to such a point, that it has scandalized the neighbors. They assured me that this young girl who they even believed to be pregnant went off shamelessly with the first man who would proposition her. This is what engaged the mother to prevent her from going out, but [illegible] because she chose the moment when she was seeing to her business.

D'Hemery.
(The police Superintendent's report on the petition.)
Ars. Arch. Bastille 12008, fol. 68 (1758)

Félicité Meunier

To My Lord Bertin, Master of Requests
and Lieutenant of Police of the City and
Prévôté and Vicompté of Paris

My Lord,

Marguerite de Grouy, widow Meunier, residing rue Saint-Honoré, across from the cul-de-sac of the Orangerie of the count de Vassures, with three children to support, whose only wealth and estate comes from tending to the infirm, takes the liberty of declaring to you, My Lord, that of her three children, the two boys give her all manner of satisfaction, but that this is not the case with Félicité Meunier her daughter whom she has watched with the greatest pain give herself to the most outrageous debauchery and sloth, vices that can lead to anything and that give her reason to fear for her family of honest folk who beseech that Your Highness might wish to obtain an order of the King to have said Félicité Meunier placed in the hospital with the offer that they will all contribute to the payment of a modest pension, their gratitude will be equal to their wishes for the preservation of Your Highness.

> Degouy Meunier, mother; F. J. Sandrié;
> J. J. Sandrié; S. Meusnier; C. Sandrié;
> P. J. Sandrié; Simon; Sandrié, uncle;
> A. Meunier, aunt; Meunier, cousin.

I the undersigned certify that for several years I have been brought complaints concerning the woman named in the present petition, who despite all of the representations made to her and the patience that has been used in her regard, nonetheless persists in her libertinage and that there is reason to fear that she might dishonor a respectable family, which I join in soliciting her detention in the hôpital de la Salpêtrière in testimony whereof I have signed the present certificate, in Paris this May 22, 1758.

> Cathelin, curé of the Madeleine
> of Ville-l'Évêque.

Ars. Arch. Bastille 12009, fol. 210 (1758)

> To My Lord
> the Lieutenant General of Police

This October 5, 1759.

My Lord,

The widow Meunier sick nurse, residing rue and faubourg Saint-Honoré has the honor of representing unto Your Highness that upon the good reports from the mother superiors in the hôpital de la Salpêtrière, and especially of Mme des Sareté, concerning the subject of Félicité Meunier her daughter, this is why she most humbly beseeches, My Lord, that he might wish to give his orders that she be freed, as the supplicant is no longer in a state to pay her pension. She hopes for this grace from Your ordinary Justice, and her wishes for the preservation of the precious days of Your Highness will be eternal.

> Widow Meunier.

Ars. Arch. Bastille 12009, fol. 215 (1758)

PARENTAL ETHOS, 1728: THE RATIONALE FOR SENTIMENT

Leclerc

To Monsieur Rossignol

I have the honor, Monsieur, of imploring Your Justice to see to the correction of Monsieur Leclerc, today all of his family implore your goodness and hope that the correction he endured will have rendered him more reasonable, his youth and his talents engage his mother to try once again to return him to the world, I am sending you her letter, and am with respect, Monsieur, Your most humble and most obedient servant.

(Illegible signature.)

Ars. Arch. Bastille 11018, fol. 134 (1728)

My Lord,

I beseech you that you might wish to grant your protection to an entire family that every day fears seeing itself dishonored by a bad subject.

I speak with regret because he is my son, but it is important even for him, that he no longer be in a state to do wrong.

You alone, My Lord, have the power to arrest his disorders by having him locked up forever.

Do not refuse help to an afflicted mother who has no other recourse left than to employ Your Justice.

I am with a profound respect, My Lord, Your most humble and most obedient servant.

Widow Leclerc.

Ars. Arch. Bastille 11018, fol. 137 (1728)

I am sending you, Monsieur, the papers that M. the Lieutenant General of Police told me to remit unto you, this M. Leclerc lodges with Monsieur Duon, place de la Sorbonne.

It would be a great charity for the whole family if he were to be locked up, because we are always afraid that he might commit some wicked deed. The grace that we request of you, is that he be seized without noise and without scandal, and even under the pretext of bringing him to M. the Lieutenant General of police.

I am, Monsieur, Your most humble and most obedient servant.

This September 30, 1728.

Montallé.

Ars. Arch. Bastille 11018, fol. 138 (1728)

My Lord,

A mother's tenderness now implores Your Authority in favor of her son, the correction that Monsieur Leclerc has just endured has brought about a great repentance for his wrongs, perhaps I am wrong to flatter myself that he is sincere.

But my son has talents, he is young and I believe that it is necessary to see once again if fear of the punishments he has suffered will not put an end to his debauches, several schoolchildren ask after him to teach them mathematics and drawing.

He promises to behave and make reparations for his past, good and reasonable folk who still have a remnant of kind feeling for him promise to be responsible for him and to watch over his actions.

God willing he will change his ways.

It is in this hope, My Lord, that I ask you for his freedom and that you might wish to order that he be released from the place where he is detained. This grace is asked of you tremblingly by one who is with great respect, My Lord, Your most humble and most obedient servant.

Leclerc.

Ars. Arch. Bastille 11018, fol. 146 (1728)

The Petit Brothers

To My Lord Hérault,
Lieutenant General of Police

My Lord,

Élisabeth Demonguenon, widow of Louis Petit, merchant grocer, has the honor of representing unto you that having lived as a widow for around nineteen years with five children to support, she made every effort to establish three of them, the fourth having given her every grief imaginable, she appealed unto Your Highness to have him locked away in Bicêtre from where he has since been released on the promise that he would lead a more orderly life. Far from doing this, she has had the pain of seeing that he has dragged into his debauches Charles Alexandre Petit his brother, the youngest, age nineteen, and made him quit the apprenticeship she had found him with a haberdasher without her being able to prevent him.

As Charles Alexandre Petit absents himself from his house daily to go to the Comédie,[17] to gamble and to frequent bad places from where he often returns drunk, abusing his domestic, he borrows money from his work to supply his debauches and he forces the domestics to lend him money, she found seventy-eight livres in his chest and on the 29th of May last he even had the boldness to send for a locksmith to open an apartment to which she had the key. Such conduct together with his lack of respect for her and his threats to her that he will grab money wherever he can and will rob a merchant if he is forced to leave, give the widow Petit reason to fear the conduct of said Charles Alexandre Petit. By which she finds herself obliged along with her family to appeal unto Your Highness so that you might be so good as to rescue her from her suffering by obtaining an order of the King to have said Charles Alexandre Petit locked away in the house of the Fathers of Charity of Charenton. She offers to pay his pension. They will be obliged to continue their wishes for the precious days of Your Highness.

> Élisabeth Demontguenon; G. Grajon,
> paternal uncle; Jourdin, paternal cousin;
> Philippe Serassieur, paternal cousin;
> E. Prignet, paternal cousin; Jacques de
> Montguenon, paternal uncle; Petit, elder
> brother; Petit, brother.

Ars. Arch. Bastille 11025, fol. 97 (1728)

> To My Lord
> the Lieutenant General of Police

My Lord,

Ones Petit de Launay and Alexandre Petit brothers, sons of the widow Petit, merchant grocer residing rue de la Truanderie most humbly represent unto My Lord, to wit that said Delaunay after having endured six months of prison in London, where he suffered the most awful misery, and having returned to the city of Paris, he rendered to his mother the duties and obedience that were her due; but on the grounds of a few youthful wrongs from before his imprisonment, she had him locked up in the hôpital de Bicêtre, which was even more surprising to De Launay as she had expressly promised him that she would forget these wrongs entirely.

With regard to Alexandre Petit locked up in Charenton, he can presume no other motive for his detention, than that during the imprisonment of his brother in England, he spoke overly ardently to his mother to put an end to it, and that she accused him of having taken some money from her, but to show the lack of grounds for this accusation, he had thought that he should report the facts as they are.

Facts:

Petit had saved up a sum of around eighty livres, his mother having found a means for opening his coffer, took this sum from him, on the suspicion, but without proof that he had taken it from her. Not long after, Petit having received a sum of one thousand eight hundred livres for his mother, kept for himself the sum of livres and gave her the surplus. (What man in these circumstances would not have done the same.)

In these circumstances the supplicants hope of My Lord's Justice that he might wish to order their release.

Ars. Arch. Bastille 11025, fol. 105 (1728)

To My Lord Hérault,
Lieutenant General of Police

My Lord,

One Jumel who has the honor of being close to M. the duke of Charost takes the liberty of presenting you with the memoir that you requested of him, My Lord, he most humbly beseeches you to have the kindness of doing him the pleasure of being willing to grant the freedom of two brothers by the name of Messieurs Petit de Launay of whom the elder of the two is in the hospital and the younger is in Charenton they were both detained eight months ago by the malice and severity of their mother who should now be fully satisfied, I pray you, My Lord, to recall that you did me the grace of promising me in Marly that you would grant the freedom of these poor unfortunate men who are worthy of compassion as for eight months they have been penitent, I hope that My Lord will grant my prayers as he had the kindness of doing with regard to Monsieur Petit de Launay who was detained in London in the debtor's prison.

Ars. Arch. Bastille 11025, fol. 110 (1728)

It is a question of knowing whether if these two brothers were to be released, they would enlist as several of their relatives have suggested.

In which case, M. de Gedayn Lieutenant Colonel of the Étampes regiment would be charmed if M. Hérault would give him permission to see them, and to enlist them if they are of the age and height to be soldiers, as even their own relatives wish they would go with him.

Ars. Arch. Bastille 11025, fol. 113 (1728)

To My Lord Hérault,
State Councillor,
Lieutenant General of Police

My Lord,

Élisabeth de Montqueron, merchant grocer, widow of Louis Petit, has the honor of supplicating You to grant her the freedom of Charles Alexandre Petit her son detained by order of the King in the house of the Brothers of

Charity of Charenton as she hopes that he will comport himself better and that he will have abandoned his bad habits.

She will continue her wishes for the precious Days of Your Highness.

Élisabeth Demontqueron.

Ars. Arch. Bastille 11021, fol. 119 (1728)

It has been around ten months, Madame, that your two children have been locked up one in Charenton, the other in Bicêtre, as this penance seems lengthy enough to recall them to more orderly conduct than in the past, I believe that you should test this by promptly making arrangements to have them released from these houses of correction from where I had not wished to liberate them without first giving you notice: I am most profoundly, Madame, your most humble and most obedient servant.

Hérault.
This March 22, 1729.

Ars. Arch. Bastille 11025, fol. 126 (1728)

To Monsieur Nogent,
in the service of Monsieur the Duke de Charost,
at Versailles

In Paris this July 9th.

Monsieur and friend,

After having made every possible diligence to discover the easiest approach to the subject of the affair of Mssrs. Petit de Launay, Mlle Saint Martin and I agreed that it would be necessary to draft a petition, which I take the liberty of sending you to present unto M. Hérault. As we agreed Thursday last when you were so good as to promise us that you would make every possible effort to endeavor to temper the anger of M. Hérault and to obtain something favorable although said Mademoiselle herself believes that you will have quite a bit of trouble especially with the eldest who is in Bicêtre and who was as you know quite well, detained in the London prisons and furthermore it is believed that he is accused of having committed swindles in his trade, but if you see that there is nothing to be done for him, I pray you not to abandon the younger brother who is in Charenton and whose case is far less messy than that of his elder brother and whose life and morals have always been most edifying and Madame his mother could only have assumed the greatest untruths about him according to the testimony of many persons and it is to be believed that her actions in this matter were driven only by vengeance and animosity and the opinions of Messieurs her sons who seek only to ruin one another and furthermore it is because they had learned that the youngest had made some movement to solicit his brother's release which you will judge is not a crime, on the contrary. It must be seen as a pure movement of fraternal charity. In short, Monsieur, you will endeavor to bring to M. Hérault's attention the wicked heart of a mother who attends only to the counsel of her sons who are married and established and consequently asks only the loss and ruin of their younger brothers so as to profit from their estate at their ease.

Whereas Mlle de Saint Martin does not have the happiness of knowing you she nonetheless charged me with assuring you of her duty and of her good faith that you and I will not have worked for ingrates, Monsieur, our procurator sends you his compliments and prays you along with myself to give us news of yourself as soon as you can so that we can know whether our petition has been successful and until then, I pray you to believe that I am perfectly, Monsieur, your most humble and most obedient servant.

Champagne, in the service of M. Duchenay.

I had hoped to convey this petition to your hands by the servants of M. the duke of Béthune as he told me just yesterday that he was going to Versailles today but as he changed his mind I am employing the ordinary route.

I also forgot to pray you to endeavor to obtain a written permission by the hand of M. Hérault that would allow me to visit them if this is possible, you will send it me alongside the first letter that you will do me the honor of writing me.

The mother of two sons, is a merchant grocer, rue de la Truanderie.

Ars. Arch. Bastille 11025, fol. 101–102 (1728)

To My Lord
the Lieutenant General of Police

My Lord,

Élisabeth de Montqueron, twenty years the widow of Louis Petit, merchant grocer in Paris most respectfully represents unto Your Highness that she left with five children, four boys and a girl whom she married to a good merchant, as well as her eldest two sons whom she also established as merchants, but she has not had the same consolation with the last two, on the contrary she has had the misfortune of seeing the third one fall into an awful disturbance and her pain became even greater when he dragged into his debauches her fourth son, one Charles Alexandre Petit age twenty, the supplicant already appealed around eighteen months ago to Your Highness to arrest the course of his disturbance and by virtue of an order of the King she had said Charles Alexandre Petit locked away in the house of the Fathers of Charenton, where he remained for one year, after which the supplicant, always full of tenderness for her children, believing this conversion to have been sufficient, consented to his release around five months ago and sent him to a merchant in Orléans thinking that his conduct had changed and that he might have lost the bad habits that he might have contracted, but she had the grief, of learning from several letters, notably the two enclosed herein that he falls further and further into libertinage, not wishing to do anything except stroll and amuse himself from morning to night and make quite considerable expenditures he bought nearly six hundred livres of superfluous clothes and linens on credit so as to better play the little master, he borrows money to support his debauches from all those who will lend it him and he mocks any remonstrance that might be made with him, and as the supplicant has reason to fear that such conduct might lead to yet more troublesome consequences still she finds herself obliged by the opinion of her family to appeal My Lord unto Your Highness, to beseech him with tears in her eyes to obtain an order of the King to have said Charles Alexandre Petit locked away by order of the King in the house of Bicêtre where the supplicant offers to pay the ordinary pension, and then to do with him as he sees fit, according to how he behaves himself and as it would please you to command, the supplicant and her family redouble their wishes for the preservation of Your Highness.

Élisabeth Demontquenon; Jourdain, paternal
cousin; E. Prignat, paternal cousin;
Belli, paternal cousin.

Ars. Arch. Bastille, 11025 fol. 124 (1728)

In Orléans this November 7, 1729.

Madame,

I am quite saddened to write you the present, my spouse and I deferred doing so for two months.

Monsieur your son goes astray instead of advancing himself, he cannot do anything perfectly; we addressed him with kindness and a just severity, nothing corrects him, he continues to do as he wishes, we do not know where he goes during the day, whom he sees at night, he says that he knows how to conduct himself, that he cannot stay and be diligent, that he needs to take a break.

I esteem Madame, unless you have a better idea that you will be so good as to retrieve him under the pretext that you have need of him. I worry that otherwise he might take a course that would displease us. We are angered by how little he has satisfied us. There is nothing we have overlooked in our attempts to change him. He does not wish to. You would have reason to be unhappy with us if we did not inform you of this. I gave him fifty-four livres in all up until now for small pleasures and voyages to Meung. He asked M. Barbier for twelve livres without my knowledge, saying that he would give them back to him upon his return, this he did not do and he even borrowed some money from him that he has not returned. [. . .]

To Monsieur Rossignol

My Lord,

Nogent, who has the honor of being close to M. the Duke of Charost takes the liberty of writing you to warn you that the widow Petit, merchant grocer rue de la Grande-Truanderie, wishes to resume and drive her cruelty to such a point as to have Étienne François Petit her son, a minor, locked away because he wants her to provide him with an account of his estate, it is right to tell you, My Lord, that this poor boy is unsafe because his unnatural mother solicits a *lettre de cachet* against him from M. the Count de Maurepas, she supplied a memoir that M. Ménard will give you when you come to Versailles. I strongly count, My Lord, that you will again be so good as to render justice unto Monsieur Petit de Launay, as you did when at my prayer you obliged his mother to pay three thousand livres that he owed in London, and in addition to all that had him released from the hospital along with his younger brother. I am again happy to inform Monsieur that Monsieur Petit has a procurator in order to make his mother render his accounts unto him and I daresay that he is making good progress. This is why she has worked upon you to do him harm, and to take away his freedom to act, in an attempt to put an end to his disputes with her, allow me, I beg you to remain with all possible respect, My Lord, Your most humble and most obedient servant.

Nogent, from Versailles
the third of December 1729.

Ars. Arch. Bastille 11025, fol. 133–134 (1728)

Monsieur,

You did me the honor of forwarding me a letter and a petition addressed unto you on the subject of one Étienne François Petit de Launay requesting the repeal of an order of the King that I was given for his arrest, he says that his mother will not do him justice with regard to the estate of his father who died twenty years ago, I arrested this young man during the time of

M. Dombreval, brought him to Saint-Lazare from whence he escaped, his mother took him back as he promised her that he would behave himself, but he again began the same life which obliged this mother to have him locked away in Bicêtre on two different occasions. Enclosed herein is a reply from this mother, I will not execute the order of the King until I have received a reply from Monsieur.

This December 15, 1729.

Langlade.

(Police Report.)

Ars. Arch. Bastille 11025, fol. 135 (1728)

To My Lord

the Lieutenant General of Police

My Lord,

Élisabeth de Montquenon, widow of Louis Petit merchant grocer in Paris represents unto Your Highness, that in the month of December last after she had exposed the libertinage and disturbance of Charles Alexandre Petit her son, age twenty, you were so good as to obtain an order of the King to have him placed in the house of Bicêtre for correction, consequent to this order he was taken there on the 6th of the month of December, but as the supplicant always felt for her children the tenderness that a good mother should and as she wishes only for their conversion, she worries that her son will not receive sufficient instruction in this house to change his disposition, she appeals unto Your Highness to beseech him most humbly to have an order delivered transferring said Charles Alexandre Petit from said house of Bicêtre to the Christian school of Saint-Yon in Rouen, where she offers to pay the ordinary pension, she will be obliged, My Lord, to continue her wishes for the preservation of Your Highness.

Élisabeth de Montquenon.

Ars. Arch. Bastille 11025, fol. 141 (1728)

To My Lord

the Lieutenant General of Police

My Lord,

Élisabeth Demonquenon widow of Louis Petit, merchant grocer in Paris, most humbly represents unto Your Highness that after she exposed the libertinage of Charles Alexandre Petit her son, you were so good as to obtain an order to have him taken to the Christian school of Saint-Yon in Rouen where she had requested that he be placed to make him return from his waywardness, as he has been there long enough and as his masters testify that he behaves himself sensibly, hoping that he will have benefited from the holy instruction that he received as he promises, with a most profound respect she beseeches, My Lord, to obtain for him an order of the King to retrieve him from there, she will be obliged to continue her wishes for the preservation of the health of Your Highness.

Élisabeth Demonqueon.

Ars. Arch. Bastille 11025, fol. 146 (1728)

Maurice Viet

To My Lord Hérault,
Lieutenant General of Police

My Lord,

One Maurice Viet age twenty-nine has the honor of most humbly remonstrating unto Your Highness that he was, by Monsieur de Guiche at the order of the King, arrested and taken forthwith to Bicêtre as said order was found by Monsieur Honnet bursar to not be in proper form he was unable to take him as moreover this order was delivered to Monsieur de Guiche around three years ago what does Monsieur de Guiche do he left the supplicant returned to His Grandeur's hotel where Monsieur de Guiche obtained an order to place him in the prisons of the Petit Châtelet where he is detained without knowledge of the reason why if it was not by the solicitations of his brothers-in-law who do everything in their power to bring about his demise by reviving an old debauchery into which he had the misfortune of falling four years ago about which Your Highness had the goodness of becoming acquainted with the facts and did him the justice that he is due he appeals My Lord, unto Your Highness and prays you do not allow yourself to be deceived most respectfully beseeching You to be so good as to release him if you judge this fit or if it is your will or to grant him any small employment in Bicêtre that Your Highness would judge fit of which he will acquit himself with honor he will pray God and offer his wishes to Heaven for the health and prosperity of Your Highness.

My Lord, although the supplicant has lost use of his right arm this is his handwriting.

Ars. Arch. Bastille 11030, fol. 246 (1728)

> To My Lord Hérault,
> Lieutenant General of Police

Monsieur Viet and Marie Gallois his wife residing in Saint-Paul parish, most humbly remonstrate unto Your Highness that Maurice Viet their son of around thirty years of age is more of a vagabond than ever, which is why they take the liberty to beseech Your Highness to grant them a *lettre de cachet* to have him taken to the château de Bicêtre, this would be the second time.

And they will pray God for the preservation of My Lord.

Ars. Arch. Bastille 11030, fol. 247 (1728)

> To My Lord Hérault,
> Lieutenant General of Police

My Lord,

One Toussaint L. Vuiet and Marie Gallois his wife most humbly beseech Your Highness that he might wish to grant the release of Maurice Viet their son by virtue of an order that was delivered to M. de Guiche around eleven months ago and as it was not executed this is what makes the supplicants request that he be released into Paris owing to the promise he made us that he will live as an honest man and better than ever before, M. Labbé Larenché went to My Lord to request of him this grace. In hopes of this, we will pray myself and my wife, God for the health and prosperity of Your Highness.

Monsieur,

In accordance with your order, I inquired into Maurice Viet's conduct, I learned that this boy was debauched and gave his family a great deal of grief, for which he was twice summoned before you, different persons with whom I spoke, told me that he was wrongly accused of being a thief, that he was never known as such, but that nobody could have given themselves more to debauchery in wine and women than he, his father is a rustic who cannot suffer him, in addition there are two sons-in-law with whom Viet has quarreled several times, who daily stir up their father-in-law's anger against him, since Monsieur De Guiche took him to the prisons of the Petit Châtelet a month ago, he has not received any aid from anyone, this boy has some talent despite having a maimed right hand, he writes perfectly well with his left hand, which could earn him his bread if he wished to settle down, I esteem that Monsieur de Guiche arrested him with slight reason, and without any other information than what he was told by the father and mother.

Ars. Arch. Bastille 11030, fol. 262 (1728)

PARENTAL ETHOS, 1758: THE DUTY TO EDUCATE

Nicolas Benoist Chapuis

To My Lord Bertin,
Lieutenant General of Police

My Lord,

Nicolas Chapuis, wigmaker residing rue Saint-Louis, Saint-Roch parish lodging with Le Roy fruit seller, most humbly represents unto you that although he always sought to give a good upbringing to Nicolas Benoist Chapuis his only son he now sees with the bitterest pain that he cannot, despite his remonstrances and all of the courses he has employed, retrieve him from the outrageous libertinage into which he has plunged himself. In fact, the supplicant fears that at any moment he will see his son arrested and taken to prison to mount the scaffold.

The supplicant does not dare to describe his son's actions, because the things he has done that deserve opprobrium are not known to the undersigned.

In consideration of this, My Lord, he beseeches you to have his son arrested to be taken to the Islands. The supplicant and his family will never cease their sincere wishes for the preservation of the precious days of Your Highness.

Langué, master of the hôpital des Quinze-
Vingts, Dorigny (son-in-law), Chapuis (father
and mother), Élisabeth Chapuis, Marianne Treynus,
Prévost (merchant grocer).

[*In the margins of the petition:*]

I the undersigned master of the Royal Hospital of the Quinze-Vingts in Paris, certify that the facts listed in the petition are truthful, that said Chapuis the younger has provoked several fights in the Enclosure of said house, that we were obliged to put him in the prison of said enclosure to arrest his violence and that I was forced to make the mother and father leave to prevent the son from having any pretext to frequent it in Paris this March 20, 1758.

Gauthier.

Ars. Arch. Bastille 11991, fol. 41 (1758)

To My Lord Bertin,
Lieutenant General of Police

My Lord,

Chapuis wigmaker rue Saint-Louis-Saint-Honoré, having at his request had Nicolas Benoist Chapuis his son placed, around six weeks ago in the cells of the château de Bicêtre for reasons of libertinage, this son now desires to enlist in the volunteers of Clermont Prince,[18] he most humbly beseeches Your Highness, to grant his consent to this son's enlistment, releasing him from said hospital by your orders to then depart to join the soldiers under the officer who enlisted him, it is only on this condition that the supplicant requests this grace and he will never cease his wishes for Your Preservation.

Chapuis, father.

Ars. Arch. Bastille 11991, fol. 47 (1758)

To My Lord
the Lieutenant General of Police

My Lord,

Nicolas Chapuis, heretofore a hair merchant [*marchand de cheveux*], residing rue des Petits-Champs at the Saint-Laurent signpost, most humbly beseeches Your Highness to grant him an order to have Nicolas Benoist Chapuis, his son age twenty-four, returned to Bicêtre prison where he was already locked away for three months, three years ago, for libertinage and from where he extricated himself by enlisting in the volunteer regiment of Clermont Prince, which he left as he was not tall enough.

This libertine has become associated with a woman who left her husband to libertine herself with him, this husband died of grief; they live together scandalously and have done several deeds that tend toward an unhappy end and the dishonor of the supplicant's family.

This is why, My Lord, he hopes for this grace from your goodness while awaiting the chance to have him sent to the Colonies. And he will never cease his wishes for the health and prosperity of Your Highness.

Chapuis.
In Paris this September 24, 1761.

Ars. Arch. Bastille 11991, fol. 50 (1758)

François Faucourt

To My Lord
the Lieutenant General of Police

My Lord,

Marie Marguerite Berthemont, widow of François Faucourt, who alive had been a veteran officer of the King, assisted by all of her undersigned family, residing rue Saint-Victor, most humbly represents unto Your Highness that she spared neither expense, nor care, in providing a good education and a Christian upbringing to one François Faucourt, age thirty-six, one of her three sons; that during his childhood she was unable to keep him in the pensions where she had placed him to study, he was placed at the silver-smith's, but the master dismissed him for disloyalty.

By order of his relatives [*avis de parents*] he was sent to the brothers of Saint-Yon in Rouen, where he remained for three years; and where was able to counterfeit himself to the point that he persuaded others of his wish to become a monk, we retrieved him and a few days later he enlisted in the regiment of the Asfeld dragoons where he remained for four years, living like a debauched dragoon, taking advantage of his furloughs only to come do violence to the supplicant, and live a debauched life in Paris. In 1749 he returned to the brothers of Charity where he had spent six weeks in 1740, stayed only another six weeks, carried off the habit, which he only sent back the next day, and hid himself in a place of prostitution. He enlisted in the regiment of the Tour du Pin. All that was left after his debauches were twenty-four livres of rent on the estate of his father, he engaged one of his brothers to give him two hundred livres of rent on annuity, which since then he has received and eaten up in debauches; he was in the regiment for five years and up until 1754. He had three furloughs that he employed engaging in awful conduct in Paris, seeing only women given to public prostitution, and the soldiers of the watch most determined to wickedness. He had joined a public whoremonger who was punished by the law, and he was entangled in disgraceful affairs for which he was put in For-l'Évêque in 1755 and in the month of August last he was placed in the Petit Châtelet for a month after being convicted for an insult that he and his companions committed in the Cours de la Reine. In the month of February last, the supplicant made a general bequest to her children of everything she owned, said François Faucourt received his third, which he consumed in debauches.

As he is given more than ever to all manner of excesses, as he no longer has anything, as he is without resources, frequenting only persons whose reputations are beyond lost, as he threatens nothing less than stabbing the supplicant and his brothers, as remonstrance has no success with him, and as she fears that this unworthy son will meet a most grievous end, which would cover an entire honest family with infamy, she most humbly beseeches Your Highness to have the charity to grant an order to have said François Faucourt locked up in Bicêtre offering that Claude Charles Faucourt, one of his brothers, a merchant jewelry-smith, rue Saint-Victor, will pay a pension of one hundred livres per year. She will wish for the health and prosperity of Your Highness.

Antoine Faucourt,
Claude Charles Faucourt,
M. M. Berthemont.

Ars. Arch. Bastille 11996, fol. 26 (1758)

My Lord,

Marie Marguerite Berthemont, widow of François Faucourt, who alive had been an officer of the King, has the honor of representing unto Your powerful protection, and most humbly beseeches you, not to grant the release of François Faucourt, one of my sons, who is locked away in the château de Bicêtre by order of the King of January 29 of the present year, this grace, you charitably granted me to avoid the clear danger to which I would have been exposed, as well as my family, the petition that I had the honor of giving you at the time, although it contained facts that were more than sufficient, was nonetheless only an abridged account of my sad life, and if today I dare to have the honor of recommending myself to your powerful protection, it is that an officer and the sergeant major of the regiment of Pitou infantry came to see me, telling me that they had enlisted said François Faucourt my son in the château de Bicêtre, I hope My Lord that you will not grant his release, because I am morally certain that great danger would result as much for my own life as for other misfortunes that would come to pass, if this unnatural child were to be released by any means and by God, I owe you everything in the world, I will never cease redoubling my wishes for the health and prosperity of Your Highness.

M. Berthemont, widow Faucourt.

Ars. Arch. Bastille 11996, fol. 41 (1758)

To My Lord
the Lieutenant General of Police

My Lord,

Marie Margueritte Berthemont, widow of François Faucourt, most humbly represents unto Your Highness, that upon the declaration of the supplicant assisted by all her family, of the disturbances and debauches of all kinds of one François Faucourt one of her sons, for whose upbringing and advancement she sacrificed everything, out of her just fear that she would see her other children and herself perish at the hands of this unnatural son who was marching with great strides toward a grievous end, who had covered an honest family with infamy, it pleased M. Bertin, on the basis of complete information, to grant an order of the King, by virtue of which said François Faucourt was arrested on January 29, 1758, and taken to Bicêtre where he is detained and for which we pay exactly one hundred livres in pension per year. The supplicant, as well as all her family, was alarmed to learn that some of said François Faucourt's companions in debauchery were planning to solicit his freedom, through false declarations, she knows that he would use this not only to give himself once again to the horrors of debauchery, but also to bring about the demise of the supplicant against whom he has out of odious ungratefulness for all the kindness she has shown him, and of all the sacrifices she made for him, sworn an implacable hatred, she most humbly beseeches you, My Lord, that you might wish to not grant the freedom of said François Faucourt, with the offer by the supplicant that she will continue to pay the pension. She has the respectful confidence that she can hope for this grace, and she will wish for the health and prosperity of Your Highness.

Marie Margueritte Berthemont.

Ars. Arch. Bastille 11996, fol. 46 (1758)

Marie Fumet

To My Lord
the Lieutenant General of Police

My Lord,

Claude Fumet water carrier residing rue Saint-Étienne faubourg Saint-Marcel has the honor of most humbly representing unto Your Highness that he has the misfortune of seeing that despite the upbringing and the good instruction that he provided to his daughter one Marie Fumet age seventeen, he has not been repaid as he had hoped. The supplicant placed her in several employments and currently she is perpetually restless, wastes her time, and to amuse herself she steals the supplicant's shirts his furniture and his belongings which she sells immediately and she even takes his money and several times she has done the same to her mistress, which gives the supplicant reason to suspect that his daughter leads a life of bad conduct and as he desires to interrupt its course and has already twice had her placed in the hospital for correction, he has observed no change, he appeals unto Your Highness's authority to beseech him to order that his daughter be locked away in the hospital to punish her for her wrongs.

In so doing the supplicant will wish to Heaven for the health and prosperity of Your Highness.

Florent de la Motte; Laborde, surgeon;
Étienne Commin; Latouz, wine merchant;
Naudin; Marcillon; Pierre Sauvier,
relative; Jean Erouar; Marianne Berthau;
Fumet wife.

Ars. Arch. Bastille 11997, fol. 215 (1758)

Pierre Lalande

To My Lord
the Lieutenant General of Police

My Lord,

Jacques Delalande gardener and his wife, have the honor of most humbly representing unto Your Highness that it is with the most extreme pain that they find themselves forced despite themselves to expose before you the bad conduct and moral depravity of their eldest son, age twenty-six. The supplicants have a large family to support, they gave their sole attention to raising their children in the fear of God and they provided them the upbringing that their state permitted them to procure, of their numerous family only two daughters remain who are the only consolation to the supplicants in their advanced age, by sharing in their pain and their labors and the son of whom they complain; in his youth they placed him with a master cobbler to learn how to earn his living, this apprenticeship and his maintenance both cost them a great deal, their son never responded to their attentions, he did not finish his apprenticeship, he returned to his father's where he showed the most complete disobedience, drinking left and right, giving himself over entirely to sloth, vagabonding, staying out all night, haunting taverns, billiard games, gambling on the bridges and behaving most dissolutely, in an interval in his dissipation he took it into his head to work and he entered the shop of a cobbler on Sainte-Geneviève hill, where he worked for a time, he soon became acquainted with the prostituted girls of faubourg Saint-Marceau, he took such a liking to them that he no longer wishes to do anything good, the supplicants have learned that the faubourg Saint-Marceau is the center of his debauches as well as the nearby little taverns outside of town, he goes out in the morning, comes back in the evening and often stays out all night, remonstrance has no effect on him, he began by selling his cobbler's tools, he picked the lock of his father's chests, he carried off his clothes and sold them, he becomes angry with him and even kicked him several times leaving him ill, he keeps the entire household in fear with his rages, he bullied them by threatening his father mother and sisters that he would beat them. In such unhappy circumstances, the supplicants appeal unto Your Highness's authority to beseech him to order that an inquiry be made into the conduct of the supplicants' son and that he then be locked away in the dungeons of Bicêtre to prevent the misfortunes that might arrive, in so doing, the supplicants will wish for the preservation of the days of Your Highness.

Jacques Lalande, M. C. Lalande, Pellert.

Ars. Arch. Bastille 12002, fol. 166–167 (1758)

Louise Marchand

To My Lord Bertin,
Lieutenant General of Police and State Councillor

My Lord,

Laurent Marchand, coachman with M. the Chevalier de Contades, dares to represent unto Your Highness that of his first marriage, all that remains is a single seventeen-year-old daughter, named Louise Marchand; that he made every effort to give her an upbringing according to his state, but he has the misfortune of having failed as she has the invincible defects of coquetry and gluttony, and to sustain them, she steals everything that she can find, which obliged the supplicant to bring her into the hotel with him, having obtained M. de Contades's permission, and despite his precautions, she found a way to take twenty-four livres from one man, and some effects from others, which he was obliged to reimburse, which is ruining the supplicant; and in fear of further unhappy consequences he was counseled to implore Your authority, My Lord, and to most humbly beseech that you might wish to have her locked away in the hospital. He hopes that Your Highness, touched by the wretched state of a father who does not have the means to place her in a convent, nor enough to pay to have her corrected would wish to grant him this grace, and he will continue his prayers for the preservation of Your health.

Cardinaux, the beadle for M. de Contades;
Février, the manservant for M. the chevalier
de Contades; Coppin, manservant
for M. de Contades; Delaserre,
secretary for M. de Contades.

Ars. Arch. Bastille 12007, fol. 213 (1758)

Inquiry by the neighborhood Superintendent
March 6, 1758.

I inquired into the life and morals of one Louise Marchand a girl of seventeen against whom her father, requests that it might please you to give your orders to have her locked away in the hospital. As this daughter comes from a first marriage, I first summoned her maternal relatives, and in the absence of any paternal relatives, I asked the opinion of the curé and several other persons of the house in which she resides and all, as much on one side as the other, declared and affirmed that not only is Louise Marchand known in the big house as a libertine, but also a thief, having been convicted of this and although it was not in their presence she was unable to deny it.

For this reason, I esteem, Monsieur, that there can be no danger in granting the father of this girl, who enjoys a reputation as an honest man, the order that he requests of you to have her locked away in the hospital.

I am with profound respect, Monsieur, your most humble and most obedient servant.

Superintendent [illegible].

Ars. Arch. Bastille 12007, fol. 214 (1758)

3 When Addressing the King

FROM USE TO ABUSE

In the eighteenth century, policing was built entirely around a dream: manufacturing the people's happiness.[1] This shaped everything the police did, from overseeing the provisioning of Paris to regulating the height of signs, from punishing blasphemy to clearing the streets of prostitutes, from banning assemblies to dissecting corpses. Day and night, they endeavored to channel the violent flow of lives that knew little discipline and had scarce reason to. How tiring these incessant tasks must have been, governed by police ordinances whose reiteration month after month attests to their inefficacy. At times the police were exhausted; each blow struck into the anthill that was Paris offered glimpses of a multitude of other spaces that needed to be cleaned up. The justice system and the police were not up to the task, contrary to what the police edicts, regulations, ordinances, or treatises would have us believe. A science of policing was in place in the eighteenth century, this much is clear, but a true police was not.

This made it possible for the *lettre de cachet* to insinuate itself, to take advantage of spaces that the ordinary justice system had left vacant. When an order of the king served as a summons it lightened the load; the efficiency of this was so great that its arbitrariness was hardly considered. The specific organizational structure of the Parisian police accentuated this phenomenon, because the police lieutenancy was simultaneously responsible for policing the city and for dispatching *lettres de cachet*. Making use of this simple means of imprisoning people served his ends.

The lieutenant general of police did not hesitate; countless *lettres de cachet* were issued for police matters. He even employed this power to go above the heads of the jurisdiction of the Châtelet, supplementing sentences handed down and demanding imprisonment without sufficient evidence.[2]

The lieutenancy was caught up in its own dream; taking advantage of its ability to dispatch *lettres de cachet*, it appropriated royal intervention as a means of palliating its own weakness, disorder, incoherence, and lack of initiative. Thus "the order of the king" sprawled outwards, its tentacles extending everywhere that the lumbering justice system, which was so poorly adapted to insubordinate Parisian sociability, had been unable to introduce itself.

Yet it would be utterly imprecise to conceive of the practice of the *lettres de cachet* as simply the functioning of a mechanism of authority that developed according to an autonomous principle of growth. If it was possible for it to reach the scale that it did, and for its arbitrariness to be considered, at least for a time, as completely acceptable, it was because families had become accustomed to turning to the state administration to resolve certain of their conflicts. They did so at times when the authority of their internal hierarchy was powerless and when seeking recourse in the justice system was neither possible (because the matter was too trivial) nor desirable (because it would have been too slow, too costly, too shameful, too uncertain). An insistent demand for state intervention came into being. Was this demand stronger in modest or poor circles than it was in those where greater resources might have been available to resolve problems of this nature (a residence in the countryside or in exile for the scandalous wife or the spendthrift son, a convent where, through means of a pension or a dowry, a troublesome daughter could be imprisoned)? It is possible. It was always the king whose intervention was solicited and his administration that looked twice before intervening. That royal authority would pay attention to a small family drama, that it would take sides with a father, a husband, a wife, etc., doing so outside of the forms of rule-governed justice, that within a family it would enforce its own values, doing so through the police apparatus and its instruments of punishment, was something that became not only allowed but actively sought after. A contact surface is generally established between the conduct of individuals and the state bodies of control and punishment. As a result, a shared morality is assumed to which both parties—those making requests and the administration that must reply—have supposedly agreed.

A certain number of consequences followed from this: political sovereignty established itself at the most basic level of social relations; from subject to subject, between members of the same family, within neighborhoods, in relationships of personal interest and labor, in relationships of hatred, love, or rivalry, the resources of "absolute" power—outside of the traditional weapons of authority and obedience—could be brought to bear, at least if one had understood how to harness them and inflect them in the desired direction. An entire chain of political authority became entangled with the threads of daily life. But, at the same time, the administration made itself—outside of the justice system—both the arbiter of and, at least in part, responsible for everyday life. The "private," all while remaining private and insofar as it remained so, could no longer remain a matter of indifference to public order. The documents we have presented here testify to this "interlocking" of the family institution into the greater administrative apparatus.

This gave rise to a complex game in which individuals, the "natural object" of the police, tried to annex its instruments and guide their effects in order to reinforce or reestablish their own power relationships within their families. The administration accepted this redirection, under certain conditions and to the extent that, without explicitly wanting to, individuals became semi-spontaneous agents of public order.[3] This overlap of tactics did not take place without ambiguity, without a good deal of imprecision and a great many "misses," through which family morality and the principles of public order nevertheless sought out a common vocabulary and rules that would be acceptable to both sides. Nor did this take place without conflicts: hatreds between the parties involved were aggravated, affirmations of individual rights in the face of families or the administration were voiced, and protests against all of these forms of arbitrariness were provoked. The quite singular practice of the *lettres de cachet* thus offers an opportunity to illustrate the concrete functioning of a power mechanism. Not, of course, as the manifestation of an anonymous "Power," oppressive and mysterious, but as a complex web of relationships between multiple partners, an institution for control and sanction. One with its own instruments, rules, and technology, whose diverse tactics varied with the goals of those who employed it or were subjected to it, their effects changing, their protagonists shifting. Adaptations were established, oppositions were reinforced; certain positions were solidified, while others were gradually undermined. From here, we can start to understand the acceptance of the "arbitrariness" of imprisonment and the unease that it provoked.

The king as the protector and judge of family activities, this image whose symbolism is quite obvious, was at the same time a daily reality in which the feeling of security provided was shadowed by a growing anxiety toward this infinite arbitrariness that was capable of striking at any moment. This explains why the practice of the family *lettre de cachet* had by the end of the Ancien Régime come to seem as if it had reached a saturation point.

Yet, there is no doubt as to the integration of this practice into mores and customs during the first half of the century; the tranquillity of families was an important cog in the maintenance of public order, which meant that it was a worthy object of the king's supreme authority. In him the private and the public were joined together; it was the repressive act that ensured this conjunction. The equation private repression/public order functioned powerfully and efficiently in the minds of all, both contemporaries and authorities. Families confided their wayward fates to the supreme office and many lieutenant generals of the police believed ardently in that public service, the preservation of the honor of families.[4]

"Through this means I have succeeded," wrote Berryer, the lieutenant general of police, "in rendering a service to honest folk such that the disorder of their relatives did not reflect upon them."[5] Lenoir was in complete agreement when he wrote:

> During M. de Sartine's administration [November 1759–August 1774], which was much longer than that of most of his predecessors, there was established between him and many families a sort of relationship of pure trust, a sentiment that he inspired by the spirit of prudence by which he was always distinguished.

Pure trust between the police and the people, paternal benevolence on the part of the king who "was ready to correct in order to prevent justice from 'punishing'"; are we not now in a pure idyll between the people, the police, and the king who imprisons in order not to punish, who withdraws freedom so that no infamy is permitted to sully families, who goes above ordinary justice, the source of dishonor . . .

Even Louis-Sébastien Mercier, who was quite strict when it came to the law and its officers, adopted this procedure and even spoke of humanity and indulgence on the part of the lieutenant general of police:[6]

> His duties are known, but perhaps it is not known that he takes care of retrieving from ordinary justice a crowd of young people from good families who, in the effervescence of passions, committed thefts, swindles, or base deeds; he spares them from public stigma: its shame would have been reflected on an entire innocent family; he performs an act of humanity, by sparing the least fortunate from the opprobrium with which they would have been covered; because our prejudices, from this point of view, are quite unjust and quite cruel.
>
> The libertine is imprisoned or exiled, and he does not pass through the hands of the hangman, thus the police remove from the tribunals culprits who would deserve to be punished; but, as these young people are withdrawn from society, only returning once their wrongs are expiated and they have been corrected, society has no reason to complain of this indulgence.[7]

Thus the family *lettre de cachet* would have led an ideal existence, it would have created harmony born out of the goodness of the king, the humanity of the police, and concern for family tranquillity. Yet this apparent equilibrium would develop fissures over time, and many arguments would be raised against this practice, which would soon come to symbolize the intolerable. The history of social practices is never as linear as the texts and discourses themselves would have us believe. A slow immersion into the judicial archives gives rise to a suspicion that here as well there was no before and after with rigid boundaries. The request for imprisonment contained within itself its own disequilibrium, potential for abuse, imprecision, and impermissible injustice. The dark violence of family secrets and of greedy testimony was too overburdened with passions, humiliations, and hatred for "the goodness of the King" to be able to act upon it definitively as a soothing balm. The good king was also a blind blade that cut too quickly and too soon.

In 1648, during the conferences in Saint-Germain[8] held between parliamentary delegates and the representatives of the sovereign, chancellor Séguier[9] was able to say: "It is necessary that the sovereign be able to arrest someone based on simple suspicions . . . in the government of States it is more expedient that innocents suffer than that the State perish because of the impunity of an individual."[10] And one after another, kings would justify their authority by invoking the necessity of secrecy and of illegal procedures for matters of State.[11] On April 8, 1759, Louis XV offered a precise explanation: these were "occasions when public good and even that of families demanded it."[12]

Abuses influenced perceptions as much as the foundations of the practice itself, and a liberal faction attacked *lettres de cachet*, although without criticizing the monarchy, of course. The reason the king was reproached, and many jurists took this tack, was that he made himself complicit in the injustices of paternal power. This was "to privilege private tyranny through public despotism," as Moreau wrote in his *Discours sur la justice.*[13] The debate was far-reaching, and it took place against a background of a discussion over liberty and the necessity of laws, which was stoked generously by Enlightenment ideas. The *lettre de cachet* violated the social contract and it was for judges to preside over the imprisonment of individuals. The idea in the public mind of justice as shameful would therefore have to be replaced by one of justice as the sole guarantor of the law. Regular remonstrances were made to the king on this theme and the Cour des Aides addressed the question energetically and opinionatedly, under the direction of Malesherbes, its first president.[14] In 1770, and then again in 1775, the Cour des Aides took a stand, with Malesherbes focusing mainly on the danger of leaving the requests from families in the hands of subordinate civil officials.[15] As we have seen, inspectors and superintendents tasked with the investigations descended into streets and neighborhoods and picked up all manner of information; nothing could be more random, precarious, and unjust than procedures of this kind. And in the private domain, the big questions finally emerged: Is shame the product of the punishment or the crime? What is this family honor that would be stained not by the wrong committed but by the judgment incurred?

REPRESENTATION AND SECRECY

The practice of the *lettre de cachet* represented a perpetual request that brought into light and placed into discourse a whole assemblage of minute agitations, quarrels between parents and children, domestic or neighborhood arguments, squabbles fueled by wine, sex, and no small number of secret passions. All of these things that made up communal life therefore had an occasion to be spoken—and written down. But if these were being recounted, it was because the king, or at least one of his representatives, was being addressed. Because of his supposed presence, ever-conscientious, benevolent or severe, depending on what was deserved, one undertook to tell him all that was going on, denouncing villains, recounting in full the infamy of the person whose elimination, at least for a time, was being requested. In short, one presented oneself to the king and one presented others to him. One staged oneself for him. One represented things and people to him in the manner that one imagined that he might represent them to himself, and as a function of what one thought were the rules of his authority and the concerns of his monarchical responsibility. Moreover, these supplicants often followed stereotypes or models that were undoubtedly transmitted by the public scribes tasked with drafting these letters or by the police superintendents whose advice was being solicited.[16] The documents that we read here are not "raw" utterances but relatively complex expressions in which the admissible representations of good and bad conduct were adjusted between individuals and the authorities.[17]

This was accompanied by astonishing contrasts. Because one was addressing the king, one of his ministers, or the lieutenant of police, one employed language that was decorative, imprecatory, or supplicating. Each of these small everyday stories had to be told with the emphasis given to rare events deserving of the monarch's attention; high rhetoric was used to dress up these trivial matters. The supplicants, with their meager knowledge—or the scribes of varying degrees of skill who moved the quill in their stead—did their best to compose the formulas or turns of phrase that they thought necessary when addressing the king or other great personages, but stuck these alongside clumsy and violent words, uncouth expressions that sprang from their hearts and which they undoubtedly thought would make their demands more forceful and truthful; thus, in the midst of solemn phrases, between two emphatic words, out gushed rough, clumsy, dissonant expressions; impatience, anger, rage, passion, and rancor bled into the obligatory and almost ritualized language. Thus spoke the wife of Nicolas Bienfait (1758):

> She takes the liberty to most humbly represent unto My Lord that said Nicolas Bienfait, delivery coachman, is a strongly debauched man who is killing her with beatings and is selling everything, having already killed his two wives of whom the first he killed with child inside her body, the second

after having dissipated and eaten her out of house and home, by his abuse caused her to waste away and die, even attempting to strangle her on the eve of her death . . . The third, he wishes to eat her heart on the grill not to mention the other murders that he has done: My Lord, I throw myself at the feet of Your Grandeur in order to implore your mercy. I hope that in your goodness you will grant me justice, because my life is at risk at every moment, I will never cease to pray the Lord for the preservation of your health.[18]

It is a strange theater in which violence, misery, and tribulation were expressed through the ceremonial obligations owed to authority. Poor people took the stage, sometimes beggars, but more often simply shabby, put on costumes, struck poses, declaimed loudly and grandiloquently in a way that to them seemed necessary for supreme power to deign to throw a glance their way. They are reminiscent of the poor jugglers who draped themselves in tawdry rags of once-sumptuous clothes to perform before the mockery of wealthy audiences. With the exception that these supplicants were staging their own lives, and doing so in front of persons of power who could decide their fates. Here we see characters out of Callot or Le Nain arriving in Versailles, desperate to make themselves heard.[19]

All at once the secret had been told to the king, the insignificant had suddenly become larger than life.[20] Once in the king's hands, it could only function in an outsize and strange manner and no other. What unusual trajectories these necessarily divulged secrets had, confided to the king so that they could then return to the shadows of their origins. The royal person was the guarantor of this unexpected metamorphosis. Through him, the secret underwent a prodigious journey; because it went all the way to the king—the supreme authority—it was kept inside the family. Thus the private remained private, even when it was made public in the place of supreme power. Here, the king played the exorcist; through him, the thing that had been written could be made to disappear. Convents and royal prisons were the dark underbelly where the secret would be swallowed whole, where its humiliation would never come to light.

What is more, this was a secret of a surprising kind because we can note that the petitions sent to the king were more often than not accompanied by the signatures of neighbors, curés, or primary leaseholders. The secret told to the king, like a secret told "to only one person at a time," was already known to those close by, once again demonstrating, if it was necessary, the extent to which family was not at all synonymous with intimacy. A painful splinter in the heart of the family group, the wrongdoing or wicked conduct of one of its members possessed an infamous face that others could not fail to notice and that sullied them. This ignominious face threatened to become theirs. The secret belonged to them to the extent that they lived it from within, because inside and outside were continually bleeding into each other, to the point that private and public life could no longer be separated.[21] Precarious living conditions, socioeconomic instability, lodgings, workshops, and shops were open to the outside, permeable to everything that seeped in from the porous outdoors, to the point of symbiosis, creating particular spaces opaque to order, but interwoven out of webs of complicity, solidarity, and conflict whose violence was almost equal to their forces of cohesion. No one could claim to be absent from the lives of others, and the experience of this lack of privacy provoked behaviors both of integration and of rejection. For those nearby, the family secret became an object to appropriate; thus, spreading the secret elsewhere, which is to say all the way to the king, was a manner of retrieving honor, of definitively repelling opprobrium back into the darkest attics, ensuring at the same time that the neighborhood was washed of all villainy.

Ordinary justice was incapable of distancing wrongdoing in this manner. Its mechanisms, its long and costly procedures, its system for conducting inquiries, subpoenaing witnesses, confronting the accused, and repeating back the witness's testimony represented a long procession of acts proclaiming judgment. Judgment meted out spectacular punishment upon the condemned, made this punishment visible to the eyes of all, placed the wrongdoer and his family on display, without returning to them either esteem or reputation. Out of a private scandal, sometimes borne by the neighborhood, Justice, with its solemn, rigid, and weighty decorum, created a public scandal that punishment could neither absorb nor diminish. On the contrary, it exhibited it in its greatest possible intensity. Punishment existed to dissuade its audience. Its public nature had no goal other than the efficient consecration of the wrong done and of the apparatus that had been put in place to see to its punishment. In this sense, Justice stripped persons of honor, humiliated and scorned them, and did so officially. The person of the king, meanwhile, allowed for the individual in question to be reappropriated at the same time as it honored those who had requested his intervention. What an astonishing process this appeal to the king was; passing through him as an intermediary meant interesting (inflecting) his will, directing (catching) his gaze, which was ordinarily turned toward matters of state, existing in his eyes, requesting that it might please him to linger over the details of lives that normally would have every reason to remain submerged in the opaqueness of the multitude. To write to the king, to oblige his hand, was to introduce oneself into History, and to compensate in a spectacular manner for one's social status. When the poor went before the court, which stigmatized and drew attention to their social conditions through its crushing system, they received nothing in exchange except shame. A petition not only made it possible to avoid losing honor, but granted upon the person who wrote it the pride of being recognized by the most important state figure.

Was this not, moreover, a dual movement? Being "touched" by the king by virtue of his decision cannot be reduced to a passive act. It required requests and argumentation, it was a way of rendering oneself prodigiously present in the king's work by inciting him to make a choice, by becoming an actor at his side, holding one's course with sufficient insistence for him to dispatch an order. To act upon the king, to be granted his *favor* in the midst of a mediocre domestic life that was often pitiable and always without glory, there was something about all this that would not escape the intellectual circles of the 1780s. "There are many cases where the King, out of his paternal goodness, has been prepared to correct in order to prevent justice from punishing" (Vergennes, 1781). "An order from the King is more favor than punishment" (Saint Florentin). "When the King, out of goodness, wishes to imprison, it is a favor" (Malesherbes, 1789).[22]

Goodness, favor, correction instead of punishment, all this was there, but it is not enough to shed light on the entirety of the unexpected site of a request for imprisonment. At the source of this royal activity was the supplicant's desire, a desire that rose to the surface in the soft shape of an avowal. An avowal that was born out of itself, without the mediation of a priest, an avowal that no one compelled, an avowal that sprang from one's lips and was impatiently dictated to the public scribe, who would be responsible for transmitting it all in due form, an avowal that corresponded ever so closely to the pact maintained between the king and his subjects, an avowal that went beyond any inquiry, including even the desire of the king. Here the petition became a site where one could produce truth by oneself; one had to tell, and do so before others had the chance to, of the wrong that had polluted the family group, to avoid at all costs the possibility of being one day found guilty by the justice system—telling oneself in order not to be told, staging one's own misfortune, representing oneself so as to never be reduced to the unfair narratives of others embroiled in the same misfortune. One spoke "oneself" in order not to be spoken about, remaining a subject without leaving the possibility open to anyone, not even the king, of making one an object.[23]

A request for imprisonment was therefore a living site assembled out of action and desire, where the production of its author's self-image projected him into a space he created out of whole cloth and did not passively experience. What's more, it was a paradoxical creation, because in order to do this he needed to clothe himself in black: the only character that one could shape before the eyes of the king was that of the "infamous man." A final avowal of submission, of dependence, especially because it had to be supported by an economic negotiation: we have not yet finished measuring the importance of this exchange within the request for imprisonment, which made it an economic site as well. Thus was the father paid to restore order to the turbulent family space . . .

In hiding the wrongdoer from the eyes of the world, imprisonment permanently washed away the stain of guilt. This erasure is rather astonishing, and it required repentance in order to work. The king corrected, so it was said, but he did not punish. And relatives did not make the mistake of arguing over this feature of correction that was also a way for the detainee to mend his ways, to regret his wrongdoings, and, through solitude, to find clarity and even, why not, innocence. Once again everything differed from the regular system: the family request for imprisonment was a site of repentance, something that ordinary justice was little interested in obtaining. In the eighteenth century, justice whipped and banished, marked and scarred the body, and sent people to the galleys, without troubling itself over other forms of correction.

This notion of correction was as absent from the legal system's procedures as it was from its problematic. The physical suffering inflicted served a twofold purpose: avenging the wrong done to society and making this visible upon the body of the condemned, striking the flesh of the delinquent enough for the punishment to become a spectacle, an intimidation, a lesson for others. The legislator was hardly thinking of guiding the criminal's soul. The soul would only become important much later, during the nineteenth century, when criminality-obsessed philanthropists[24] would lend prisons the atmosphere of convents, in which the guard's eye[25] was there to provoke repentance, fight evil, and compel amendment.

In this sense, and yet also in an altogether different manner, the eighteenth-century convents and houses of detention were not spaces dedicated primarily to repentance. Family requests for imprisonment calling for repentance prefigured the large philanthropic projects of the next century. In this way, these families could distinguish what they were doing from standard justice, which linked infamy with the spectacle of punishment without ever erasing the former. The royal order represented another path entirely. It smoothed over contempt twice. It alone had the ability to bury a secret and allow for the rebirth of the wayward and impious person. The theater of the restitution of honor could finally be brought to its climax, and the sacred and repentance were at the heart of this scene.

Without knowing, of course, that in doing so it would plant the seed of its own demise. A day would come when maintaining the honor of families would seem trivial, when the vagaries of domestic life would seem too common, too vulgar, to be taken into serious consideration. Similarly, this site where the force of the king translated itself into arbitrariness day after day would come to appear odious rather than necessary: imprisoning a thirty-two-year-old son for his absence took up too much time and too much space in the lives of inspectors, superintendents, and police lieutenants for this torrent of requests not to be dammed. Reticence, suspicion, and then indignation seeped into the popular mind to the point of paralyzing the mechanism of the *lettre de cachet.* The more the private distinguished itself from public order, the more tribulations, of the young or even of lovers and spouses, came to be seen as necessitating first and foremost the intervention of the head of the household. The law and its supremacy were the order of the day; the refusal of the injustice of arbitrariness, of the good pleasure of the king, became increasingly forceful. It was crime that was the target of punishment by laws made for all, not dissipation (turbulence), unimportant trifles that the just authority of the father should know how to resolve. The detainees themselves protested against the years of imprisonment that had ruined their bodies and broken their spirits. Complaints came in from all sides, attacking these abusive orders that caused the disappearance from society of defenseless beings who had only scratched the social order.

This is how the slow transformation began. In maintaining the honor of families, the king would lose his own through a complex and irreversible movement carried out in the name of new liberties.

THE END OF THE *LETTRES DE CACHET*

The motives that led to the disappearance of family *lettres de cachet* were as complex and contradictory as the functioning of the institution itself.

It is easy to imagine that this practice of imprisonment would provoke displeasure on the part of its victims, worry among those who risked becoming its objects, and even distrust on the part of those who made use of it (given the possibility of consequences or a backlash that could be difficult to control). In short, this represented a very large portion of the population; placing the supreme power of the sovereign at the service of the public did not take place without posing a threat to all. Nonetheless, we should note that, in the general critique of the *lettre de cachet,* its use for reasons of family discipline was relatively more accepted than were its other uses. We are all, of course, familiar with the famous protests against it, such as Mirabeau's.[26]

But it is remarkable that in the discussions that took place at the Assemblée Constituante over detention by order of the king, there was a tendency to distinguish those obtained by family request from other kinds; as if, in these cases, the king exercised a more legitimate power than when he locked up his enemies.[27] While Abbé Maury, as we might have expected, objected to liberating all of the detainees on the grounds that some of them might well "injure the interests of society," Fréteau requested that all those who were imprisoned by family request be found, until family courts could be organized (except in cases of minor misdeeds).[28] And Robespierre complained that in these discussions, the primary focus was always on "persons imprisoned at the solicitation of their families," and not those who "were often detained for their virtue alone, for having allowed themselves to let slip a few indications of energy and patriotism."[29]

But we should not believe that this distinction between the needs of families, which had to be respected, and the arbitrariness of political despotism, which had to be guarded against, resulted in a pure and simple acquiescence to detentions requested by relatives or spouses. In fact, these procedures had been problematic for quite some time. They were a problem for jurists and philosophers who wished, on the basis of general principles, to reserve to a systematically codified law and the courts charged with enforcing it the responsibility of punishing, along a sliding scale, those who deserved it. But it was also problematic for all those who, being closer to the real functioning of the administration, were confronted with its internal difficulties. This was the case for certain police superintendents themselves, who were swamped with investigations and tired of having to waste time and energy meticulously reviewing domestic details that they considered trivial. They were evidently exhausted by the prospect of this enormous assignment that they were being asked to undertake, but they were also fed up with a task that they perhaps came to believe was not theirs to do, but rather the responsibility of the relatives themselves. Would they be expected to investigate youthful amusements forever, solely on the pretext that the parents of these youths were unable to restrain their offspring? Malesherbes expressed in more general terms his worry about the legitimacy of the reasons that could push families to request the imprisonment of one of their own. He was struck by the fact that sometimes reasons were not given, as if the family's desire was in itself sufficient. He suspected that in many cases—and especially in those involving husbands and wives—what lay behind these requests were simple incentives of personal interest or passion: "There are no *lettres de cachet* more abused than these because there are none that are solicited with more ardor." But he was especially perplexed by differences in motivations based on the class of the persons soliciting the letters, and by the resulting impossibility of laying down general principles—which were the only kind that an administration should recognize. When it came to aristocrats, it was a question of defending what they considered to be attached to the privilege of their blood:

> A patrician family will be indignant over a gentleman who, through very ignoble conduct, derogates his birth. What is called a base act is placed at the level of actions that public order cannot permit itself to tolerate from a man of standing. It would seem as if a family's honor demands that we remove from society any individual who, out of vile and abject morals, causes his parents to blush. Plebeians have other prejudices, which are perhaps grounded in a very healthy morality, but to which they are too tightly attached. There are wrongs of which everyone disapproves, but which people of standing and what we might call people of the world think of as pardonable and which in the judgment of a bourgeois family are inexcusable offenses. Pure and simple morality has been relegated to the lower orders. It would be desirable for these simple morals to be those of the nation as a whole, but they are not, and we cannot go so far as to deprive of their liberty all those who have allowed themselves to indulge in the common vices of their century.[30]

Malesherbes here provides a clear definition of the basic difficulty of establishing a rational policy for family *lettres de cachet*: not all social groups understood family in the same way. The aristocracy wished to make its own specific prejudices into principles for constraining individuals. On the other hand, those who had no privileges to bring to bear referred to more general moral rules; but these rules were never effectively applied, even by those who requested them. The *lettre de cachet* should be neither the tool of individual arrogances nor the establishment of abstract universalism; it should only, if we follow Malesherbes's logic, impose sanctions on deviations from a general moral consensus.

The famous circular drafted by Breteuil in March 1784 after he was named minister in the Maison du Roi did not put an end to imprisonment for family reasons; it was an attempt to establish rational principles for its operation and to impose limitations on it.[31] Among the imprisoned, Breteuil distinguished three categories of individuals who were to remain imprisoned, but about whom the principle for their imprisonment had to be understood in detail. There are "the mentally alienated": they must be detained to the extent that they are "incapable of behaving themselves in the outside world, or even to the extent that their rages make them dangerous."[32] There are those who committed delinquent acts that were not brought to the attention of the justice system: Breteuil did not seem to think that it was illegitimate or even disadvantageous for the state if certain wrongs escaped from the heaviness of the "afflicting or dishonoring punishments" of rule-governed justice. Finally, there are those who did not "trouble public order," but who indulged in "libertinage," by which Breteuil meant the two traditional elements of bad conduct: "debauchery and dissipation," sex and money.[33] Moreover, Breteuil did not contest the idea that families should be able to have someone imprisoned for these reasons. But he did wish to place a number of limitations on this practice.

1. Some of these limitations concerned the judicial status of persons: "An adult person who is master of his rights and no longer under paternal authority must no longer be imprisoned, even at the request of united families, so long as there has been no crime that might arouse the vigilance of public authority." In the courts, the practice of imprisonment must take place fully within the law, and no family bonds should be allowed to trump the judicial guarantees recognized as belonging to each person in general.

2. Other limitations were focused on establishing boundaries for that uncertain domain called honor, which had been so important to the practice of internment. Breteuil argued that honor, which is a trait of an individual (who has the right to defend it, but also the freedom to abandon it), must not be conflated with "the unpleasantness" that others, particularly family members, feel in response to seeing this person compromise his honor. A man debasing himself by a shameful marriage, or ruining himself through impulsive spending, or persons "seeing before their eyes a sister or close female relative of indecent morals," these are all forms of unpleasantness. As for the boy or the girl in question, "the type of dishonor in which they cover themselves reflects upon them alone, and since their relatives in no way share in this dishonor, it seems to me that they have no right to the intervention of the authorities."

3. Breteuil also sought to distinguish between that which might be considered to be reprehensible disorder and that which is only the result of conflicts and hatred within the family. From this point of view, spousal requests for imprisonment seemed to him to be the most suspicious: "It is only with the greatest circumspection that we should receive complaints of husbands against wives, or those of wives against husbands." With respect to the petitions that came from parents, Breteuil was a little more willing to give them the benefit of the doubt, on the condition that they were authenticated by other members of the family: "up until now, the agreement of the father and the mother has sufficed. But fathers and mothers are sometimes too unfair, or too strict, or too quick to become alarmed, and I think that we should

always require that at least two or three of the closest relatives sign, alongside the father and mother, these memoirs that contain requests for orders."

4. Finally, the circular emphasizes the distinction that should be made between punishment and correction. Imprisonment at the family's request must not operate as a substitute or analogy for judicial punishment, but should aid in the transformation of the individual. A first prerequisite of this transformation was that this imprisonment should be neither too long nor too severe: because, as Breteuil wrote, imprisonment itself was felt as a punishment, and even, if it lasts too long, as "the severest punishment for those whose sentiments have not been utterly annihilated or degraded." Second, it also required that the internal conditions of incarceration not be overly severe, that attention be paid to the improvement of detainees for as long as the detention lasted, and that it be ended once this improvement had been observed. "Independent of other considerations that can contribute to delaying or hastening their release, it is fair that its timing depend above all on how they have behaved themselves, the degree of change that has occurred in them, and what we can expect or fear from them once they become free again." In order to track this potential progress with more certainty, Breteuil requested that the police officials go to the houses of detention themselves, and not rely simply on what the guards told them, but rather interrogate the prisoners themselves and "have them give an account in their presence of everything bearing on their case."

This circular was important. We can see distinctions being drawn between the categories of honor, libertinage, dissipation, and disorder, which had for such a long time allowed imprisonment in the name of traditional social ties to operate. We can make out an attempt to shift this practice of imprisonment into a framework of the general rights of persons. We can also see a clearer delineation of the idea that imprisonment should be reserved above all for sons and daughters who were still under the power of their parents. And at a time when imprisonment began to take its place on the list of possible legal punishments, Breteuil's circular emphasized the idea of a specialized kind of detention, one whose goal would not be the punishment of acts committed but rather the modification of individuals.

Such would be the problems that legislators would have to resolve from this point on. On the one hand, they had to reduce the demands of families over their own members to the power of parents over children alone, and give justifications for the exercise of this power that were less particular than the honor of a family line and less general than the necessities of public order. On the other hand, they needed to present these measures in legally valid form, all while keeping them carefully separated from the judicial procedures of punishment. In sum, they needed to find a way for parents to retain a right to imprisonment that would be validated and controlled by public power, without calling upon the intervention of the latter's right to pursue and punish crimes.

In his project of providing a general organization of justice and the police, Sieyès separated "domestic reasons" from the rest.[34] These were admissible when "a father, a mother, a tutor, or a family" found themselves "gravely alarmed or worried about the conduct of a child, a pupil, a relative, or second-degree kin." But the wishes of relatives could only be enforced with the sanction of two mechanisms. One would represent the family unit in a wide sense; it was necessary to consult "at least eight family members, relatives, and friends of the accused to know whether the complaints were based in fact." One represented the police and judicial apparatuses: the police bureau would be responsible for the investigation. This would then be forwarded to the *chambre de police*, which would play the role of public official before a criminal court, which alone could decide to grant the requested imprisonment in a house of correction. Sieyès dreamed of parental correction, but of one that was closely shepherded by a family consensus, a meticulous police investigation, and a judicial verdict.[35]

This was a vast apparatus, and we might wonder whether, in the minds of those who conceived of it, the intention had been to render its use as difficult as possible, or whether they wished to restore an acceptable form of legitimacy to a practice that was indispensable, but whose arbitrariness had been disqualifying. The reintroduction of corrective imprisonment for children would in fact be a subject of debate over the different projects and measures that would later be adopted under the Revolution and then the Empire. We will not retrace the history of these discussions and these measures here. We will simply note that the Code of 1803 (articles 375–383) would legally organize paternal correction (let us not forget that this was a civil code).[36] The old practice of family imprisonment would be forced to retreat to the confines of the rights of parents over minors. Along with the corrective task assigned to these measures, less importance would be given to the exigencies of family honor than to the needs of society. Thus, the houses of correction that opened at this time, such as, for example, the maison de Bazancourt,[37] would provide a routine founded "upon impressions that were all aimed toward moral correction and the instilling, through regular tasks, of an inclination toward work . . . The correction of children from less fortunate classes will over time gradually reduce the number of men whose first youthful waywardness quickly leads to depravity and crime."[38]

Afterword to the English Edition

ARLETTE FARGE
Translated by Lara Vergnaud

On the thirtieth anniversary of Michel Foucault's death, the French publishing world, so fond of commemorations, marked the occasion with articles, book reprints, and publications about the man behind the author, the work, the intellectual, the philosopher, the writer, and the historian.

This is how Éditions Gallimard came to request a reprint of *Disorderly Families*, a book written by Michel Foucault and myself, which appeared in 1982, two years before his death.

Writing an afterword thirty years after the author has passed away is a tall order, though it is perhaps necessary for all those international readers who neither followed nor are aware of the vicissitudes of Foucauldian publications. Even if he was known abroad, notably in the United States and Brazil, Foucault was still not "heard" in France by his historian colleagues in the way he would have wanted, though his role as a "specific intellectual" reflecting on, among other subjects, the penitentiary system had brought him intense renown. We weren't far removed from 1968 and the explosion of overly rigid barriers between knowledge and action *[savoirs et actions]*.

Today, the task of adding an afterword to a book that was so "unusual" for its time has been imparted to me, an honor I accept joyfully and with humility. The book's publication date in France (ed. Archives/Gallimard, 1982) is not insignificant; it followed a long period of silence from the author. After the publication of the first volume of his *History of Sexuality, The Will to Knowledge*, in 1976, Foucault had in fact subsequently announced that other volumes would rapidly follow. But nothing he announced was to appear. Instead, in 1982, bookstores received a short book: *Disorderly Families*, written by two people, whose coauthor (me) was far from well known at the time. Its publication was a surprise and somewhat mysterious.

It's important to explain the genesis of this work and the reasons a young (at the time) female historian with few publications to her name was associated with the project. In 1975, Gallimard published Foucault's magnificent *Discipline and Punish: The Birth of the Prison*, a pioneering look at penitentiary institutions, their systems of thought, and the debut of the notion of docile bodies and social control. My sole publication, however, was a dissertation directed by Robert Mandrou, director of studies at the EHESS, on food theft in eighteenth-century Paris, based on trials of minor crimes maintained at the National Archives.[1] The thesis was published by Éditions Plon as part of the History and Mentalities collection directed by Georges Duby and Robert Mandrou.

My thesis director (known for, among other things, his work on witchcraft trials) had guided me toward police archives that struck him as underexploited, thus opening the door to an astonishing universe lying in wait at the National Archives, home to piles of thousands of sheaves of handwritten correspondence from *commissaires* and police lieutenant generals, arrest records, interrogations, and witness statements about thousands of incidents. These archives didn't contain major criminal proceedings (parricides, murders, assassinations, infanticides) but rather records of trials for theft, criminal acts, fighting, and brawls whose perpetrators belonged notably to classes deemed disadvantaged. These sheaves (whose rows spanned miles) were not yet well preserved at the time, as they had never been opened.

I therefore proceeded with caution, for they were barely legible and at times stained or torn. I opened those documents and to this day, I have stuck with them. Obsessional? No, I don't think so. And thus, without any intention, the focus of my future research was decided: from within those archives sprang, in every form, the outlines and interiors of a hidden and unknown existing world, at that time unfamiliar to us, from which escaped thousands of characters filled with affects and hopes, disillusionment and baseness, thoughts and desires, fantasies that were often disappointed, thwarted or successful loves. They had names, faces, professions, they loved one another, fought one another, stole, and hated each other, but they made history, a history in which the "greats," the major figures, who knew them so little, scorned them, robbing them even of their faculty to exercise their own judgment, and constructed, in order to coerce and render docile, systems that ultimately served to ignore or dismiss [*méconnaître*] them.

This unknown world of *gens de peu* (people of modest means), as they were referred to during the 1970–80s, was there, in those sheaves, and I wanted to draw an intricate portrait of its inhabitants, their lives, who they were, their emotions and fortunes, the meaning of their struggles, and all of it with genuine emotion.

1975, Publication of *Discipline and Punish*: I've never met Michel Foucault or attended his classes at the Collège de France, but I jump at his book. Having lived in the United States, I haven't followed his seminars, but while abroad I developed a passion for the birth of feminist movements.[2]

Just released, the book sparks as much admiration as it does veritable controversy, the latter mostly on the part of historians. How dare a philosopher, venturing into the historical field, disrupt traditional academia, systems of causality, and the habitual rationalism? What's more, his frequent use of the neutral pronoun *one,* which could be applied to anyone and erases all subjectivity, further aggravates the situation. For that matter, his limited use of footnotes is viewed as contempt for academic conventions or even evidence. The historians are bristling. But I don't realize it right away; I'm dazzled by the intellectual performance, the formidable intelligence, the new and original questions suddenly offering a new dimension to knowledge. I'm so admiring that I begin to question whether I shouldn't work on something besides penitentiary systems. Within the traditional historical milieu, silence nonetheless remains the norm all too often.

Later: I cross the Boulevard du Montparnasse on my way to meet with a fellow historian. When I arrive at the café, I see a book on the table: *Discipline and Punish.* At that instant, my colleague points out (I hadn't previously noticed) that I am quoted in it several times. Surprised, I don't pay this much mind beyond our meeting. Time goes by. In 1979 or 1980, I receive a telephone call from Michel Foucault asking to meet me in regard to a potential collaboration. How can I express my surprise and emotion when faced with such a request? There were so many disparities between us: social status, age, book publications, international prestige, classes whose audience threatened to spill out beyond the large lecture hall at the Collège de France . . .

During our meeting, he explains that he wants to publish a fair number of requests for imprisonment sent to the king and to write accompanying interpretations and analysis. At this point, I understand that he appreciates the way in which I read "these manuscripts from the past" from poor families who addressed the king in an extraordinarily direct way, without the intermediary of ordinary justice. I had, of course, read, in 1975, his article in the *Nouvelle Revue Française* (Gallimard) titled "Lives of Infamous Men," which conveyed his admiration for and emotional attachment to the grievances addressed to the highest power in the kingdom: the king. With rigor, emotion, and lyricism, he spoke of lives illuminated solely by "the light of justice," thanks to which they were able to be preserved. The intelligent, controlled, and impassioned lyricism of his opening sentences touched me enormously. He spoke of the men and women of *vies brèves,* brief lives, a term he preferred to *nouvelles* in the literary sense of the term.[3] The unique and unfailing beauty of his writing gave a specific tone to the text. For Foucault, those singular lives were also *vies poèmes,* life-poems.[4] Speaking of emotion in those days represented a real break from the traditional way of writing about history. He wrote: "I admit that these 'short stories,' suddenly emerging from two and a half centuries of silence, stirred more fibers within me than what is ordinarily called 'literature' . . . [If] I made use of documents like these . . . it was doubtless because of the resonance I still experience today when I happen to encounter these lowly lives reduced to ashes in the few sentences that struck them down."[5]

Reading about the emotional and physical resonance Foucault experienced was a revelation for me, encouraging and comforting. All the more so because, as a woman, known for being sensitive, my perspective as a historian was often put in doubt, sullied by attributes that historical science didn't want to understand and on which it had casually shut the door. Having chosen to focus my research on judicial archives, the road ahead was sometimes difficult and combative. It was necessary to maintain, in the most intelligent way possible, that spoken words, the unique situation of every human being, their discourse formed "events" that could be social or religious, political or affective, and more often than not were filled with emotion.

The Wonder and the Work: After my initial shock, we got to work. Some of the letters had already been recopied by one of Foucault's assistants, Éliane Allo, and by one of his friends, who was very ill and to whose child we granted all the rights.

Like many at the time, he copied the archives at the Bibliothèque de l'Arsenal by hand; I did the same. In reality (and I know this method has become obsolete and antiquated), copying petitions, interrogations, expressions of grief, and police recommendations offers a way to make direct contact with another flesh-and-blood person who also "exists," and has for so many years. A hand-to-hand struggle made possible by a sheath of manuscript. I must admit that I continue to operate in this fashion under the curious gaze of onlookers and surrounded by the clicking of computers. Writing, physically recording something with pen and paper, is a sensory act that brings the very distant, close.

Some of our work sessions took place at his home, during which we sifted through the texts, interpreted them, endeavored not to choose the most extravagant ones, established the contexts in which each "poem-life" was written, noted the violence, baseness, impact of domination, and so on. These hours of work were punctuated by discussions on the current events that had us both captivated: for example, Mitterrand's rise to power, the state of prisons and psychiatric hospitals in France, but also films and various events or occurrences that would have Foucault burst out laughing. Once we had more or less made our selection, we would sometimes work in his small office at the Collège de France, situated at the very top of a spiral, wooden staircase, in sessions I remember well. All our working hours were quite rich, learned (thanks to him), and generous: when it came time to determine the form of the publication in concrete terms, we discussed it together.

Increasingly attached to the beauty of these texts no doubt, to their odd manner of beginning with sumptuous phrases addressed to the sovereign, before continuing with remarks penned by the public letter writer, which had been whispered in his ear, Michel Foucault contended that it was necessary to publish the archives, the dossiers of requests for imprisonment, without any commentary, so that all that remained visible was the "sublime" of these unraveled lives laid bare in hatred and grief alike, facing a sovereign who shone as bright as the sun. In my opinion, in imagining that publication format, he "saw" a tableau wherein misery would challenge glory.

This did not strike me as the best solution, however. On the one hand, the public had been waiting for Foucault's next work, which still hadn't arrived, since the first volume of *The History of Sexuality*: *The Will to Knowledge*. A collection of texts on a subject different from that announced did not bode well for its publication. On the other hand, on a more intellectual level, it struck me that we would be forgoing a large number of analyses, reflections, interpretations, and systems of thought, which could only be understood by the public if we put them in writing. All the more so given that this type of family letter had a rather short life: police lieutenants wearied of so many investigations, the elites didn't understand why the king would take an interest in such an undignified class of people, and the sovereign himself grew tired of the exercise.

We discussed this calmly and he agreed to write about and interpret the texts. This led him to take on a new task—dividing the topics and themes on which we could write and reflect. Furthermore, attempting the critical, political, anthropological, and emotional analysis of this precise moment in history allowed for reflection on historical ruptures and discontinuities, both themes dear to Foucault.

Parents–Children, Husbands–Wives: It was 1980. Society was still very marked by the events of 1960 and we had entered the great period of feminism. I was an activist (we used to say we were making "women's history"); Michel Foucault was defending homosexuality and at the same time took the feminist movement very seriously. Which didn't stop him from joking about it at times. He was quite worried about having to write about husband–wife relations, believing he didn't know the theories coming from the United States very well and fearful of being criticized by such a combative movement. We laughed about it together. So we wrote the parents–children and husbands–wives chapters separately (I took on the latter). We exchanged our writing as much as possible in order to better harmonize with, understand, and learn from each other. We then drafted the introduction and conclusion together.

In the table of contents, we refused to note who wrote what, which led to some curious assumptions by others.

Our shared endeavor has stayed with me. I can't put into words how this period created a "before" and "after" me. Nobody could have remained unaffected, given our differences in intelligence, by an encounter of such intensity.

Book Publication, 1982: The book was published two years before his death in Paris at the Hôpital de la Salpêtrière. It appeared in Gallimard's "Archives" collection, led by Pierre Nora. And—quite the surprising phenomenon—a good deal of time passed between the completion of the book's writing and its publication. The day it came out, a large gathering assembled at the Gallimard offices, including editors, directors, the publisher's press agents, as well as many guests. Speeches, talks, a warm reception. I didn't say much. For that matter, I had never told my historian colleagues that I was writing the book because the atmosphere between the philosopher and historians was, after all, quite tense. Indeed, in 1980 Michelle Perrot assembled several contributors in order to produce a book of commentaries about *Discipline and Punish* titled *L'Impossible prison: Recherches sur le système pénitentiaire au XIX* siècle.*[6] Within the work, the historians react, discuss, and refute, in terms of both form and substance; Michel Foucault defends himself brilliantly with a vigor and force as much poetic as historically grounded.

In short, *Disorderly Families* appeared in a vast media desert, apart from one broadcast on *Lundis de l'Histoire* on France Culture, on the initiative of Roger Chartier. No reactions in the newspapers apart from (and I can't recall whether this was *Le Figaro* or *Le Monde*) a dozen sentences calling the book *poujadiste*, penned by Emmanuel Todd.

I know that Michel Foucault was deeply saddened and appalled by this rejection and blanket silence (I was at the École des Hautes Études at that time, where the only colleague who mentioned the work to me was Jacques Revel). Foucault was never even invited to the École to discuss the texts or give a lecture.

In 1982, undiscouraged, Michel Foucault and I decided to once again work together, using eighteenth-century police archives, on family secrets as well as letters from parents and children, demands for release, and texts or poems written during the period of imprisonment. He went to the United States for a while, as he often did. In 1984, he became ill, then came news of his death, earth-shattering, not least because of the secrecy he had hoped to maintain about his condition.

2014, thirty years later: *Disorderly Families* is reissued with a pretty cover, and not a line is changed. Countless features and press articles appear in newspapers and magazines, alongside testimonials. Books are published about him, related to his life, his works, or the philosophical disagreements provoked by Foucauldian thought. But little appears about our project. In the meantime, and notably thanks to Judith Butler and many others, feminism seizes on Foucauldian thought as a basis for analysis and reflection that aim to bring feminism and the history of women toward the history of gender, queer and transsexual studies, and homosexuality. I can't help but think that he would have been quite surprised.

As for me, today I'd like to address the reader directly. I want to share— all these years later—a few disarmingly simple musings and memories:

> I remember his laugh
> I remember his conviction when talking about singular lives and making them actors in history
> I remember his love for cinema
> I remember love for his black cat
> I remember his erudition, his passion for books, literature, reasoning, the desire to convince, the subversive desire *(volonté)*
> I remember his appetite for thinking outside the box, for breaking down barriers between disciplines
> I remember his appreciation for the disparate, which deconstructed what we call "the real" *(le réel)*
> I remember his desire that we each learn the fable of obscure lives
> I remember that he always spoke of true lives
> I remember his vocabulary: strategies and power
> I remember how much he liked ruptures and discontinuities, rifts and cracks
> I remember what he thought of those in power and the "characters out of Céline, trying to make themselves heard at Versailles"
> I remember his writing, to which I don't want to append any adjectives given that, for me, it is the writing of history
> I remember his fierce love of the shameful and shameless
> I remember his activism and his fight for the prisons
> I remember the lifelong lesson he imparted on me that the *quelconque*, the whatever, was only able to appear under the impetus of power
> I remember that the *quelconque* is so serious that it must know how to defy power
> I remember meeting and working with Michel Foucault

Notes

EDITOR'S INTRODUCTION

I thank Philippe Artières and Daniel Defert for their generosity in talking to me about this project, and the librarians at IMEC and BNF for helping research its critical reception. Finally, I thank Shai Gotler, Rachel Mattson, and David Temin for their meticulous research assistance.

1. A *lettre de cachet* was "a letter written by order of the King, countersigned by his secretary of State, and sealed with the King's seal *(cachetée du cachet)*," (Joseph-Nicolas Guyot, *Répertoire universel et raisonné de jurisprudence civile, criminelle, canonique et bénéficiale,* vol. 10 [Paris: Visse, 1785], 479).

2. When Farge and Foucault were searching for a title, they encountered various difficulties. Foucault liked the idea of *Dérangement des familles* because *dérangement* brings with it connotations of madness, unsettlement, and malaise. His editors demurred, on the grounds that malicious readers might think instead of intestinal disorders (the other usage of *dérangement*). He and Farge settled instead on *désordre,* a word that has its own echoes across several of the letters, such as that of Pierre Germain Béranger. See Arlette Farge, "Souvenir d'un dérangement," *Le Magazine littéraire,* no. 435 (October 2004): 54. Likewise, the English translation has its own challenges. We had considered "Families in Disarray" to capture the disregard for usual orders and arrangements; "disarray," however seemed too pallid in the face of the conflicts in the letters. "Familial Disorders" seemed more full-throated but limited these disorders to a family setting. In the end, "Disorderly Families" seemed best to capture the unruliness of the letters, their whiff of unreason, and the refraction of these plaints through family relations. Elsewhere Farge comments that "disorder" captures people's "simultaneous desires for encounter and rupture" (Arlette Farge, *Fragile Lives: Violence, Power and Solidarity in Eighteenth-Century Paris,* trans. Carol Shelton [Cambridge: Harvard University Press, 1993], 285).

3. The classic texts that globally treat these letters of arrest are Frantz Funck-Brentano, *Les Lettres de cachet à Paris: Étude suivie d'une liste des prisonniers de la Bastille (1659–1789)* (Paris: Imprimerie nationale, 1903); Frantz Funck-Brentano, *Les Lettres de cachet* (Paris: Librairie Hachette, 1926); Marc Chassaigne, *La Lieutenance générale de police de Paris* ([1906], Geneva: Slatkine reprints, 1975), 146–60; Claude Quétel, *Les Lettres de cachet: Une légende noire* (Paris: Perrin, 2011); Vincent Milliot, *Un Policier des Lumières* (Seyssel: Éditions Champ Vallon, 2011).

4. Michel Foucault, *History of Madness,* ed. Jean Khalfa, trans. Jonathan Murphy and Jean Khalfa (New York: Routledge, 2006), xxxviii.

5. Cf. Michel Heurteaux, "La délation, poison latent," *Le Monde,* May 15, 1983. In contrast to the anonymous letters denouncing neighbors that were sent to local police under Vichy, these letters were signed and quasi-public knowledge.

6. For a discussion of this history, see Quétel, *Les Lettres de cachet,* 12–16.

7. Likewise, Foucault initially believed the letters were an illustration of royal power until his archival work. He and Farge will comment on this point in nearly every interview or essay on the project. See Michel Foucault, "Confinement, Psychiatry, Prison," in *Politics, Philosophy, Culture: Interviews and Other Writings, 1977–1984,* rev. ed., ed. Lawrence D. Kritzman (New York: Routledge, 1990), 187.

8. The thirteen regional *parlements* in Ancien Régime France were high courts of appeal with no legislative powers. In the years leading up to the French Revolution, the *parlement* in Paris sought to contest royal authority over several jurisdictions, and occasionally the king used the *lettres de cachet* to regulate those disputes.

9. Arlette Farge describes Foucault's response as one of near "physical vibration" ("Souvenir d'un dérangement," 54).

10. Radio broadcast with Roger Chartier (moderator), André Béjin, Arlette Farge, Michel Foucault, and Michelle Perrot, "À propos les 'lettres de cachet,'" *Les Lundis de l'histoire*, Radio France Culture, recorded on November 27, 1982, and broadcast on January 10, 1983. Consulted at IMEC, audio recording C127(I) and at the Bibliothèque Nationale de France (Inathèque).

11. Foucault lays down several ground rules for the texts to be selected: that these persons have existed; that their lives be obscure; that they present these lives tersely in "a fistful of words"; that they not easily fall into formulaic scripts of highway robbers and the like; that their words evoke that queer sense of beauty mixed with dread. See Michel Foucault, "Lives of Infamous Men," in *Power: Essential Works of Michel Foucault, 1954–84*, vol. 3, ed. James Faubion, trans. Robert Hurley et al. (New York: New Press, 2000), 159–60; Gilles Deleuze, "A Portrait of Foucault," in *Negotiations*, trans. Martin Joughin (New York: Columbia University Press, 1995), 108–10.

12. *Herculine Barbin, dite Alexina B* includes the memoirs of self-discovery for a young hermaphrodite and is prefaced by a short essay more interpretive than the historically oriented essays in *Disorderly Families*. See *Herculine Barbin: Being the Recently Discovered Memoirs of a Nineteenth-Century French Hermaphrodite*, trans. Richard McDougall (New York: Vintage, 1980).

13. Critical attention might group this volume alongside *I, Pierre Rivière* (1973) and the memoir *Herculine Barbin* (1978); the first produces the police dossier around Pierre Rivière's parricide (discovered in the Departmental Archives of Calvados) along with a collection of essays written by Foucault's research seminar participants. See *I, Pierre Rivière*, trans. Frank Jellinek (Omaha: University of Nebraska Press, 1982). Both of these texts contain a biographical dimension lacking in the letters, however. One might also read the letters alongside the untranslated *L'Impossible prison*, which brings together French scholars from a variety of disciplines to reflect on practices of imprisonment and their analysis. See *L'Impossible prison*, ed. Michelle Perrot (Paris: Seuil, 1980). In addition to substantive questions around lives lived on the margins, such readings raise questions of history, historical interpretation, and methodology. Farge compares *Disorderly Families* to these works in her interview with Laurent Vidal, "Arlette Farge, le parcours d'une historienne," *Genèses*, no. 48 (2002/3): 115–35.

14. For a collection of essays that analyze the different dimensions of the GIP, see *Active Intolerance: Michel Foucault, the Prisons Information Group, and the Future of Abolition*, ed. Perry Zurn and Andrew Dilts (New York: Palgrave Macmillan, 2015). This activist context, along with the then-contemporary resonance between the letters and the 1974 trial of Dr. Mikhail Stern in the USSR emerge clearly in Foucault's interview with *Apostrophes* as well as in the discussion recorded in "Confinement, Psychiatry, Prison," and in Deleuze, *Negotiations*, 108–10.

15. Foucault specifically references the *lettres de cachet* in *History of Madness*, 47, 81, 119, 125, 130, 382, 420ff., 446; *Abnormal: Lectures at the Collège de France, 1974–75*, trans. Graham Burchell, ed. Arnold Davidson (New York: Palgrave Macmillan, 2004), 37, 53; *Psychiatric Power: Lectures at the Collège de France, 1973–1974*, trans. Graham Burchell, ed. Jacques

Lagrange (New York: Palgrave Macmillan, 2008), 7, 125; *The Punitive Society: Lectures at the Collège de France, 1972–1973*, trans. Graham Burchell, ed. Bernard Harcourt (New York: Palgrave Macmillan, 2015), 125–41.

16. Foucault mentions this assistant, Christiane Martin, in his January 15, 1975, lecture in *Abnormal* (37, 53). Christiane Martin first encountered Foucault after taking a sociology course with his partner, Daniel Defert, who took her under his wing. Of modest means, she was employed by Foucault as a research assistant to help maintain her student status and earn some money; after her death, Foucault arranged for the royalties from *Désordre* to go to her daughter. I thank Daniel Defert for sharing this account with me on July 6, 2013. Arlette Farge recounts a similar story in an interview with Laurent Vidal, "Arlette Farge, le parcours d'une historienne," 115–35.

17. This essay was initially published in *Cahiers du chemin* 29, January 15, 1977, 19–29.

18. In 1964, Foucault signed a contract for a volume that should have appeared in the Archives collection established by Pierre Nora at Julliard. Earlier volumes list as forthcoming the title *Les Fous: Michel Foucault raconte, du XVIIe au XIXe siècles, de la Bastille à Sainte-Anne, le voyage au bout de la nuit* (The Mad: From the Bastille to Sainte-Anne, Foucault tells the story of the voyage to the end of the night in the 17th to 19th centuries). See David Macey, *The Lives of Michel Foucault* (New York: Vintage, 1995), 453.

19. Deleuze finds the conception of infamous men to be "infused with a quiet gaiety. It's the opposite of Bataille: the infamous man isn't defined by excessive evil but etymologically, as an ordinary man . . . It's a man confronting Power, summoned to appear and speak" (Deleuze, *Negotiations*, 108).

20. Foucault, "Lives of Infamous Men," 169, 171.

21. See Foucault, Preface to the 1961 edition, *History of Madness*, xxxi, xxxiii.

22. I thank Philippe Artières for this felicitous phrasing. The question of arrangement or "collage" is touched on in Philippe Artières, Jean-François Bert, Pascal Michon, Mathieu Potte-Bonneville, and Judith Revel, "L'Atelier de Michel Foucault," in *Lieux de Savoir: Les mains de l'intellect*, vol. 2, ed. Christian Jacob (Paris: Éditions Albin Michel, 2011), 960.

23. French historian Roger Chartier views *Désordre* as a means to "lay bare the thought within texts that, on the one hand, are surrounded by a formal juridical apparatus; and, on the other hand, seem directly linked to experiences, usually unhappy, of daily lived experience." See "Retour à l'archive," in *Foucault aujourd'hui*, ed. Roger Chartier and Didier Eribon (Paris: L'Harmattan, 2006), 53; my translation.

24. Farge reflects on this collaboration in a number of essays and interviews, including Arlette Farge, "Michel Foucault et les archives de l'exclusion," in *Penser la folie* (Paris: Éditions Galilée, 1992); Arlette Farge, "Travailler avec lui," in *"Dossier Michel Foucault: La rupture permanente," Le Monde*, September 19–20, 2004, iv–v; interview with Laurent Vidal, "Arlette Farge, le parcours d'une historienne," 115–35; and interview with Sylvain Parent, "Entretien avec Arlette Farge," *Tracés: Revue de Sciences humaines* [Online], May 2004, published January 26, 2009, consulted October 12, 2012. See also Leon Antonio Rocha, "'That Dazzling, Momentary Wake' of the *lettre de cachet*," in *Foucault, the Family and Politics*, ed. Robbie Duschinsky and Leon Antonio Rocha (New York: Palgrave Macmillan, 2012), 17–88.

25. The book cited in *Discipline and Punish* is *Le Vol des aliments à Paris au XVIIIe siècle* (Paris: Plon, 1974) (Macey, *Lives of Michel Foucault*, 453). Farge and Foucault also shared a common affection for historians Philippe Ariès and Robert Mandrou, whose work affected their

own interest in a "history of mentalities." Ariès backed away from both the demography and the Marxism that was connected to the *Annales* school; both Ariès and Mandrou rejected ideas of "collective unconscious" and instead pushed to (re)discover the history that emerged from daily life. See "Le Style de l'histoire," interview with Arlette Farge and F. Dumon and J-P. Iommi-Amunategui, *Le Matin*, no. 2168, February 21, 1984, 20–21, in Michel Foucault, *Dits et Écrits II* (Paris: Gallimard, 2001), 1471.

26. Interview with Vidal, "Arlette Farge, le parcours d'une historienne."

27. Foucault proposed this division, indicating both his reluctance to write on heterosexual relationships and his fascination for the children dreaming of escape from their families. For her part, Farge explains that she preferred the "acerbity and violence" from the letters on married life. For an account of the division of labor, see Farge's interview with Vidal, "Arlette Farge, le parcours d'une historienne," 119, and Farge, "Souvenir d'un dérangement," 53.

28. Foucault, "Lives of Infamous Men," 168.

29. Farge and Foucault, "Marital Discord," *Disorderly Families.*

30. Farge and Foucault, "Parents and Children," *Disorderly Families.*

31. Farge, "Travailler avec lui."

32. Foucault, "Lives of Infamous Men," 168.

33. For a longer discussion of the complexities of comparing families to royal politics, see the essay "Marital Discord" in this volume, and the discussion of historical research in note 3.

34. Classic interventions include Keith Michael Baker, *Inventing the French Revolution* (Cambridge: Cambridge University Press, 1990); Jean-Louis Flandrin, *Families in Former Times: Kinship, Household, and Sexuality*, trans. Richard Southern (Cambridge; Cambridge University Press, 1979); Joan Landes, *Women and the Public Sphere in the Age of the French Revolution* (Ithaca, N.Y.: Cornell University Press, 1988); Sarah Hanley, "Engendering the State: Family Formation and State Building in Early Modern France," *French Historical Studies* 16.1 (spring 1989): 4–27; Lynn Hunt, *The Family Romance of the French Revolution* (Berkeley: University of California Press, 1993). French historians tend to contest both that the eighteenth century reflects the slow, even centralization of royal power and the Habermasian claim that something like a public sphere emerges only at the end of the century. For an overview of the dispute, see Roger Chartier, "Discourses and Practices: On the Origins of the French Revolution," in *On the Edge of the Cliff*, trans. Lydia Cochrane (Baltimore: Johns Hopkins University Press, 1997), 72–80; and Suzanne Desan and Jeffrey Merrick, eds., *Family Gender and Law in Early Modern France* (University Park: Pennsylvania State University Press, 2009), xi–xxvi. For essays that rethink the family from a Foucauldian perspective, and are specifically informed by *Le Désordre des familles*, see Duschinsky and Rocha, *Foucault, the Family and Politics.*

35. In his lecture of January 14, 1976, Foucault explains: "juridical systems, no matter whether they were theories or codes, allowed the democratization of sovereignty, and the establishment of a public right articulated with collective sovereignty, at the very time when, to the extent that, and because the democratization of sovereignty was heavily ballasted by the mechanisms of disciplinary coercion . . . In our day, it is the fact that power is exercised through both right and disciplines, that the techniques of discipline and discourses born of discipline are invading right, and that normalizing procedures are increasingly colonizing the procedures of the law, that might explain the overall workings of what I would call a 'normalizing society'" (Michel Foucault, *Society Must Be Defended: Lectures at the*

Collège de France, 1975–76, English series ed. Arnold Davidson, trans. David Macey [New York: Picador, 2003], 37–39).

36. Readers of Foucault have often risked overstating the coherence of power relations, or identifying a late "turn" to ethics in Foucault's writing. Foucault voices his frustration with these misreadings and clarifies the imbrication of power, self-cultivation, and knowledge around historically variable modes of subjectivity in the course summary for *Subjectivity and Truth.* In their discussion of "avowal" in Foucault's lectures on nineteenth-century criminology and ancient truth telling, Fabienne Brion and Bernard Harcourt argue the same point ("Editor's Preface," in *Wrong-Doing, Truth-Telling: The Function of the Avowal in Justice,* ed. Fabienne Brion and Bernard Harcourt, trans. Stephen W. Sawyer [Chicago: University of Chicago Press, 2014], 4–6). I have also defended this claim in *Crisis of Authority* (Cambridge: Cambridge University Press, 2013).

This sense is reinforced by the course summary for *Subjectivity and Truth* in which Foucault contextualizes what will turn out to be a course on the ancients by explaining that he proposes to examine the different and variant mechanisms of power that establish the subject "as a possible, desirable, or even indispensable object of knowledge." Those lectures promise to examine the intersections of subjectivity and governmentality; the experiences of the lives in *Disorderly Families* are just one schema among many possible. Although this broader context disappears from the lectures actually given in *Subjectivity and Truth,* it helps to contextualize how Foucault understood the implicit political and theoretical stakes of *Disorderly Families.* See Michel Foucault, *Ethics: Essential Works of Foucault, 1954–1984,* vol. I, ed. Paul Rabinow, trans. Robert Hurley et al. (New York: New Press, 1997), 87–92.

37. Foucault, "Lives of Infamous Men," 168.

38. These retorts are very explicitly presented in Farge and Foucault's interview with Yves Hersant, "L'âge d'or de la lettre de cachet," in *Dits et Écrits II,* 1170–71. Farge and Foucault use the phrase "speaking so as not to be spoken about" ("se dire pour ne pas être dit") in "When Addressing the King" (this volume), and again in the radio broadcast "À propos les *lettres de cachet.*"

39. In *Society Must Be Defended,* Foucault acknowledges that while sovereign power is at its height in the seventeenth century, it coexists alongside a later disciplinary power and its administration through the apparatuses of governmentality. If sovereignty targets security and territory, then discipline targets individuals. By the time of *Security, Territory, Population,* Foucault clarifies: "sovereignty is exercised within the borders of a territory, discipline is exercised on the bodies of individuals, and security is exercised over the whole population" (English series ed. Arnold Davidson, trans. Graham Burchell [New York: Picador, 2009], 11).

40. Foucault writes at length about the role of the police and their connection alternately to royal power and governmentality in the April 5, 1978, lecture for *Security, Territory, Population,* 333–61.

41. Foucault briefly mentions the creation of the lieutenancy, its complicated jurisdiction, and the *lettres de cachet* in *History of Madness,* 124–26; *Théories et institutions pénales: Cours au Collège de France, 1971–1972* (Paris: Gallimard, 2015), 34n11, 95–96, 99n19, as well as the connection of the police to capitalist production (95); and at greater length in *The Punitive Society,* 126–34.

42. Lieutenant General Nicolas Delamare, in his *Traité de la police,* writes: "The first legislators of the famous [Greek] republics, considering life to be the basis of every other good that is the object of police, and considering life itself, if not accompanied by a good

and wise conduct, and by all the external aids necessary for it, to be only a very imperfect good, divided all of police into these three parts, the preservation, the goodness, and the pleasures of life." See "Idée générale de la police," in *Traité de la police*, vol. I, 2d rev. ed. (Paris: Michel Brunet, 1722), 3.

The classic work on bread, politics, and policing is Steven L. Kaplan, *Bread, Politics and Political Economy in the Reign of Louis XV*, 2d ed. (New York: Anthem Press, 2015 [1976]); and Steven L. Kaplan, *Provisioning Paris* (Ithaca, N.Y.: Cornell University Press, 1984). Bernard Harcourt has written about the contradictions between free markets and the *police des grains* in *The Illusion of Free Markets* (Cambridge: Harvard University Press, 2013). For specifics on the policing techniques involved, see Milliot, *Un Policier des Lumières*, 147–48.

43. See David Garrioch, "Bread, Police, and Protest," in *The Making of Revolutionary Paris* (Berkeley: University of California Press, 2002), 132–41.

44. Milliot, *Un Policier des Lumières*.

45. The edict of 1708 named about forty *inspecteurs*; the edict of March 1740 brought that number down to twenty and distributed them across the *quartiers de police* under the authority of the *commissaires*. One of the *commissaires*, or superintendents, who contributes letters to this volume is Jean-Baptiste-Charles Lemaire, from the quartier Maubert. Lemaire attains this position after serving as an investigating officer for Châtelet, working in the quartier Saint-Benoît (1751), then on the Île de la Cité (1755), and Maubert (1757), before taking charge as *commissaire* (1757–79). He has a reputation for moderation and competence, qualities that lead to his rapid promotion by Lieutenant General Antoine de Sartine. He writes his *Mémoire sur la police* between 1768 and 1771, at Lieutenant General Sartine's request.

46. Foucault discusses the mounted constabulary in *Security, Territory, Population*. My gloss here does not begin to capture the jurisdictional conflicts around policing. For lengthier discussion of these bodies, see Farge and Foucault's "Introduction" (note 14) and "Parents and Children" (note 4). For more details on these different policing bodies, see Alan Williams, *The Police of Paris, 1718–89* (Baton Rouge: Louisiana State University Press), 67–111.

47. As lieutenant general, d'Argenson distinguished himself by destroying the Jansenist monastery of Port-Royal in 1704, by improving street lighting, and by the financial scandals of his later career. He used the lieutenancy to move toward a "new police" freed from the jurisdictional constraints of the *parlements*. D'Argenson was particularly concerned with libertinage, gambling, and prostitution. Foucault finds that his judgments as lieutenant general move madness toward the world of morality. D'Argenson's son, Marc-Pierre de Voyer de Paulmy, later held the same position twice for short periods of time.

Antoine de Sartine begins service as a judge at Châtelet at age twenty-three and is ennobled following his purchase of the office of Criminal Lieutenant. In 1759, he became lieutenant general and served one of the longest terms in that office, from 1759 until 1774. Sartine had a reputation for moderation, improved the street lighting in Paris, doubled the presence of firefighters, and created a free drawing school for workers—all of which commanded the respect of other European cities. In addition, he used the *lettres de cachet* as both threat and punishment, increased the policing of billiard parlors, and expanded the role of police informants *(les mouches)*—all of which earned him popular ill will. In the guise of emphasizing the police as a public force, under Sartine the jurisdiction of the police extends to include a more deliberate monitoring of "at-risk" populations, and specifically the reading of personal letters and the use of a network of spies. See Jacques Michel, *Du Paris de Louis XV à la Marine du Louis XVI: L'œuvre de Monsieur de Sartine* (Paris: Éditions de l'Érudit, 1983); Quétel, *Les Lettres de cachet*, 168–76.

48. Indeed, René Hérault took the position of lieutenant general in August 1725 in the midst of a violent uprising of women over high bread prices, which originated in the notoriously autonomous neighborhood of the Faubourg Saint-Antoine. He remained lieutenant general until December 1739, when he was replaced by his son-in-law Claude-Henri Feydeau de Marville. The classic text here is Steven L. Kaplan, *Bread, Politics, and Political Economy in the Reign of Louis XV* (The Hague: Martinus Nijhoff, 1976).

49. Nicolas Berryer's career unfolds under the protection of Madame de Pompadour. After working as a lawyer for the Chambre des requêtes de l'Hôtel in 1728, he goes on to serve as an adviser to the *parlement* of Paris (1731), as a civil servant in Poitou (1743–47), and then lieutenant general of police (1747–57). This was a stepping stone to more prestigious positions, including being secretary of state for the Marine from 1758 to 1761, and finally Garde des Sceaux. Berryer was part of the "new police" that sought to demonstrate and defend its power through more punitive measures aimed at protecting public order.

50. Turmeau de la Morandière, *Plan de Police contre les Mendians, les Vagabonds, les Escrocs, les Filles de débauche et les Gens sans aveu* (Paris: Dessaint Junior, 1764); cited in Milliot, *Un Policier des Lumières*, 183.

51. Used in this context, the word for clarifications in French is interestingly allusive. The sense here is of the king's publicity piercing the shadow of obscurity in everyday lives. Paradoxically, his visibility can protect the secrecy of the familial disturbances confided in the letters. In a later radio interview, Farge comments that these investigations often obscure more than they illuminate. Deleuze will later elaborate: "The infamous man's a particle caught in a shaft of light and a wave of sound." The phrase also resonates with the Enlightenment *(les Lumières)* and with Nietzsche's analogy of the split between doer and deed to lightning *(éclair)* and its flash. See roundtable with Roger Chartier (moderator), André Béjin, Arlette Farge, Michel Foucault, and Michelle Perrot, "À propos les 'lettres de cachet'"; Deleuze, *Negotiations*, 108.

52. Proposals to deport beggars and vagabonds to France's colonies in Louisiana, Mississippi, and elsewhere date at least to the seventeenth century. These proposals were backed by royal edicts of 1718, 1719, and 1720. Following a series of complaints—that these policies were backed by thuggery and applied inhumanely, and that they had an adverse effect on seasonal agricultural labor—the edicts were revoked by royal declaration on July 5, 1722. Rumors that these policies were being resurrected surfaced in 1750, when the increased vigilance of the police led to rumors that children were being arrested in the streets of Paris and deported. See Robert Schwartz, *Policing the Poor in Eighteenth-Century France* (Chapel Hill, N.C.: University of North Carolina Press, 1988); Arlette Farge, *Vanishing Children of Paris*, trans. Claudia Mieville (Cambridge: Harvard University Press, 1991).

53. Foucault, "L'âge d'or de la lettre de cachet," 1170–71. See also the discussion of Farge's later claim that the letters tell "the history of a secret" in note 20 of the essay "When Addressing the King" in this volume.

54. Funck-Brentano, *Les Lettres de cachet à Paris*, 44–94; Milliot, *Un Policier des Lumières*, 294.

55. Quoted in Milliot, *Un Policier des Lumières*, 294. Malesherbes served briefly as minister of the Maison du Roi for Louis XVI between 1775 and 1776. He used the system of remonstrances to curb the letters of cachet, by outlining the corrupt nature of their administration in his *Les Remontrances* (1775). A year after defending the king before the French National Convention, Malesherbes and his family were guillotined in 1794.

56. These letter-writing manuals, or *secrétaires*, were printed and circulated as part of the *Bibliothèque bleue*, a collection of books known for the blue color of the paper on which they

were often printed. The term *secrétaire* has a varied history, referring alternately to a person or to a book. In the context of aristocratic domesticity, *secrétaires* are employed by a lord to write letters; in the judiciary, the *secrétaire* records the proceedings; in tragedies, they refer to the figure of confidant. Other sources offer a different differentiation by functional roles and clearer hierarchy. Antoine Furetière's *Dictionnaire universel* (1690) distinguishes between those officers in service to the king who dispatch commands and warrants on his order, authorized with his own signature. Next in rank are clerks for lawyers and lords, and lowest are those scribes who write for the populace. See *Dictionnaire universel* which is permalinked at http://gallica.bnf.fr/ark:/12148/bpt6k50614b/f1888.image. See also Roger Chartier, ed., *Correspondence: Models of Letter-Writing from the Middle Ages to the 19th Century*, trans. Christopher Woodall (Princeton. N.J.: Princeton University Press, 1997), 59–62. The original French volume is more comprehensive, with essays that trace the internalization of epistolary practice by workers, domestic servants, and those outside of Paris: *La Correspondance: Les usages de la lettre au XIXe siècle* (Paris: Fayard, 1991).

57. To this point, the file of François Dubois, filed by Farge and Foucault under "Marital Discord," includes a near-exact copy of one such letter. The only differences are a modernization of certain words (e.g., *aussy* becomes *aussi*)—and of course the names signed at the end of the second letter show a slight increase in prominence.

58. Michel Rey, "Police et sodomie à Paris au XVIIIe siècle: Du péché au désordre," *Revue d'histoire moderne et contemporaine* 29.1 (January–March 1982): 113–24. See also Nina Kushner, *Erotic Exchanges: The World of Elite Prostitution in Eighteenth-Century Paris* (Ithaca, N.Y.: Cornell University Press, 2013).

59. Foucault writes at length about the Great Confinement *(Grand Renfermement)* and the creation of the Hôpital général in *History of Madness*. See also Schwartz, *Policing the Poor in Eighteenth-Century France*, 50–92; Thomas McStay Adams, *Bureaucrats and Beggars: French Social Policy in the Age of the Enlightenment* (Oxford: Oxford University Press, 1990); Jacques-Guy Petit, *Histoire des galères, bagnes et prisons (XIIIe–XXe siècles): Introduction à l'histoire pénale de la France* (Toulouse: Privat, 1991); Pierre Deyon, *Le temps des prisons: Essai sur l'histoire de la délinquance et les origines du système pénitentiaire* (Paris: Éditions Universitaires, 1975).

60. Farge, interview with Laurent Vidal, "Arlette Farge, le parcours d'une historienne," 120. Foucault seemed compelled to speak about the political climate rather than his own publications. He canceled a planned TV appearance to promote *Désordre* and instead appeared on Christine Ockrent's program to discuss the deteriorating situation in Poland. See Macey, *The Lives of Michel Foucault*, 455; Deleuze, *Negotiations*, 108–9.

61. See interview with Laurent Vidal, "Arlette Farge, le parcours d'une historienne," 120–21.

62. Foucault, *Society Must Be Defended*, 32.

63. Michael Ignatieff, "At the Feet of the Father," *Times Literary Supplement* [London], April 22, 1983, 409.

64. Emmanuel Todd, "Ce que révèlent les lettres de cachet: Une anthropologie de la vie familiale au dix-huitième siècle," *Le Monde*, May 11, 1982. Farge recalls this review as characterizing *Disorderly Families* as a text with *"poujadiste"* politics. The brief review does not use that term and is largely descriptive. Farge responds to the charge of *poujadisme* in her interview with Laurent Vidal, "Arlette Farge, le parcours d'une historienne," 121. Another review was later published in the same newspaper: Michel Heurteaux, "La délation, poison latent" (Denunciation, a slow-working poison), *Le Monde*, May 15, 1983.

65. For an overview of these debates, see Roger Chartier, "History between Narrative

and Knowledge," in *On the Edge of the Cliff*, 13–27. For attention to how these debates differently played out on both sides of the Atlantic, see Suzanne Desan and Jeffrey Merrick, "Introduction," in *Family, Gender, and Law in Early Modern France*, xi–xxvi. For an overview oriented toward archives and the challenges of biography/autobiography, see Philippe Artières and Dominique Khalifa, "L'historien et les archives personnelles: Pas à pas," *Sociétés & Représentations* I.13 (April 2002): 7–15; and Philippe Artières, Arlette Farge, and Pierre Laborie, "Témoignage et récit historique," *Sociétés & Représentations* I.13 (April 2002): 201–6.

66. See Carlo Ginzburg, *The Cheese and the Worms: The Cosmos of a Sixteenth-Century Miller*, trans. John Tedeschi and Anne Tedeschi (Baltimore: Johns Hopkins University Press, 2013 [1980]); Giovanni Levi, *L'eredità immateriale: Carriere di un esorcista nel Piemonte del seicento* (Turin: Einaudi, 1985); Michel de Certeau, *The Practice of Everyday Life*, trans. Steven Rendall (Berkeley: University of California Press, 2011 [1980]); Jacques Le Goff and Pierre Nora, eds., *Constructing the Past: Essays in Historical Methodology* (Cambridge: Cambridge University Press, 1985 [1974]).

67. These comments come specifically in the preface to the French edition: Carlo Ginzburg, *Le Fromage et les vers: L'univers d'un meunier du XVIe siècle*, trans. Monique Aymard (Paris: Flammarion, 1980), 13.

68. Ibid.

69. Such was the charge made by Carlo Ginzburg when he writes that "an aestheticizing irrationalism" allows Foucault to present Pierre Rivière, for example, as "'a mythical being, a monstrous being who escapes definition because he emerges from no discernible order.' One swoons before an absolute 'outside' which, in reality, is the fruit of a refusal to analyze and interpret" (ibid.). Farge defends Foucault on these points in her presentation "L'Archive et l'histoire du social," given at the colloquium L'Effetto Foucault, Milan, summer 1985. Consulted at IMEC, dossier FCL 5.11.

70. Richard Brody, "Goings on about Town," *New Yorker*, June 28, 2008.

71. *Mémoires secrets pour servir à l'histoire de la République des Lettres en France depuis 1762 jusqu'à nos jours*, 36 vols. (London, 1777–89), 35: 278. Imprisoned at least five times, Honoré Gabriel Riqueti, comte de Mirabeau angrily denounced the *lettres de cachet* as an arbitrary use of royal power. Mirabeau wrote the treatise *Des Lettres de cachet et des prions d'état* following his 1777–80 detention at the château de Vincennes by a *lettre de cachet* requested by his father in the face of excessive debts. A more moderate figure in the French Revolution, he both supported a constitutional monarchy and was an early advocate for the abolition of slavery.

72. Foucault calls attention to this entanglement, contrasts it to the clear distinctions between so-called personal and political in ancient Greece, and concludes that the emergence of a world dominated by individualism is far from linear ("Le Style de l'histoire," in *Dits et Écrits II*, 1473–74).

73. By the time of her collaboration with Foucault, Farge had already examined street life in *Vivre dans la rue à Paris au XVIIIe siècle* (Paris: Gallimard, 1979). To examine the social sites of precarious existence, Farge wrote *Fragile Lives*. That such sites have no legal status and yet exercise a powerful political effect—that of collective opinion—is a contradiction examined in *Subversive Words*, trans. Rosemary Morris (College Station: Pennsylvania State University Press, 1995). Farge also reflects on these spaces in her interview with Sylvain Parent, "Entretien avec Arlette Farge," *Tracés: Revue de Sciences humaines* (May 2004), online

January 26, 2009, consulted October 12, 2012. For a discussion of the imbrication of public and private as it bears on the family, see Jean-Louis Flandrin, *Families in Former Times*.

74. Arlette Farge, "Protesters Plain to See," in *A History of Women in the West: Renaissance and the Enlightenment Paradoxes*, vol. 3, ed. Arlette Farge and Natalie Zemon Davis, trans. Arthur Goldhammer, series eds. Georges Duby and Michelle Perrot (Cambridge: Harvard University Press, 1993), 489–507; Natalie Zemon Davis, "Women on Top," in *Society and Culture in Early Modern France* (Stanford, Calif.: Stanford University Press, 1975), 124–51.

75. Michel Foucault, "About the Concept of the 'Dangerous Individual' in Nineteenth-Century Legal Psychiatry," in *Power: Essential Works of Foucault, 1954–1984*, vol. 3 (New York: New Press, 2000), 176–200.

76. If initially the unruly are described as "bad subjects" who are implicitly outside of society, then by the late eighteenth century, as the charge of the police becomes even more oriented toward "public safety," the category of "dangerous subject" becomes more frequently used. Confronted with the dilemma of imprisonment, the eighteenth-century revolutionaries increasingly turned to medical categories (of insanity, for example) to decide the terms of regulation and confinement. In his January 14, 1976, lecture, Foucault explains: "Disciplines will define not a code of law, but a code of normalization, and they will necessarily refer to a theoretical horizon that is not the edifice of law, but the field of human sciences. And the jurisprudence of these disciplines will be that of a clinical knowledge" (Foucault, *Society Must Be Defended*, 38). See also Foucault, *History of Madness*, 88–90; 109ff.; 388–93.

77. I take these terms from Chartier. See *On the Edge of the Cliff*, 8.

78. Foucault in the interview "Le Style de l'histoire," *Dits et Écrits II*, 1473; emphasis in the original.

79. One example is a book written by the collective Maurice Florence (Foucault's pseudonym in certain newspaper editorials) that presents montages of identity papers, letters, and photos of French immigrants and asylum detainees. See *Archives de l'infamie*, Collectif Maurice Florence (Paris: Les Prairies Ordinaires, 2009). One member of the collective reflects on this project in an interview between Mathieu Potte-Bonneville and Pierre Lauret: "La vraie vie," *Cahiers philosophiques* 4.120 (2009): 112–27.

80. Foucault, "Lives of Infamous Men," 160, 167.

81. Ibid., 165; Foucault, *Abnormal*, 360.

82. Michel Foucault, "Débat avec M. Foucault," in *L'Impossible prison*, 50.

83. Roger Chartier, *The Order of Books* (Stanford, Calif.: Stanford University Press, 1994).

84. Chartier, *On the Edge of the Cliff*, 3–4.

85. These connotations can be found in Alfred Boyer, *The Royal Dictionary, French and English, and English and French* (London, 1764); William Cobbett, *A New French and English Dictionary, Parts 1–2* (London: Mills, Jowett, and Mills, 1833); Alfred Havet, *The French Manual* (New York: D. Appleton and Company, 1876).

86. Foucault explains: "In this system, though, confession does not play the eminent role that Christianity had reserved for it. For this social mapping and control, long-standing procedures are used, but ones that had been localized up to then: the denunciation, the complaint, the inquiry, the report, spying, the interrogation. . . . The single, instantaneous, and traceless voice of the penitential confession that effaced evil as it effaced itself would now be supplanted by multiple voices" (Foucault, "Lives of Infamous Men," 166).

87. Foucault makes these distinctions in the course summary for *Subjectivity and Truth*, in *Ethics*, 87–92. In her examination of the 1820s Nanette Leroux case study, historian

Jan Goldstein suggests that interiority does not socially or medically take full force until the late nineteenth century (Jan Goldstein, *Hysteria Complicated by Ecstasy: The Case of Nanette Leroux* [Princeton, N.J.: Princeton University Press, 2010]).

INTRODUCTION

1. [With this opening sentence, Farge and Foucault refer to an ongoing debate with Jacques Léonard, Carlo Ginzburg, and other historians. Foucault's 1977 essay "The Lives of Infamous Men" likewise opens with the line "This is not a book of history"—a line that underscores Foucault's very different use of archives from that of historians. Both projects emerge from an encounter between a flesh-and-blood author and the lives that pierce through the gloom of historical distance and archives. This sentence implicitly challenges the aesthetic of neutral, anonymous academic and reasoned analysis and responds to criticisms by Léonard and others that Foucault wasn't really a historian. In 1977, Jacques Léonard insists on writing "The Historian and the Philosopher" as the opening essay to the volume *L'Impossible prison* (connected to a 1976 conference on penitentiary history organized by Michelle Perrot) (ed. Michelle Perrot [Paris: Seuil, 1980]). If the conference presaged the reception that would soon greet Foucault's *Discipline and Punish,* then Léonard's critical essay marks the ambivalent relationship between Foucault and historians. In it, Léonard sarcastically congratulates Foucault for his deftness in writing "historical fiction" (164) and bemoans his own inability "to appreciate the exactitude of all the claims held by Foucault" (ibid.). Angrily, Foucault insists on writing a response, the essay "Poussière et nuage"; both essays introduce the volume. See Jacques Léonard, "L'historien et le philosophe: À propos de *Surveiller et punir: Naissance de la prison,*" *Annales historiques de la Révolution française* 49 (1977): 163–81; Roger Chartier, "History between Narrative and Knowledge," in *On the Edge of the Cliff,* trans. Lydia Cochrane (Baltimore: Johns Hopkins University Press, 1997), 13–27. For a more detailed account of Foucault's relation to historians in France and elsewhere, see Gérard Noiriel, "Foucault and History: The Lessons of a Disillusion," *Journal of Modern History* 66 (September 1994): 547–68.

In a 1982 interview, when asked how she and Foucault work differently from mainstream historians, Farge responds that they sought "to avoid breaking up social relationships into pieces"—here the family, there sexuality—and Foucault adds that they refused a division between ideas and actions (Entretien avec Yves Hersant of *L'Express,* "L'âge d'or des lettres de cachet," in *Dits et Écrits II* [Paris: Gallimard, 2001]), 1170–71). Some twenty years and a generation of scholarship later, Farge revisits these trade-offs between the false objectivity and false immediacy of first-person accounts in an interview with Philippe Artières and Pierre Laborie: "Témoignage et récit historique," *Sociétés & Représentations* 1.13 (2002): 199–206. She reflects on the initial joint project in Arlette Farge, "Michel Foucault et les archives de l'exclusion," in *Penser la folie* (Paris: Éditions Galilée, 1992).—Ed.]

2. [When *Désordre* was published, Arlette Farge had recently finished her book *Délinquance et criminalité: Le vol d'aliments à Paris au XVIIIe siècle* (1974)—a book that Foucault cited twice in *Discipline and Punish*—as well as *Vivre dans la rue à Paris au XVIIIe siècle* (1979). Farge was one of numerous historians, including Paul Veyne, Michelle Perrot, and Maurice Agulhon, who were deeply influenced by Foucault and his move away from attention only to the words and deeds of official public order. Among many other books, Farge later published *Fragile Lives* (1993), *Subversive Words* (1995), and *Allure of the Archives* (2013), texts that each differently challenge what counts as an archive, and which experiences bear on the internalization of existing order and its externalization through the ordinary practices

of lived experience. See *Délinquance et criminalité: Le vol d'aliments à Paris au XVIIIe siècle* (Paris: Plon, 1974); *Vivre dans la rue à Paris au XVIIIe siècle* (Paris: Gallimard-Julliard, collection Archives, 1979); *Fragile Lives: Violence, Power and Solidarity in Eighteenth-Century Paris,* trans. Carol Shelton (Cambridge: Harvard University Press, 1993), *Subversive Words: Public Opinion in 18th Century France* (University Park: Pennsylvania State University Press, 1995); and *Allure of the Archives,* trans. Thomas Scott-Railton (New Haven: Yale University Press, 2013).—Ed.]

3. [Foucault draws on brief excerpts from the *lettres de cachet* as early as *History of Madness* (1961); they are also mentioned briefly in the lecture series *Théories et institutions pénales* (1971–72), *The Punitive Society* (1972–73), and *Abnormal* (1973–74). Most of the work on *Le Désordre des familles* comes on the heels of *Discipline and Punish* (1975). In the 1978 lectures for *Security, Territory and Population,* Foucault traces the police and their effect on circulation of persons and goods; they serve as the hinge between the "circulation of men and goods in relation to each other" and "juridical sovereignty." In *Discipline and Punish* the attention to policing and circulation emerges in Foucault's discussion of workshops, policing, and incarceration. Additional archival work motivates the far more interpretive essays that compose *I, Pierre Rivière.* See *History of Madness,* ed. Jean Khalfa, trans. Jonathan Murphy (New York: Routledge, 2006); *Théories et institutions pénales: Cours au Collège de France, 1971–1972,* ed. Bernard Harcourt (Paris: Seuil/Gallimard, 2015); *The Punitive Society: Lectures at the Collège de France, 1972–1973,* ed. Arnold Davidson, trans. Graham Burchell (New York: Palgrave Macmillan, 2015); *Abnormal: Lectures at the Collège de France, 1974–1975,* ed. Arnold Davidson, trans. Graham Burchell (New York: Palgrave Macmillan, 2004); *Security, Territory, Population: Lectures at the Collège de France, 1977–1978,* ed. Arnold Davidson, trans. Graham Burchell (New York: Palgrave Macmillan, 2007); *I, Pierre Rivière,* trans. Frank Jellinek (Omaha: University of Nebraska Press, 1975).—Ed.]

4. [The archives of the Bastille include the original administrative records of the Ancien Régime that were originally kept at the Bastille. These were later moved to a different building, the Bibliothèque de l'Arsenal, which is an administrative part of (although physically distinct from) the Bibliothèque Nationale de France. Farge writes movingly about the experience of working in these archives in *Allure of the Archives.* Much earlier, Frantz Funck-Brentano drew on these archives to write his classic work that surveys and indexes the recovered *lettres de cachet* dating from 1659 to 1789 (Frantz Funck-Brentano, *Les Lettres de cachet à Paris* [Paris: Imprimerie nationale, 1903]). The abbreviation for the dossiers marks their location: Bibliothèque de l'Arsenal, Archives de la Bastille, or Ars. Arch. Bastille.—Ed.]

5. [Immediately after the storming of the Bastille, its archives (containing copies of police registers, *lettres de cachet,* police and judicial archives, records of daily administration) were scattered into the gutters of Paris. The Paris Commune (1789–95) quickly realized that it was about to lose the historical record of royal absolutism, and issued a civic appeal that the documents be returned. Some six hundred thousand were returned and are the basis of what serves today as the archives of the Bastille.—Ed.]

6. The definition of *lettre de cachet* is very general: "Letter written by order of the King, countersigned by a secretary of State and stamped with the seal of the King" (Joseph-Nicolas Guyot, *Répertoire universel et raisonné de jurisprudence civil, criminelle, canonique et bénéficiale,* vol. 10 [Paris: Visse, 1785]).

7. [The Maison du Roi (literally, the "King's Household") had military, religious, and domestic branches. Its reference to the intimacy of household signals the prestige and status implied by proximity to the king. Because the Maison du Roi is an official institution without contemporary equivalent, the term has been left untranslated. For a historical

overview of its composition and organization, see Lucien Bély, ed., "Maison du Roi," in *Dictionnaire de l'Ancien Régime* (Paris: Presses Universitaires de France, 2010), 777–78.—Ed.]

8. This contradicts the argument made by François-Xavier Emmanuelli, "Ordres du Roi et lettres de cachet en Provence à la fin de l'Ancien Régime: Contribution à l'histoire du climat social et politique," *Revue historique*, 252.512 (October–December 1974): 357–92. In fact, requesting imprisonment was not an undertaking pursued by the well-off alone. The outline of a socioprofessional analysis of these sources finds that around half to two-thirds of them involved people of little means.

9. [Foucault discusses the spatialization of new social categories through reference to such entourages in *History of Madness* (416, 427). He refers to the "social entourage" of "the family, parents, doctors, the lowest levels of police" in "Two Lectures." In *Society Must Be Defended*, the translation is more literal: "immediate entourage" (*l'entourage immédiat*, 32). See Michel Foucault, *Power/Knowledge: Selected Interviews and Other Writings, 1972–1977*, ed. and trans. Colin Gordon (New York: Pantheon, 1980), 101; Michel Foucault, *Society Must Be Defended*, ed. Arnold Davidson, trans. David Macey (New York: Picador, 2003). For her part, Farge works with the spatialization of street and neighborhood, and the social authority they cement, in her concept of *voisinage*. See Arlette Farge, *Effusion et torment, le récit des corps* (Paris: Odile Jacob, 2007), 77–111.—Ed.]

10. [Farge and Foucault here insert themselves amid historians such as Carlo Ginzburg or Robert Mandrou who sought to excavate the culture and actions of ordinary people in, respectively, sixteenth-century Italy and seventeenth-century France. Where Ginzburg's "micro-histories" sought to recover lost voices, Farge and Foucault understood themselves to be doing something else: to find traces of the intersections and relationships that bind public power and private persons. Hence their attention to relationships that compose what Foucault might term the "grid of intelligibility" by which individuals enter into the political field. For a more detailed discussion of this volume's engagement with scholarship in History, see the Editor's Introduction to this volume.—Ed.]

11. [In the Introduction to *Fragile Lives*, Farge writes: "Emotion. The word is out! It is a word which is almost taboo for anyone who professes to be a student of social matters. But as I understand it, emotion is not, as is commonly believed, an exclusion of reason nor a kind of sugary sentimentality to be used for coating over whatever sections of reality it encounters with a uniform gloss . . . Emotion opens up into an attitude which is proactive rather than passive, allowing one to lay hold of the written word in order to take it, not as the result of research, but as a means of apprehending social life and thought" (3–4). In *Fragile Lives*, much as in *Désordre*, Farge organizes her archival work around the axis of key relationships: those between parents and children, husbands and wives, men and women, and workshop owners and workers. Differently from *Désordre*, she insists also on collective events and displays of power, to trace the intersection of public and private relationships of power. "From these sketches there emerges a picture of precariousness and strength," she writes, "along with a determination not to allow oneself to be abused or sold short" (6).—Ed.]

12. [Some of the most notable persons imprisoned by *lettre de cachet* include the Marquis de Sade, the moderate revolutionary Mirabeau, the satirist Voltaire, and the encyclopedist Diderot.—Ed.]

13. [The exact number of *lettres de cachet* can only be estimated. French historian of the Ancien Régime Frantz Funck-Brentano lists the number of prisoners *embastillés* between 1659 and 1789 at 5,279. More recently, historian Claude Quétel has estimated around

one hundred thousand letters were written over 130 years, with about sixty thousand from the Paris region. In that same period, the French population grew from twenty to twenty-eight million. Most intriguingly, Quétel's research confirms Farge and Foucault's larger claim—that most *lettres de cachet* did not concern acts of state—a claim that flies in the face of received knowledge. From the passionate writings of Mirabeau, to the enigmatic story of the Man in the Iron Mask (reportedly a political rival to Louis XIV imprisoned on an island off France's coast, in the Château d'If), the letters have often been associated with state intrigues. See Claude Quétel, *Les Lettres de cachet: Une légende noire* (Paris: Perrin, 2011).

More recent scholars have surveyed the letters more broadly to include those that led to imprisonment at lesser prisons than the Bastille, and to extend research beyond Paris. This research reveals that the letters were more than a means to control political dissent; that they were not part of the popular resentments that incited the French Revolution; and that, quite to the contrary, the letters were discontinued in 1784 by the Baron de Breteuil, minister to the Maison du Roi, because they were *too* popular and overwhelmed the police. The overwhelming majority of letters were written by family members—indeed, these compose 97.8 percent of those from Caen. The classic text is Funck-Brentano, *Les lettres de cachet à Paris*. See also Farge, *Fragile Lives*; Quétel, *Les Lettres de cachet*, 317ff.; Claude Quétel, "Lettres de cachet et correctionnaires dans la généralité de Caen au XVIIIᵉ siècle," *Annales de la Normandie* 28.2 (1978): 127–59; Lynn Hunt, *Family Romance of the Revolution* (London: Routledge, 2013). For an overview of policing techniques and practices, along with the memoirs of Lieutenant General Lenoir, see Vincent Milliot, *Un Policier des Lumières* (Seyssel: Éditions Champ Vallon, 2011). For a reading of these letters as part of a broader genre of epistolarity, see Elizabeth Wingrove's two articles "Philoctetes at the Bastille," *Cultural Critique* 74 (winter 2010): 65–80; and "Sovereign Address," *Political Theory* 40.2 (February 2012): 135–64; as well as her manuscript *Agony of Address*.

Different generations of scholars have characterized these letters in different terms. In the early twentieth century, Funck-Brentano concentrated attention on those political prisoners imprisoned in the Bastille, as well as the theater performers imprisoned in For-l'Évêque. As scholars realized that most letters characterized family affairs, French historians Nicole Castan and Claude Quétel expanded the scope of inquiry to include those imprisoned in the region of Languedoc or the city of Caen; Quétel has also argued that most of these letters come from persons of relatively modest means. See Nicole Castan and Yves Castan, *Vivre ensemble: Ordre et désordre en Languedoc au XVIIIᵉ siècle* (Paris: Gallimard, 1981); Quétel, *Les Lettres de cachet.*—Ed.]

14. [The police lieutenancy was created in April 1674 with the aim of centralizing police power in royal hands, and consolidating (or suppressing) the proliferation of police jurisdictions. Before 1674, procedures of "policing" and "justice" had a hazy cohabitation. Initially, provosts of legal order could act from the legitimacy either of law or of police. Police superintendents reported alternately to Parisian institutions with different legal jurisdictions, to religious authorities, or to the French regional courts. Following a 1666 investigation by royal adviser Pierre Séguier, the position and jurisdiction of the police lieutenancy were reformed; despite these efforts to disentangle justice and police systems, the *lettres de cachet* allow the police to arrest people at their discretion without due legal process. The lieutenant generals mentioned in this volume include d'Argenson, Berryer, Bertin de Bellisle, and Hérault. See Milliot, *Un Policier des Lumières*; Alan Williams, *The Police of Paris: 1718–1789* (Baton Rouge: Louisiana State University Press, 1979); Quétel, *Lettres de Cachet*, 123–79; Farge, *Fragile Lives*, 11–13, 139–40; David Garrioch, *Neighbourhood*

and Community in Paris,1740–1790 (Cambridge: Cambridge University Press, 1986); David Garrioch, *The Making of Revolutionary Paris* (Berkeley: University of California Press, 2004), 132–41.—Ed.]

15. [In the absence of regularized police, a *décret de prise de corps* (literally, a decree to "seize the body") enabled a judge to arrest someone accused of a crime. In his true-crime collection, lawyer François Gayot de Pitaval gives the example of a husband issuing such a decree against his pregnant, adulterous wife "to ensure that she didn't continue to live in disorder, or to hide the state of her person." See *Causes célèbres, curieuses et intéressantes de toutes les cours souveraines avec les jugements qui les ont décidées,* vol. 16 (Paris, 1892), 123.—Ed.]

16. [In this introduction, along with subsequent essays, Farge and Foucault quote liberally from the letters that follow. The quotations were not attributed in the original 1982 text and are not attributed here; the effect is to allow the repeated phrases and voices from the letters to rise up and form a collective murmur.—Ed.]

17. Germain-Louis Martin, "Lois, édits, arrêts et règlements sur les associations ouvrières au XVIIIᵉ siècle, 1700–1792," doctoral thesis, Paris, A. Rousseau, 1900.

18. [Along with the move to centralize police jurisdiction came an effort to centralize control over the corporations associated with craft workshops. Regulation of these workshops was stormily shared by the guilds and the king's administration. Into this murkiness of jurisdiction, the lieutenant generals were authorized to issue police orders and to regulate matters that bore on public order, even as the craft guild's own police were authorized to regulate conflicts. For example, apprentices who felt badly treated—treatments the masters believed were authorized by the terms of apprenticeship—would often disappear only to be arrested on the capacious charge of "libertinage." With the destruction of the archives of the corporations in an 1871 fire, historians now have records only of those conflicts that made it into royal police archives. Foucault writes briefly about such disorders in his discussion of the policing of developing urban centers in *Security, Territory, Population* (107, 119, 333–45), and Farge in *Fragile Lives.* For more on the workshop, see also Garrioch, *Neighbourhood and Community in Paris, 1740–1790,* and Steven Kaplan, "L'apprentissage au XVIIIᵉ siècle: Le cas de Paris," *Revue d'histoire moderne et contemporaine* 40.3 (July–September 1993): 436–79.—Ed.]

19. Cf. Frantz Funck-Brentano, *La Bastille des comédiens, le For-l'Évêque* (Paris: Éditeur Albert Fontemoing, 1903). [Actors and actresses could be imprisoned at For-l'Évêque for failing to respect the king's ordinances around theatrical productions, for failing to demonstrate proper respect to their publics, or for pushing their theatrical representations beyond what was deemed politically or morally responsible. These actors were part of the Chambre du roi, a jurisdiction that in equal measure brought them royal protection and punishment; technically, actors were "loaned" to the public by the king. Their association with For-l'Évêque, rather than the other sites of internment, testified to their special place in ancien régime society. Directors, and more rarely playwrights, could also be imprisoned there. See ibid,, 151–257.—Ed.]

20. Bibliothèque de l'Arsenal, Archives de la Bastille (cited from here on out as Ars. Arch. Bastille), ms. 10141. [Inspector Jean Poussot kept a journal for the years 1747–48 in which he noted the "they say" rumors whispered about Paris, rumors whose circulation led to the uprising of 1750. Among other claims, those rumors claimed that children were being kidnapped to populate France's overseas colonies. Riots broke out in May 1750 in response to police arrests of vagabonds, beggars, and (it was feared) children. See Ms. 10029, folios 124–55.—Ed.]

21. [Émile Zola famously refers to Les Halles as "the belly of Paris." Since the twelfth century, Les Halles served as one of the city's largest marketplaces located in the very heart of the city. Policing of this neighborhood would include the usual attention to petty theft and prostitution, but also to those selling wares or foodstuffs without the proper seal of quality from the guild or syndic. Police often found themselves charged with the task of *distraint*, or the seizure of unlicensed tools and merchandise. More than just a marketplace, Les Halles was also a home to groups bound by family, neighborhood, and occupational ties. For more information, see Garrioch, *Neighbourhood and Community in Paris, 1740–1790*.—Ed.]

22. [Police in eighteenth-century France had a very different organization and purview than their contemporary counterparts. Police inspectors worked effectively as direct agents of the king, rather than in response to complaints from the neighborhood, and those not tied to a jurisdiction could seek out whichever persons and places they chose. Inspector Poussot kept a register over sixteen years in which he noted the name, surname, nickname, age, occupation, place of birth, and current address of the offender. Next to these were listed the date of arrest, decision-making authority, and prison. Poussot also noted the circumstances surrounding the arrest, the offender's past, and other pieces of contextual information. Arrests could also be made, of course, by writing a *lettre de cachet* and effectively summoning police investigation into whatever disturbance of public order was alleged in the letter. Comparing the two sorts of arrest reveals the differing priorities and conceptions of "order" on the part of populace and king. For a vibrant account of the incessant coming and going of Parisian street life, see Farge, *Fragile Lives*; Louis-Sébastien Mercier, *Tableau de Paris*, 12 vols. (Paris: Virchaux & Compagnie, 1781–89); Jeremy Popkin, ed., *Panorama of Paris: Selections from Tableau de Paris* (University Park: Pennsylvania State University Press, 1999).—Ed.]

23. [Farge uses similarly figurative language in *Fragile Lives* and *Subversive Words* to capture the ebb and flow of human lives, in and out of public spaces. See especially her chapter "At the Workshop Door" in *Fragile Lives* (131–68).—Ed.]

24. [Drawing on police registers and memoirs (and sometimes, more obliquely, on the *lettres de cachet*), historians have established that men seeking sex with other men in eighteenth-century Paris cruised the streets, public parks, and certain taverns. These efforts often encountered police efforts at entrapment through use of informants (see the Editor's Introduction to this volume). By and large, few of these arrests were prosecuted. See Michel Rey, "Parisian Homosexuals Create a Lifestyle, 1700–50: The Police Archives," trans. Robert A. Day and Robert Welsh, in *'Tis Nature's Fault: Unauthorized Sexuality during the Enlightenment*, ed. Robert Purks Maccubbin (Cambridge: Cambridge University Press, 1988), 179–91; Michael Sibalis, "The Regulation of Male Homosexuality in Revolutionary and Napoleonic France, 1789–1815," in *Homosexuality in Modern France*, ed. Jeffrey Merrick and Bryan Ragan (Oxford: Oxford University Press, 1996).—Ed.]

25. [The police relied on a network of spies, known as *mouches* or *mouchards*; for a longer discussion, see the Editor's Introduction. Far from trustworthy, the *mouches* often developed ties with the populations they surveyed—and then reported on one another. See Farge, *Fragile Lives*, 140ff.; Milliot, *Un Policier des Lumières*, 57, 178ff.; Quétel, *Les Lettres de cachet*, 162–69.—Ed.]

26. [A fascination with the body and sexuality of the king was one of the effects of the entanglement of public and personal spaces. The sexual profligacy of Louis XIV and Louis XV was taken as a sign of the degeneracy of France itself. Both kings also inspired

fascination with sexual intrigues in the Court, often read as lessons for behavior within the family. See Jeffrey Merrick, "Sexual Politics and Public Order in Late Eighteenth-Century France," *Journal of the History of Sexuality* 1.1 (July 1990): 68–84.—Ed.]

27. [Lieutenant General Marc René d'Argenson was particularly aware of the potential for scandal among clergy members. Often dioceses preferred to chase disorderly clergy members toward another parish, and inevitably Paris, which soon found itself home to the drunk and sexually scandalous. See Quétel, *Les Lettres de cachet*, 141–43; and Williams, *The Police of Paris*, 104–11.—Ed.]

28. Cf. Henri Debord, *Contribution à l'histoire des ordres du Roi au XVIIIᵉ siècle d'après les registres du secrétariat d'État à la Maison du Roi, 1741–1775* (Paris: F. Loviton, 1938).

29. [The *lettres de cachet* did not stipulate the length of imprisonment; that decision usually was made by the lieutenant general. Often, subsequent letters would ask that the duration of imprisonment be shortened (often because the prisoner was financially needed at home) or lengthened (if family members feared the prisoner's return or felt greater proof of repentance was needed). See Funck-Brentano, *Les Lettres de cachet à Paris*; Quétel, *Les Lettres de cachet.*—Ed.]

30. [The French word *placet*, usually rendered as "plaint" or "petition," has Latinate etymological roots. Where the original Latin phrase indicates consent or approval, a *placet* is a succinct written request for grace, a favor, or justice. In reference to the Latin phrasing, Foucault later reflects on the use of *placet* as a personal means to indicate judgment or approval in his lectures on Serenus, the Roman Stoic. See Michel Foucault, *Wrong-Doing, Truth-Telling: The Function of the Avowal in Justice*, ed. Fabienne Brion and Bernard Harcourt, trans. Stephen W. Sawyer (Chicago: University of Chicago Press, 2014), 101, 116, 121nn24–25.—Ed.]

31. [The more well-to-do families could use the *lettres de cachet* as a means to incarcerate unfaithful wives or husbands, hustle scandalous children off to the nicer houses of detention, and generally muffle public scandal. If occasionally a minister or Louis XIV read a letter from a commoner, by Louis XV that practice all but disappears, and these letters are handled by the lieutenant general. For more discussion, see the Editor's Introduction. Farge and Foucault's description largely follows Funck-Brentano, *Les Lettres de cachet à Paris*, xxiii–xxiv.—Ed.]

32. [Successor to the throne just before his fifth birthday, Louis XIV grew up marked by the experience of living under the regency of his mother, Anne d'Autriche, and the revolutionary incitements of La Fronde, whose members sought to protect feudal privilege from royal absolutism. Later known as the Sun King, Louis assumed power in 1661. Louis XV reigned as king of France from September 1715 until his death in May 1774. Louis XV succeeded his grandfather at age five; until his majority, his uncle, the Duke of Orléans, served as Regent. His reign is often characterized as weak and indeterminate, and his sexual dalliances were associated with the enervating of France's power. Under Louis XV, the phrase *lettres de cachet* comes into general usage and the letters become issued increasingly by the lieutenant generals as "letters of anticipation" of a later order by the king. During this period, the use of these *lettres de cachet* increased significantly, although the length of imprisonment decreased. In 1757, Louis XV was stabbed in the side by Damiens, in the incident that opens Foucault's *Discipline and Punish.* See Quétel, *Les Lettres de cachet à Paris*, 46.—Ed.]

33. See Nicole Castan, *Justice et répression en Languedoc à l'époque des Lumières* (Paris: Flammarion, 1980), 201; as well as the pages dealing with *lettres de cachet* in Jean-Claude Perrot,

Genèse d'une ville moderne: Caen au XVIIIe siècle (Paris-The Hague: Mouton, 1975), facsimile published by Éditions de l'EHESS, 2001. See also Claude Quétel, *De par le Roy, essai sur les lettres de cachet* (Toulouse: Privat, 1981).

34. [Those persons submitting *lettres de cachet*, often illiterate, would seek out a public scribe to convey their thoughts using the proper format and formal address. See the Editor's Introduction.—Ed.]

35. [The *locataire principal* was the primary leaseholder for a building. The owner of a building would rent the entirety of the building to this principal leaseholder, who then delimited the living units that he would sublet. The spaces on the ground floor and first floor were reserved for merchants and their shops. Often these subletting arrangements were not formalized with leases, and so the principal leaseholder could evict people without notice if their rent was in arrears or if they were disorderly. The principal leaseholder was responsible to the police for the order of the house, and for monitoring the entrance of the door onto the street; these leaseholders were the precursors to the concierges that emerged toward the end of the eighteenth century. See "At the Sign of the Camel: Ways of Living in and Ways of Managing in Lyon during the 18th Century," *Cahiers d'histoire* 38.1 (1993): 25–54; Garrioch, *Neighbourhood and Community*, 33–36.—Ed.]

36. [The *convulsionnaires* are religious pilgrims who would fall into religious ecstasy before the tomb of the Jansenist religious leader, François de Pâris. *Lettres de cachet* were heavily used by Louis XV to quash this Jansenist movement. The Jansenists believed in predestination; this challenge to Catholic doctrine and religious hierarchy was understood equally as a challenge to political absolutism and as the kernel of a proto-democratic political discourse. Damiens, who attempts to kill the king and whose story opens *Discipline and Punish*, was a domestic for several prominent Jansenists in the *parlement* of Paris. See Dale K. Van Kley, *The Jansenists and the Expulsion of the Jesuits from France, 1757–1765* (New Haven, Conn.: Yale University Press, 1975); Dale K. Van Kley, *The Damiens Affair and the Unraveling of the Ancien Régime, 1750–1770* (Princeton, N.J.: Princeton University Press, 1984).—Ed.]

37. [Jean-Charles-Pierre Lenoir begins his career as an adviser to Châtelet in 1752, then moves up to *lieutenant particulier* (1754) and *lieutenant criminel* (1759) before buying the office of *maître des requêtes* (1765). Lenoir was a prototypical example of the public servant emergent from the merchant bourgeoisie who realized his social aspirations and a certain economic enrichment through his office. Having survived the French Revolution, Lieutenant General Lenoir publishes his memoir in part to counter the extracts from the Bastille archives published by the revolutionaries. In contrast to those accounts of policing that fold it into a story of centralization, Lenoir's memoir veers between personal, administrative, and political registers, and suggests a police in transition. For an overview of policing techniques and practices, along with Lenoir's memoir, see Milliot, *Un Policier des Lumières*. For an overview of changes in police administration, see Steven Kaplan and Vincent Milliot, "La police de Paris, une 'révolution permanente'? Du commissaire Lemaire au lieutenant de police Lenoir, les tribulations du Mémoire sur l'administration de police (1770–1792)," in *Réformer la police: Les mémoires policiers en Europe au XVIIIe siècle*, ed. Catherine Denys, Brigitte Marin, and Vincent Milliot (Rennes: Presses Universitaires de Rennes, 2009), 69–115.—Ed.]

38. Bibliothèque municipale d'Orléans, Fonds Lenoir, ms. 1423, fol. 21: Sûreté. Recall that Marc René d'Argenson was lieutenant general of police from 1697 to 1718; Berryer from 1747 to 1757; Sartine from 1759 to 1774.

39. [Louis Auguste le Tonnelier, the Baron de Breteuil, was a minister in the Maison du

Roi from 1783 to 1788. Breteuil's 1784 circular sought to limit the use of the *lettres de cachet*, and to make it harder to abuse their discretionary power. Nonetheless, he acknowledges the need to keep imprisoned both those already charged and those posing a discernible threat to public safety.

As the *lettres de cachet* grew in popularity, the police became overwhelmed with requests for arrest. The prisons became overburdened, all the more because the arrests brought lengthy and indeterminate stays in prison—often themselves the subject of further letters to the police requesting the early release of some prisoners (often needed back at home to work or care for children) or the continued incarceration of others (whose families feared they had not sufficiently improved). As discussed in the later essay in this volume "When Addressing the King," the Baron de Breteuil circulated an announcement ending the practice and stipulating guidelines for terms of incarceration in 1784.—Ed.]

40. [Lieutenant general of police from 1757 to 1759, Bertin de Bellisle was preoccupied with public health, and so with regulating the sale of fruits and vegetables at Les Halles; increasing the presence of the police in that market; forbidding the sale of cadavers by grave diggers; and seeking to improve the illumination of public streets. He became involved in a dispute among members of the wigmakers guild in 1765. As new positions of "master" were foreclosed, apprentices began to set up shop on their own and the guilds were overrun with complaints. Determined to bring an end to the conflict, Bertin had the police posted outside the residence of the apprentice Grignon who was leading the charge. But these efforts were to no avail—having confided these plans to his own wigmaker, Bertin soon discovered that Grignon had gone into hiding. See Farge, *Fragile Lives*, 133–35.—Ed.]

I. MARITAL DISCORD

1. [The language of *tableau* evokes Louis-Sébastien Mercier's twelve-volume work *Tableau de Paris*. See note 6 in "When Addressing the King."—Ed.]

2. This survey studied, as we said earlier, the years 1728, 1756, 1758, 1760.

3. [For a long time, scholars presumed that the *lettres de cachet* reflect a homology between absolute power of the monarch and the absolute power of the father within the family. In 1903, Funck-Brentano writes that with the *prisonniers de famille* "we discover the Ancien Régime in one of its most characteristic aspects: authority nearly absolute of the father over the family, or, by default, over the 'familial assembly' *[l'assemblée de famille]*, an authority exercised in the name of common interests" (Frantz Funck-Brentano, *Les Lettres de cachet à Paris* [Paris: Imprimerie nationale, 1903], xxii). Anglophone scholars picked up this homology, most notably in the work of Sarah Hanley, and have emphasized that the political pact rested on a patriarchal pact. More recently, scholars have sought to challenge whether the authority of the family and that of the king were seen as directly commensurable; increasingly, that claim appears to be a nineteenth-century retrospection of political power onto family organization. Instead, many historians (including Arlette Farge) argue that the family should instead be understood as a site of conflicting relationships, not always subordinate to the rule of the father. See Sarah Hanley, "Engendering the State: Family Formation and State Building in Early Modern France," *French Historical Studies* 16.1 (spring 1989): 4–27; Arlette Farge, "Protesters Plain to See," in *A History of Women in the West: Renaissance and the Enlightenment Paradoxes*, vol. 3, ed. Arlette Farge and Natalie Zemon Davis, trans. Arthur Goldhammer, series eds. Georges Duby and Michelle Perrot (Cambridge: Harvard University Press, 1993), 489–507; Natalie Zemon Davis, "Women on Top," in *Society and Culture in Early Modern France* (Stanford, Calif.: Stanford University

Press, 1975), 124–51; Joan Landes, *Women and the Public Sphere in the Age of the French Revolution* (Ithaca, N.Y.: Cornell University Press, 1988); Suzanne Desan and Jeffrey Merrick, eds., *Family, Gender and Law in Early Modern France* (University Park: Pennsylvania State University Press, 2007).—Ed.]

4. It should be noted that out of all the requests taken together (requests for imprisonment by parents, requests for imprisonment by spouses), there were only a few more men imprisoned than women: 195 men, 181 women.

5. In 1728: 13 years, was the average length of marriage before a request was made.

In 1756: 14 years.

In 1758: 13 years.

In 1760: 11 years.

6. [The promised definition for *infamy* never quite materializes. Broadly, *infamy* refers to something shaming and dishonorable. More narrowly, it sometimes serves as a euphemism for clandestine sexual, and especially homosexual, behavior. Speaking to its broad sense, Foucault writes an essay published separately titled "Lives of Infamous Men." For a more specific attention to homosexuality, see Michel Rey, "Parisian Homosexuals Create a Lifestyle, 1700–50: The Police Archives," trans. Robert A. Day and Robert Welsh, in *'Tis Nature's Fault: Unauthorized Sexuality during the Enlightenment*, ed. Robert Purks Maccubbin (Cambridge: Cambridge University Press, 1988), 179–91.—Ed.]

7. Ars. Arch. Bastille, ms. 11994, fol. 74 (year: 1758).

8. Ars. Arch. Bastille, ms. 12083 (year: 1760). The letters from this dossier are not collected in this volume.

9. [Because summonses for arrest were publicly posted, the *lettres de cachet* were comparatively discreet; they did away with such summonses as well as with the publicity of a trial. Farge offers an overview of the dynamics of honor in "The Honor and Secrecy of Families," in *History of Private Life: Passions and Renaissance*, vol. 3, series eds. Philippe Ariès and Georges Duby, volume ed. Roger Chartier, trans. Arthur Goldhammer (Cambridge: Harvard University Press, 1993), 579–607. For an account of the preoccupation with shame and the regulation of social misfits as connected to eighteenth-century French politics, see Jill Locke, "Rousseau's Pariahs, Rousseau's Laments," in *Democracy and the Death of Shame: Political Equality and Social Disturbance* (Cambridge: Cambridge University Press, 2016).—Ed.]

10. Ars. Arch. Bastille, ms. 11988, fol. 274 (year: 1758).

11. [For many years, the police and the palace of justice shared jurisdictions; Châtelet functioned simultaneously as a police headquarters, prosecutor's office, royal palace of justice, and prison. Until 1667, the civil lieutenant of Châtelet was both the official head of judicial matters and the de facto head of the police. These civil and criminal lieutenancies split in 1667, with the office of lieutenant general of police taking its own jurisdiction in 1674. As a prison, Châtelet was known to have the worst conditions, given its proximity to nearby slaughterhouses, sewers, and the Seine (which often flooded the lower levels). The Petit Châtelet was located across the Seine, on the site of what is today Place St.-Michel. In addition to having a prison extension of the Grand Châtelet, it was also a customhouse. Following the demolition of the Petit Châtelet in 1780, the Hôtel-Dieu was enlarged to accommodate some of the extra prisoners; others were sent to the Grand Châtelet. See Jacques Hillairet, *Gibets, piloris et cachots du vieux Paris* (Paris: Éditions de Minuit, 1956); Lucien Bély, ed., "Commissaires du Châtelet de Paris," and "Lieutenant Général de Police," in *Dictionnaire de l'Ancien Régime* (Paris: Presses Universitaires de France, 2010), 296–97, 739–40.—Ed.]

12. [The National Archives have a unique history of their own, one that opens up an extraordinary window onto the workings of justice in France, and especially Paris. These archives include data on police expenditures, correspondence of certain lieutenant generals, the archives for the policing of the central market Les Halles, documents from the Maison du Roi, from the keeper of the seals, boxes containing the *lettres de cachet*, and finally the famous Y series. The Y series (a reference to its cataloging system) collects criminal complaints filed with the superintendent of the Petty Criminal Court, along with registers from the guard, commissioners, and inspectors, and covers acts of violence between 1720 and 1755. The material in the Y series includes everything from reports on evidence and interrogation about which storekeepers failed to sweep their sidewalk. The fonds Joly de Fleury of the procurators general of Parlement are also useful, along with the papers for the secretary of state for the Maison du Roi. The archives available today are a fraction of those initially maintained; approximately six thousand registers (maintained by police and royal administrators) and boxes of letters, edicts, decrees, and censored materials were burned in May 1871 by the members of the Paris Commune. These losses include three hundred boxes of additional *lettres de cachet.* See Arlette Farge, *Allure of the Archives* (New Haven: Yale University Press, 2013). Alan Williams has an extensive overview of the holdings and catalog system used by the Archives Nationales, the Archives de la Préfecture de Police, the Bibliothèque Nationale, and other libraries in his *The Police of Paris: 1718–1789* (Baton Rouge: Louisiana State University Press, 1979), 305–8. Bernard Harcourt traces the variegation of police reporting in *The Illusion of Free Markets* (Chicago: University of Chicago Press, 2011), 22–25ff.

13. This, moreover, only applies to Paris, as we have already emphasized.

14. Registers of these clarifications are preserved in the Archives de la Préfecture de Police (Series AB 405, for example) and in the Bibliothèque de l'Arsenal (as was that of police inspector Sarraire). [Farge comments repeatedly on the paradox that police investigations often obscure more than they clarify. For a discussion of *éclaircissement*, see note 48 in the Editor's Introduction.—Ed.]

15. [On average, families paid between one hundred and six hundred livres a year to cover the pensions of detainees. Correspondingly, prisons varied in terms of their quality and privileges. The franc was not introduced as a unit of currency until 1795. To put this cost in perspective, an ordinary servant earned about 150 livres a year.

[The two primary sites of Parisian imprisonment, Bicêtre and the Salpêtrière, find their history in the earlier Edict of 1656 that sought to imprison the poor, vagrants, vagabonds, and beggars. The Hôpital général de Paris was not a hospital oriented toward the sick but instead ostensibly offered shelter—hospitality—to the poor. It opened in April 1656 with some six thousand vagrants who were swept up in the teeth of the *Grand Renfermement, or Great Confinement.* Henry IV donated six buildings for the Hôpital, including the Salpêtrière (originally a gunpowder manufactory) and Bicêtre (a château from 1400). The latter was intended for men, the former for women. Bicêtre housed a mixture of the poor and indigent (some with minor illnesses), and a large population of men recovering from venereal disease; the Salpêtrière had a similar population, as well as those arrested for prostitution. In *History of Madness*, Foucault describes the imprisonment of the insane in these two sites (Michel Foucault, *History of Madness*, ed. Jean Khalfa, trans. Jonathan Murphy [New York: Routledge, 2013]). In fact, the populations of both prisons was mixed. Bicêtre housed 187 men for insanity out of its 3,650 inmates in 1789; in the same year, five hundred insane people and epileptics were housed in the Salpêtrière out of seven thousand. Tragically, most of these inmates were killed in the September massacres of 1792, when the revolutionaries feared a counterrevolutionary plot arising from Parisian prisoners. Léon Bernard comments: "Only the poorest, most rootless, and the less clever generally ended up in the Hôpital général" (*The Emerging City* [Durham, N.C.: Duke University Press, 1970], 134–35). See also Quétel, *Les Lettres de cachet: Une légende noire* (Paris: Perrin, 2011); Hillairet, *Gibets, piloris et cachots du vieux Paris.*—Ed.]

16. Arlette Farge, *Le Miroir des femmes* (Paris: Éditions Montalba, 1982), 70.

17. Postmortem inventories and marriage contracts among the lower orders testify to its importance. Cf. the master's thesis of Bernadette Oriol, "Maîtresses marchandes lingères, maîtresses couturiers, ouvrières en linge aux alentours de 1751," Université de Paris VII, 1980.

18. [Throughout this translation, we have chosen to translate *mauvaise conduite* as "bad conduct." Similarly, *mauvais sujet* is translated as "bad subject" (see "Parents and Children"). In both cases, the first translation is marked, and the phrases are consistently translated in the letters that follow. For more discussion of these phrases, see the Editor's Introduction.—Ed.]

19. [Questions of circulation are paramount for understanding the complicated topographies of eighteenth-century Paris. The language of circulation and trajectories speaks to the borderlands of public versus familial spaces, and site public space as that which opens upon exiting from a privately owned building. The language of circulation, and the preoccupation with vagabonds, index a time when the economic precarity of certain professions, along with an unevenly developed market, threaten to spill over into political precarity of riots and unrest. See Arlette Farge, *Fragile Lives: Violence, Power and Solidarity in Eighteenth-Century Paris,* trans. Carol Shelton (Cambridge: Harvard University Press, 1993); David Garrioch, *Neighbourhood and Community in Paris, 1740–1790* (Cambridge: Cambridge University Press, 1986); Robert Schwartz, *Policing the Poor in Eighteenth-Century France* (Chapel Hill: University of North Carolina Press, 1988); Lucien Bély, "Mendiants et Vagabonds," in *Dictionnaire de l'Ancien Régime* (Paris: Presses Universitaires de France, 2010), 815–16.—Ed.]

20. [*Debauchery* had an extensive meaning in eighteenth-century French, with nearly a whole page of definitions and usage in the *Dictionnaire universel.* Although it could be used in a playful sense, to indicate merrymaking among "honest people," it also indexed moral and social disorder. "To debauch" meant to live with corrupted mores, to throw oneself toward vice, to leave the path of virtue. According to the *Dictionnaire universel,* "good-for-nothings debauched lots of people, and drew them toward gambling, carousing with women, and frequenting the cabarets." The dictionary of the Académie Française for 1762 defines *debauchery* as disorderliness, or excess in drink and food, or incontinence. Starting in 1713, "public debauchery" falls under the jurisdiction of the lieutenant general, or occasionally the criminal court at Châtelet. Under Lenoir, sentences of exile for debauchery almost entirely disappear, and instead prostitutes are imprisoned for three to six months; these sentences harden in the second half of the century. Foucault discusses debauchery in *History of Madness* (84–90), and then again in the context of unreason (106, 109). See Antoine Furetière, *Dictionnaire universel,* 1727 edition, revised and expanded by Henri Basnage de Beauval and Jean-Baptiste Brutel de La Rivière. See also the online *Dictionnaires d'autrefois* project at https://artfl-project.uchicago.edu/; Garrioch, *Neighbourhood and Community,* 76; Erica-Maria Benabou, *La Prostitution et la police des mœurs au XVIIIe siècle* (Paris: Éditions Perrin, 1987).—Ed.]

21. Jean Terrassin Dessessarts, ms. 11006, Ars. Arch. Bastille (year: 1728).

22. [Couples could ask for a *séparation de corps* (divorce) or *séparation de biens* (financial separation). Usually, such petitions were made after long episodes of domestic violence. Divorce was rarely granted, but occasionally women could obtain a financial separation that allowed them at least to protect their dowry from creditors. France legalized divorce in 1792, but then abolished that practice in 1816. Divorce was not legalized again until 1884. On the difficulties of obtaining divorce, see Giacomo Francini, "Divorce and Separations in Eighteenth-Century France: An Outline for a Social History of Law," *The History of the Family* 2.1 (1997): 99–113; and Julie Hardwick, "Seeking Separations: Gender, Marriages, and the Household Economies in Early Modern France," *French Historical Studies* 21 (1998): 157–80. On women as disorderly, see Sarah Hanley, "Engendering the State: Family Formation and State Building in Early Modern France," *French Historical Studies* 16.1 (spring 1989): 4–27; and on domestic violence, see Desan and Merrick, *Family, Gender and Law in Early Modern France.* For the connection between sexual and political orders, see Jeffrey Merrick, "Sexual Politics and Public Order in Late Eighteenth-Century France: The Mémoires Secrets and the Correspondance Secrète," *Journal of the History of Sexuality* 1.1 (July 1990): 68–84; David Garrioch, "The Paternal Government of Men: The Self-image and Action of the Paris Police in the 18th Century" in *A History of Police and Masculinities, 1700–2010* (New York: Routledge, 2012), 35–54. For works that think the political, economic, and sexual lives of women together, see Julie Hardwick, *Family Business: Litigation and the Political Economies of Daily Life in Early Modern France* (Oxford: Oxford University Press, 2009); Janine Lanza, *From Wives to Widows in Early Modern Paris* (Farnham: Ashgate, 2007); Jennifer Ngaire Heuer, *The Family and the Nation: Gender and Citizenship in Revolutionary France, 1789–1830* (Ithaca, N.Y.: Cornell University Press, 2007).—Ed.]

23. Ars. Arch. Bastille, ms. 11027. [The letters from this dossier were not included in the final collection.—Ed.]

24. Ars. Arch. Bastille, ms. 11004, fol. 12 (year: 1728).

25. [This kind of "neighborhood" was a social description rather than a geographic one, and described the neighbors who acted as a single social entity. The discussion of the "gaze of others," then, needs to be carefully situated. Foucault evokes the gaze earlier when he discusses the clinical gaze in *History of Madness* and in the discussion of panopticism in *Discipline and Punish.* If the sixteenth-century medical gaze came to reside in the doctor–patient relationship of the nineteenth century, and if the nineteenth-century panoptic gaze moved between juridical and carceral relationships, then here Farge and Foucault tell the story of the eighteenth-century social gaze that comes to reside in conventional social relationships that regulate shame. Jacques Donzelot's *The Policing of Families* charts the emergence of the social sector, and its connections to crime, poverty, and the family best embodied by the "social workers" of the nineteenth century. As boundaries between public and private become renegotiated, Donzelot argues that the state actively works to create the family as a locus of responsibility, to organize it around a "head," and to insist on the family as an end in itself (Jacques Donzelot, *The Policing of Families* [New York: Pantheon Books, 1979]). Farge and Foucault's account, then, charts the circulations around newly emergent social categories. For an account of the regulation of shame and social misfits as connected to eighteenth-century French politics, see Locke, "Rousseau's Pariahs, Rousseau's Laments." For more on the social gaze and its effects, see Foucault, *History of Madness,* 486ff.; and Arlette Farge, "Michel Foucault et les archives de l'exclusion," in *Penser la folie* (Paris: Éditions Galilée, 1992).—Ed.]

26. [Foucault uses the term "entourage" elsewhere in his writings, usually to denote

those involved in some form of normalization. See note 9 in Farge and Foucault's Introduction.—Ed.]

27. [Preoccupations with visibility are common to this period of *Lumières* (Enlightenment; literally, Lights), one in which the streetlights of Paris, City of Lights, were replaced with gas lamps, so as to improve safety and policing. These preoccupations with light and visibility have found an important echo in contemporary reflections on French philosophy and political order. Examples range from Martin Jay's excoriation of French contemporary philosophers (including Foucault) for their lack of vision, to Jacques Rancière's association of visibility and the sensory broadly speaking to policing and police order. See Martin Jay, *Downcast Eyes: The Denigration of Vision in Twentieth-Century French Thought* (Berkeley: University of California Press, 1994), and Jacques Rancière, *Dis-agreement*, trans. Julie Rose (Minneapolis: University of Minnesota Press, 2004).

28. [The lieutenant general generally has three domains of responsibility: first, to maintain public order (cleanliness, safety, circulation, building inspection, confiscation of arms, and the monitoring of gambling houses, prostitutes, and vagabonds); second, to secure the provisioning of the city (regulation of markets, of price and quality of various commodities, of the circulation of goods); third, to police the trades (with attention to approved monopolies, conflict between master craftsmen and their workers, observation of holidays). By the time of d'Argenson, forty-eight *commissaires du quartier* (superintendents) serve under the lieutenant general; from 1740 onward, these are complemented by twenty inspectors, tied either to a neighborhood or to a speciality (e.g., public safety, morals, contraband) that permits them to move about. See Bély, "Lieutenant Général de Police," 739–40. For a more extensive discussion, see the Editor's Introduction.—Ed.]

29. [The letters excerpted here are not in the dossiers collected in this volume. Jean-Étienne Dominique Esquirol (1772–1840) was a French psychiatrist who worked with Philippe Pinel at the Salpêtrière. With the financial backing of Pinel, Esquirol founded a *maison de santé* in 1801 in the neighborhood of Ivry, just opposite to the Salpêtrière, before being named the medical director of Charenton (an asylum that has since been renamed to bear his name). Esquirol also influenced the building of St. Yon at Rouen, with a similar attention to the layout of the buildings, courtyards, and baths. In the nineteenth century, his research gave birth to a wave of asylum reform born of moral indignation at the conditions of previous institutions. Esquirol figures prominently in *History of Madness*, where Foucault argues that the Charenton of the Brothers of St. John foreshadows that of Esquirol, just as the Salpêtrière foreshadows Charcot. See Pierre Pinon, *Charenton Hospital* (Liège: Mardaga, 1989); Jeanne Mesmin d'Étienne, "La folie selon Esquirol: Observations médicales et conceptions de l'aliénisme à Charenton entre 1825 et 1840," *Revue d'histoire du XIXᵉ siècle* 40 (2010); Foucault, *History of Madness*, 388.—Ed.]

30. Archives de la Préfecture de Police, AB 405. Quartier Saint-Denis, Rapports sur placets, 23 juillet 1779 au 19 avril 1786.

31. Ars. Arch. Bastille, ms. 11006, fol. 267.

32. Ars. Arch. Bastille, ms. 11021, fol. 13.

33. We should also mention that for every dossier from the [Bibliothèque de l'] Arsenal in which we found requests for imprisonment, the request was always followed by a *lettre de cachet.*

34. [In the eighteenth century, a *communauté* referred either to a group organized by a set of rules (such as a religious order, sect, cult, or parish) or to a society organized around a common interest (often a professional society). For more on the involvement of the

police in these contexts, see Steven Kaplan, "Réflexions sur la police du monde du travail, 1700–1815," *Revue Historique* 261.1 (January–March 1979), 17–77. —Ed.]

35. Arsenal, ms. 11989, fol. 249 (year: 1758).

36. [*Surprendre la religion* indicates something obtained fraudulently, through artifice or deception. Literally, "to surprise or unsettle one's beliefs." This phrase avoids insult by suggesting an excess of piety led to this startlement. See *Dictionnaire de l'Académie française,* 4th ed. (1762), available online through the *Dictionnaires d'autrefois.*—Ed.]

37. Arsenal, ms. 11013, fol. 127 (year: 1728).

38. Arsenal, ms. 11939. [The letters from this dossier were not included in the final collection.—Ed.]

39. [Sainte-Pélagie was a women's prison for those arrested for debauchery. Administered by nuns, it was founded by Marie Bonneau, widow of M. de Beauharnais de Miramion, as part of her effort to turn around wayward young women. Some women entered Sainte-Pélagie voluntarily. Those imprisoned by *lettre de cachet* came from a certain social class, and were believed to have dishonored their family or to be at risk of public scandal; those who misbehaved were often sentenced to the danker conditions of the Salpêtrière. In 1792, the buildings of Sainte-Pélagie were converted to a political prison, at which point its conditions deteriorated rapidly. See Hillairet, *Gibets, piloris et cachots du vieux Paris,* and also the flamboyant *Les prisons de l'Europe* by Auguste Maquet and Jules-Édouard Alboize du Pujol (Paris: Administration de librairie, 1845).—Ed.]

40. [The phrase *rentrer en soi-même* is difficult to translate. Quite literally, it suggests being recollected to oneself and so suggests the personal movement of recoil mixed with reflection, all motivated by social disapproval. The phrase does not yet carry the strong psychological overtones, or sense of interiority, that it will acquire by the nineteenth century. For an extended discussion of the difficulties of this translation and its historical permutations, see the Editor's Introduction.—Ed.]

41. Taking all the years together, half of the wives who requested the imprisonment of their husband later requested his release; only a third of husbands did the same.

42. Catherine Duprat, "Punir et guérir: En 1819, la prison des philanthropes," in *L'Impossible prison: Recherches sur le système pénitentiaire au XIXe siècle,* ed. Michelle Perrot (Paris: Éditions du Seuil, 1980), 64–124.

LETTERS FOR "MARITAL DISCORD"

1. [The company of the Lieutenant of the Short Robe was initially formed to regulate vagabonds and to respond to those who resisted paying taxes. If initially this company had a partly judicial function, that role diminishes over the eighteenth century and ends with the edict of July 1783. These officers also escorted criminals, including Robert-François Damiens, from Foucault's *Discipline and Punish,* to their executions; Damiens was the last person to be executed by drawing and quartering. These officers are described in reference to their short, military robes that distinguish them from their colleagues in the civil and criminal lieutenancies who wear a long robe befitting their more judicial functions.—Ed.]

2. [Inspector Roussel keeps a double-entry register of interrogations and arrests for the years 1739–51. See ms Bastille 10136.—Ed.]

3. [Étienne-François Stainville was first count of Stainville and then duke of Choiseul. Advancing through his career under the protection of Madame de Pompadour, mistress to king Louis XV, the duke de Choiseul was active in suppressing the Jansenist revolt against royal authority. He later served as minister of foreign affairs in 1758, and

until 1770 remained an active presence in the highest offices. Choiseul is known for his efforts to strengthen French military presence in Europe and beyond, and for his colonization of the Antilles and San Domingo. He also did much to strengthen political ties between France and Austria, including support for the marriage of Louis XVI and Marie-Antoinette—Ed.]

4. [The phrase "to mislead or deceive the religion" *(surprendre la religion)* evokes the shock and disbelief provoked by some new event. It avoids insult by suggesting that an excess of piety, rather than credulity, led to this startlement.—Ed.]

5. [Louis-Daniel Rossignol begins his career in the police in 1730 and serves as secretary to several lieutenant generals. His son becomes ennobled by patent letter and goes on to serve as consul general for Russia—an indication of how offices within the lieutenancy were often the stepping stones for career advancement.—Ed.]

6. [An archaic term for public gambling houses.—Trans.]

7. [*Comédie* here might refer to the national playhouse known as the Comédie française, or to theatergoing more generally.—Ed.]

8. [An idiom meaning "ruined" or "penniless"; it suggests being reduced to sleeping on straw.—Ed.]

9. [An idiomatic phrase, "bad commerce" indicates that someone is dishonest in his or her business dealings.—Ed.]

2. PARENTS AND CHILDREN

1. [Single women were not allowed to live with men to whom they were not married; widows likewise were not to be sexually available. In *Fragile Lives*, Arlette Farge notes that the charge of concubinage in the context of long-term relationships often masks concerns about succession, inheritance, or some other issue. See Arlette Farge, *Fragile Lives: Violence, Power and Solidarity in Eighteenth-Century Paris*, trans. Carol Shelton (Cambridge: Harvard University Press, 1993). 74ff.).—Ed.]

2. [For more on marriage as a "site"—that is, as a social space with its own regulations—see Sarah Hanley, "Social Sites of Political Practice in France: Lawsuits, Civil Rights and the Separation of Powers in Domestic and State Government, 1500–1800," *American Historical Review* 102.1 (February 1997): 27–52. Farge refers to this theme of thinking marriage and the family as a "place" in "Concerning Parents and Children," in *Fragile Lives*, 42ff.—Ed.]

3. [Such itinerancy is usually captured in the language of vagabondage. More precisely, according to a declaration in 1764, vagabondage refers to those who haven't exercised a trade or a profession for six months. They are known as *sans aveu* (those without vows); that is, nobody speaks for them *[les avoue]*, nobody acknowledges them. The number of vagabonds seems to grow toward the end of the eighteenth century, in conjunction with the demographic explosion, economic crisis, and restrictions on the commons. The world of vagabonds is crisscrossed with variation. Younger and less permanently poor than those called "beggars" *[mendiants]*, vagabonds include those fleeing their families or debts, and domestics, former soldiers, peddlers, day workers, or artisans. See Lucien Bély, "Mendiants et Vagabonds," in *Dictionnaire de l'Ancien Régime* (Paris: Presses Universitaires de France, 2010), 815–16; Alan Williams, *The Police of Paris* (Baton Rouge: Louisiana State University Press, 1979), 189–95; Arlette Farge, *Vivre dans la rue à Paris au XVIIIe siècle* (Paris: Gallimard-Julliard, collection Archives, 1979), 163–243.—Ed.]

4. [The dossier for Antoine Cotte was not included in the original volume.—Ed.]

5. [The dossier for Marie-Françoise Coucher was not included in the original volume. —Ed.]

6. [The Guard was created in 1667 as the failures of the traditional watch *(guet)*, itself a patrol of venal offices created in the thirteenth century, became apparent. Composed of three units (one mounted), the Guard surveyed the city from a mix of stationary guard-houses and patrols. In 1725 it counted approximately 450 men, by 1760 about 725 men, and by 1788 it had grown to 1,000. Soldiers of the Guard held salaried positions paid out bimonthly, and most were sons of small farmers or artisans. For more detail about the history and function of the Guard, see Williams, *The Police of Paris*.—Ed.]

7. [Most working-class parents sought to secure an apprenticeship for their children, and were less concerned about the continuity of the trade than that these children stayed in the neighborhood; the poor were unable to do so. Girls were the economic responsibility of their parents until they married; parents might intervene in the case of death or abandonment. In the face of children unwilling to work, parents sometimes asked the authorities to intervene. See David Garrioch, *Neighbourhood and Community in Paris, 1740–1790* (Berkeley: University of California Press, 2004), 102–14.—Ed.]

8. [Such merchants of haberdashery would sell items connected to fashion and clothing, such as needles, thread, buttons, ribbons, laces, and so on. See Alfred Franklin and Émile Levasseur, eds., *Dictionnaire historique des arts, métiers et professions exercés dans Paris depuis le treizième siècle* (Paris: H. Welter, 1906), 478–81.—Ed.]

9. [Especially in the smaller workshops, the social relations between master and apprentices or journeymen were strong. Workers, then, could not be unpredictably absent without these absences becoming known throughout the trade. See Garrioch, *Neighbourhood and Community*, 102–11.—Ed.]

10. [The main character in a picaresque novel, *The Adventures of Gil Blas* by Alain-René Lesage, in which Gil Blas finds himself obliged to help robbers, threatened with imprisonment by *lettre de cachet*, and then enjoys a series of misadventures as a valet.—Ed.]

11. [The protagonist from the novel *Manon Lescaut* by Antoine François Prévost. This short novel recounts the adventures of Des Grieux and Manon Lescaut as they run away first to Paris and then to New Orleans, to which Manon has been deported as a prostitute. It offers a romanticized version of some of the social relations associated with the *lettres de cachet*; indeed, Prévost flees to London to avoid being imprisoned under a *lettre de cachet* issued by a prior.—Ed.]

12. [In eighteenth-century writing, "resipiscence" often functions similarly as the phrase *rentrer en soi-même*. According to the *Dictionnaire de l'Académie française* (1762), it suggests a recognition of faults followed by amends. It carries with it an awareness of public opinion. Foucault finds it absent in certain of Bicêtre's carceral practices from this period: "The notion of resipiscence is quite foreign to the whole system . . . The men chained to the walls of the cells were not seen as people who had lost their reason but as beasts filled with snarling, natural rage" (*History of Madness*, ed. Jean Khalfa, trans. Jonathan Murphy [New York: Routledge, 2006], 147). In *The Punitive Society*, Foucault notes: "There is a reference here to resipiscence, which is as much remorse in the moral sense as return to health; a reference, also, to the instrument of a regular life, to a regularity of social life as well as of a monastic rule observed in a community." The manuscript (folio 12) continues: "The other essential element is not arbitrariness, it is correction. With all the possible ambiguities of this word, which designates a pedagogy, a cure, a religious repentance, and a moral conversion." See

Michel Foucault, *The Punitive Society: Lectures at the Collège de France, 1972–1973,* trans. Graham Burchell, ed. Bernard Harcourt (New York: Palgrave Macmillan, 2015), 130.—Ed.]

13. [The French policy of sending criminals to the colonies originated in 1682 and was renewed multiple times into the eighteenth century. Sending criminals to the colonies seemed a way to relieve the crowding in Parisian prisons and hospitals, to minimize potential future threats to public order, and to fill the "empty colonies" with inhabitants. In May 1719, a royal order opened Bicêtre, l'Hôpital général, la Pitié, and the orphanage known as l'Hôpital des Enfants-Trouvés to the Company of the West, a charter company directed by John Law with territory in Louisiana. In 1719, approximately two thousand prisoners sailed for Louisiana, Mississippi, and Dauphine Island. These prisoners were mostly men, but included some women, including couples who were married in a mass ceremony and promised a dowry (often subsequently stolen by the guards overseeing their travel). By 1720, the creation of empressment gangs in rural areas, combined with reports of rough treatment en route to the colonies, created a violent backlash among the poor. The last ship of prisoner colonists associated with the Company of the West sailed with eighty-one women from Salpêtrière to Dauphine Island in 1721. Others continued into the late eighteenth century, facilitated by the decree of July 15, 1763, but never with much success. References to "the Islands" usually indicate the islands in the French West Indies (including Île de la Désirade, Saint-Domingue, Martinique, Guadeloupe, and Tortuga).

Back in France, a series of revolts broke out between December 1749 and May 1750 related to rumors of child abductions at the hands of the police. Lieutenant General Berryer had implemented a harsh policy against begging, vagrancy, and vagabondage. A number of teenagers were picked up in the course of these arrests, giving rise to the accusation that these children were being sent to Louisiana and Mississippi to populate the colonies. For more on these riots of 1750 and the charges of abduction, see Arlette Farge and Jacques Revel, *The Vanishing Children of Paris: Rumor and Politics before the French Revolution,* trans. Claudia Mieville (Cambridge: Harvard University Press, 1993); Christophe Romon, "L'Affaire des 'enlèvements des enfants' dans les archives du Châtelet (1749–50)," *Revue historique* 587 (July–September 1983); Farge, *Fragile Lives,* 55–62; Vincent Milliot, *Un Policier des Lumières* (Seyssel: Éditions Champ Vallon, 2011),308–20. Foucault has a general discussion of imprisonment and the colonies in *History of Madness,* 401–06. See also James D. Hardy, "The Transportation of Convicts to Colonial Louisiana," *Louisiana History: The Journal of the Louisiana Historical Association* 7.3 (summer 1966): 207–20; and Jacques Hillairet, *Gibets, piloris et cachots du vieux Paris* (Paris: Éditions de Minuit, 1956).—Ed.]

14. [Gabriel-Charles Rousseau de Villejouin served as governor of Île de la Désirade, an island in the archipelago of the Antilles and part of the administrative unit of Guadeloupe. His brother, Gabriel-Michel Rousseau de Villejouin, emigrated to St. Domingue (today's Haiti) and lived through the Haitian slave revolt; his family later emigrated to Louisiana. See Hardy, "The Transportation of Convicts to Colonial Louisiana," 207–20.—Ed.]

15. [The Hôpital général gathered under a common administration, overseen by the king, the different hospitals across the city. These were not hospitals in the modern sense, but almshouses and houses of detention oriented toward the poor. The Hôpital général brought together la Pitié (which housed children eight years and older), Bicêtre (a prison for men), and the Salpêtrière (its female counterpart) and later various orphanages (including l'Hôpital des Enfants-Trouvés) and Sainte-Pélagie (a women's prison for those arrested for debauchery). The Hôpital général's funding came from three sources: charitable gifts; a percentage taxed on public fines, the confiscation of goods, theater ticket sales, wine,

and salt; and, finally, a tax on the revenues of religious communities. The prison of Saint-Lazare was more respectable and usually housed errant clergy members and dissolute sons of the best families. It never grew larger than fifty-six people prior to the Revolution. Most prisoners were arrested by *lettre de cachet*, the pensions cost 600 livres (compared to the more usual 150 livres) and families often paid even more for linens, heating, and medicine. For some prisoners, the pension cost grew to 1,000 to 1,200 livres. See Hillairet, *Gibets, piloris et cachots*; Frantz Funck-Brentano, *Les Lettres de cachet à Paris: Étude suivie d'une liste des prisonniers* (Paris: Imprimerie nationale, 1903); Isabelle Robin and Agnès Walch, "Géographie des enfants trouvés de Paris aux XVIIᵉ et XVIIIᵉ siècles," *Histoire, économie et société* 6.3 (1987): 343–60.—Ed.]

16. [Emer de Vattel, *The Law of Nations* (London: G. G. and J. Robinson, 1797), book I, chapter 13, §83. The full text for §84 reads: "The internal police consists in the attention of the prince and magistrates to preserve every thing in order. Wise regulations ought to prescribe whatever will best contribute to the public safety, utility and convenience; and those who are invested with authority cannot be too attentive to enforce them. By a wise police, the sovereign accustoms the people to order and obedience, and preserves peace, tranquility, and concord among the citizens. The magistrates of Holland are said to possess extraordinary talents in this respect:—a better police prevails in their cities, and even their establishments in the Indies, than in any other places in the known world."—Ed.]

17. [Such education was not easily or obviously available. *Éducation*, translated consistently here as "upbringing," connotes moral instruction as much as book learning. Public education emerged as a political ideal along with the French Revolution, and then was extended and institutionalized by Jules Ferry in a series of laws in 1881–82.—Ed.]

18. [Beginning in the 1750s, a panic around depopulation seized France and convinced intellectuals that the luxuriant living of the Sun King was rotting France from within. Some charged that libertinage and intemperance were the source of the degeneracy—even as demographers demonstrated that the French population was expanding. Others, such as the abbé Jaubert, charged upper-class women with a putative decline in breast-feeding and moral education as they became distracted by fashion. Foucault cites the abbé Jaubert in his lectures for *Security, Territory, Population* as he argues that the emergence of the "population" as a natural datum shifts governance from the obedience of political subjects toward the management and administration of populations. See Michel Foucault, *Security, Territory, Population: Lectures at the Collège de France, 1977–1978*, ed. Arnold Davidson, trans. Graham Burchell (New York: Palgrave Macmillan, 2007); 71.—Ed.]

19. Abbé Pierre Jaubert, *Des causes de la Dépopulation et des moyens d'y remédier* (Paris: Chez Dessain, 1767), 157–68.

LETTERS FOR "PARENTS AND CHILDREN"

1. [Son of Jérôme Phélypeaux, Jean-Frédéric Phélypeaux (also the count de Maurepas) was part of the administrative nobility of Versailles under Louis XV and occupied offices passed down through the right of inheritance. He entered into the Maison du Roi in 1718, and from there served as Minister of the Marine (1723–49). After a brief exile from Paris, he returned to serve as chief adviser to Louis XVI, and used this position to liberalize the grain markets and to appoint sympathizers such as Turgot, Malesherbes, and Vergennes to key positions. Maurepas justified the use of *lettres de cachet* to solve disorders around the grain riots, by arguing that sometimes the state needed to act swiftly and decisively.—Ed.]

2. [An *intendant* is a public official.— Ed.]

3. [Likely a misspelling of Phélypeaux.—Ed.]

4. ["Island" here refers to the jurisdiction that contains Paris and is known as the "Île de France."—Ed.]

5. [A lemonade-maker infused both alcoholic and nonalcoholic drinks. A number of drinking establishments existed in eighteenth-century Paris, and their names reflected either what type of alcohol was sold or the type of establishment. If the *marchands de vin* or *de bière* sold wine and beer and served it on-site, the *limonadier* served wine, spirits, and infused refreshments to those willing to drink without sitting down. They were authorized to sell wines from Spain, Provence, Malavasia, and La Ciotat; muscat dessert wine; liqueurs; flavored lemonades; ice creams; and sorbets. The *limonadiers* also were a potent political force. Their union formed in 1674 and was allowed to grow to 250 masters. In 1704, these master-ships were refunded and the king proposed to license 150 masters at a higher sum; after ten years of dispute, the initial organization was retained. A century later, the *limonadiers* became active in the anarcho-syndicalist movement in France in large part because of the precarious nature of the profession. See Alfred Franklin and Émile Levasseur, eds., *Dictionnaire historique des arts, métiers et professions exercés dans Paris depuis le treizième siècle* (Paris, 1906), 434–35.—Ed.]

6. ["H." here indicates "Honorable Fathers"; the French equivalent is "Reverend Fathers."—Ed.]

7. [*Mainmorte* refers to the inalienable ownership of property; *gens de mainmorte* are the legal persons affected by this status (notably, serfs whose property reverts to their lord, or to the church, which holds property in perpetuity). The *greffe des gens de Mainmorte* is the office that manages the documentation for such persons and property.—Ed.]

8. [These were flat round coins with images imprinted on them that were used for gambling, much like casino tokens today—Trans.]

9. [The French Guards were a regiment in the military branch of the Maison du Roi. Together, the French and Swiss Guards comprise four thousand men. These forces were complemented by the brigades of the Prevost of the Island (about 150 men, centered in Île-de-la-Cité at the center of Paris), which include the mounted constabulary *(le maréchaussée)* and two hundred members of the Company of the Lieutenant de la Robe Courte of Châtelet (lieutenant of the short robe, in contrast to the longer robes of the military), which was charged with policing the tribunals and the prisons. The French and Swiss Guards were called upon only when the guard and the short robe needed help. Many of the French Guards later defected during the Revolution. Foucault briefly discusses the mounted constabulary in *Security, Territory, Population*, English series ed. Arnold Davidson, trans. Graham Burchell (New York: Picador, 2009), 335–36. See Alan Williams, *The Police of Paris: 1718–1789* (Baton Rouge: Louisiana State University Press, 1979), 71–89, and Lucien Bély, ed., "Maison militaire du Roi," in *Dictionnaire de l'Ancien Régime* (Paris: Presses Universitaires de France, 2010).—Ed.]

10. [A cutting tool with a wooden handle and a curved blade. These served purposes common to both the knife and the axe. In France, the billhook was often used in connection with viticulture to prune and harvest grapevines. Pierre Rivière used a billhook to kill his mother and two siblings.—Ed.]

11. [Marie Lescombat was an adulterous wife who famously had her husband stabbed by her young lover, her husband's own apprentice. This *fait divers*, or true story, garnered a great deal of public attention and she was arrested and hanged in 1755.—Ed.]

12. [The place de Grève was public square often thought of as the "forum of the Pari-

sian people." It gained notoriety as a site for public executions, including that of Robert-François Damiens, but it also was the site where workers gathered to protest (hence the phrase *faire la grève* or "go on strike") and where the masses gathered to consolidate their victories in July 1789. It is now the square in front of the town hall, and since 1802 has been named the Place de l'Hôtel de Ville de Paris. See "Hôtel de Ville," in Frédéric Lock, *Dictionnaire topographique et historique de l'ancien Paris* (Paris: Librairie de l'Hachette, 1855), 187ff.—Ed.]

13. [Surgeons in eighteenth-century France exercised a wide range of professional competencies; they also served as dentists, and more surprisingly, as barbers. Indeed, for many centuries, the barber and surgical professions were quite close; between the sixteenth and eighteenth centuries, this proximity was institutionalized through the formation of a common guild. This history originates in the church's twelfth-century condemnation of any invasion of the flesh, an act that pushed everything from shaving to dentistry to minor surgeries beyond the faculty of medicine. Adept with razors and working close to the flesh of the body, many barbers treated abscesses and open wounds, applied sticking plasters, and drew blood. Their professional identities were defined by their tools. Although the royal edict of November 1692 began to separate the two professions, many surgeons continued to work as barbers, especially in small towns. The two professions were not rendered cleanly distinct until a 1743 edict that prohibited surgeons from also serving as barbers. The letters in this dossier thus provide additional insight into the corporate guilds that brought surgeons and barbers together; their reorganization and the subsequent new alignment of barbers and wigmakers; the high stakes of apprenticeships and the constant threat that these be abandoned; and the role of corporate bodies in "constructing the social"— for many years independent of legal organization. For an essay that uses the connection between surgeons and barbers to untangle the complex social, economic, and political relations of eighteenth-century corporate bodies, see Christelle Rabier, "La disparition du barbier-chirurgien: Analyse d'une mutation professionnelle au XVIIIᵉ siècle," *Annales Histoire, Sciences Sociales* 2010/3 (65th year): 679–711.—Ed.]

14. [A statue of Moses, or Moyse, had been placed at the corner of the rue Princesse, next to the rue du Four. The hôtel here was built sometime in the seventeenth century. See *Recherches critiques, historiques et topographiques sur la ville de Paris*, vol. 5, ed. Jaillot (Paris: A.-M. Lottin the elder, 1774), 79.—Ed.]

15. [Foucault reads the *lettre de cachet* for Pierre Béranger in his January 15, 1975, lecture for his course, *Abnormal*. Afterwards, he comments: "Perversity and Danger. You can see how today we find again, at the same level, reactivated in a modern institution and knowledge, a vast practice that judicial reform at the end of the eighteenth century was supposed to have got rid of. This is not just the result of a kind of archaism. Rather, as crime becomes increasingly pathologized and as the expert and judge swap roles, this form of control, assessment, and effect of power linked to the characterization of an individual becomes increasingly active" (Michel Foucault, *Abnormal: Lectures at the Collège de France, 1974–75*, trans. Graham Burchell [New York: Palgrave Macmillan, 2004], 38). Foucault argues that a third term, the "abnormals," emerges along with a set of practices and discourses that are neither judicial nor medical but that derive from "the power of normalization."—Ed.]

16. [An order of canons regular founded in Prémontré (a town in northeastern France) in 1120 by St. Norbert, and subject to Augustinian rule (meaning that they have to earn their living). As canons regular, they live in community and share their property in

common. Their work involves preaching and the exercise of public ministry. The order was largely devastated during the French Revolution. Ironically, many of Foucault's papers are now maintained by l'Institut Mémoires de l'Édition Contemporaine (IMEC) at Abbaye d'Ardenne, itself a Premonstratensian abbey.—Ed.]

17. [*Comédie* here might refer to the national playhouse known as the Comédie française, or to theatergoing more generally.—Ed.]

18. [The volunteers of Clermont-Prince were an irregular corps formed in 1759 to counter the threat of German light troops. They take their name from their two proprietors: Clermont and later his nephew the Prince de Condé.—Ed.]

3. WHEN ADDRESSING THE KING

1. [In the well-known *Dictionnaire universel de police* (1786–90) by the lawyer Nicolas Toussaint Lemoyne Des Essarts, policing is defined as the art "of governing men and doing them well, the art of rendering them happy as much as possible and as much as they should be for the common interest of society." Later, in the presentation of the judicial function of the lieutenant general of police in Paris, Des Essarts writes that under his lead the police should "maintain order and discredit its abuse, to do good and impede evil, and finally force men to recognize that they are interested in conducting themselves well *[se bien conduire]* in order to be happy" (Nicolas Toussaint Lemoyne Des Essarts, *Dictionnaire universel de police*, vol. 8 [Paris: Moutard, 1790], 343, 526). For a longer discussion of Des Essarts, and a comparison of his language of management to the earlier paternalism of Delamare in his own *Traité de la police* (1705), see Vincent Milliot, *Un Policier des Lumières* (Seyssel: Éditions Champ Vallon, 2011), 277ff. Foucault comments on Delamare's earlier invocation of felicity (327), his emphasis on the "goodness of life" and "preservation" (334), and the organization of police (334ff.) in *Security, Territory, Population: Lectures at the Collège de France, 1977–1978*, ed. Arnold Davidson, trans. Graham Burchell (New York: Palgrave Macmillan, 2007).—Ed.]

2. [Farge and Foucault refer here to Châtelet's double jurisdiction that enables it both to try and to investigate arrests. See the earlier discussion in note 11 in "Marital Discord."—Ed.]

3. [In this passage, Farge and Foucault suggest that the *lettres de cachet* gradually rewrite and redirect the connections between social relations and political sovereignty. These claims echo those made earlier by Foucault in *Society Must Be Defended*, in which he writes that "an important phenomenon occurred in the seventeenth and eighteenth centuries: the appearance—one should say the invention—of a new mechanism of power which had very specific procedures, completely new instruments, and very different equipment . . . This nonsovereign power, which is foreign to the form of sovereignty, is 'disciplinary' power" (Michel Foucault, *Society Must Be Defended: Lectures at the Collège de France, 1975-1976*, ed. Arnold Davidson, trans. David Macey [New York: Picador, 2003], 35–36). One might read the letters, then, as an illustration of an indeterminate agency in which the grudging "democratization of sovereignty" simultaneously conceals the mechanisms of a new, disciplinary power "and erases the element of domination and the techniques of domination involved in discipline" (37). Importantly, this period becomes one in which social norms and the gaze of others have not yet settled into mechanisms of normalization and discipline.—Ed.]

4. [A number of commissioners, lieutenant generals, and police inspectors have written memoirs, including Lieutenant Generals Berryer, d'Argenson, and Lenoir. These memoirs often seek to grapple with implications of police surveillance and to place this policing

in broader political context. After Nicolas Delamare's 1705 *Traité de la police* (which evokes policing in the age of Enlightenment and adopts the tone and organization of an encyclopedia), comes the defense of new policing practices from commissioner Jean-Baptiste-Charles Lemaire in *Mémoire sur la police de Paris*, written in the 1760s. Delamare writes at the request of Lieutenant General Antoine de Sartine, who was himself polled by Empress Maria Theresa of Austria about the best mechanisms for policing. Where these memoirs addressed the structure of the police, by 1790 Lenoir's memoirs offer a view onto policing as it shifts from a judicial to an administrative function. Although Lenoir seeks to rise above the autobiographical, his memoirs never quite achieve a historical perspective. These memoirs are published in Milliot, *Un Policier des Lumières.* See also Marc-Réne d'Argenson, *Rapports inédits du lieutenant général de police Réne d'Argenson (1697–1715), publiés d'après les manuscrits conservés à la Bibliothèque nationale* (Paris: P. Cottin, 1891). Also useful are the "bulletins" that circulate information and updates from the police spies *(les mouches)*, to the moral police, to the vice squad, all the way to the lieutenant general. For example, Inspector Jean-Baptiste Meusnier kept from 1731 to 1753 a notebook with an edited selection of bulletins sent to the lieutenancy. These bulletins tracked the private lives of actresses, dancers, and singers. See Vincent Milliot, Un Policier des Lumières (Seyssel: Éditions Champ Vallon, 2011), 178; Arlette Farge, *Dire et mal dire; Bulletins de la police secrète rédigés pour le lieutenant général de police, 1740–1781 (Paris: Seuil, 1992),* mss. Bastille 10167–69.—Ed.]

5. [Under the lead of Lieutenant General Berryer, the police developed its central administration, both by employing more administrators (around fifty by 1789) and by proliferating their specialities. These numbers leave out, of course, the network of spies, clerks, and relays, as well as the informal police contacts in the neighborhoods. Under Berryer, there were about three thousand paid informers, at a cost of 1 million *livres* in 1753; by 1780, there were three times fewer spies for eighty thousand *livres* (Milliot, *Un Policier des Lumières,* 190). Popularly known as the "infamous Monsieur Beurrier [Mr. Butterman]," Lieutenant General Berryer became associated with indiscriminate police harassment and detention. Notably, Berryer advocated arresting children on the claim that they were vagrants or street urchins; yet many working-class children served as messengers and go-betweens for the family business. Arlette Farge and Jacques Revel, *The Vanishing Children of Paris: Rumor and Politics before the French Revolution,* trans. Claudia Mieville (Cambridge: Harvard University Press, 1993), 49.—Ed.]

6. [Louis-Sébastien Mercier's twelve-volume *Tableau de Paris* (1781–89) stages eighteenth-century daily life in a series of street scenes. Mercier takes his reader on a ramble across the city—commenting on the interactions of police spies, actresses, workers, parish priests, peddlers, and others—and observes ordinary mores and conventions with a biting wit. In his essay *Du théâtre, ou Nouvel essai sur l'art dramatique* (1775), Mercier critiques the closed sessions of the Comédiens du roi that limited the plays performed in Paris to a royal troupe. Drawing an analogy between political and theatrical representation, he cast the playwright as "legislator" who spoke as the "public orator of the oppressed" and the actors as those who served despotism by silencing the public voice. For these claims, first a *lettre de cachet* and then an *arrêt de conseil* (order of arrest) were ordered against Mercier. See Paul Friedland, *Political Actors: Representative Bodies and Theatricality in the Age of the Revolution* (Ithaca, N.Y.: Cornell University Press, 2002), 82; Louis-Sébastien Mercier, *Tableau de Paris,* 12 vols. (Paris: Virchaux & Compagnie, 1781–89).—Ed.]

7. Mercier, *Tableau de Paris,* vol. I, chapter 63, "Lieutenant Général de Police."

8. [The conflicts over jurisdictional authority of the multiple courts, and the balance

of political power between the royal court and the *parlements*, has a long history that dates back to 1648. Rather than serving as legislative bodies, the French *parlements* functioned as courts of appeal that defended the feudal liberties of chartered towns. The *parlements* chafed against the consolidation of absolutist political power under Louis XIII and Louis XIV. Even as negotiations concluded over the treaty of Westphalia—an event often used to index the rise of the nation-state—the conflict between royal power and the local *parlements* grew into a series of civil wars known collectively as the Fronde. The royal court was obliged to move to the château de Saint-Germain, where it eventually held a series of conferences from September 25 to October 4 between parliamentary delegates and sovereign representatives. The *parlementaires* made a number of demands that sought to counter royal absolutism, including a reduction in taxes, constitutional reforms, and the abolition of the *lettres de cachet*. Acting as regents for the young Louis XIV, Queen Anne d'Autriche and Cardinal Mazarin temporarily accept some of these demands—but they keep in place the *lettres de cachet*. See Sharon Kettering, *Judicial Politics and Urban Revolt in Seventeenth-Century France* (Princeton, N.J.: Princeton University Press, 2015).—Ed.]

9. [Chancellor Pierre Séguier, head of the royal Grand Council *(Grand Conseil)*, was particularly hated by the *parlementaires* and was forced into retirement in 1650. In 1666, Louis XIV appoints Séguier to the Conseil de Police and charges him with studying and then proposing reforms to the Parisian police. For many years, the proceedings at Châtelet had been managed by a civil lieutenant (responsible for disputes between individuals and corporations) and a criminal lieutenant (responsible for crimes committed). Justice and policing mixed. On the basis of the Conseil's deliberations, Louis XIV decides in March 1667 to consolidate police power under a single lieutenant of police charged with maintaining public order, guarding against fires and floods, provisioning and cleaning the city, as well as judging flagrant violators of police order. These two posts will be formally joined in 1674 and the position renamed as lieutenant general of police; its origin speaks to the initial close connection between policing and royal power. See Alan Williams, *The Police of Paris, 1718–1789* (Baton Rouge: Louisiana State University Press, 1979).—Ed.]

10. François-André Isambert, *Recueil général des anciennes lois françaises depuis l'an 420 jusqu'à la Révolution de 1789*, vol. 17, May 14, 1643–August 19, 1661 (Paris: Belin-Leprieur, 1829), 93, 94.

11. Philippe Megrin, *La Réforme de la lettre de cachet au XVIIIe siècle* (Paris: É. Larose, 1906).

12. Jules Flammermont and Maurice Tourneaux, eds., *Remontrances au Parlement de Paris au XVIIIe siècle*, vol. 2, 1755–68 (Paris: Imprimerie Nationale, 1895), 185.

13. [Jacob-Nicolas Moreau is a jurist and propagandist known as a defender of royal power, a public figure who (by the 1750s) had come to attack the philosophes and republican theorists he considered to be threats to social and political order. In *History of Madness*, Foucault quotes from Moreau's *Discours sur la justice*: "A family finds a viper in its breast, a cowardly individual who is capable of bringing dishonor. To avoid any such mishap the family swiftly makes a decision which the courts should follow, and any sovereign has a duty to look favorably on any such family deliberations," (Michel Foucault, *History of Madness*, ed. Jean Khalfa, trans. Jonathan Murphy [New York: Routledge, 2013], 90–91). Moreau thus aligns familial and sovereign authorities. Farge and Foucault quote from this broader passage in *Discours sur la justice* that reads: "It is the Prince's humanity that allows him to deprive a lunatic of his frenzy, to enable a virtuous family to escape from a tormenting shame. Behold the rule of power. To abuse it would be to promote private tyranny through public despotism—to serve with the most noble motivations, the most

vile interests, and to make the Prince executive and minister of the injustices of paternal power, through an almost sacrilegious desecration. Listen to public outcry, rather than the cry of the Courts, that cry of slavery that is no more than the echo of the orders and wishes of the Master. Lend an attentive ear to what is said, far from you, by the multitude that is so indignant as it complains and mutters. Doubtless its voice will never be your rule, but it is almost always just when it applauds authority; and when it blames authority, this voice at least is a useful warning that should render authority more circumspect" (162–63). In *History of Madness*, Foucault develops this connection between the use and abuse of words, and the transition from considering such abuse as blasphemy to an affair of civic order (92); this connection is similar to Foucault's preoccupation with "avowal" in the lectures he gives at the Université Catholique de Louvain in 1981. See Nicolas Moreau, *Discours sur la justice*, vol. 1 *(Versailles: De l'Imprimerie du Roi, 1775)*; Michel Foucault, *Wrong-doing, Truth-telling*, ed. Fabienne Brion and Bernard Harcourt, trans. Stephen W. Sawyer (Chicago: University of Chicago Press, 2014).—Ed.]

14. [The Cour des Aides, an excise board, was created in 1389 and primarily heard appeals about juridical decisions on fiscal matters. The court had no jurisdiction on those taxes established on the authority of the king, but reserved the right of formal complaint *(remontrance)*. Under Malesherbes, the Cour des Aides unsuccessfully demanded the suppression of the *lettres de cachet* in 1779 on the grounds that they had become increasingly arbitrary. See Jean Egret, "Malesherbes, Premier Président de la Cour des Aides (1750–1775)," *Revue d'histoire moderne et contemporaine* 3.2 (April–June 1956): 97–119.—Ed.]

15. [Chrétien-Guillaume de Lamoignon de Malesherbes served briefly as minister of the Maison du roi for Louis XVI between 1775 and 1776. He used the system of remonstrances to curb the *lettres de cachet*, by outlining the corrupt nature of their administration in his *Les Remontrances* (1775). These essays were distributed to the public in clandestine editions, and resulted in his own exile by *lettre de cachet* to his country house. Nonetheless, the public was increasingly convinced that it had been deprived of its voice by a tyrannical government; that the problem could not be overcome by restoring the influence of the *parlements*; and that the Estates-General, not called since 1614, needed to meet. A friend of the economic liberal Anne-Robert-Jacques Turgot (whose policies contributed in part to the bread riots of 1775), Malesherbes was a leading proponent of representative, rather than direct, politics. More than Turgot, he acknowledged the heterogeneous nature of public opinion; in contrast to the philosopher Condorcet, he was not convinced that popular opinion was always the most rational. He shared with these contemporaries, however, the conviction that men of letters, or professional representatives, could forge unified public opinion from particularist views, and thus give the public a voice, albeit one premised on the exclusion of the multitude. In 1792, Malesherbes defended the king before the French National Convention. Malesherbes was later guillotined, along with his older sister, his daughter and her husband, and his granddaughter and her husband. See Paul Friedland, *Political Actors: Representative Bodies and Theatricality in the Age of the Revolution* (Ithaca, N.Y.: Cornell University Press, 2002).—Ed.]

16. [Because many of those seeking *lettres de cachet* were not literate, letter writers consulted either public scriveners or *secrétaires*—letter-writing manuals that contained model letters for a variety of occasions. For all that the letters may strike modern readers as ornate and elaborate in their phrasing, the eighteenth-century art of writing imagined a reader who heard these words read aloud. Interestingly, some evidence suggests that Lieutenant General Lenoir used a *secrétaire* to aid in writing his memoirs. See Roger Chartier, *L'Ordre du*

livre (Aix-en-Provence: Éditions Alinea, 1992); Milliot, *Un Policier des Lumières*, 69. See also the discussion in the Editor's Introduction.—Ed.]

17. [Farge convinced Foucault not to publish the letters without an interpretive apparatus by arguing that readers needed some contextualization. In the 1983 France Culture radio broadcast on *Disorderly Families*, both argue that "raw utterances" don't exist—even archival materials are already staged for an audience in some way. For more on this specific collaboration and Farge's general approach to archival work, see Farge's interviews with Laurent Vidal, "Arlette Farge, le parcours d'une historienne," *Genèses*, no. 48 (2002/3): 115–35; and Sylvain Parent, "Entretien avec Arlette Farge," *Tracés: Revue de Sciences humaines* (online), May 2004, published January 26, 2009, consulted October 12, 2012. See also Roundtable with Roger Chartier (moderator), André Béjin, Arlette Farge, Michel Foucault, and Michelle Perrot, "À propos les 'lettres de cachet,'" *Les Lundis de l'histoire*, France Culture, January 10, 1983, consulted at Inathèque.—Ed.]

18. [Nicolas Bienfait was imprisoned at Bicêtre in 1758. Farge and Foucault did not include his full dossier (ms. 11987).—Ed.]

19. [Farge and Foucault here call attention to the juxtaposition of baroque court life with the emotional weather of ordinary people rendered on a less grandiose scale. Much as the etchings of Jacques Callot (1592–1635) and the paintings of the Le Nain brothers (c. 1600–1648) captured scenes from daily life—shorn of the fancy dress, simpering manners, and ornament of eighteenth-century "high" society—the letters capture the lives and speech of everyday people. Within these letters, the embellishments of formulaic legal expressions jostle with the direct vernacular recorded by the scriveners, much as styled social conventions jostle with the rougher practices of daily life.

[In other characterizations of these same letters, Foucault will refer to the letter writers as "characters from a novel by Céline" to capture the ragged existences that people their pages. See Michel Foucault, "Lives of Infamous Men," *Cahiers du chemin* 29, January 15, 1977, 171.—Ed.]

20. [In using the language of "secret," Farge and Foucault call attention to the play of secret and publicity that governs both royal authority and its invocations with the letters. Absolutists would characterize the king's authority in terms both of secret and mystery—the mystery of his person, his healing touch—and of its visibility through public spectacle. Paradoxically, by making visible one's misfortunes to the king, a family could shield itself from scandal. In the course of the 1750s, as conflicts rage between royal power and alternately the Jansenists and the *parlements*, publicity begins to take on a different meaning as political disputes emerge over the authority of the public and public opinion. See Keith M. Baker, "Memory and Practice: Political Representations of the Past," and "Public Opinion as Political Invention," in *Inventing the French Revolution* (Cambridge: Cambridge University Press, 1990); and Roger Chartier, "The Public Sphere and Public Opinion," in *The Cultural Origins of the French Revolution*, (Durham, N.C.: Duke University Press, 1991), 34–37. For more discussion in this volume of the language of secrecy, see "Marital Discord" and note 9.—Ed.]

21. Arlette Farge, *Vivre dans la rue à Paris au XVIIIᵉ siècle* (Paris: Gallimard, 1979). [In this text, Farge argues that the street is a privileged space with a multiform sociability that invades what will later be considered as private spaces.—Ed.]

22. [Charles Gravier, count of Vergennes (1717–87), is romantically rumored to have issued the *lettre de cachet* that prompted General Lafayette to flee France for the American colonies; Louis Phélypeaux, count of Saint Florentin, served as a minister in the Maison

du Roi (1749–75) for Louis XV, during which he made notorious use of the *lettres de cachet*; Malesherbes, minister in the Maison du Roi (1775–76) supported the *lettres* but sought to curb their abuse. For more context around Malesherbes, see note 15 above. Farge and Foucault appear to have taken these three quotes, cited in the same order, from Frantz Funck-Brentano, "Les lettres de cachet," in *Revue des deux mondes*, vol. 113 (Paris: May & Motteroz, 1892), 828.—Ed.]

23. [The word that Farge and Foucault use throughout this paragraph is *aveu*. Questions of truth telling have a long history in Foucault's works, from their first treatment in the clinic in *History of Madness* to the attention to juridical confession associated with *Discipline and Punish* as well as *I, Pierre Rivière*, and finishing with the lectures that treat truth telling in the ancient world. As Fabienne Brion and Bernard Harcourt note, *aveu* has a slightly different meaning than "confession" in the French context; it signals a juridical, rather than a religious, context. Brion and Harcourt, then, translate *aveu* as "avowal" in the lectures that Foucault gives at the Université Catholique de Louvain in 1981. Given the historical proximity of those lectures and this book (first published in 1982), and the similar juridical contexts, "avowal" is used here as well. It underscores the different performances being staged: with the mechanisms of power laid bare, both accusers and penitents turned to avowal to attract the king's attention and so raise their plight to public concern. "Avowal" also presses the point raised in the Introduction regarding "the self"—for all that those imprisoned were encouraged to "look inwards" and reflect on themselves, this return did not involve the fully interiorized self so familiar from the nineteenth century. See Fabienne Brion and Bernard Harcourt, eds. *Wrong-Doing, Truth-Telling: The Function of the Avowal in Justice*, trans. Stephen W. Sawyer (Chicago: University of Chicago Press, 2014), 271–321.—Ed.]

24. Catherine Duprat, "Punir et guérir: En 1819, la prison des philanthropes," in *L'Impossible prison: Recherches sur le système pénitentiaire au XIXe siècle*, ed. Michelle Perrot (Paris: Éditions du Seuil, 1980).

25. Cf. Jeremy Bentham, *Panopticon* (London: T. Payne, 1791), and "The Eye of Power," an interview with Michel Foucault published as a preface to Jeremy Bentham, *Le Panoptique* (Paris: Belfond, 1977). [See also Michel Foucault, "The Eye of Power," in *Power/Knowledge: Selected Interviews and Other Writings, 1972–1977*, ed. and trans. Colin Gordon (New York: Pantheon, 1980).—Ed.]

26. [Mirabeau angrily denounces the *lettres de cachet* while detained at the château de Vincennes by *lettre de cachet* requested by his father in the face of excessive debts. Mirabeau is imprisoned at least five times—first, in 1773, at the family château, then at Manosque (a city in the Alps of southern France), then at the fortress on the isle of If, then briefly at Vincennes before sojourning at the fortress of Joux in eastern France, followed by the château de Dijon, and then once more at Vincennes, from 1777 to 1780. His work *Lettres de cachet et prisons d'État*, condemns these letters as an instrument of arbitrary power. See Fred Morrow Fling, "Mirabeau, a Victim of the Lettres de Cachet," *American Historical Review* 3.1 (October 1897): 19–30.—Ed.]

27. [The French Assemblée Constituante is convoked on June 17, 1789, when the Estates-General declare themselves to be the National Assembly. It formally is seated on July 9, 1789, and votes to found a constitutional monarchy in December 1791. Although the general sentiment of the Assembly was to reform the constitution, a great deal of disagreement existed over whether the constitution needed only reform to eliminate various abuses of power or whether it should be entirely rewritten. The demands put forward in

the *cahiers de doléances* demonstrated a real lack of uniformity around the *lettres de cachet*, with some calling for their elimination and others their modification. As Farge notes, the language of these debates circles around the inchoate "public interest." For his part, Foucault comments that the Committee on Begging nominated five people to visit various houses of confinement. It decided that prisoners should not be forced to mix with the mad, but (more pityingly) that the mad needed some special form of assistance. In March 1790, the edicts stemming from the Declaration of Human Rights set out to free those imprisoned by *lettre de cachet* within six weeks, unless they have been sentenced, charged, are awaiting trial, or are mad. Then, "requests poured in from all sides for the Assembly to draw up a text that would protect the public from the mad," and so injunctions to postpone such liberation for the mad were passed later in 1790 and again in 1791. See Arlette Farge, *Subversive Words: Public Opinion in 18th Century France* (University Park: Pennsylvania State University Press, 1995); Foucault, *History of Madness*, 420–24.—Ed.]

28. [Abbé Maury (1746–1817) was a clergy member and conservative deputy to the Assembly who supported the use of the *lettres de cachet* in the name of public safety; Fréteau de Saint-Just (1745–94) was a Jansenist, former *parlementaire*, and elected member of the Second Estate; Robespierre goes on to serve on the notorious Committee of Public Safety during the Terror. In the discussion of the *lettres de cachet*, Robespierre comments: "You will not extricate the wretched from the dungeons of despotism to transfer them to the prisons of justice." See Timothy Tackett, *Becoming a Revolutionary: The Deputies of the French National Assembly and the Emergence of a Revolutionary Culture, 1789–1790* (Princeton, N.J.: Princeton University Press, 2014). Robespierre's comments appear in *Archives Parlementaires de 1787 à 1870: Recueil complet*, Assemblée Nationale Constituante, vol. 12, March 16, 1790, 201.—Ed.]

29. Archives parlementaires de 1787 à 1860, Jérôme Mavidal and Émile Laurent, eds., *Recueil complet des débats législatifs et politiques des Chambres françaises*, vol. 11, *Du 24 décembre 1789 au 1er mars 1790* (Paris: P. Dupont, 1880, débats de février et mars 1790), 661ff.; vol. 12, *Assemblée nationale constituante du 2 mars au 14 avril 1790* (Paris: P. Dupont, 1881), 161.

30. Malesherbes, *Mémoire inédit sur les lettres de cachet, adressé à Louis XVI en 1789, collection of M. Alf. Bégis.*

31. [As minister to the Maison du Roi, Baron de Breteuil publishes this circular in March 1784 in an effort to curb both the usage and the duration of imprisonment. In *History of Madness*, Foucault adopts a more institutional perspective on the practices of the *lettres de cachet* and their status. One the one hand, he characterizes the 1784 circular as newly conceding that "If a mature individual dishonors himself by marrying badly, ruins himself with inconsiderate expenditure, gives himself over to debauched excesses and keeps low company, none of these things in themselves seem sufficiently powerful motives to deprive of their liberty persons who are *sui juris* [i.e., legally competent to manage their own affairs]" (91). On the other hand, the logic of delineating and institutionally demarcating the line between reason and unreason remains intact: "This was the first step: reducing as far as possible the practice of confinement where it was simply a result of a moral fault, a family conflict, the more benign aspects of libertinage, but maintaining it in principle, and with one of its major significances to the fore: the locking up of the mad" (420). See Foucault, *History of Madness*, 420–22. The wording of the circular is presented at length in Claude Quétel, *Les lettres de cachet: Une légende noire* (Paris: Perrin, 2011), 309–12.—Ed.]

32. [In *History of Madness*, Foucault argues that initially the eighteenth century worked with a largely undifferentiated category of alienation (*aliénation*) and the more precise characteristics of frenzy (*fureur*) and imbecility (*imbécillité*). If frenzy implies all acts of violence

against others, death threats, and "a rage that went so far as to turn against the self," its other extreme is the passivity of imbecility. Frenzy and imbecility gradually become the two poles between which madness oscillates and finds its place. Both poles were pushed outside of society, and confined so as to be better surveyed. In talking about the changes in how madness was perceived, in so short a time as 1721 to 1733 at Saint-Lazare, Foucault writes: "Forms now multiplied and doubles appeared; imbeciles were now to be distinguished from the weak-minded and the senile; disturbance, disorder and extraordinary sentiments were now no longer the same thing, and there was even a difference between the alienated *(aliénés)* and the insane *(insensés)*, a division that seems enigmatic in the extreme to our eyes." Madness becomes established as an object of perception (88–90; 109ff.; 388–93).—Ed.]

33. [In literature, the libertine initially appears in the seventeenth century as someone who, in the name of liberty of conscience, refuses Catholic dogma. In literary works, it later becomes associated with a pleasure in cruelty (as in the eighteenth century's *Dangerous Liaisons*). In these letters, libertinage more simply connotes a dissipation or waywardness, one often connected to gambling or sexuality. Foucault somewhat differently understands libertinage (and the work of Sade), by juxtaposing libertinage with reason; libertinage thus becomes an unreason forced underground so as to keep reason unsullied. "Libertinage, in the 18th century, was the use of reason alienated in the unreason of the heart," Foucault writes, one that instead rests in the service of the heart's desires. Libertines thus demonstrate a "refusal of truth [that is] the result of moral abandonment" (*History of Madness*, 100). He later notes that often those confined but not labeled mad were locked up as libertine (390). Their unreason lurked in dark regions of the soul, and was unavailable to any moral conduct that might lead them toward truth. To return to oneself, then, is to vacate these regions of unreason and to make oneself available to moral conduct.—Ed.]

34. [Famed for writing the pamphlet *What Is the Third Estate?*, the Abbé Sieyès was trained as a clergyman and political writer both. Following the Revolution, he was a member of the Assemblée Constituante (where this proposal was first heard) and the third National Assembly. Sieyès was later instrumental in the coup d'état that allowed Napoleon Bonaparte to take power in 1799.—Ed.]

35. This proposal, drafted in 1789, was distributed to the Assemblée Constituante in 1790. Cf. *Archives parlementaires*, vol. 12, March 14, 1790. [The proposal was titled "Aperçu sur la réorganisation de la justice et de la police en France," and the relevant discussion about families is on pages 43–47 of the original pamphlet.—Ed.]

36. [The Napoleonic Civil Code of 1803, articles 375–383, contains a chapter on paternal power. The code empowers fathers to imprison a child under sixteen for a month, and a child over sixteen for six months in a letter requesting address and addressed to the court. The court retains the right to abridge the request. The father is obliged to cover the expenses of confinement and may request additional periods of arrest should new irregularities arise. Mothers lack such empowerment unless they are able to convince two paternal relatives to sustain the request. The child, if he owns personal property, may lodge a protest to the court of appeal.—Ed.]

37. [L'Hôtel Bazancourt was a correctional home for young boys. When street expansion destroyed the building in 1832, the boys moved to the Maison de Refuge. Following the edict of September 30, 1807, the population of young girls in this Maison had been itself transferred to the former convent de la Madeleine. At this women's prison, they became known as "Madelonnettes," where supposedly they learned by example "the practice

of Christian virtues and the working life." See *Musée des familles: Lectures du soir,* vol. 4 (Paris: 1836–37), 256.—Ed.]

38. Romain Fresnel, *Considérations qui démontrent la nécessité de fonder des maisons de refuge* (Paris: J. Renouard, 1829). The paternalist Bazancourt house of correction was opened during the first years of the Restoration.

AFTERWORD

1. [Published as *Délinquance et criminalité: Le vol d'aliments à Paris au XVIIIe siècle* (Paris: Plon, 1974).—Ed.]

2. [After finishing her diplôme d'études approfondies in the History of Law (a degree equivalent to a master's degree), Arlette Farge went to Cornell University in 1969. At the time, the black student movement and feminist movement were in full force, and the first courses on women's history were taught. See her interview with Perrine Kervran, "À voix nue," France Culture, November 11–15, 2013, https://www.franceculture.fr/emissions/voix -nue/arlette-farge-15#.—Ed.]

3. [*Nouvelles* can be translated as both "news" and "short story."—Ed.]

4. [Foucault writes about these "poem-lives" in "Lives of Infamous Men," in *Power,* ed. James D. Faubion, trans. Robert Hurley and others (New York: New Press, 2001), 159.—Ed.]

5. Ibid., 158.

6. Jacques Léonard, "L'historien et le philosophe," and Michel Foucault, "La poussière et le nuage," in *L'Impossible prison: Recherches sur le système pénitentiaire au XIXe siècle,* ed. Michelle Perrot (Paris: Éditions du Seuil, 1980); with the participation of Maurice Agulhon, Nicole Castan, Catherine Duprat, François Ewald, Arlette Farge, Alexandre Fontana, Carlo Ginzburg, Remi Gossez, Pasquale Pasquino, Michelle Perrot, and Jacques Revel.

Glossary of Places

Barrières: The *barrières* refer to the city's custom barriers. Just beyond the custom barriers were taverns, known as *guinguettes*, that were cheap haunts favored by workers, because fewer taxes meant lower drink prices. The *guinguettes* were less established than the wine shops, cabarets, or cafés found in city neighborhoods and served a rough, itinerant clientele.

cemetery of the Saints-Innocents: The sisters of Saint Catherine (*filles hospitalières de Sainte-Catherine*) washed the dead from prisons (and notably Châtelet) or drowned in the Seine— about fifteen bodies a night—wrapped them in cloth, and delivered them to this cemetery for burial.

Charenton: An insane asylum that also received prisoners sent by *lettres de cachet*. The Brothers of Charity founded the prison in 1645 as a hospital for sick paupers. By the end of the century, it grew to include buildings for those confined by *lettre de cachet*, and those otherwise needing punishment. The Marquis de Sade died in Charenton in 1814.

château Bicêtre: Built on the site of a thirteenth-century castle fallen into ruin, Bicêtre was built in the seventeenth century under Louis XIII, initially as a hospital for injured soldiers. It was among the buildings later donated by Louis XIV to found the Hôpital général. A prison for convicted criminals, the complex also housed a treatment center for venereal disease and a hospice for the poor. Bicêtre housed men, while its counterpart, the Salpêtrière, housed female prisoners (with a special dormitory for prostitutes). Philippe Pinel began his notorious work with the insane at Bicêtre. The Dortoir de la Visitation, on the second floor of one of the "new" buildings of Bicêtre, was specifically for children. Psychiatrist Jean-Baptiste Pussin begins his career at Bicêtre in 1780, nine years after spending a period there as a child being treated for tuberculosis.

Châtelet [Petit Châtelet, Grand Châtelet]: Broadly speaking, Châtelet served as the royal palace of justice. The forty-eight *commissaires* (superintendents) and the thirty-seven *procureurs* worked out of the Châtelet, which made it a center of police command as well as the equivalent of the local courts and prosecutors' office. The Châtelet thus functioned as a police headquarters, prosecutor's office, and prison. By the mid-eighteenth century, the power of local notables, ecclesiastical councils, and the Hôtel de Ville had waned and the Châtelet became the real center of local government. The prison of Châtelet had the reputation of housing the worst criminals in the dankest of conditions. Neighborhood slaughterhouses left the ground fetid with drying blood, and nearby sewers oozed into the Seine. Although its jurisdiction was abolished in 1790, the prison continued to house 350 prisoners. On September 2, 1792, approximately 216 of these prisoners were massacred by revolutionaries who feared a counterrevolutionary plot arising from the prisons.

Collège des Quatre Nations: The Collège des Quatre Nations was one of the colleges of the University of Paris. Founded by Cardinal Mazarin in 1661, the "four nations" in its name refer to four territories that had come under French control through the Treaty of Westphalia (1648) and the Treaty of the Pyrenees (1659).

Comédie-Française: Created in 1680, the state theater had its own troupe of actors. These could be arrested for dramatizing false representations of political order; if so, these actors usually were sent to For-l'Évêque.

Conciergerie: In the Middle Ages, the Conciergerie was the site of a Merovingian palace. Part of the building was converted to a prison in 1391. In 1757, it held Robert-François Damiens, the famous criminal who attempted regicide, along with noted political prisoners. Others, held in its dungeons, enjoyed less hospitable quarters. Later, during the French Revolution, it held Marie Antoinette in the days leading to her trial and execution, along with approximately 2,700 others before they were guillotined.

cours de la Reine: A garden promenade along the Seine that goes from place de la Concorde to the place du Canada.

cour du Palais: In this case, the cour du Palais refers to ancillary buildings of the Louvre that housed workshops for, among others, master clockmakers engaged by the king.

Enfants-Trouvés: Literally a hospice for "found children," l'Hôpital des Enfants-Trouvés was founded by St. Vincent de Paul around 1640 to house abandoned children. In 1648, the foundlings were moved to Bicêtre, and then because of the high mortality rates, to a hospital near St. Lazare; and then in 1670 l'Hôpital des Enfants-Trouvés was founded as a unit of the Hôpital général. Around 70–80 percent of these children died before reaching adulthood. By the eighteenth century, over ten thousand children have overwhelmed the system and are scattered between multiple institutions. In 1801, Enfants-Trouvés moved to a hospice on rue de l'Enfer (Hell Street); which later expanded to share space with the hospice for the faubourg St. Antoine.

For-l'Évêque: Initially a prison of the Inquisition run by the Church, For-l'Évêque was transformed into a secular prison run by the monarchy in the 1670s. In addition to those arrested by *lettres de cachet*, it also housed debtors and theater performers. It was considered a mid-range prison, in terms of the comfort, freedom, and social rank of many of the prisoners.

Hôpital général: Opened in April 1656 with some six thousand vagrants, the Hôpital grouped together Bicêtre, Salpêtrière, La Pitié and other establishments under a common administration. Designed for the poor of Paris, it was founded at the same time as the "Lieutenant du Prévôt pour la partie de police" who was charged with watching over the safety of Paris. Henry IV donated six buildings for the Hôpital, including the Salpêtrière and Bicêtre. The latter was intended for men, the former for women. Upon its expansion, the institution averaged around ten thousand inmates. Fashioned by Colbert, a minister for Louis XIV, as a workshop for able-bodied vagabonds who would labor as a form of correction (and fund the Hôpital through sale of the products), the Hôpital général quickly devolved into an institution that housed multiple categories of persons, including young orphans, venereal cases, epileptics, "lunatics," and "imbeciles." Most of those swept up in the teeth of the Great Confinement *(Grand Renfermement)* were directed here.

Hospitaliers: Refers to those members of a religious order who shelter, feed, and care for the indigent.

Hôtel-Dieu: A poorhouse, the Hôtel-Dieu had a bad reputation among the indigent of Paris but took all comers. It was nearly bankrupt by the 1750s.

Île Saint-Denis: This island is its own district, or commune, five miles from Paris.

Les Halles: The central covered, fresh-food market in Paris, called "the belly of Paris" by Émile Zola. It was demolished in 1971 to be replaced by a shopping mall.

les Invalides: A home and hospital for sick, disabled, or aged military veterans, erected at the behest of Louis XIV in the 1670s.

l'hôpital Quinze-Vingts: See Quinze-Vingts.

l'hôpital Saint-Lazare: See Saint-Lazare.

Mississippy: In 1750, many speculate that children are being kidnapped so as to populate Mississippi. Earlier royal edicts from 1718 to 1720 had likewise deported prisoners to French overseas colonies.

parish of St. Médard: Housing the tomb of François de Pâris, the cemetery of Saint-Médard often was visited by the convulsionnaires de Saint-Médard, or those religious pilgrims who would fall into religious ecstasy before the tomb of the Jansenist leader, François de Pâris. *Lettres de cachet* were heavily used by Louis XV to quash this Jansenist movement. The Jansenists believed in predestination; this challenge to Catholic doctrine and religious hierarchy was understood both as a challenge to political absolutism and as the kernel of a proto-democratic political discourse.

Petit Châtelet: Petit Châtelet was a prison located in what is now known as the place St.-Michel. Bringing together the varied roles of the procurator general, it contained his lodging, the prison extension of Grand Châtelet, and controlled goods entering the city that proceeded through a narrow passage stretching through the ground floor; it was destroyed in 1782. "Châtelet" on its own would refer to Grand Châtelet.

la Pitié: Established by Henry IV as part of the Hôpital général, the Pitié took in orphaned or unruly children.

place Maubert: Located near the Sorbonne, the place Maubert was (and continues to be) home to a bustling marketplace.

prison de Saint-Martin-des-Champs: The prison of Saint-Martin housed teenagers as well as "public girls" or prostitutes arrested for soliciting. Conditions in Saint-Martin were harsh; these young girls slept on the tile floor, perhaps softened with straw, and mostly were fed bread and water. In 1719, 184 young women from this prison were married to 184 young men from Bicêtre and other Parisian prisons, and then sent to populate French Louisiana.

Prison of Brunoy: The prison of Brunoy is located about fifteen miles outside of Paris. In 1785, approximately two hundred to three hundred stoneworkers showed up at the château de Brunoy, where the king's brother was staying, to protest a new tariff on journeymen. Little trace remains of the strike, suggesting that perhaps *lettres de cachet* were used to quiet the protesters.

prison of Saint-Germain-des-Prés: This prison was found in a corner of the Abbey of Saint-Germain des Prés. It later was the site of one of the more bloody and horrific massacres of September 2, 1792.

Puits Certain: A public well *(un puits)* paid for and established by Robert Certain, the curé for the church St. Hilaire.

Quinze-Vingts: This hospital was founded by King Louis IX in the thirteenth century as a "refuge for the blind." Its name reflects its three hundred beds – or, 15 x 20 – and derives from an archaic numbering system. The hospital gave its name to the surrounding area of the faubourg Saint-Antoine, near the Bastille.

Saint-Lazare: The detention house of Saint-Lazare included those clergy members arrested for their lack of discipline. It also included those young men from the best of families who were accused of libertinage, gambling, and dissipation. Most prisoners were arrested by *lettre de cachet*, the pensions costs six hundred livres (compared to the more usual one hundred livres), and families often paid even more for linens, heating, and medicine.

Sainte-Pélagie: Sainte-Pélagie was a prison for women arrested for debauchery or for living a disorderly life. It was for those women of better means than the poor imprisoned in the Salpêtrière, although these women could be sent to the Salpêtrière for bad behavior.

Salpêtrière: Part of the Hôpital général complex, the hospital—a converted gunpowder manufactory—took in poor women and their young children. Converted to a combination of almshouse and prison in 1656, the Salpêtrière also housed women who were mentally or physically ill, elderly married couples, pregnant women, or nursing mothers, and those imprisoned for vagrancy, prostitution, or "libertine behavior."

School of Saint-Yon of Rouen: Built in 1705 and west of Paris in Rouen, this school contained three establishments: a boarding school for the middle class, a school for unruly children, and a house of correction. The first two sets of children conducted the same studies but ate at separate tables. The last set was sent here rather than prison by the *lettres de cachet*, so as to protect their family from scandal. These included children but also adults who were members of the nobility, upper bourgeoisie, or a religious order, as well as some with mental illness. The school was run by the Brothers of Christian Schools.

"signpost of the Red Rose next to Salt Storage": The salt granary *(grenier à sel)* was originally located near Châtelet and then moved to the rue Saint-Germain-l'Auxerrois. The signpost *(l'enseigne)* may indicate an auberge, especially since the area contained housing for officials associated with the salt trade.

Name Index

Rolet, Louis (nephew of Louise), 215, 216

Rolet, Louise (nun; aunt of Louis), 215, 216

Rolland (police *commissaire*, quartier Saint-Benoît), 60

Rossignol (secretary for the police lieutenancy), 84, 101, 106, 164, 174, 194, 214, 231, 238, 300

Rousseau, Claude, 38

Rousseau De La Mouche, Mme (relative of one of the first presidents of the Parlement de Paris; the first president is a high magistrate named by the king), 108

Rousseau de Villejouin, Gabriel-Charles (1709–81; governor of La Désirade), 131, 132, 302

Roussel (police inspector), 59

Roy [Leroy], François (unemployed, soldier; son of Catherine Galenby and Vincent Roy), 154, 155, 156

Roy, Vincent (merchant; husband of Catherine Galenby, father of François Roy), 154, 155

Sabin (Parent), François (saddler; husband of Marie Anne Laville), 61, 62

Saffard, François (husband of Madeleine Belot, grandfather of Madeleine Marguerite Chapé), 165, 166, 167

Saint-Christ (prostitute; sister of Madeleine Tiquet), 121

Saint-Florentin, Louis III Phélypeaux, count of (1705–77, minister of King Louis XV), 56, 58, 77, 98, 118, 119, 120, 157, 181, 182, 183, 184, 205, 259, 303, 304, 310

Salé [Sallé] (lawyer for Marie Antoinette Guichard), 206, 207

Sandrié (uncle of Félicité Meunier), 230

Sarraire, Étienne François (inspector from 1760 to 1771), 295, 329

Sartine, Antoine Gabriel de, count d'Alby (1729–1801; lieutenant general de police from 1759 to August 1774), 6, 7, 26, 27, 254, 280, 292, 307

Sarty, de (steward of the Salpêtrière), 115

Saussay, Nicolas (master sculptor for Étienne Dupuis), 226

Sauvage, Guillaume (son of Louise de Laurent and Jérôme Sauvage), 202, 203

Sauvage, Jérôme (ballet organizer; husband of Louise de Laurent, father of Guillaume), 202

Sauvier, Pierre (relative of Claude Fumet), 246

Savard (brother-in-law of Marie Madeleine Hébert), 179

Séguier, Pierre (1588–1672), 255, 288, 308

Serassieur, Philippe (cousin of the Petit de Launay brothers), 233

Seray, Anne Catherine (daughter of Gabriel Seray and Anne Charlotte Muideblé), 170

Seray, Gabriel (master locksmith; husband of Anne Charlotte Muideblé, father of Anne Catherine Seray), 169, 170

Sieyès, Emmanuel Joseph, known as the Abbé Sieyès (1748–1836), 266, 313

Sivert, Thérèse [Marie Thérèse] (wife of Nicolas Pichard), 64

Solor, Charles de (uncle of Étienne Dupuis), 225

Soucy, de (police *commissaire*, quartier Saint-Germain-l'Auxerrois), 177, 199, 200

Stainville, Étienne-François, count of Stainville, then duke of Choiseul (1719–85; minister from 1758 to 1770), 78, 299

Süe (surgeon for Marie Marguerite Fournier), 84

Tagon (lemonade maker; neighbor of Anne Hubert), 169

Terrassin des Essarts [Dessessart, Dessessarts] Jean (tailor; husband of Madeleine Dessarle), 44, 90, 91, 92, 93, 296

Arlette Farge is director of research in modern history at the Centre national de la recherche scientifique (CNRS), Paris, and the author of more than a dozen books, including *Fragile Lives: Violence, Power, and Solidarity in Eighteenth-Century Paris* and *The Allure of the Archives.*

Michel Foucault (1926–1984) was a French philosopher who held the chair in the History of Systems of Thought at the Collège de France. He is considered one of the most influential political theorists of the twentieth century and left an indelible mark on philosophy, the humanities, and the social sciences. Among his most notable books are *Madness and Civilization, Discipline and Punish,* and *The History of Sexuality.* The University of Minnesota Press published *Speech Begins after Death* (2013) and *Language, Madness, and Desire: On Literature* (2015).

Nancy Luxon is associate professor of political science at the University of Minnesota and author of *Crisis of Authority: Politics, Trust, and Truth-Telling in Freud and Foucault.*

Thomas Scott-Railton has translated *The Allure of the Archives* by Arlette Farge, *The Most Sublime Hysteric* by Slavoj Žižek, and *Citizenship* by Étienne Balibar.